Rana P. B. Singh

Cultural Landscapes and the Lifeworld

Literary Images of Banaras

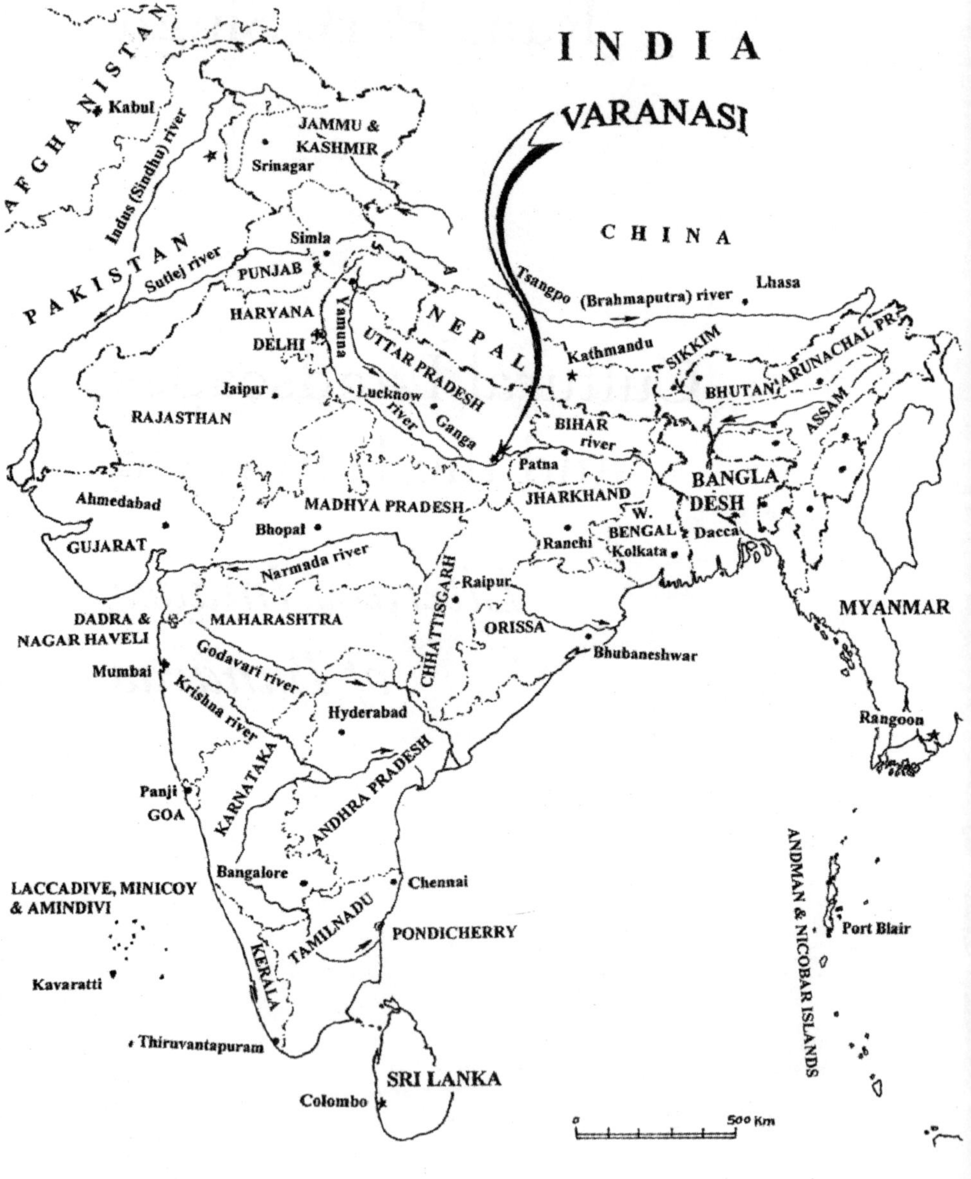
INDIA
VARANASI
CHINA
AFGHANISTAN
Kabul
JAMMU &
KASHMIR
Srinagar
Indus (Sindhu) river
PAKISTAN
Sutlej river
Simla
PUNJAB
HARYANA
DELHI
Yamuna
NEPAL
UTTAR PRADESH
Tsangpo (Brahmaputra) river
Lhasa
Kathmandu
SIKKIM
BHUTAN
ARUNACHAL PR.
ASSAM
Jaipur
RAJASTHAN
Lucknow
river
Ganga
BIHAR
river
Patna
BANGLA
DESH
Ahmedabad
MADHYA PRADESH
JHARKHAND
W.
BENGAL
Dacca
Bhopal
Ranchi
Kolkata
GUJARAT
Narmada river
CHHATTISGARH
Raipur
MYANMAR
DADRA &
NAGAR HAVELI
MAHARASHTRA
ORISSA
Bhubaneshwar
Godavari river
Mumbai
Krishna river
Hyderabad
Rangoon
ANDHRA PRADESH
KARNATAKA
Panji
GOA
ANDMAN & NICOBAR ISLANDS
Bangalore
Chennai
LACCADIVE, MINICOY
& AMINDIVI
TAMILNADU
PONDICHERRY
Port Blair
KERALA
Kavaratti
Thiruvantapuram
SRI LANKA
Colombo
0
500 Km

Rana P. B. Singh

Cultural Landscapes and the Lifeworld

Literary Images of Banaras

Based on the writings of:

Kabir, Tulasi, Mirza Ghalib, Bhartendu Harishchandra, Rudra Kashikeya, Bhishma Sahni, Raja Rao, Shivprasad Singh, Abdul Bismillah, Kashinath Singh, Pankaj Mishra

INDICA

Pilgrimage & Cosmology Series: 6

Cover illustration:

Cataloguing Data:

Singh, Rana P. B. (b. 1950)

Cultural Landscapes and the Lifeworld. Literary Images of Banaras.

Based on the writings of: Kabir, Tulasi, Mirza Ghalib, Bhartendu Harish-chandra, Rudra Kashikeya, Bhishma Sahni, Raja Rao, Shivprasad Singh, Abdul Bismillah, Kashinath Singh, Pankaj Mishra.

398 pp., 55 Figures/Maps.

Indica Books, Varanasi, 2004.

1. Religious Studies; 2. Literature; 3. Cultural Geography; 4. Heritage Studies.

Sponsored by: Society of Heritage Planning and Environmental Health

1st edition published in 2004 by

Indica Books
D 40/18 Godowlia
Varanasi - 221001 (U.P.)
India
E-mail: Indicabooks@satyam.net.in

ISBN: 81-86569-45-6

Printed in India by
First Impression, New Delhi, 09811224048, 22484045 & published by Dilip Kumar Jaiswal for Indica Books, D 40/18 Godowlia, Varanasi - 221001 (U.P.), India

dedicated

to

Shivprasad Singh

(1928 – 1998)

the great literary craftsman and luminous novelist who through his trilogy of historical-cultural novels on Kashi, covering three eras of Banaras, has re-constructed the broken links of historical warp and cultural weft, and exposed for all of us the 'lifeflow' of Indian culture from the Vedic, through medieval to the present period. The three of his novels are the basic sources for three chapters in this book.

Varanasi: Light and Dark

Kashi : thou of many names, many glories,
philic and phobic both.
Banaras : where juice is ready every time,
yet people thirst all the time.
Varanasi : city between the Varana and Asi rivers,
where people enjoy the flowing sewers.
Kashi: known as the City of Light,
also of delight and plight.
Shmasana : the city of burning corpses,
making pits of garbage-ashes.
Jnanavapi : where the well of wisdom lies,
however always the rumour flies.
Holy Tirtha : the city of divine realm,
now changing to devil's helm.
The Abode of Vishvesvara — Lord of the Universe,
where the people are diverse.
Here Police inspector Bhairava lives,
but all the time people weep!
Annapurna assures for almsgiving,
however the dwellers enjoy hemp!
Ganesha watches the deeds as witness,
who can measure people's dullness!
This is Shiva's "Forest of Bliss",
yet the motto : to kill and kiss!
The flowing Ganga calls for eternity,
worshippers follow the path of disparity!
Good and bad: both the apexes everywhere,
one is free to march anywhere.
O Kashi! Bowing we to thy personality,
bliss and wish for our stability.

Rana P.B. Singh

Contents

PREFACE & ACKNOWLEDGEMENTS

All literature has a cultural and social tradition that projects the personality of a place, 'the intrinsic reality': *"Where Cultural Symbols Meet"*. In India, the city of Varanasi (also called Kashi or Banaras) is known as the Cultural Capital of India and also the holiest city of the Hindus. Naturally, with this inherent quality the city has drawn literary attention, which in turn produced creative writings based on the people and landscape of this city. Among them fourteen such literary works are taken here into consideration. Both levels, microscopic and telescopic, are implied in this context, with the aim to reflect upon a long time span, going back into the ancient past and touching what is at present.

The present book consists of sixteen chapters arranged chronologically according to the period when their action takes place. Both the glories and pitfalls of culture are highlighted in their perspectives and contexts while comparing with other contemporary writings. Everywhere the *puranic* mythologies are cited to illustrate their religious connections. This approach I hope will help in understanding the holistic personality of this city in all the possible ways, topophilic and topophobic both.

Finally, at the end, an integrated essay based on all the chapters, "Varanasi: Multiplicity of Images", is added to project the total picture of the city at a glance. I tried my best to reflect without any bias the bad and good scenes while presenting portraits of Varanasi, however the readers are free to make their own reflections. Of the total fourteen main chapters ten are based on writings in Hindi, one in Persian, and three in English. This does indicate that the local colour can be perceived mostly through the local language or dialect, and the folk and oral traditions prevailing there.

The first and foremost sense of obligation is due to all those authors whose writings inspired me and have been taken as settings for narrating the scenes in this book. Many established writers and literary geographers have shown me the right track and the way to follow during the last one and a half decades in my march on the road; among them I am especially grateful to professors Anne Buttimer

(Cork, Ireland), Denis E. Cosgrove (Egham, UK), Ramesh Dhussa (Drake, USA), Ashok K. Dutt (Akron, USA), G. Eichinger Ferro-Luzzi (Rome, Italy), Reginald G. Golledge (Santa Barbara, CA, USA), Edward T. Hall (Evanston, USA), John S. Hawley (Columbia, USA), (late) Ron G. Lister (Dunedin, N.Z.), David Lowenthal (London, UK), Philip Lutgendorf (Iowa, USA), Kenneth R. Olwig (Trondheim, Norway), Douglas C.D. Pocock (Durham, UK), J. Douglas Porteous (Victoria, Canada), Edward Relph (Toronto, Canada), Cristopher L. Salter (Columbia, USA), David Seamon (Manhattan, USA), Jamie Scott (North York, Canada), and (late) Paul Simpson-Housley (North York, Canada), who passed away in March 2002. In Banaras Hindu University, (late) Prof. Shivprasad Singh, Prof. Kashinath Singh and Prof. Shukdeo Singh, all from the Hindi Department, were rational critics and inspirers. For information concerning Tulasi's role in the development of Hanuman worship and Hanuman's shrines, I am especially thankful to my friend Dr. István Keul (Free University of Berlin, Germany).

Many scholars had published their detailed and critical reviews and constructive suggestions on the first edition, published under the title *Where Cultural Symbols Meet* (1989). The list includes my mentor-'Guru' (late) Prof. R.L. Singh, Dr. Marc J. Katz, Prof. Mary L. Nolan, Prof. Ramesh Dhussa, Dr. D.P. Dubey, Prof. Masaaki Fukunaga, Prof. L. Eugene Thomas, and Prof. A.K. Tripathi (for the reviews, see *National Geographic Journal of India*, 36 (1-2), 1990: 129-146). Their comments are taken care of in this expanded and completely re-written edition.

Prof. A.K. Tripathi, Professor of English in Banaras Hindu University, has been kind enough to edit the entire book and suggested many improvements; I'm thankful to him. The entire book has been finally revised in the congenial environment of the Karlstad University (Sweden) where I was a Linnaeus-Palme Visiting Professor in May 2002 and June 2003. The support of my intimate friends, Prof. Gerhard Gustafsson and Dr. Marc Katz (Karlstad) has always been a great source of inspiration. Nevertheless, I am solely responsible for any inconsistency.

A personal sense of obligation is due to a great personality of Banaras, Dr. Bhanu Shankar Mehta, *the Banarasi par excellence*, whose blessings gave me the insight to work on the literary images and experiential reflections. My friend and noted peregrinologer Dr. D.P. Dubey (Allahabad University) has been a great source of help in getting original writings and making available the ancient source materials which are illustrated in the text. Mr Sushil Tripathi, a serious and senior journalist, was kind enough to provide several inside stories of modern Banaras. Communication scholar Dr. Vishvanath Pandey and critical sociologist Dr. Ashok Kaul, both from Banaras Hindu University, have been inspiring critics. My friend and study partner Ms. Vrinda Dar, a social activist, has also supported this project in several ways. The academic and moral support by the three British friend-associates of the Schumaker College, living at Devon (UK), viz. the painter and author John Lane, the poet and author Kathleen Raine, and the great and insightful wanderer Satish Kumar have inspired and directed me to continue my constant journey. The seniour journalist and social activist Dr. Dhirendranath Singh has also been a great source of support in this project. I am thankful to my friend Mr. Rakesh Singh of Harmony Bookshop (Assi Ghat, Varanasi) for his kindness in making available to me many of the relevant publications that helped the writing and re-writing, and also encouraging me in several ways.

Alvaro Enterria and Dilip Jaiswal, the publishers and partners of Indica Books (Varanasi), have been a spirit behind the contract, progress and the final product. It is thankless to thank them because they are the companions along the sacred path and writing. However, I express my special gratitude to Mr. Alvaro, the man *par excellence*, who as copy-editor, has taken the challenging task of questioning sympathetically, criticising rationally and friendly suggesting, a task which has paved my path smoothly to improve the book in several ways by answering, adding and changing. In this march he put me in a state of pleasant stress and strain which I will cherish with love. His sense of *genius loci* is roaming throughout this work. And, we reciprocally enjoyed our company with the pleasure of common sharing.

Writing a book about the lived experience of landscape and people preferably needs a humanistic environment where built and social systems together form a collective condition for understanding and expressing the scenes. My family, wife Manju 'Usha', our two sons, Pravin and Prashant, our two daughters, Prabha and Pratibha, and our son-in-law Ravi and their son Abhishth 'Ballu' have created this setting. They have made the setting multifaceted — tense, easy, harmonious and many times sentimental while claiming and blaming, without which it was not possible to march on the road of literary-perceptive exposures. How can I express my deep gratitude to my wife who sacrificed so many good days in order to provide me free time; she has always been a source of inspiration and a silent observer! Dr. Ravi Shankar, a co-pilgrim, my old student and now my son-in-law, is a companion on the sacred march; to him I express my deep sense of appreciation for his rational criticism and inspiration. In all the ways they deserve my gratefulness and obligation. I'm thankful to Pravin, my eldest son, who did the scanning and the firsthand typesetting of most of the book.

Let me very humbly warn the reader that the task of writing this book completely lacks the intention of geographic orientation, but I do confess that it is also an essential part of geography to describe the place-exposures based on common experiences. I hope that the work will help in reviving the sense of geographicality as propounded by the great French geographer Vidal de la Blache and most recently by many leading literary geographers like Ted Relph, Den Cosgrove, Ken Olwig, and Jamie Scott, etc.

Mr Tripurari Shankar, a senior citizen and established advocate of Banaras, has always supported me in difficult days and encouraged me to constantly work on this project. He warned me while citing an epithet expressing the place-ballet as in Kabir's *sakhi* (cf. Yugeshvara, 1994: 482, *pada* 69):

Rāma jharokhe baiṭh ke, sabkā mujarā leya,
Jaisī jāko cākari, taisī munasaba deya.

Being non-attached and sitting on the world-tower,
Enjoy the world-play from the lattice-window every hour;
As you sow, so you reap, Destiny grants it so.

For reading this book, a pre-requisite of literary taste and sensibility to experience landscape and people would be a great help. Without undue claim, very humbly I can place on record that this is the first book of its nature, which describes all the literary sources on the city lifeworld of Banaras. I hope that the book will help the scholars and seekers of the cultural experiences in several respects and that they will enjoy it. The book is completely re-written and an expanded form of the earlier edition (1989), and has four new chapters and a new introduction.

Rana P. B. Singh
Asi Ghat, Varanasi:
Vasant Navaratri-1 Samvata 2060; 2 April 2003

~1~

Geography of Literary Images, and Search for Identity in India

1. Introduction

Literature as a source material for the understanding of culture, people and belief systems is now realised as one of the basic means of intimate sensing. In fact, "evocative descriptions of geographical places by novelists and poets are of great benefit to both students of literature and students of geography" (Mallory and Simpson-Housley, 1987: xi). Of course, imaginative literature is the creation of an individual's interaction with the environment, the depth of its exposure depends upon the intensity of intimate sensing, experiences, and finally the art of expression for the larger mass. In the early 20th century it has already been noted that, "...Some novelists have had an even clearer vision for the facts of geography that are of most significance to the average man than do professional writers on geographic thought" (J.K. Wright, 1926: 490). Even before, Wright has strongly emphasised the inherent quality of creative literature, which preserves closely the sense of place and the culture of the inhabitants. He has remarked that "Some men of letters are endowed with a highly developed geographical instinct. As writers they have trained themselves to visualise even more clearly than the professional geographer those regional elements of the earth's surface most significant to the general run of humanity" (Wright, 1924 b: 659). About the richness of contents in the novel Lukács's observation is cited as a message by Edward Said:

"The novel is the epic of a world that has been abandoned by God. The novel hero's psychology is demonic; the objectivity of the novel is the mature man's knowledge that meaning can never quite penetrate reality, but that, without meaning, reality would disintegrate into the nothingness or inessentiality ...Irony, with intuitive double vision, can see where God is to be found in a world abandoned by God ...Irony... is the highest freedom that can be achieved in a world without God. That is why it is not only the sole possible *a priori* condition for a true, totality-creating objectivity but also why it makes that totality — the novel — the representative art-form of our age: because the structural categories of the novel constitutively coincide with the world as it is today" (cf. Lukács, 1971: 84, 92-93, as cited in Said, 2001: 459).

Although Carl Sauer did not mention directly the exploration of literary works in geographic studies, what he emphasised clearly draws the attention of future researchers towards literature (cf. Sauer, 1925; see Dhussa, 1992: 77). Remember that geography's traditional attachment has been to particular places and the people who live there. The narration of such attachment moves around the sense of place (*genius loci*), the lived-in space and landscape which can also be derived from the knowledge and consciousness we have of the world we live in (Lando, 1996: 9). It seems that by this march towards place consciousness and humanistic approach the traditional regional geography is taking a new turn, as the French geographer Vidal de la Blache and the American doyen of geography Carl Sauer had once established.

Since long before the emergence of humanistic geography, there had been interest in describing the territorial settings in novels and stories that included the scenes of landscapes, regional identity and geographical phenomena. In Italy there was a strong tradition of this concern. In his work on the explanation of tides in classical Antiquity, R. Almagiá (1903/4) relates that "not only geographers but also philosophers and poets were intrigued by the phenomena of flood and ebb". In the early 20th century O. Marinelli (1902) made an argument on the importance of artistic renditions in the description of regions, while complaining that regional geography was becoming "an unwieldy and untidy collection of facts, data and figures". After eighty years this has been strongly supported by John Hart (1982) through his appeal for a good regional geography that would be fun to read, "written with imagination, flair, style, vevere, dash, panache, enthusiasm... and... flamboyance".

Wright's provocations are seriously considered by many geographers seeking alternatives for a better understanding of man-environment interaction through the exposures of inherent qualities in place of the illusionary quantitative abstractions. This alternative has encouraged to rediscover the literary heritage of geography (Pocock, 1981a: 9). In this context the quest for understanding starts from what Heidegger called 'being-in-the-world', a pre-scientific account which deals with the everyday, immediate or original relationship that people have with their surroundings (Relph, 1986:16).

This quest in geography is transferred so as to understand 'man-in-the world', but with the phenomenological approach both 'man' and 'world' are analysed in relativistic perspective which an individual intimately perceives and experiences. This experience need be described in relation "to the ties of the region, landscape, space and place that link people to the earth — his way of experience and fate" what French historian Eric Dardel called *geographicality* (Pickles, 1985: 44; also Relph, 1986: 17). Many writers have preserved the in-depth insights of this aspect in their writings, which can be taken as source material to understand the *geographicality* of the local place and landscape.

The noted American historical geographer David Lowenthal (1961) wrote that 'any one who inspects the world around him is in some measure a geographer'. The knowledge a society acquires is based on personal geographies created from past recollections, present experiences and future expectations. Past is a memory, future is an imagination and present is a lived experience. Literature is a valuable storehouse which captures all the emotions and reactions to the environment at different places in different times (cf. Lowenthal, 1985).

2. Geography, Literature and Cultural Landscape

Cultural geography is concerned with culture, cultural area, cultural history, and cultural ecology. And cultural landscapes, considered as an end product of human interaction, consist of topography, vegetation, structure, and settlement patterns. Cultural landscapes are both the cause and the effect of cultural values, cultural institutions, and human behaviour, which interact with the natural environment. In other words, "Culture is the agent, the natural area is the medium, the cultural landscape is the result" (Sauer, 1963: 343). The exposition and understanding of cultural landscapes, thus firstly should be explained through the perspective of human behaviour, followed with the ideas and traditions continued and maintained since the ancient past. All these three elements are related to one another and all reflect and affect the others. Literature and its interpretation are one of the prime resources and ways to narrate the cultural landscapes and their distinct and varied characteristics. Culture is defined as "learned behaviour" and consists of several critical elements: language and dialects, religion and rituals, society and ethnic groups, diet, clothing and wealth, politics and power game, and several such combinations. The elements of culture are specific, located in space, purposeful, rule-following, rule-making, and communicating and interacting with people in different ways and on different occasions — they altogether converge to make a place-ballet.

In general, the dynamic and complex nature of cultural landscapes allows geographers to conceptualise landscape as text (a post-modern way of saying it), which, like a book, can be read and written by individuals and groups for very different purposes and with many different interpretations. The messages embedded in the landscape can be read as signs about values, beliefs, and practices from various perspectives, e.g., settling process and cohesiveness among peoples; the marginality of lower castes in the suburbs and the higher castes in the central part of the city; lanes and alleys as dividing lines between two social groups; place distinction and its unique place-ballets; and so on. Landscapes both produce and communicate meanings which one attempts to read and understand in all its complexity and contradictions in this course.

The first attempt, of course without surety, to utilise literature for analysing regional geography was by the British geographer H.C. Darby (1948) who detailed the regional geography of Thomas Hardy's Wessex. Successive writings followed Darby's line and mostly considered regional novels capturing the full flavour of a rural region, especially a single novelist's depiction of a single region. Pocock's (1981a: 12-13) all three traditions fall into this general category, viz. word-painting, which develops a holistic expression having full vision of a region; the geography *behind* literature, where literature is examined in the context of the physical processes involved in its formation while comparing the regional reality; and the search for geography in literature, "treating writings as a literary quarry from which to construct a more general literary topography" (Pocock, 1981a: 13). Jay's work (1975) of reconstructing the Black Country from the works of Brett Young is one of the best known examples of the third tradition.

All the above three approaches are labelled as 'traditional' by Porteous (1985: 118). Works by Aikens (1979), Cosgrove (1979, 1984), Gilbert (1972), Hoy and Elbow (1976), Lanegran (1972), Murton (1976), Salter (1978), and Wyckoff (1979) have also followed similar perspectives. The latest by S. Daniels (1988) has paved the path of literary geography as one of the fascinating fields of practice where landscape, image and text are integrated to describe the geographicality of the region. During the late 1970s the philosophical dialogues have created an atmosphere for adding new dimensions in the subject, especially by focusing in a humanistic approach, which already received recognition in the wider field of human geography.

The field of studying literary images and narrations broadly emphasises the following five themes, viz. the methodological and theoretical aspect, the subjective use of imaginative literature, the exploration of factual information from an objective viewpoint, the application of literary works in teaching and portraying landscape, and portraying imaginary landscapes with respect to utopian literature (Dhussa, 1992: 77). Edward Said (1978: 55) has eloquently related his reflections thus:

"For there is no doubt that imaginative geography and history help the mind to intensify its own sense of itself by dramatizing the distance and difference between what is close to it and what is far away. This is no less true of the feelings we often have that we would have been more 'at home' in the sixteenth century or in Tahiti.

Yet there is no use in pretending that all we know about time and space, or rather history and geography, is more than anything else imaginative. ...Scholars now do know more about the world, its past and present, than they did, for example, in Gibbon's time. Yet this is not to say that they know all there is to know, nor, more important, is it to say that what they know has effectively dispelled the imaginative geographical and historical knowledge I have been considering. We need not decide here whether this kind of imaginative knowledge infuses history and geography, or whether in some way it overrides them. Let us just say for the time being that it is there as something *more* than what appears to be merely positive knowledge".

In Europe, some symbols of political history, like the Basilique du Sacré-Coeur in Paris, were studied by Harvey (1979). This paper opens a new dimension to analyse the sacredscape (sacred places, sites, symbols, monuments, etc.) as text of culture and value system. This idea has encouraged geographers to expand their concern to landscape studies. The dilemma of integrating *yin* and *yang*, low and high, river and mountain, and similar mythical codes of belief systems has shown how such codes manifested over the sacredscape in different dynasties and ideologies, e.g. in the case of Manchu landscape (Forêt, 1995).

3. Intimate Sensing and Humanistic Focus

"Since the body is the measure of all things for man, language and literature abound with comparisons of the human body to places, landforms and buildings" (Lutwack, 1984: 77). This refers to the 'body-earth metaphor' mostly expressed through an intimate sensing — "the appraisal of land and life at ground level, *and* is by far the more complete for it involves not only the visual sense but also sound, smell, taste and touch, body and soul as well as knowledge" (Porteous, 1986a: 250). To handle intimate sensing, naturally a holistic framework and approach is needed. Many of the practitioners of literary geography have followed a humanistic frame in this context. This can be better explained if the traditional tools of literary criticism are also to be taken together. The well-known source is Lutwack's *The Role of Place in Literature* (1984); this is a groundbreaking study of the uses of metaphors and images of place in literature. The author is familiar with the works in geography of a similar nature, it is therefore that this book provides substantially potential insights for future work. This issue has already been strongly supported by Tuan (1978), and Mills (1982).

From its beginning Geography has implied its concern to etymology, i.e. *graphein*, the ability to describe while expressing states of mind, moods, or simply milieus, and thus helped in widening our understanding of the world. Literary resources have been considered very important in this march (cf. Caviedes, 1996). The contemporary epistemological reflections in geography turned to a holistic understanding of man-environment interaction with acceptance and elaboration of the aesthetics and landscape symbology in the context of *genius loci* which is vividly narrated in the literary sources (cf. Lando, 1996). The search for meaning, messages and narration are now common themes in landscape analysis and cultural geography (Osborne, 1996). Despite the social and performance context of cultural memory, events of the past are still remembered by the process of maintaining the continuity of the traditions or through the social memories inscribed in landscape (cf. DeLyer, 1999; Osborne, 1998; Hoelscher, 2003). In the post-modern epoch in geography, a search for alternative representation and interpretative advancement are important with a view to be part of the contemporary world and also communicative skill (Lamme, 1996).

While appraising linguistic refinement and cultural poignancy, Olwig (1981, 1984) has used passages of novels and pieces of poetries to analyse the transformation of landscape and their preservative measures. Olwig's recent saga, *Landscape, Nature, and the Body Politic* (2002), explores the origins and lasting influences of two contesting but intertwined discourses that persist today when we use the words landscape, country, scenery, nature, national. Olwig tracks these ideas though Anglo-American history, starting with the seventeenth-century conflicts between the Stuart kings and the English Parliament, and the Stuart dream of uniting Scotland with England and Wales into one nation on the island of Britain. This book shows how the concept of landscape has historically affected theatre, literature, art, nation building, law, racism, nature conservation, and wilderness movements.

The interactions among people-place-vision and the insight through literary and art sources while comparing with personal experiences and field investigation help in reaching quite closer to the reality. Cosgrove (1979, 1984, and 1985) has been successful in analysing the evolution and formation of landscape in this way. Logical connections, historical events and symbolism — all together have been taken to prepare the portrait of the landscape. The literary works should "be interpreted according to the antinomies of home: away, insider: outsider, roots: rootlessness; and place: placelessness" (Porteous, 1985: 120). Porteous' works (1986b, 1987) dealing with the writings of Malcolm Lowry are examples in this direction; they provide a guideline for the geographers' march in this direction. The dilemma of insider-outsider perspectives is further described by Seamon (1981), and more recently in India by Singh (1985); of course, in both the cases urban regions have been taken as base.

Being an insider researcher, one has to be sensitive to, and critical of the researcher's role in shaping the narrations portrayed by the writers. Further, by use of participatory observation the mythology, the imagery tradition and the belief systems to be reinforced to understand the present lifeworld (cf. Delyser, 2001). Being an insider is not simple, and it has been pointed out that even 'native anthropologists' are insiders only in certain regards: "We all belong to several communities simultaneously… [P]eople born within a society can be simultaneously both insiders and outsiders, just as those born elsewhere can be outsiders and, if they are lucky, insiders too" (Narayan, Kirin 1993: 676).

While making critical remarks, Silk (1984) has classified the main characteristics of current work in Geography and Literature into three major approaches — the formalist approach, the culture-and-society tradition, and the Marxist approach. He has argued that "a materialist analysis is necessary which views literature (and art in general) as one of the many practices in a society based on a particular mode of production, and that examination of the intrinsic features of any text — 'the words on the page' — must be linked with that of its extrinsic features" (Silk, 1984: 151). But beyond this lies the state of mind and soul, which could be understood through experiential feelings and focus on a humanistic approach. In fact, "traditional and humanist approaches are complementary" (Porteous, 1985: 120).

The emotional bonds and value assignment to a place is the subject of variation according to the vital power a place possessed. The creative literature fully absorbs this power and the aesthetic quality to make the place alive like an organic reality. D.H. Lawrence (1964: 6) has rightly noted that, "Different places on the face of the earth have different vital effluence, different vibration, different chemical exhalation, different polarity with different stars; call it what you like. But the spirit of place (*genius loci*) is a great reality". The writers who preserved the spirit of place and extended its reflection have been successful in describing the lived experiences in relation to place (cf. Cosgrove, 1984). In this context Heidegger's "being-in-the-world" could be expanded with the consideration of the self-individual as microcosm of the universe. This acceptance would lead to describe any place or landscape not in reference to individuality, but as part of a global identity (Cosgrove, 1984: 92). Therefore, the description of lived experiences by an author also reflects to the world, as any place has a complex history and global interrelationship.

With a view to analysing a novel in a manner that the incidents and characters may speak for themselves, Heidegger's method of phenomenological approach would be appropriate. Accordingly, the essence of the method is "to let that which shows itself be seen from itself in the very way in which it shows itself from itself" (Heidegger, 1962: 58). In unintentional fashion, it has been attempted to present within a historical context a phenomenological interpretation of a specific real-world description. Heidegger in accordance with the general argument proposes this (cf. Seamon, 1984: 46). With an idea similar to Heidegger's, using experiential background and the explanation of the life philosophies of the farmers of the Östmark parish, Värmland, Sweden, Gustafsson and Wahlström (1990) attempted to analyse the goals of the society and the meaning of development. Of course they have not taken literary source as a tool, but their humanistic constructs are useful in the literary interpretation. Their paradigms and approaches are taken into serious consideration in Indian context (cf. Rana Singh, 1994). On the issue of representation of space in novels, Edward Said (1993: 94) has rightly remarked that, "As the conclusions of the novel confirm and highlight an underlying hierarchy of family, property, nation, there is also a very strong spatial *hereness* imparted to the hierarchy...The narrative explores, moves through, and finally endows these places with confirmatory positive and/or negative values. This moral commensuration in the interplay between narrative and domestic space is extendable, indeed reproducible, in the world beyond metropolitan centres like Paris or London".

One can say in reaction that the philosophic and reference frames as given are the subject of philosophic and literary discussion, what being a geographer does one find in such an analysis or essay. Buttimer (1984: 261) has made an appealing challenge in this context: "After all, when scientists and humanists come together, what does a geographer have to bring to the meeting? One contribution is surely explication of landscape — reading the face of the earth as the texts in which civilisations have inscribed their ongoing dreams and realities". Both the perspectives in relation to landscape and people emerge: the place as hostile and alien state, keeping man far from a human potential (*placelessness*); and the place as true home (*placefulness*). This may be interpreted on psycho-environmental scales, i.e. an aversion (*topophobia*), and strong affection (*topophilia*). For a balanced value assignment to a text, both the senses are required in an experiential-reflective exposition.

Another dimension of humanistic literary geography is related to the horizon of meaning-metaphor-simile-milieu, which respectively opens the inside realities, symbolic expression, comparison with contrasts, and the contextual conditioning (cf. Buttimer, 1984). These together help to understand the 'lifeworld' of a place or region. The lifeworld refers to "the culturally defined spatiotemporal setting of horizon of everyday life" (Buttimer, 1976: 227). For such approach phenomenology provides a helpful ground in understanding the underpinning humanistic socio-cultural life.

In the late 1930s the question of 'the urban frame of mind' (*L'âme de la ville*) was considered as one of the noble subjective dimensions in geography. According to George Hardy, "novelists have captured regional personalities far better than geographers" (Hardy, 1939: 146, ref. Buttimer, 1971: 113-4). Geography should also be "studied in the manner of '*Geosophy*' — the study of geographic knowledge from any and all points of view, ...covering the geographical ideas, both true and false, of all manner of people" (Wright, 1947: 10).

How the variety of religious myths and symbols, rituals and values and heroes and histories have played their role is the major concern of an anthology edited by a geographer, viz. "And the Birds Began to Sing" (Scott, 1996). This collection covers the whole range from Native American to New Zealand, and in between India.

Post-colonial writings offer concrete opportunities to discover our world 'within' the self and 'beyond' the self that are simultaneously present, of course sometimes seen and sometimes unseen. The inherent essence of sacrality in the landscape and culture has been the major concern in this paradigm shift (see Scott, 1999 and 2001). The roots of a culture are interpreted in the process of sacrality, manifesting the spatiality of time, temporality of space and their resulting tradition of cultural wholes — cosmology. Issues like ethical codes, spiritual experience, institutionalisation of religious life, changing values in terms of socio-political transformations are the other concerns in this direction. Scott summarises, "Contemporary international literatures representing the interplay between the religious and the geographical thus offer concrete opportunities for us to discover in ourselves and in our neighbours that simultaneous presence of the seen and unseen, the material and the mysterious, which animates Eliade's sense of sacred space" (Scott, 2001: xxviii).

The use of literary images for attracting tourists sometimes produces adverse effects, like Jackson's 1884 novel *Ramona*, which was responsible for saturating California's landscape through the heavy pressure of tourists, and ultimately inspired a romanticised false past for the region. However, tourism and boosterism intertwined to create attractions that were both profitable as well as meaningful (DeLyser, 2003, 2004).

4. Literary Geography: a search for identity in India

Analysis of images, landscape, people and society based on fictional writings on India or by Indian writers are relatively few (Dutt and Dhussa, 1983). The researches presented in this field can be arranged into two main categories. One, utilisation of information found in ancient and religious scriptures for the purpose of re-constructing the geographic environment of the time that is depicted in a particular ancient work like the *Puranas*, the *Mahabharata*, and the *Ramayana*, etc. This type of literary work can be called "the objective use of creative writing" (Dhussa, 1992). Ali's monumental work, *The Geography of the Puranas* (1966) is a model of 'objective use'. Mukerji's (1969a and b) writings on the climatological data in the *Yajur Veda* and rural settlements in the *Jatakas* are the other pioneer and early examples in this direction. The second type of literary geographic works fall under "the subjective use of creative writings". In the latter category experiential, contextual and interpretative aspects of spatial phenomena are explored. The works by Ramesh Dhussa, and Rana Singh are recent representatives in the second category.

In an International Symposium on "Urban India: Society, Space and Image" held at Duke University, USA in 1970, for the first time three papers were presented by a sociologist, a historian and a linguist dealing with urban images. They have approached the city as it is reflected in the literature of modern and ancient India (Fox, 1970: xi). There the city "appears through the perceptions of its denizens, through the urban images of Indian writers".

Apte (1970) described the pre-1940 Bombay (Mumbai) in the context of the ensuing post-war depressed valuation of the middle class. His writing narrates pure fantasy and a mixture of various experiences and imagination (*ibid:* 199). He concluded that "the various aspects of urbanisation as reflected in Marathi literature are not much different from those in other societies" (*ibid:* 212).

Zelliott (1970) has taken several works in the English language written by Indians to analyse the general perception of the theme of 'the City of Hell'. She concludes that although "urban personality is often malevolent, there are exceptions". Among such scenes, any sharp dichotomy does not appear between rural and urban (*ibid:* 223). Her remarks are similar to that raised by Apte (1970). Ramanujan (1970) emphasised the urban images of ancient India. He feels that "sometimes the best focussed image of a city is the literacy one, sensitive to both structural design and the significance of detail" (*ibid:* 224). Comparing Tamil and Sanskrit literature with respect to the continuity of city and country, he has remarked that, "in contrast to Sanskrit, early Tamil aesthetics makes no clear distinction between *bhava* and *rasa,* the raw everyday feelings and the refined emotions of art and poetry" (*ibid:* 242).

In contrast to the above approach, Gemmill (1980) highlighted the city as jungle, as revealed in Indo-English novels, while following the line of literary criticism. The idea of landscape aesthetics and placelessness is not given emphasis by him.

The first article attempting to explore the geography of Jhabwala's *Householder* is by Tewari and Saxena (1978). Two more articles were published by Indians in Indian journals. The first one is by Dutt and Dhussa (1983), which deals with novelist Sarat Chandra's perception of the Calcutta (Kolkata) region, emphasising the migratory behaviour of Bengalis. Their two earlier articles (1976, 1981) highlighted the contrasting images and landscape of Calcutta, and the Bengali home region. In both the studies Sarat's writings are taken as a base. In a later article Dhussa and Bhardwaj (1988: 33-40) dealt with the picture of India as drawn by expatriate imaginative writers — Backhory (1979),

Gurudutt (1978), Ved Mehta (1973), V.S. Naipaul (1968, 1977) and Rama Rau (1945), and described both the positive and negative visions with critical appraisal. Another major study based on a novel was by Singh (1985, 1994) to reflect upon the personality and lifeworld of Banaras; the historicity and religious personality of the city have been compared with treatises, *puranic* literature and other contemporary writings. This study helps to understand the insider-outsider and intrinsic-extrinsic dilemmas of the city's landscape and people.

Philip (1986) has examined the perceived picture of India as revealed by Nirad Chaudhuri, R.K. Narayan and Ved Mehta in length. The analysis was laid on the psychological processes of transformation of culture and alien civilisation. He further sketches an evolutionary progression from loss to recovery of self. The writings of these authors are the representatives of three images of India: sense of selfhood, Indianness, and de-cultured / polarised culture, respectively.

The fictional townscape of Malgudi as portrayed by R.K. Narayan in his ten novels and some of his other stories are studied in detail by Allen Noble (1976, 1980). Noble has emphasised the three stages of the evolution and exposition of the development of the townscape of Malgudi, an imaginary small town which possessed the varied gamut of Indian culture. Contrary to the common perception of Malgudi, Bery (1997: 8) opines that the Hindu orthodoxy of R.K. Narayan "probe limitations and contradictions in Hindu world views and identities" by problematising such doctrines as *dharma*, *moksha* and *karma*. With an objective to study the interaction of religion, ideology and social practice in Malgudi, a fictional symbol of "Little India" was studied by Kanaganayakam (2001); she concludes that "In Narayan's Hindu world, old gods hold hegemonic sway over a traditional sacred landscape" (*ibid.*: 332).

The pioneer work in tracing out the route and landscape associated with Rama's exile was presented a century ago by Pargiter (1894). Using the *Ramayana* as source, the paper traced and detailed out the narration of places where Rama had travelled and lived during his exile. This paper inspired many scholars to follow a similar approach of narration by describing the place and landscape as in the ancient texts. Pargiter's classical paper has been re-examined in the light of a literary, folklore and cultural-archaeological context by Rana Singh (1991); however he has not arrived at a conclusive answer in search of the exile route. Tamasker's (1956, 1969) works are other examples of using the *Shiva Purana* and the *Upanishads* in narrating the natural landscape. In another article Rana Singh (1999/1992) attempted to project the contributions of Hindu geographic thought in terms of nature and cosmic integrity, emphasising the five gross elements of organic entity as described in the Vedic and Puranic literature and also the symbolic forms attached with them. Dhussa (1992: 79) comments on this paper saying, "This is one of the best examples using literature in exposition of deep ecology and cosmology".

Recently attempts have also been made to discuss social divisions and psychological crosscurrents in the rural world around Calcutta, especially in historical perspective (Ray, 1983). Moreover, the culture-specific themes in Tamil short stories are also analysed in relation to a whole religious system — it has founded a new dimension of research in anthropology and cultural studies. With the use of participatory observations and detailed field study this will be proved as one of the major approaches to approach the inside realities and even in understanding invisible qualities (cf. Eichinger Ferro-Luzzi, 1983, 1987).

For interpreting Tamil literature and the different local cultures the life-long and great contributions of Eichinger Ferro-Luzzi (1980-2002) will always be remembered in the field of the literary geography of South India. In her early writing she has narrated the changing perspectives and paradoxical reasoning in the use of symbols and their association with Hindu gods, e.g. the interconnectedness among myths, meanings, metaphors and milieu (*idem*. 1980). This theme has been further elaborated in her book, *Cool Fire* (*idem*. 1983). Various nature images, including anthills, have been the object of veneration according to the regional traditions and beliefs (*idem*. 1987). Using similies and metaphors in the writings of Ramamirtham she has vividly projected the salience of certain aspects of nature and culture in the Tamil mind, which represent the regional identity (*idem*. 1990 and 1992).

Further, with a detailed cultural analysis of Ramamirtham's 132 short stories, cross-cultural aspects and ethnographic details are narrated by Eichinger Ferro-Luzzi to reflect upon everyday lives (*idem*. 1995). Examining the role of water and water-related rites she has explained the well-known fertility of the Indian Imagination and concludes that water is conceived as a metaphor and symbol of both purity and sexual passion as well as equated with fire (*idem*. 1997). The Indian classification of five gross elements making the organic web of life is vividly portrayed in Tamil literature, and finally describes the earth as goddess conceived as *shakti*, energy, which is immaterial and impalpable (*idem*. 1999). Taking Tamil folktales as the base, she has pursued an ethnographic survey and a theoretical construct to understand values, beliefs and interests of people in maintenance of their regional culture (*idem.* 2002b). She adds that the relationship between thought and reality, the memory and metaphor as narrated in the Tamil idiomatic expression 'mental monkey', should be understood with reference to philosophical premises and the life-philosophy of people (*idem.* 2002a).

A notable contribution on the subjective use of literature and geographicality in the form of first doctoral dissertation has been presented by Ramesh Dhussa (1986), which deals with the urban images of Delhi (also Dhussa, 1994, and *forthcoming*). This work has paved the path for a deeper understanding of the subjective, humanistic and experiential dimension of creative modern literature in India. Dhussa (1992: 83) has very rightly remarked that "India has an exceptionally rich storehouse of both ancient and modern literature; scholars from various disciplines, including geographers, should make extensive use of such a rich literary heritage".

Bose's (1996) study of the short stories and novels of the Indo-American writer Bharati Mukherjee is an example of a cross-cultural context which seems to advocate the intriguing notion of Hindu reincarnation as a metaphor for the changes of identity such emigration involves. Her novel focuses on the Hindu goddesses Durga and Kali, who serve as sources of strength for Indian women in North America (cf. Scott, 2001: xix). Some of the ethnographic studies of tourits sites, tourists' perception and reflections and the supporting literature attempt to understand and uncover both meaning and practice in the arena of change, e.g. in case of Taj Mahal (cf. Edensor, 1998).

The ideology of space as narrated in Raja Rao's *Kanthapura* is a trial to replace the idea of the colonial system of exchange and also the brahminical code of rigid rules which sustained the socio-economic life in the past (Mondal, 1999: 105). An attempt by a geographer to study Anita Desai's *Fire on the Mountain*, specially in terms of Hindu sacred geography, is a noble effort to unite geography and literature in search of the interpretative codes concerning the cultural notion of landscape and value system, and also their changes, especially during the colonial period (cf. Scott, 1999: 33). Desai's novel is a good resource to interpret the inter-relationship and distinction between *karma* and *dharma* on the scale of space and time.

5. Literary images of Banaras: the present book

The present book attempts to analyse literary images of a single city based on the writing of several writers. Banaras, perceived as the cultural capital of India and the holiest city of the Hindus, has been taken here as a case study. Ten writers are considered independently and their writings are arranged chronologically, from the ancient to the contemporary, into fourteen chapters.

This book is a modest attempt to capture the spirit and images of 'Varanasi through time' as evoked by the writings of ten authors from a variety of different backgrounds. This work presents images of the city of *rasa*: Kashi, Varanasi, Avimukta, Thaganam Sthanam, Benares, and Banaras (all appellations of Varanasi) based on the perceptions of various writers. Banaras is the oldest and holiest city of India. Hindus perceive Banaras as such a sacred place that if one leaves this world in Varanasi then his or her soul will undoubtedly go to heaven.

One of the perspectives taken into the background is the appraisal of the richness of information that has been drawn from varied literary sources. The book begins with the ancient period, associated with the mythical king Divodasa, and also presents images of the medieval period. The following chapters begin with the fifteenth-century reformer poets Kabir and Tulasi, and continue through the 19th century with poets like Mirza Ghalib and Bhartendu. The 20th century is portrayed with many writers such as Raja Rao, Abdul Bismillah, Shivprasad Singh, Kashinath Singh, and Pankaj Mishra. All these writers stem from various philosophical, cultural, linguistic and religious backgrounds. This richness of resources has generated kaleidoscopic images of the city of Varanasi from temporal, spatial and, of course, experiential points of view. The selection includes an entire array of authors ranging from 'Banarasi' natives such as Kabir, Tulasi, and Bhartendu to visitors like Ghalib, and including the expatriate Indian writer Raja Rao. With this collection of writers we get 'insider' views along with the perceptions of 'outsiders'. The subject matter of the book is divided into sixteen chapters. The 1st chapter is a critical appraisal and synoptic review of the emerging field of literary geography and the search for identity in India. The following fourteen chapters chronologically evoke the images of Banaras based respectively on the writings of each author. The last chapter (16) presents summary and conclusion.

Of course, the chapters are arranged into a chronological order, each chapter brings its own unique perspective to appraising lifeworld and place-attachment. The spatial and temporal dynamics of culture and landscape in the form of 'city images' have been colourfully portrayed by presenting both sides of exposition, i.e. hard realities (materialistic pleasure) and glorious images (spiritual vision). That is how the city is called Banaras, where always ready (*Bana-*) to serve the 'juice' of life (*-ras*). Lowenthal (1975: 3), has rightly remarked that, "...The linements of the world we live in are both seen and shaped in accordance, or by contrast, with images we hold of the other worlds — better worlds, past worlds, future worlds. We constantly compare the reality with the fancy. Indeed, without the one we could neither visualise nor conceptualize the other". Variety, distinction and assimilation are all woven to form the cultural personality of this city (known as "Banarasi", or "Banarasian" in English).

6. References

Agnew, J.A. & Duncan, J.S. (eds.) 1989. *The Power of Place: Bringing together Geographical and Sociological Imaginations*. Unwin Hayman, London.

Aikens, C.S. 1979. Faulkner's Yoknapatawpha Country: A place in the American South. *Geographical Review* (New York), vol. 69 (3): 331-334.

— 1981. A Geographical Approach to William Faulkner's '*The Bear*'. *The Geographical Review*, 71 (4): 446-456.

Almagiá, R. 1903/4. La dottrina della marea nell'antichitta classicà. *Revista Geografia Italiana*, 10: 480-493, and 11: 13-23.

Barnes, T.S. & Duncan, J.S. 1992. Eds. *Writing Worlds: Discourse, Text and Metaphor in the Representation of Landscape*. Routledge, London.

Barrell, J. 1982. Geographies of Hardy's Wessex. *Journal of Historical Geography*, 8 (3): 347-361.

Bordessa, R. 1988. The City in Canadian Literature, Realist and Symbolic Interpretations. *The Canadian Geographers*, 32: 269-270.

Buttimer, Anne 1971. *Society and Milieu in the French Geographic Tradition*. Rand McNally & Co., Chicago.

— 1976. Grasping the Dynamism of Lifeworld. *Annals, Association of American Geographers*, 66 (2): 277-292.

— 1984. Perception in Four Keys: A Commentary. In, T.F. Saarinen et al., eds. *Environmental Perception and Behavior*. Univ. of Chicago, Dept. of Geography, Res. Paper 209: 251-263.

Caviedes, César N. (Guest Editor) 1996. Geography and Literature. *GeoJournal* 38 (1): 1-136.

Cosgrove, Denis E. 1979. John Ruskin and the Geographical Imagination. *Geographical Review*, 69 (1): 43-62.

— 1974. *Social Formation and Symbolic Landscape*. Croom Helm, Beckenham, Kent.

— 1975. Prospect, Perspective and the Evolution of Landscape Idea. *Transaction, Institute of British Geographers*, NS, 10: 45-62.

Cosgrove, Denis E. & Daniels, Stephen (eds.) 1988. *The Iconography of Landscape: Essays on the Symbolic Representation, Design and Use of Past Environment*. Cambridge University Press, Cambridge.

Cresswall, T. 1993. Mobility as Resistance: A Geographical Reading of Kerouac's '*On the Road*'. *Transaction, Institute of British Geographers*, 18: 249-262.

Daniels, Stephen J. 1988. *Landscape, Image, Text.* Polity Press (Basil Blackwell), Oxford.

— & Rycroft, S. 1993. Mapping the Modern City: Alan Sillitoe's Nottingham novels. *Transaction, Institute of British Geographers*, 18: 460-480.

Darby, H.C. 1948. The Regional Geography of Thomas Hardy's Wessex. *Geographical Review*, 38 (4): 426-443.

DeLyser, Dydia 1999. Authenticity on the ground: Engaging the past in a California ghost town. *Annals of the Association of American Geographers* (Washington, DC), 89 (4): 602-632.

— 2001. "Do we really live here?" Thoughts on insider research. *The Geographical Review* (New York), 91 (1-2): 441-453.

— 2003. Ramona memories: Fiction, tourist practices, and placing the past in Southern California. *Annals of the Association of American Geographers* (Washington, DC), 93 (4): 886-908.

— 2004. *Ramona Memories*. University of Minnesota Press, Minneapolis.

Drabble, M. 1979. *A Writer's Britain: Landscape in Literature*. Knopf, New York.

Eliade, Mircea 1959. *The Sacred and the Profane*. Harcourt Brace Jovanovich, New York.

Forét, Pierre 1995. The Manchu Landscape Enterprise; Political, Geomantic and Cosmological Readings of the Gardens of the Bishu Shanghuang Imperial Residence at Chengde. *Ecumene*, 2: 325-334.

Gilbert, E.W.1972. British Regional Novelists and Geography. In, E. W. Gilbert ed. *British Pioneers and Geography.* David & Charles, Newton Abbot, Devon: 116-127.

Gilbert, E. & Simpson-Housley, P. 1997. Places and Spaces of Dislocation: Lady Oracle's Toronto. *The Canadian Geographer*, 43 (3): 235-248.

Gilbert, E., Carter-Park, D., Simpson-Housley P., & Scott, J. 1996. Battles from Below: A Literature of Oppression. *GeoJournal*, 38 (1): 19-28.

Gunn, C. 1974. The Non-Western Novel as a Geography Text. *Journal of Geography*, 73 (1) : 27-34.

Gustafsson, Gerhard & Wahlström, Lage 1990. Geography and Life Philosophies: Some Experiences from a Western Point of View with a Reference to Östmark Society, Sweden. *National Geographical Journal of India*, 36 (1-2): 86-94.

Hardy, George 1939. *La Géographie Psychologique.* Gallimard Pub., Paris.

Hart, John F. 1982. The Highest Form of the Geographer's Art. *Annals, Association of American Geographers*, 72 (1): 1-29.

Harvey, David 1979. Monument and Myth. *Annals of the Association of American Geographers*, 69 (3): 362-381.

Heidegger, Martin 1927. *Being and Time.* (Transl. J. Macquarrie & E. Robinson). Harper & Row Publs., Inc., New York. Reprinted 1962.

Hoelscher, Steven 2003. Making Place, Making Race: Performances of Whiteness in the Jim Crow South. *Annals of the Association of American Geographers*, 93 (3): 657-686.

Hoy, D.R. & G.S. Elbow 1976. The Use of Literary Works in Teaching Latin American Geography. *Journal of Geography*, 75: 556-569.

Jay, L.J. 1975. The Black Country of Francis Brett Young. *Transaction, Institute of British Geographers*, 66: 57-72.

Lamme, A.J. III 1977. The Use of Novels in Geography Classrooms. *Journal of Geography*, 76: 66-68.

— 1996. Speaking with the Same Voice: Geographic Interpretation and Representation of Literary Resources. *GeoJournal*, 38 (1): 41-48.

Lando, Fabio 1996. Fact and Fiction: Geography and Literature, A Bibliographical Survey. *GeoJournal*, 38 (1): 3-18.

Lanegran, D.A. 1972. The Pioneers' View of the Frontier as Presented in the Regional Novel *'Giants in Earth'. International Geography* 1: 350-352.

Lanegran. D.A. & S.A. Toth 1970. Geography Through Literature. *Places*, 3 (I) : 5-12.

Lawrence, D.H. 1964. *Studies in Classical American Literature.* Heinemann. Pub., London.

Ley, David & M.S. Samuels (eds.) 1978. *Humanistic Geography: Prospect and Problems.* Maaraufa Press, Chicago.

Lloyd, W.J. 1976. Landscape Imagery in the Urban Novel: A Source of Geographic Evidence. In G.T. Moore & R.G. Golledge eds., *Environmental Knowing* : 279-285.

Lowenthal, David 1961. Geography, Experience and Imagination: Towards a Geographical Epistemology. *Annals, Association of the American Geographers*, 51 (2): 241-260.

—1975. Past time, Present Place: Landscape and Memory. *The Geographical Review* (AGS, New York), 65 (1): 1-36.

— 1985. *The Past is a Foreign Country.* Cambridge University Press, Cambridge.

Lowenthal, David & Bowden, M.J. (eds.) 1976. *Geographies of the Mind. Essays in Historical Geography.* Oxford University Press, New York.

Lukács, Georg 1971. *The Theory of the Novel*, trans. Anna Bostock. Merlin Press, London.

Lutwack, Leonard 1984. *The Role of Place in Literature*. Syracuse University Press, Syracuse.

Mallory, William S. & Paul Simpson-Housley 1987. Eds. *Geography and Literature. A Meeting of the Disciplines.* (12 essays). Syracuse University Press, Syracuse.

Marinelli, O. 1902. Alcune questioni relative al moderno indirizzo della geografia. *Revista Geografia Italiana*, 9 : 217-240.

Mills, W.J. 1982. Metaphorical Vision: Changes in Western Attitudes to the Environment. *Annals, Assoc. of the American Geographers,* 72: 237-253.

Moore, G.T. & R.G. Golledge 1976. Eds. *Environmental Knowing.* Dowden, Hutchinson & Ross, Stroudsberg. PA.

Murton. Brain J. 1976. Waituhi : A Place in Maori, New Zealand. *New Zealand Geographer*, 35 (1): 24-33.

Narayan, K. 1993. How Native is a "Native" Anthropologist? *American Anthropologist* 95 (3): 671-686.

Olwig, Kenneth R. 1981. Literature and 'Reality': The Transformation of the Jutland Heath. In, *Humanistic Geography and Literature*, eds. D.C.D. Pocock; Croom Helm, London: 47-65.

— 1984. *Nature's Ideological Landscape: A Literary and Geographical Perspective on its Development and Preservation of Denmark's Jutland Heath*. Allen-Unwin, London.

— 2002. *Landscape, Nature, and the Body Politic: From Britain's Renaissance to America's New World.* Foreword by Yi-Fu Tuan. The University of Wisconsin Press, Madison & London.

Osborne, Brian S. 1988. Fact Symbol and Message: Three Approaches to Literary Landscapes. *The Canadian Geographer*, 32: 267-269.

— 1996. Texts of Place: 'A Secret Landscape Hidden Behind the Everyday'. *GeoJournal*, 38 (1): 29-39.

— 1998. Constructing Landscapes of Power: The George Etienne Cartier Monument, Montreal. *Journal of Historical Geography*, 24 (4): 431-458.

Pickles, John 1985. *Phenomenology, Science and Geography.* Cambridge University Press, Cambridge.

Piveteau, J.L. 1991. Imaginaire littéraire et territorialité. *Cahiers de l'Institut de Géographie de Fribourg*, 8: 121-126.

Pocock, Douglas C.D. 1971. The Novelist's Image of North. *Transaction, Inst. of British Geogr.* (NS), 4: 62-76

— 1981a. Ed. *Humanistic Geography and Literature: Essays on the Experience of Place.* Croom Helm, London.

— 1981b. Place and the Novelist. *Transaction, Institute of British Geographers*, NS, 6: 337-347.

Porteous, J. Douglas 1985. Literature and Humanistic Geography. *Area*, 17 (2) : 117-122.

— 1986a. Intimate Sensing. *Area*, 18 (3) : 250-51.

— 1986b. Inscape: Landscapes of the Mind in the Canadian and Mexican Novels of Malcolm Lowry. *Canadian Geographer*, 30 (2): 123-131.

— 1987. Deathscape : Malcolm Lowry's Topophobic View of the City. *Canadian Geographer*, 31 (1): 34-43.

Reiner, T.S. & M.A. Hindery 1984. City Planning, Images of Ideal and Existing City. In, L. Rodwin & R.M. Hollister, eds. *Cities of the Mind.* Plenum Press, New York: 133-147.

Relph, Edward C. 1981. *Rational Landscapes and Humanistic Geography.* Croom Helm, London.

— 1985. Landscapes Methods and the Geographical Imagination. Unpubl. mss.

— 1986. Geographical Experiences and Being-in-the-World: The Phenomenological Origin of Geography. In, R. Mugerauer & D. Seamon, eds. *Dwelling, Place and Environment.* M. Nijhoff Pub., The Hague: 15-31.

Robinson, Brian 1996. Charles Dickens and London: The Visible and the Opaque. *GeoJournal*, 38 (1): 59-74.

Said, Edward W. 1978. *Orientalism. Western Conceptions of the Orient.* Routledge & Kegal Paul, London. With a 'New Afterward' reprinted by Penguin Books India, New Delhi, 2001.

— 1993. *Culture and Imperialism.* Vintage, London.

— 2001. *Reflections on Exile and other Literary and Cultural Essays.* Penguin India, New Delhi.

Salter. C.L. 1978. Signature and Settings: One Approach to Landscape in Literature. In, Karl W. Butzer, ed. *Dimensions of Human Geography.* Univ. of Geography, Res. Paper 186: 69-83.

Salter, C.L. & W.J. Lloyd 1977. *Landscape in Literature.* Resource Paper for College Geography, Assoc. of Amer. Geog., Washington, DC No. 76-3.

Sauer, Carl O. 1925. The Morphology of Landscape. *University of California Publications in Geography*, Publication 2 (2): 19-54, reprinted in 1963 in his anthology, *Land and Life*, UCP, Berkeley: 315-350.

— 1963. *Land and Life* (*Selection from Carl Sauer's writings*, ed. John Leighly).University of California Press, Berkeley.

Scott, Jamie 1996. Ed. *'And the Birds Began to Sing': Religion and Literature in Post-Colonial Cultures*. Cross/Cultures 20. Edition Rodopi Press, Amsterdam & Atlanta GA.

— 1999. Geographies of the Sacred and Post-colonial Literatures. In, *Spirit of Place: Sources of the Sacred?*, eds. Michael Griffith & James Tulip. CSRLA, Australian Catholic University, Sydney: 50-74.

— 2001. Mapping the Sacred Across Postcolonial Literatures. In, *Mapping the Sacred*, eds. Jamie Scott & Paul Simpson-Housley, op. cit. : xv-xxxiii.

Scott, Jamie & Simpson-Housley, Paul (eds.), 2001. *Mapping the Sacred: Religion, Geography and Postcolonial Literatures*. Editions Rodopi Press BV, Amsterdam & Atlanta.

Seamon, David 1976. Phenomenological examination of imaginative literature: a commentary. In, Moore & Golledge, eds. *Environmental Knowing*: 286-290.

— 1981. Newcomers, Existential Outsiders and Insiders: Their Portrayal in Two Books by Doris Lessing. In Pocock, ed. : 85-100.

— 1984. Heidegger's Notion of Dwelling and One Concrete Interpretation as Indicated by Hasan Fatby's *Architecture for the Poor. Geoscience and Man* 24 (30 April): 43.53.

Shortridge, J.R. 1991. The Concept of the Place-defining Novel in American Popular Culture. *The Professional Geographer*, 43: 380-291.

Silk, C.P. & J.A. Silk 1985. Racism, Nationalism and the Creation of a Regional Myth: The Southern States after the American Civil War. In, J.A. Rurgess & J.R. Gold, eds. *Geography and Media,* Croom Helm, Beckenham, Kent: 165-191.

Silk, J.A. 1984. Beyond Geography and Literature. *Environment and Planning,* Ser. D. *Society and Space* 2: 151-178.

Simpson-Housley, Paul & Preston, Peter 1994. Eds. *Writing the City: Eden, Babylon and the New Jerusalem*. Routledge, London (UK).

Tuan, Yi-Fu 1976. Literature, Experience and Environmental Knowing. In G.T. Moore & R. G. Golledge, eds. *Environmental Knowing*: 260-272.

— 1978a. Literature and Geography: Implications for Geographical Research. In D. Ley & M.S. Samuels, eds. : 194:-206.

— 1978b. Sign and Metaphor. *Annals, Assoc. of American Geographers*, 68: 362-372.

— 1990. Realism and Fantasy in Art, History, and Geography. *Annals, Association of American Geographers*, 80 (4): 435-446.

Wang, X.L. 1990. Geography and Chinese Poetry. *The Geographical Review*, 80 (1): 43-55.

Wright, John K. 1924 a. The Geography of Dante. *Geographical Review*, 14: (2) : 319-320.

— 1924 b. Geography in Literature. *Geographical Review*, 14 (4): 659-660.

— 1926 a. Bibliogeographical Sources for Geographical Fiction. *The Geographical Review*, 16 (4): 499-501.

— 1926 b. A Plea for the History of Geography. *ISIS*, 8: 477-491.
— 1947. *Terrae Incognitae*: The Place of Imagination in Geography. *Annals, Assoc. of American Geographers*, 37 (1): 1-15.

Wyckoff, W. 1979. The Prairie Novel and the European Immigrant: New Perspectives for the Geography Classroom. *Journal of Geography*, 78: 226-230.

References on India

Ali, S. Muzaffer 1966. *The Geography of the Puranas*. People's Publishing House, New Delhi.

Apte, Mahadeo L. 1970. Reflections of Urban Life in Marathi Literature. In, R.G. Fox ed. *Urban India*: 199-214.

Bery, Ashok 1997. 'Changing the Script': R.K. Narayan and Hinduism. *ARIEL: A Review of International English Literature*, 28 (2): 7-20.

Bose, Brinda 1996. In Good Faith? Shadows of Hinduism on Expatriate Identity in the Fiction of Bharati Mukherjee. In, *'And the Birds Began to Sing': Religion and Literature in Post-Colonial Cultures*; Ed. Jamie Scott. Cross/ Cultures 20. Edition Rodopi Press, Amsterdam & Atlanta GA: 293-300.

Buckhory, Somdutt 1979. *The Call of the Ganges*. Vikas Publ. House, New Delhi. [pub. in Hindi 1972. *Ganga ki Pukar*; Abha Publ., Delhi]

Desai, Anita 1977. *Fire on the Mountain*. Penguin, Harmondsworth.

Dhussa, Ramesh C. 1981. Literary Geography: A Bibliography. *Journal of Cultural Geography*, vol. 1 (2), Spring-Summer: 113-117.
— 1986. *Urban Images of Delhi through Literature: A Study in Humanistic Geography*. Unpublished Ph.D. dissertation in Geography, Kent State University, Kent, Ohio (USA).
— 1990. Premchand's Writings: A Goldmine of Geographic Images. *National Geographical Journal of India*, 36 (pts. 1-2): 95-108.
— 1992.Trends of Literary and Humanistic Geography of India. *National Geographical Journal of India*, 38: 75-86.
— 1994. Phenomenology of Place: An Inquiry in Indian Cultural Context — Case of Delhi. *National Geographical Journal of India*, 40: 157-170; also in *The Spirit and Power of Place*, ed. Rana P.B. Singh. N.G.S.I., Varanasi, Publ. 41.
— n.d. *Literary Geography of an Indian Region: The Middle Ganga Plain*. Forthcoming.

Dhussa, Ramesh C. & Surinder M. Bhardwaj, 1988. Delhi as Viewed by Expatriate Writers. *National Geographical Journal of India*, 34 (1): 33-41.

Dutt, Ashok K. & R.C. Dhussa 1976. The Contrasting Images and Landscape of Calcutta through Literature. *Proceedings, Assoc. of American Geographers* 8: 102-106.

— 1981. Novelist Sarat Chandra's Perception of his Bengali Home Region: A Literary Geographic Study. *GeoJournal*, 5 (1) : 41-53.

— 1983. Novelist Sarat Chandra's Perception of Bengalis in Probash (Foreign Lands): A Literary Geographic Study. *National Geographical Journal of India*, 29 (3-4): 188-206.

Eck, Diana L. 1982. *Banaras, City of Light.* Alfred Knopf, New York. Reprinted: Penguin India, New Delhi.

Edensor, Tim 1998. *Tourists at Taj: Performance and Meaning at a Symbolic Site*. Routledge, London.

Eichinger Ferro-Luzzi, Gabriella, 1980. The Female *Lingam*: Interchangeable Symbols and Paradoxical Associations of Hindu Gods and Goddesses. *Current Anthropology*, 20: 45-54, and 62-67.

— 1983. *COOL FIRE: Culture Specific Themes in Tamil Short Stories*. Edition Herodot, Göttingen.

— 1987. *The Self-Milking Cow and the Bleeding Lingam. Criss-Cross of Motifs in Indian Temple Legends.* Otto Harrassowitz Verlag, Wiesbaden.

— 1990. Tamil Culture in its Literary Similies and Metaphors. *National Geographical Journal of India*, 36 (1-2): 109-116.

— 1992. Creativity in Tradition: A contemporary Tamil writer's similies and metaphors. In, Mariola Offredi, ed. *Literature, Language and the Media in India*. Manohar Publs., New Delhi: 95-106.

— 1995. *The "Incomprehensible" Writer. Tamil Culture in Ramamirtham's Work and Worldview*. Harrassowitz Verlag, Wiesbaden.

— 1999. Hindu perceptions of Earth. In, *The Perceptions of the Elements in the Hindu Traditions*. Studia Religiosa Helvistica. Eds. Maya Burger and Peter Schreiner. Peter Lang, Bern: 29-57.

— 1997. Water in Modern Tamil Literature. *Revista delgi Studi Orientali* (Universita di Roma "La Sapienza"), vol. LXX, Fasc. 3-4 (1996): 353-366.

— 2002a. The Mental Monkey: The Mind in Modern Tamil Literature. *Zeitschrift der deutschen Morgenlandischen Gesellshaft* (Harrassowitz Verlag, Wiesbaden), Band 152 (H. 1): 113-131.

— 2002b. *The Maze of Fantasy in Tamil Folktales*. Harrassowitz Verlag, Wiesbaden.

Fox, Richard G. 1970. Ed. *Urban India: Society, Space and Image*. Program in Comparative Studies on Southern Asia, Duke University, Durham, Monograph No. 10.

Gemmill, Janet P.1980. The City as Jungle in the Indo-English Novel. In, A.G. Noble & A.K. Dutt, eds. *India: Cultural Patterns and Process*: 45-67.

Gurudatt 1978. *Yatra ka Anta* ('End of the Journey'); in Hindi. Bhartiya Sahitya Sadan, New Delhi.

Kanaganayakam, Chelva 2001. Charting a Secular Ganges: Revisiting Malgudi and Little India. In, *Mapping the Sacred: Religion, Geography and*

Postcolonial Literature, eds. Jamie Scott & Paul Simpson-Housley. Editions Rodopi Press BV, Amsterdam & Atlanta: 317-334.

Mehta, Ved 1973. *Portrait of India.* Penguin Books, Middlesex, UK.

Mondal, Anshuman 1999. The Ideology of Space in Raja Rao's Kanthapura. *Journal of Commonwealth Literature*, 34 (1): 103-114.

Mukerji, Anath Bandhu 1969a. Climatological Lore in the Yajur Veda. *The Indian Geographical Journal of India*, 12 (1 & 2): 18-25.

— 1969b. Rural Settlements in the Jatakas. *Geographical Review of India*, 31 (2), June: 17-32.

Naipal, V.S. 10968. *An Area of Darkness.* The McMillan & Co., New York.

— 1977. *India: A Wounded Civilisation.* Penguin Books, Middlesex, UK.

Noble, Allen G. 1976. The Emergence and Evolution of Malgudi: An Interpretation of South Indian Townscapes from the Fictional Writings of R.K. Narayan. *Proceedings, Assoc. of Amer. Geogr.*, 8: 106-110.

— 1980. Malgudi: The South Indian Townscape of R.K. Narayan. *Deccan Geographer*, vol. 18 (January-June): 803-811.

Noble, Allen G. & Ashok K. Dutt 1980. Eds. *India: Cultural Patterns and Process.* Westview Press, Boulder CO.

Pargiter, F.E. 1894. The Geography of Rama's Exile. *Journal of the Royal Asiatic Society*, (April): 231-264.

Philip, D.S. 1986. *Perceiving India Through the Works of Nirad C. Chaudhari, R.K. Narayan and Ved Mehta.* Sterling Publ., New Delhi.

Ramanujan. A.K. 1970. Towards an Anthology of City Images. In, R.G. Fox, ed. *Urban India*: 224-244.

Rama Rau, Santha 1945. *Home to India.* Harper & Brothers, Inc., New York.

Ray, Rajat K. 1983. The Rural World of Tarashankar Banerjee: Social Divisions and Psychological Crosscurrents. In, Peter Robb ed. *Rural India.* SOAS Collected Paper No.6. Curzon Press, London: 275-314.

Shinde. S.B. 1988. 'Region' in the Regional Marathi Novels: A Socio-geographical Analysis. A paper in the *IX Annul Conference of the Institute of Indian Geographers* (Abstract VIII-12). Varanasi. Feb. 14-16.

Singh, R.L. & Singh, Rana P.B. 1990. Eds. *Literature and Humanistic Geography.* National Geographical Society of India, Varanasi, Res. Pub. Series: No. 37; 11 essays and book reviews.

Singh, Rana P.B. 1985. The Personality and Lifeworld of Varanasi as Revealed in Shivprasad Singh's Novel: A Study in Literary Geography. *National Geographical Journal of India*, 31 (4): 291-318.

— 1989. *Where Cultural Symbols Meet. Literary Images of Varanasi.* Tara Book Agency, Varanasi.

— 1990. Literary Images, Cultural Symbols and Intimate Sensing: The Ganga River in Varanasi. *National Geographical Journal of India*, 36 (1-2): pp. 117-128.

— 1991. Rama's Route after Banishment: A Geographic Viewpoint. *Journal of Scientific Research* (B.H.U., Varanasi), vol. 41 B (Earth Sciences): 39-46.

— 1994. Modern Varanasi: Place and Society in Shivprasad Singh's Novel *Street Turns Yonder*. In, *Writing the City: Eden, Babylon and the New Jerusalem*, eds. Paul Simpson-Housley & Peter Preston. Routledge, London (UK): pp. 220-240.

— 1999. Nature and Cosmic Integrity: A Search in Hindu Geographic Thought. In, Anne Buttimer & Luke Wallin, eds. *Nature and Identity in Cross-Cultural Perspective*. Kluwer Academic Publishers, Dordrecht (Netherlands): pp. 69-86. [Reprinted from *GeoJournal*, vol. 26 (2), 1992: pp. 139-147]

Singh, Rana P.B., Singh, Ravi. S. & Rana, P.S. 2002. Sacred Geography of Goddesses in Kashi (Varanasi). *Journal of Geography*, vol 3 (Theme: Social Geography, eds. H.N. Sharma & A.K. Bhagabati; Dept. of Geography, Gauhati University, Guwahati, AS, India), October: pp. 11-35.

Tamaskar, B.G. 1956. Geographical Knowledge in the Upanishads. *National Geographical Journal of India*, 2 (2): 101-114.

— 1969. Geographical Genesis of Hell in the Maha Shiva Purana. *Geographical Knowledge*, 2 (2): 128-132.

Tewari, A.K. & Rajni Saxena 1978. Geography of the Householder. *Deccan Geographer*, VI (2) : 433-441.

Twain, Mark 1898. *Following the Equator. A Journey around the World*. The American Publ. Co., Hartfort.

Zelliott, Eleanor 1970. Literary Images of the Modern Indian City. In, R.G. Fox, ed. *Urban India*: 215-223.

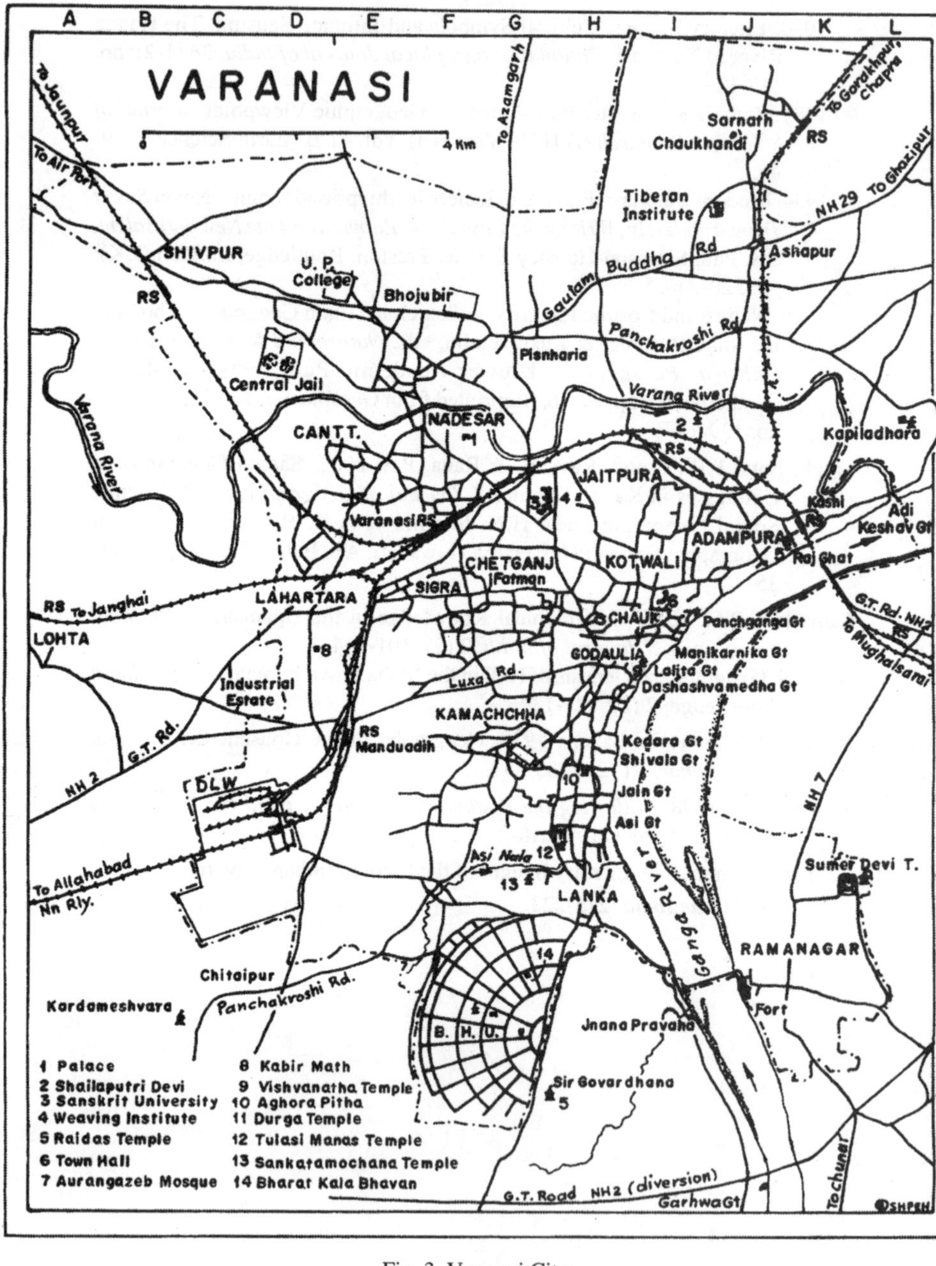

Fig. 3. Varanasi City.

~2~

The Lifeworld in Ancient Banaras: Shivprasad Singh's *The Primordial Fire*

1. Introduction: Canvas and Context

While living, working and experiencing Kashi, the novelist Shivprasad Singh (1928-1998) planned to have three novels on the city, one each on a historical period, viz. the ancient, the medieval, and the modern. His latest novel, ***Vaishvanara*** ('The Primordial Fire', 1996; hereafter referred as **VS**:) is first in the series.[1] The focus of his consideration has been the 'lifeworld' that refers to "the culturally defined spatio-temporal setting or horizon of everyday life" (Buttimer, 1976: 227). The ancientmost mythology which goes back to the period of the *Rig Veda* (ca. 13th century BCE) and flourished in different versions till the 10th century CE recounts the life and deeds of Divodasa, the legendary king of Kashi. This has been taken as the canvas for the novel *Vaishvanara*. Covering such a vast span of time would certainly result in slipping through many aspects, issues and contents. It was a difficult job to give importance to certain aspects from the complex and diversified story of Divodasa. However, the novelist has been successful in covering and linking the tales.

The novelist felt ashamed for the present-day cultural crises. He said "I know how much our intellectuals are copy-cats and feel proud of their knowledge of ignorance. If the stories of the *Bible* or the *Quran* are discussed, people enjoy with pride and glory, but they show their distaste and disbelief in the Vedic stories. The present novel also attempts to document the culture and life in the Vedic period — the ideal society, the humanistic thoughts, the knowledge of herbal medicine, and above all the universalism and social cohesiveness" (VS: 8).

The present novel deals with the culture and life of the central Ganga valley in the ancient period (12th century BCE - 4th century CE). Vedic, post-Vedic and early Puranic literature are taken as sources for the imaginary construction of landscape and life. On the basis of the ancient mythologies, it can be concluded that before ca. 1000 BCE the Kashi region was well settled and under the sovereign control of the kings of the Kashya clan, who gave it the name Kashi (Motichandra, 1985: 26). An early Purana, *Matsya* (180.68), mentions that after the glorious reign of Alarka the city was also called Alarkapuri.

The novelist challenges the historical assumption that Kashi was not mentioned in the Vedic literature. He quotes the *RigVeda* (RgV), which describes a 'sacred metre' (*richa*) composed by Kashiraja ('the king of Kashi'), by name Prataradana (RgV, 10.179.2, cf. VS: 7). Citing further the story of Bhishma's preaching that refers to the fight between Prataradana and Videha as incidence of the past, the novelist illustrated his viewpoint about the historicity of the state of Kashi (VS: 8). According to the Puranic sources king Prataradana was the 10th in the lineage of Manu, the primordial man described in the Hindu creation theory; this can be exemplified from a 9th century text, *Bhagavata Purana* (9.1.7). It is quite possible that the Puranic literature represents a walking-over and systemisation and elaboration of the traditions which had already been current for some time in the remote past.

The story of Divodasa and Prataradana represents the incidence of an early ancient period by referring to the migration and expansion of the Aryans from the northeast part of Bharata/India (Motichandra, 1985: 24). Prataradana was the son of Divodasa, who defeated the Haihaiyas and re-gained his crown over Kashi, which had been earlier lost by his father. Again in the later part of life Prataradana was defeated by the non-Aryan chiefdom Kshemaka. He made the palace his own fort (VS: 467). Kshemaka, who was a king, stopped all the Brahmanic rituals and learning of the Vedas, which was directly a great loss to Brahmins because their livelihood depended upon these activities (VS: 468). After the passage of time Prataradana's son Alarka killed Kshemaka and re-established his own sovereignty. The *Panchavimsha Brahmana* (15.37) narrates that the Brahmin sage Bharadvaja later became the priest of Divodasa and had helped to return his crown. The medieval text *Vishnu Purana* mentions that the king Divodasa sought refuge with Bharadvaja, and by his favour he had a son named Pratardana who destroyed his opponent Haihaiyas ruled by their king Vitahavya, and re-established the kingdom of Kashi (cf. Sherring, 1886: 381). Using imaginary incidences and plots of minute stories, the novelist has successfully woven the details of the culture and social life of ancient Banaras.

The story referring to Shiva's involvement in getting Divodasa out of Kashi is clearly a later version; most probably in the later Puranic mythologies this story is elaborated in so many ways (cf. Eck, 1982: 53). The earlier *Puranas* accounting the story of Divodasa and the rivalry of the Kashis and the Haihaiyas are the *Brahmanda Purana* (2.3.67-78) and the *Vayu Purana* (92), both dated ca. 6th-7th century CE. One of the speculations tells us that the story of Divodasa as a man and king of unspotted purity and of the strictest integrity "may be conceived to have resisted the encroachments of Hinduism on its first approach to Banaras, but was eventually obliged to succumb to it, and to surrender his crown to the Brahmanical invaders (*associates of Shiva*)" (Sherring, 1868: 83-84). But Sherring (*ibid.*) has wrongly speculated that Divodasa was a Buddhist, because during that period nowhere was Vajrayana Buddhism mentioned in the Vedic literature; however Tantric rituals are described at many places that were based on the indigenous belief systems.

2. The issue of Aryan expansion

There is no common agreement as to when the Aryan came and settled in the central Ganga valley. Most likely the heavy pressure of population encouraged the Aryans to migrate from their major areas of concentration in northwest India, the Indus valley, mostly along the Sarasvati river (that vanished around 1750 BCE). The core was the township of Harayupiya (Harappa) in the Sarasvati basin, referred as Brahmavarta (Fig. 4). The *Mahabharata* (3.83.4 and 205) mentions this land as Kurukshetra. Chaudhury (1966: 49) mentions: "The Vedic Aryan settled down in the Punjab, but they could not remain satisfied with it, nor confined to it. For one thing, they were a restless warrior folk with a wanderlust. Next, they had come into India, not simply as an aristocracy, but as a complete society". They initially spread in masses up to the coast of the Gulf of Kutch (Gujarat). From the sea route the Aryans also developed contact and promoted business in southeast Asia and other nearby islands (VS: 58). Around 1000 BCE another stream of Aryan migrants went to Bhrigukachha and from there to Mahishmati ('source of the Narmada river'). And, the other one went to Pratishthan (Allahabad), Ayodhya and Kashi (VS: 439).

According to another view (based on remote sensing data) a catastrophic drought and epidemic in ca. 1750 BCE (VS: 8) were the main factors resulting in the drying of the course of the Sarasvati river. The settlers were bound to search for an alternative land for survival

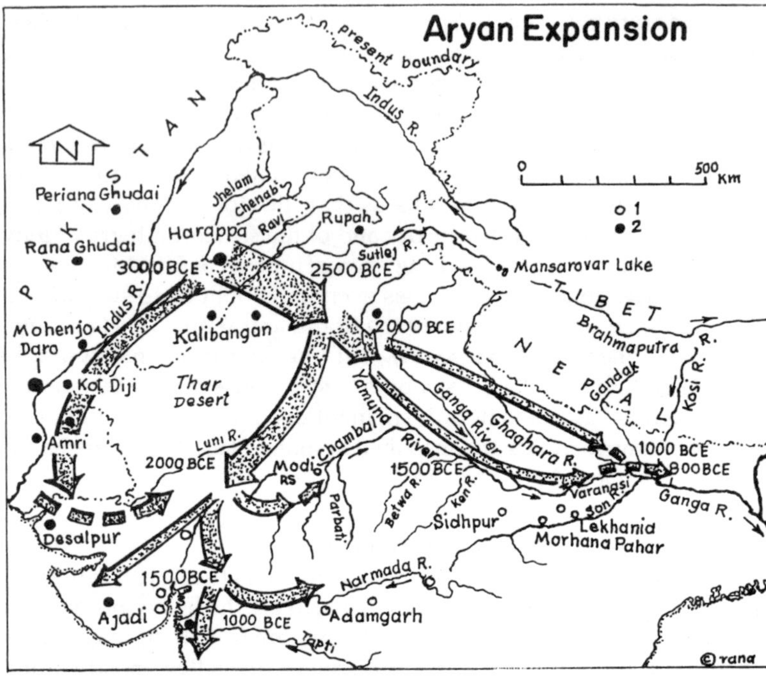

Fig. 4. Aryan expansion, From Harappa & Mohenjo Daro to the Kashi Region; (1) Late stone age site, and (2) Pre-Harappan and allied sites (after Singh, Rana, 1977: 33).

and subsistence. The drought was so intense and widespread that people even ate the meat of dead animals. One of the sages said (cf. RgV, 4.18.13) that "leaving aside the religious codes, I have eaten the boiled intestine of a dead dog; I have seen how my wife took her last breath because of the lack of food. Even in this crucial time the gods did not help us. Finally, O Shyena ('Rays of Light'), you offered the rains to us" (VS: 87, also p. 8). The *Shatapatha Brahmana* (1.4.1.15-17), a ca. 8th century BCE text, narrates the story of Aryan expansion. It says that from the dried bed of the Sarasvati river a noble Aryan group marched towards the east under the leadership of Videgha Mathava and in the course of time reached the bank of the Sadanira (Gandaki) river. They established the kingdom of Koshala. Another branch, named Kashya, at the same time established its separate kingdom, which was called Kashi. The *Ramayana*, another contemporary text, also described Kashi as a kingdom and an important city (Motichandra, 1985: 26). It is obvious from these sources that Kashi was well known as a glorious kingdom in the ancient past, around 1000 BCE. The archaeological evidences further support this on the basis of the scientific analysis of chronosequence of non-occluded/ occluded phosphate ratio of the vertical profile of anthrosols in the Rajghat area of Varanasi, which has been dated from 800 BCE to CE 800. The results support the fact that residential settlement during this time span was uninterrupted (cf. Eidt, 1977: 1330-31).

The Puranic history tells us that the Chedi-Haihaiyas and the Yadus were frequently attacking Kashi to impose their sovereignty, however they were always defeated (VS: 114). The great grandfather of Prataradana, Kshatravridha, explained that "we Aryans came here to settle down and make this territory of Kashi (*Janapada*) great and ultimately our own kingdom. Let us not fear war or attacks by the neighbouring states" (VS: 116). For the first time in the ancient history a Great War led by the Yadu clan of the Haihaiyas spread from Gandhara (Afghanistan) to Saptasindhu, following the path leading to the dark side of humanity. The whole of northwest India suffered calamities like rape and killing, and was set on fire — altogether a ghostly dance! Kshatriyas lost their moral code of conduct, which resulted in the killing of their own brothers and cousins (VS: 194).

The dwellers of Kashi believed that long before their occupancy, some tribes like the Mundas inhabited the area (VS: 77). The later Aryan settlers referred to these original settlers as *anarya* (non-Aryan) and *dasyu* (enemy). Dhanvantari once said that "I've walked from Kashi to the central part of Bharat (India) up to Nagpur, and found a predominance of black-faced tribes, the Mundas. They worshipped *Singabonga* ('Surya', the Sun god). The Sun was their patron deity, followed by the ancestors" (VS: 78). On another occasion Dhanvantari recalled that there was a kingdom of Kiratas in the Central Himalaya, and their chief deity was Shiva. They had also built a temple of Trilokeshvara (Shiva). In the early period of Aryan invasion in ca. 9th century BCE the king Mandhata defeated the Kiratas and made them slaves (VS: 68). Malaria (*'takma'*) was a common epidemic resulting in the loss of lives everywhere (VS: 18, 19, 28, 30, 50, 70, 82). In spite of all the preventive care, it was difficult to check the high fever and save the lives. Tribes like the Mundas and the Kiratas were the worst hit (VS: 68). These tribes dominantly inhabited the southern part of the city (cf. VS: 340).

The ancient tradition about the original site was carried continuously by the descendant migrant settlers, one of whose traditions is the festival of oil lamps. The novelist narrates, "Today again a memorial celebration will be held, comparable to that which our ancestors celebrated at Sumeru (Pamir) plateau. The lighting of the lamps in a circular form was spectacular. The sliced meat pieces were arranged into an iron stick, roasted on the open fire, and enjoyed with the juice of Soma; who will not remember!" (VS: 82). According to Wilkins (1882: 69) the Soma-plant of the *Rig Veda* refers to *Asclepias acida* of Roxburgh, and that's how Soma as a god represents the juice of the Soma-plant.

3. Mythology and history of ancient Kashi

The Chedis (Karttivirya) were rivals of the Prataradana's family and occasionally tried to defeat them, but always failed (VS: 28). Karttavirya was the sovereign of the Haihaiya tribe, endowed by the favour of the mystic-sage Dattatreya. One of the metres (*richas*) of the *Rig Veda* (10.179) describes Pratardana, the king of Kashi.

Buddhist literature refers to the ancient city Kashi as Varanavati. The main city was settled around the confluence of the Varana to the Ganga, today known as Raj Ghat, and was expanded in the south up to Madhyameshvara. The *Mahabharata* (6.10.30) refers to the old name of Varana as Varanavati. The *Atharva Veda* (4.7.1) also refers to the city as Varanavati, which connotes the city grown along the Varanavati (Varana) river; the text (AV, 5.22.14) also refers to Kashi as a kingdom.

The ancient site of the shrine of Avimukteshvara (Shiva) is not known, however it is believed that after the passage of time its replicated form was built near the present Jnanavapi (VS: 11). Avimukta was also known as Devadeva; the *Mahabharata* says (*Vanaparva*, 84.18) that after reaching the Avimukta Kshetra one can get high religious merit by worshipping Devadeva. In the later Puranic period the image of Devadeva had been established separately; presently there is one in Dhundhiraj Gali, near Brahmavaivarta Kupa.

The *Rig Veda* (10.81.4) says, "Who is the host of all, host of all the life substance, host of the human beings; the only answer is the 'trees' " (VS: 88). Among the herbal plant, *tulasi* (*Ocimum sanctum*) together with black pepper was used as a common preventive herb against cold and cough, and was called Vrinda, 'the wife of Vishnu' (VS: 56). The Adusha plant (Malabar nut tree, *adhatoda vasika*) was used by the oracles for exorcism (VS: 160), while the yellow mustard (*'siddhaitha'*) used for hypnotism (VS: 167). The spicy paste made of *amalaki* (*Emblic myrobalans*) was a common chutney (VS: 364). Among the seasonal fruits the local specie of mango (*Magnifera indica*) was famous for its sweetness and fragrance and beautiful look (VS: 491). "There were reserved forests known for the healing and herbal plants where sages perform meditation and austerity" (VS: 79). It is a fact that every plant has some medicinal value for curing one or other disease (VS: 80).

> Where was the old city of Kashi, in the ancient past there was no river, no human habitat, but only forests. In those days of the past, a divine being, Ishana, came on the earth and saw a great *linga* that touched the sky in the upper part, and in the lower reached the netherworlds. Thereafter two gods, Brahma (the creator) and Vishnu (the preserver) came from the heavens while fighting among themselves over the issue of their own supremacy. With a view to ending their fight, Ishana suggested that one of them should go to the sky and the other to the netherworlds and check the respective ends of the *linga*. The one who will return first will be considered stronger and greater. Brahma riding on a swan, his vehicle, flew up to the sky, and Vishnu in his Boar-form entered into the earth. Both, fully tired and unsuccessful in their attempt, returned in despair. Vishnu innocently accepted his defeat. Brahma falsely claimed that he had reached to the end, but failed to prove it. Ishana, in fact a form of Shiva, became angry with Brahma and cursed him that the devout people will not offer you oblations and will not worship you. The *linga* was beyond any limit, far away from vision and absolutely undescribable. That is how it is called Vishveshvara or Avimukteshvara. (VS: 325)

"Passing by the four generations of the kingdom, I, Divodasa, accept the power of the crown placed upon my shoulders by the kindness of all our respected ancestors and the people" (VS: 212). The mythology of Divodasa starts in the *Rig Veda*. It is eulogised even in the later *Puranas,* and especially, in a more elaborate form, in the KKh, dated ca. 11th-14th century (cf. Eck, 1982: 53). The legend of Shiva's involvement and the expulsion of Divodasa from Kashi by the demon Nikumbha and the later control of the kingdom by the demon Kshemaka is vividly described in the *Brahma Purana* (11.40-54), a ca. 6th century text. Of course the novelist concentrated on the Vedic period, and in several contexts he took the narration from the KKh and elaborated it. According to the KKh (44.29-34), "Divodasa made Kashi his capital and ruled his kingdom well. The earth flourished and the people prospered under his leadership. He became the epitome of the *dharmaraja,* the just and righteous king. During Divodasa's glorious rule, Kashi was a city of flawless harmony, and it was said to surpass the heavens in excellence."

In the *Upanishads,* Prataradana, the king of Kashi, was also called Ajatashatru (cf. *Brihadaranakya U,* 2.1.1; also *Kaushikeya U,* 4.1), who taught Gargi. He is referred to there as one of the greatest sages and yogis (VS: 498).

4. Vaishvanara, the Sun Supremacy

"The sun, wind and fire are brothers. Of the realm of light the chief is the Sun, of the sky the Wind, and of the earth the Fire. ... All the organic life is the product of the two basic elements according to their dominance the organic life is also classified in two groups — Fire and Water" (VS: 23).

The *Rig Veda* (1.59.2) prays to Vaishvanara:

> O Vaishvanara!
> You're the head of the realm of light
> And also the navel of the Earth.
> You're called Vishvareta by the gods.
> You've shown the radiant path to human beings. (VS: 5)

The fire of the ethereal breath (*prana*) is the form. Offering grains to the fire generates energy. The body depends on the substance of grains. This is the supreme bliss; but for process and continuity it sucks the juice from all the five gross elements, viz. earth, water, fire, sky and air. The essence of this juice is *virya* ("the seed"). For any growth always a liquid of creation is required from which the seeds of sustenance get birth (VS: 269).

The Sun — the fire element of nature, and the Moon — the liquid element of nature, together interact to make energy which is symbolised in the form of Vaishvanara, "the Primordial Fire" (VS: 18).

'There are twelve Sun images (excluding the one at the centre, the Samba) in Kashi. These are not independent images. Each one is a distinct form of the same vital power. The Aryans believed that if all the forms will settle at one site and at one time, this will turn into a great fire — complete dissolution. Remember that the Sun moves along the circuit of twelve zodiacs, representing twelve months, and thus forms a *mandala.* ... The shadow and images are created by the will of Shiva, who is the patron deity of the city and the maker of its fate' (cf. VS: 237). Even today the pilgrimage to the Sun images (Aditya Yatra) is a common practice. In this pilgrimage, three distinct sites are Lolarka at Lolarka Kund in the south, Yama at Sankata Ghat in the east and

Uttara at Bakaria Kund in the north. The central shrine of Samba is at Suraj Kunda in the west to where the rest of the 12 Sun images orient for alignment.

Each of the thirteen forms of the Sun god Aditya (Surya), including the one at the centre of the circle, has a specific place closely connected to each other in terms of cultural astronomy, zodiacs, and division of time — altogether put into the web of mythology. According to astrological correspondences all the Sun images of Varanasi are associated with their respective zodiacs and with their correspondent planets and parts of the body. These relationships are also linked with the tissues of the body whose relations constitute the person's physiological processes. Astrologers interpret the horoscopes by understanding the role and impact of various planets with respect to the zodiac and the sun (cf. Singh and Malville, 1995: 75-78). This is a complicated pattern and process related to the complex system of faith healing. The complex network and structure of the spatial pattern of solar shrines and their association with the movement of the sun throw light on the cosmological sense of city planning in the ancient period. Probably this pattern is older than the Brahmanical tradition, but in course of time it has been superseded by the Brahmanical (in fact Shaiva) tradition. In Varanasi, the sun is directly involved in the making of cosmic ordering at one end, and in the life of the city at the other.

Of course while each and every Sunday is prescribed for Sun worship, it becomes even more auspicious if Sunday falls on the 6th or 7th day of the lunar month. On the occasion of a solar eclipse, taking a holy dip in the river Ganga and worshipping the Sun god is a special ritual. If Sunday falls on the 6th or 7th day of the light fortnight (waxing) in *Margashirsha* (November-December), that provides the most auspicious time for taking a holy bath in the tank at Lolarka Kunda. The annual festival takes place on the 6th day of the light fortnight of *Bhadrapada* (August-September).

The etymology of the name Alarka, son of king Prataradana, the grandson of Divodasa and the great grandson of Dhanvantari, refers to the Sun god; the city was also sometimes called Alarkapuri (VS: 451).

5. The territory of Kashi and Physical Landscape

Kashi is the most sacred land (VS: 329). Among the seven sacred abodes of Vishnu as narrated in the ancient texts, Kashi served as the supreme, the centre, bestower of the highest merit (VS: 331).

In the early rainy season Matsyodari was not converted into a lake. Enough waters from the Ganga and Varana both came into it.

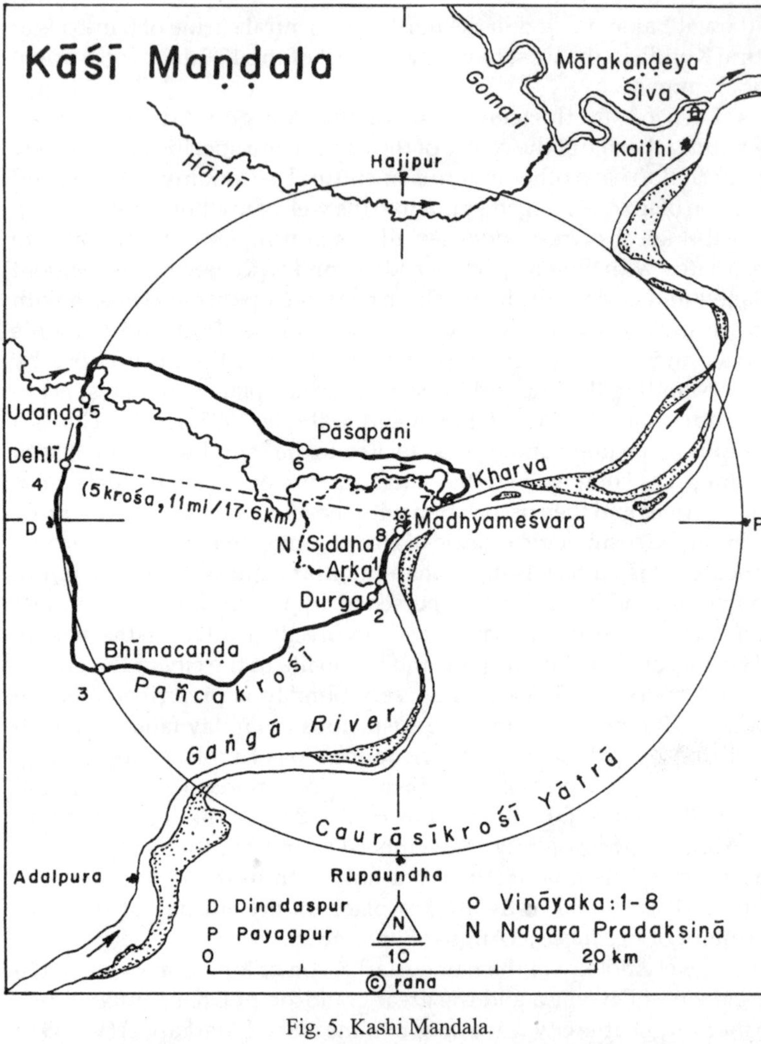

Fig. 5. Kashi Mandala.

Mandakini, another stream, before entering the Chakrapushkarini, a big lake, turned to the west and formed a big pond, and then proceeded further towards the Ganga (VS: 336). The *Linga Purana* accounts (LP as in KKT, p. 127) that during the peak season, flood water from the Ganga reached the Matsyodari and touched the temple of Omkar-eshvara and the Kapalamochana tank (cf. Sukul, 1977: 63). The novelist's description is very close to the ancient drainage system of the city as given in one of the oldest Puranas.

One of the characters narrates, "I've walked several times across the temple of Markandeshvara at the confluence of the Gomati to the Ganga, but never found any cave where the non-Aryan rivals get shelter" (VS: 428). This temple settled on a raised ground was famous for the performance of marriage ceremonies (VS: 297). And, this tradition is still continued by the attendance of thousands of couples every year. This site once had ghats made of stone steps, palatial buildings and great compounds. This territory was called Nagaloka ('the realm of snakes') (VS: 297). The archaeological excavations at a little distance from Saidpur support the existence of an ancient city, however it is doubtful whether it had any direct connection to the city of Kashi. The *Mahabharata* (Anushashana, 31.18) mentions the second site of Kashi that Divodasa developed near the confluence of the Gomati to the Ganga (Fig. 5) after his defeat. Unfortunately no historical or archaeological evidences have been found to support this viewpoint. In the course of time the city grew along the left bank of the Ganga, and by the turn of the 3rd century BCE we find enough description of the city in the *Jatakas*, the Buddhist literature (cf. Vishvakarma, 1987: 15-17).

Chunar, ca. 38 km southwest of Varanasi, was at the margin of the territory of Kashi, but there are legends referring to the use of hilly tracks and caves therein by the non-Aryan tribes. "Once he arrived at Charanadri (Chunar) the story of the Dwarf-Form of Vishnu (Vamana) flashed to his mind, who by his three footsteps measured the three mythical realms (*lokas*) of the universe" (VS: 431). Ancient Hindu mythology relates that Vamana, the 5th incarnation of Vishnu, measured the earth in three paces, of which the first was placed on the hillock at Chunar. This gave the name Charanadri (cf. Singh and Rana, 2002: 243).

The Vindhya range was under the control of Karttavirya Arjuna, the sovereign of the Chedi-Haihaiyas (VS: 183). In fact, both Charanadri (Chunar) and Vindhyachala, as also the Yogamaya temple (the old Vindhyavasini temple, near the present Anandamayi Ashram) fall under the territory of Kashi (VS: 434). It is believed that Vindhyavasini is one among the most ancient Hindu goddesses and that she has an important role in the rise of the Hindu theology of the Great Goddess. Since the early centuries of the current era, the goddess received a special position in the Shakta pantheon either in the form of Uma (Shiva's spouse) or as the supreme creative energy, Yogamaya ('Yogic

Delusion') — also called Vindhyavasini (cf. Tiwari, 1985: 89-90). Her face is described as owl-faced, three-eyed, four-armed, riding on a lion or a tiger, and assisted by Ganesha and a Bhairavi (Singh, 1997: 246-247).

The Yogamaya temple, at the right side of the Ganga basin, is surrounded by the Vindhyan hills like Kairamali, Mauli (Rohitashva), Sphatika and Gurupadgiri, and was inhabited by the Mundari tribe (VS: 505-06, 507). Gurupadgiri has many caves (e.g. presently, Durgakhoha near Chunar). The Vindhya range continues up to the Magadha region in south Bihar (VS: 521). The indigenous tribes had their habitats in the hills and caves in Charanadri (Chunar), Vindhya range (VS: 428).

The outer limit of the sacred territory of Kashi was expanded even beyond the confluence of the Gomati to the Ganga in the northeast. Taking Madhyameshvara as centre, a circle with a radius of five *kroshas* (11 miles/ 17.6 km) makes a circumference of eighty four *kroshas* (296 km/ 168 miles) which is considered as the archetypal limit of Kashi (cf. VS: 341, 411, 423, 406; see *Padma Purana*, as in TS: 100). Symbolically, this territory represents the limit of universe. In another description, as in the *Linga Purana* (cf. KKT, p. 40), from Krittivasa or Madhyameshvara in all the directions one *krosha* (2.2 miles) distance delimits the sacred territory of Avimukta/ Kashi (VS: 329). A similar description is also given in the *Skanda Purana*, and in medieval treatises like the *Tirthachintamani* and *Tristhalisetu* (cf. Sukul, 1977: 51-52).

From the port at Bhrigukaccha (Gujarat, Kathiawad) good quality horses were imported. Of course, in Kathiawad crossbreed horses were available, which were reasonably good but not the best (VS: 413). The ancient kingdom of Kashi maintained close ties with the southeast countries. "The ships from the country of Champa were regularly coming to Kashi (VS: 243). Through the water channel of the Ganga our ships go to the sea. And, by the sea route we have our business in southeast Asia, including the nine island countries, viz. Indradvipa (Andaman), Nagadvipa (Nicobar), Saumyadvipa (Sumatra), Yavadvipa (Java), Gandharvadvipa (Philippines), Varunadvipa (Borneo), Kasherudvipa (Kasheru), Gabhastibhana (Malacca, Malaya), Singhala (Sri Lanka) and Kumarika" (VS: 243; cf. Fig. 6).

The close ties to distant areas were noticed on the occasion of invitations for marriage ceremonies. "The preparation of the marriage ceremony (of Prataradana) was in its full swing. The list of specially invited guest includes Nagaraja Ashvatara and Madalasa of Kanyakubja, Devarata — the representative of the great sage

Fig. 6. South East Asia as known to the ancient Indians.

Vishvamitra, sage Bhargava Rama (Parashurama), king Bahu of Saketa, Karandham of Vaishali, Janaka-I of Mithila, Amritastava of the Chedi dynasty Kaushami, and Yayati's son Puru of Pratisthana (Allahabad). With gratitude all have given their consent and assurance to attend the celebration" (VS: 256).

The sacred circular territory called Chaurashikroshi, recording a circumference of 296 km, was reduced to only ca. 88 km (five *kroshas*) and marked as the outer limit of the city. Most probably by the 11th century CE the frame of the archetypal circuit had already lost its importance. Moreover, in the ancient past nowhere is any reference of the Panchakroshi route observed. According to the novelist's perception, even in the ancient period the Panchakroshi route was not given importance. In fact, only isolated spots were marked as reference points but in no way the full route; most of the area was covered with forest and woodlands. "The outer limit of the sacred territory was marked by the Panchakroshi route, however the route and the marked signs along the route were in isolation for decades, therefore the two-*krosha* inner circle (Avimukta) is accepted for arrangement of security" (VS: 260).

"The kingdoms of Kanyakubja, Kashi and Saketa together make the Trikshetra region, which was propitiator of the theist culture (Hindu). Videha was out of this region, and followed the anti-theist beliefs (Buddhist)" (VS: 272). Kashi, Koshala and Vaishali made an agreement for mutual friendship and common goals (VS: 491).

The Dakshinapatha ('the southerly route') of ancient India passed through Varanasi, Allahabad, Chitrakut, central India, and so on. The novelist is fully confused with the spatial orientation and the historicity of the route. "I heard from Sarthavahanas that the Dakshinapatha passes through Mathura and Gopachala and reaches to Kaushambi and Revan" (VS: 465).

Of course, one of the narrations tells us that a fair was held at Bhrigupura across the Ganga. And, Bhrigu's hermitage was also a shelter of rebels and their activities were doubtful and not favourable to the descendants of Divodasa (VS: 483). This hermitage could not be identified with Bhrigu Kshetra (in Ballia town, 140 km east of Varanasi), as it was out of the territory of Kashi.

6. The Temples and Sacred Spots

"Kashi is a city of legitimate and respectful people. The supreme god, Shiva, blesses them. This is the Avimukta Kshetra ('never forsaken by Shiva'). The city lies on Shiva's trident. Here is the 'Forest of Bliss' (*anandavana*), always auspicious to the visitors. At any cost nobody would be willing to sell his landed property in this holy land" (VS: 426). The novelist's narration of *trikuta* symbolising Shiva's trident, refers to the three mounds in Varanasi, not what he describes as the Vindhyan remnants (cf. VS: 50). In fact, there are no remnants of the Vindhyan range in the city territory.

Between Raj Ghat and the Ganga-Varana confluence, in the western part is the temple of Avimukteshvara (VS: 326). In the ancient period Avimukteshvara and Vishveshvara were synonymous (VS: 363). It is also not true that the king Pratardana had changed the name of Raj Ghat to Dattatreya Ghat (cf. VS: 503). In the old literature Varana Sangam (confluence) Ghat was mentioned, not Raj Ghat. Moreover, Dattatreya Ghat is an example of 18th century architecture, built by Bajirao Peshva in 1735 and later on repaired and rebuilt by queen Baijabai of Gwalior in 1830.

The temple of Jamadagnishvara was built by Parashurama in honour of his father (VS: 400). In memory of Dhanvantari he also built there a rest house for pilgrims and a school of Ayurveda (VS: 427). It was queen Madalasa's wish to built a temple of Pratardaneshvara, named after her husband, however it was later named Madaleshvara (VS: 503).

In the northeast of the present Lat Bhairava was the temple of Bhismachandika, at walking distance in the south from Shailaputri Temple at the bank of the Varana (cf. Motichandra, 1985: 4). This was different from the present Bhimachandi Temple along the Panchakroshi pilgrimage route. Says the novelist, "this is a haunted place — the temple of Bhishmachandika. People say that there is a great cremation ground where corpses walk. I've never paid a visit but I know the route" (VS: 155). He added further, "as we were reaching it, the forest was becoming dense, the owls' voices were becoming more fearful. The shriek of crickets gave the impression of sounds coming from a sitar's broken wires. Soon I saw two jackals passing into the bushes. The thorny creepers occupied the acacia bushes. In the darkness, fire-flies were jumping from one bush to another" (VS: 156). The area around Bhishmachandi was used as a safe refuge by criminals and rebel non-Aryans (VS: 475). The *Linga Purana* says (as in KKT, cf. Motichandra, 1985: 147) that there was a water pool where Kotitirtha and the shrines of Kotishvara and Bhishmachandika were found.

On the occasion of Prataradana's marriage the lane going to Vishveshvara was decorated with Banyan trees (vata, *Ficus indica*), sandalwood pastes and incense. ... The auspicious tress planted on both sides of the lane included margosa (nima, *Azadirachta indica*), mango (amra, *Magnifera indica*), ashoka (*Saraea Indica asoca*) and nyagrodha (nimbu, *Citrus aurantifolia*) (VS: 257). Surprisingly the novelist missed to mention the Ashvatha/ Pipal (*Ficus religiosa*), the most sacred tree, and the two sacred grass species, viz. kusha and durva. These trees and plants were very highly eulogised in Vedic literature, and even today they are considered sacred and are used in rituals.

According to one of the prescriptions, first of all one should take a holy dip in the Ganga, and then pay a visit to Vishveshvara; Parashurama followed the same tradition (VS: 321). If one observes minutely the sanctum sanctorum of Vishveshvara Temple, it would be obvious that all the architectural forms symbolise the distinct altar of the archetypal universe (VS: 271). It is notable that even the 15th century temple of Vishveshvara, which was demolished by order of the Mughal emperor Aurangazeb in 1669, was also based on the archetypal plan of Indian astronomy and ancient architectural designs (cf. Singh, 1994: 199-205; cf. Figs. 7, 8 and 9). Vishveshvara has been the main *jyotiralinga* ('linga of light'); in fact Vishveshvara and Avimukteshvara were synonymous (VS: 324, 325). One of the priests informed Parashurama that if you want to worship Rudra (the oldest form of Shiva), then first you have to take a holy dip in the Ganga at Manikarnika Ghat and then visit Avimukteshvara, presently called

Fig. 7. Western part of the ancient Vishvanatha temple in the early 19th century (Prinsep, 1833).

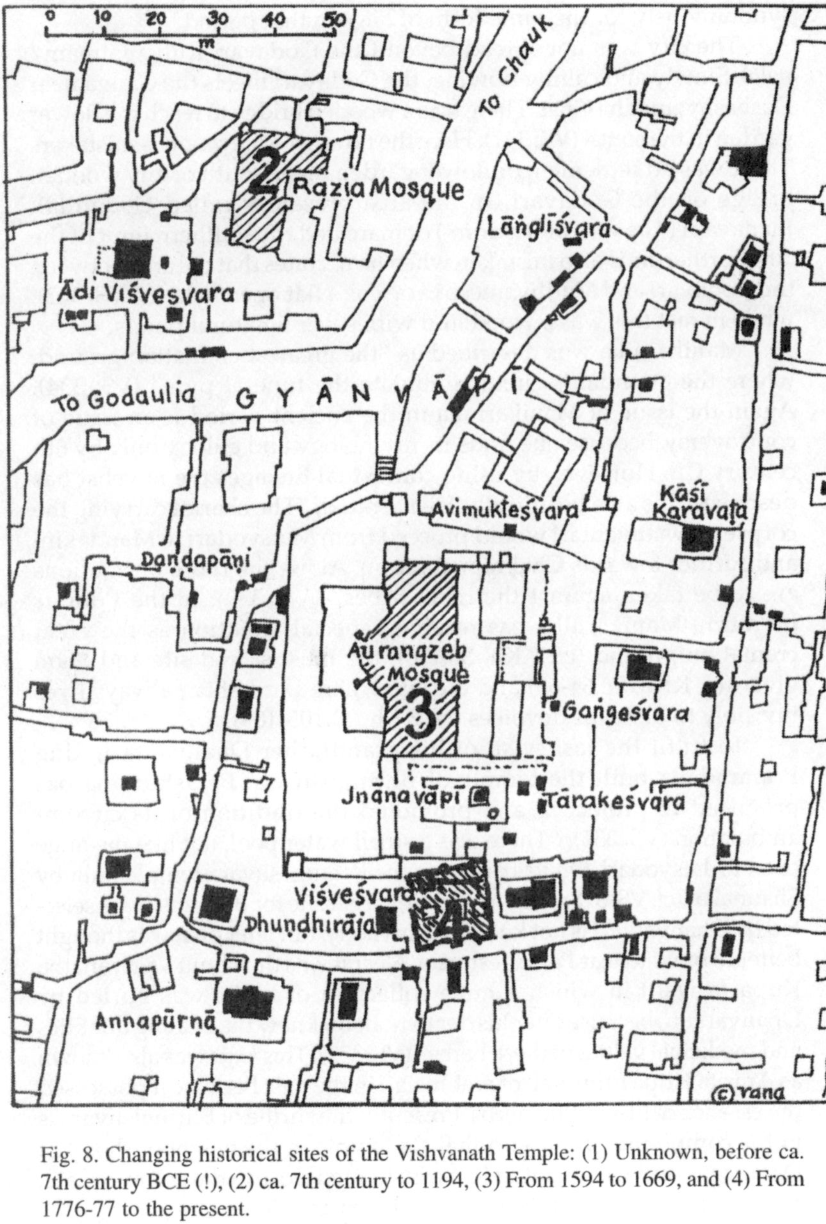

Fig. 8. Changing historical sites of the Vishvanath Temple: (1) Unknown, before ca. 7th century BCE (!), (2) ca. 7th century to 1194, (3) From 1594 to 1669, and (4) From 1776-77 to the present.

Vishveshvara (VS: 325). Perhaps, these two names were used synonimously for the same form of *linga* in that period.

The city was not spread beyond the Godavari Kulya (stream/*nala*). Slowly and calmly flowing, the Godavari meets the Ganga near Dashashvamedha Ghat. There was a wooden bridge to reach the flower garden in the south (VS: 341). Here the novelist's narration is mistaken. There was no settlement or flower garden in the south or any wooden bridge on the Godavari (in the area presently called Godaulia). Jnanavapi ('the well of wisdom') demarcated the southern limit of the city. Further, he is also mistaken when he narrates that the area between the Godavari and Madhyameshvara was a flat open field (cf. VS: 342), while in fact this was a woodland with several natural ponds.

Manikarnika was described as "the greatest cremation ground, where the attendants circumambulate the funeral pyre" (VS: 334). Again the issue of Manikarnika in the ancient period is an issue of controversy, because one finds its mythology and eulogy only by 6th century CE. However, by using contextual linkages the novelist has described this area beautifully. He narrated, "The chariot carrying the corpse of Dhanvantari would proceed from Matsyodari to Mandakini and further towards Chakrapushkarini. Along the route precautions are to be taken against the rebel tribes" (VS: 339). In the Puranic literature Manikarnika has received special attention as the great cremation ground (cf. KKh, 33.110), the most sacred site and boon giver (cf. KKh, 26.64-65) and the site where Lord Shiva always lives invisibly to bless his devotees (cf. KKh, 33.105-109).

To fulfil the last wish of his grandfather Dhanvantari, king Prataradana built the temple of Bhringishvara. Parashurama has promised to protect it, and promoted the tradition of its circumambulation (VS: 331). "There was a small water pool, not like the huge one of Matsyodari. On its bank was the Patangeshvara temple built by Shaunaka"(cf. VS: 328). Where was the earlier site for Bhringishvara selected by Dhanvantari is not known to anybody. But later on it was thought better to build it near Patangeshvara. Near it was then built Vaidyanatha Kupa (a well) in which a huge collection of herbs was buried by Dhanvantari, because after his death nobody knew the healing qualities and medicinal values of those herbs" (VS: 332). This *kupa* was also known as Amrita Kupa ('the well of ambrosia') in the past because it possessed the essence of life-saving herbs. Presently the shrine of Bhringishvara is in the compound of the Vriddhakala temple in the neighbourhood of Daranagar, and Dhanvantari Kupa is situated close to the entrance gate. Vaidyanatha Kupa and Dhanvantari Kupa are identical.

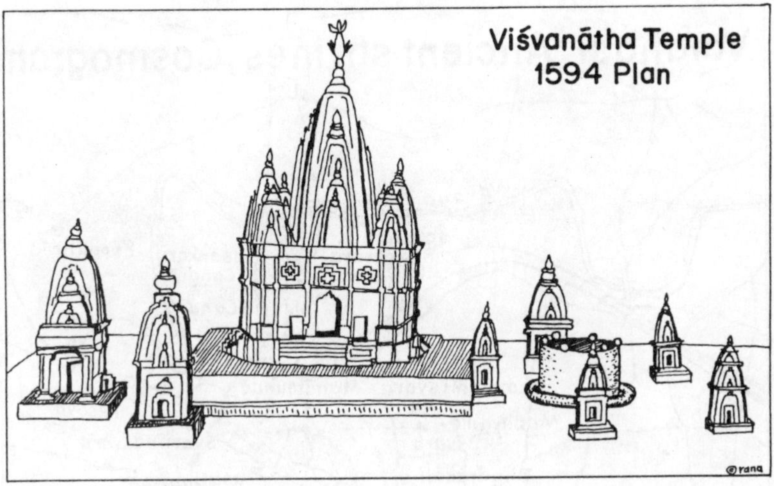

Fig. 9. Vishvanath Temple: Model view of the 1594 plan.

"According to the ancient legends, Svarlineshvara, Avimukteshvara and Madhyameshvara together form a sacred triangle area (*trikantaka*). Independently, they are also known as *jyotirlingas*" (VS: 326-27; Fig. 10). This Trikantaka group is described in the older version of the *Linga Purana* (as in KKT, p. 123). Madhyameshvara is a self-born (*svayambhu*) *linga*, which sprouted from the earth to please Shiva's devotees (VS: 329). There was a narrow lane amidst the forest which leads to Madhyameshvara (VS: 442); in fact, the temple is an isolated landmark surrounded all around by forests (VS: 474).

> Like in the sheath system (*hridaya chakra*), Madhyameshvara, unique in appearance, is the *axis mundi* of the earth, which provides peace and prosperity to the devotees. This attracts a large mass of visitors in comparison to Avimukteshvara and Svarlineshvara. Geographically situated between Raj Ghat and Manikarnika, this temple is the heart of the city. Even in the cosmic dissolution the infinite spire that always stands without disappearance is called Madhyameshvara. Metaphorically, the Varana is perceived as Ida, the Asi as Pingala and the Matsyodari as Shushumna arteries in the sacred body of the city. Madhyameshvara is the source of Shushumna. This is the cosmic structure of the body of Kashi. (VS: 328)

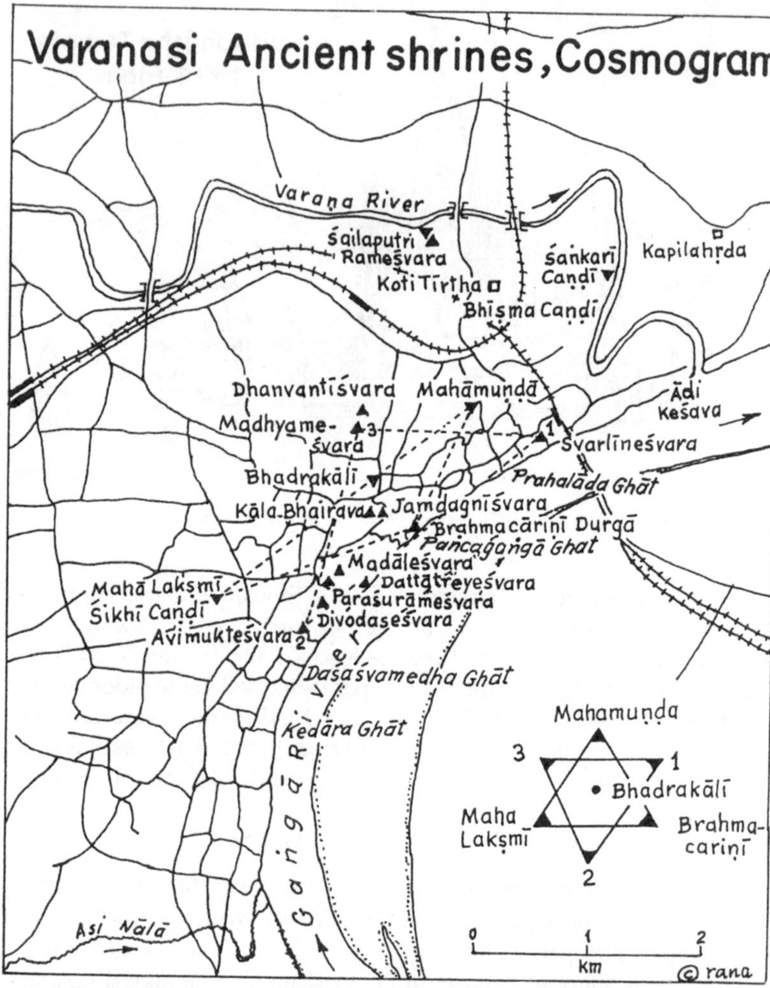

Fig. 10. Varanasi:
Ancient shrines of Shiva and Devis and emerging Shrividya Cosmogram.

"There was a palace near Svarlineshvara, and a wealthy neighbourhood, called Alkapuri, or Alarkapuri" (VS: 469). "The military commander of king Alarka decided to make Kashi the most sacred and glorious site of pilgrimage (*mahatirtha*), and provide for its maintenance too." (VS: 477).

The *Mahabharata* (*Aranyaka* canto, 82.69-70) mentions only two sacred places of Kashi, viz. Vrishabhadhvaja at Kapilahrida (Kapiladhara) and Markandeshvara Tirtha at the confluence of the Gomati with the Ganga. However, these sites were not so important in the legends of Divodasa. Perhaps for this reason the novelist has not described them. The novelist has omitted to describe one of the most notable sacred sites and shrines of the ancient period, i.e. Dashashvamedha. This sacred spot has links with the story of Divodasa. With the support of Divodasa, Brahma performed ascetic rites and sacrificed ten horses, that's how the name Dashashvamedha ('ten horses sacrifice') was given to this place (cf. Sherring, 1868: 141-142).

7. The Social World

"Said Prataradana, 'I don't want to break the traditions. I am a supporter of the *yajna* culture, but not at all a blind follower of any ritualistic tradition. ... Of course, it is quite difficult to know which are the good traditions and also which are valuable for life" (VS: 119).

Parched barley mixed with molasses, honey and milk was the common diet (VS: 34). Sweetmeats have also a long tradition in the history of Kashi. Even during the ancient days people enjoyed sweetmeats made of milk and cheese, such as Kshiramohan (now *khiramohan*) and Alupa (now *barafi*), which are even now very popular (cf. VS: 435).

Almost all the people were against sacrifice, because society was dominated and administered by the noble thoughts given by the great sages (VS: 22). This was the Aryan tradition. However the non-Aryan tribes always preferred animal sacrifice to invoke the spirits of energy.

As for the arranged marriages, there was nothing like the predetermined destiny of bride and groom. Any youngster was free to choose his/her partner (VS: 247). Inter-caste and inter-clan marriages were also noticed, though of course they were not common (VS: 250).

In many incidences the Tribals reacted against the Aryans; they said, "Why should we follow the *Vedas*. Only a few among the sages are the real creators of the sacred metres. Most of the Brahmins are engaged in luxurious life and worldly pleasures, and they are hypocrites as they teach others lessons of morality and ethics while they themselves never practice them" (VS: 78).

For a Mahabrahmin, a Brahmin engaged in cremation rites was considered as degraded, and his visits to the home of the mourners were restricted; this practice is followed even today. They are allowed to receive donations and ask alms in the cremation area where the rituals are performed. It is doubtful that this practice goes back to the

Vedic period as the novelist presumes (VS: 334). Following the *Garuda Purana*, a 7th century text, many of the folk traditions of cremation rites are accepted by Kashi-dwellers without considering their relevance and rationality (VS: 338). The Brahmin priests narrate that these rituals are based on the *Atharva Veda* (canto 18). The cremation rites follow successive steps like preparing the funeral pyre, setting up an earthen pot in a holy fig, etc. (VS: 350). As described in the *Vayu Purana*, another text of the same period, the period of post-cremation rites covers thirteen days, and on the 10th day the tonsure rite is held. The later text also prescribes that on this occasion the donation of a *nila-varna* ('blue') bull is more auspicious. On the buttock of the bull the signs of a trident and a circle will be branded with a hot iron stamp to mark its sanctity, and a paste of turmeric and mustard oil will be smeared for healing the wound (VS: 358). The advice of a Nila bull is described in the *Mahabharata* (3.87.10-12) while prescribing the steps and ways to perform ancestors' rites, especially at Gaya. Since Varanasi falls under the group of "The three holy pillars for ancestors' rites", a similar tradition prevailed there, as in the other two sites: Prayaga (Allahabad) and Gaya.

Based on the Vedic tradition, the novelist strongly supports the idea of stopping animal sacrifice. The *Rig Veda* (10.134.6) also speaks out against animal sacrifice (VS: 271):

> Convey even to the gods, that
> animal sacrifice is a direct killing.
> By the sacred verses and acts too
> *Yajna* becomes fruitful.
> By acceptance you will understand.

The *Rig Veda* (1.164.34-35) is the basic source for understanding the meaning of *yajna* (VS: 268):

> The universal quest —
> Let me know, where's the end of the Earth?
> Also, what is the navel centre of the world?
> What is the speed of the time-horse?
> What is the language of the infinite sky?
> The answers are —
> The surface-altar is the end of the Earth,
> The *yajna* site is the navel centre of the world,
> Soma is the speed of the time-horse,
> The cosmic soul is the language of the infinite sky.

"By the death of a noble man, we loose a light, and at this site we keep the oil lamp in an earthern pot, and by this way we make ourselves happy in illusion (VS: 457). When a spiritual happening takes place or the procession of carrying the corpse of a noble man or sage proceeds, the city dwellers pay their homage and respects by their emotional tears as expression of good memories. Similarly when an inhuman person or his associate dies, the dwellers very simply abuse them openly and also make this a tradition. While getting satisfied performing condolence or mockery, they spend money from their own pocket. ... Even for their dead pet or domestic animals like horses, cows and monkeys the dwellers arrange a common procession for their cremation (VS: 433-434).

Whenever side-shows are performed, a common ocurrence everywhere in the city, Kashi-dwellers never miss such occasions of fun and laughter (VS: 436). Some examples are bull fighting, cock fighting, abusive dialogues between two people, or processions in agitation. For such open recreations they donate money to the players or organisers according to their will and capacity (cf. VS: 434).

In a different context the novelist has explained the problem of a generation gap, resulting in conflict between father and son. "Tolerating the foolishness of his sons was a painful practice and was not suited to his nature"(VS: 387). "Even an adopted but devoted and respectful son is far better than a hundred disobedient sons of one's own" (VS: 390). "Every father in his lifetime wants to see his son established in the right way and at the height of glory" (VS: 222).

8. Tantric Culture: The Other Side

Tantric culture in Varanasi in the ancient past as described by the novelist is mostly based on his imagination and citations from the late 7th-8th century CE traditions. "South of Mahavana (great forest) surrounding Shankhudhara was Bhadravana, where was a fort of Kapalika tantrics" (VS: 179). The Tantric rituals include even human sacrifice (VS: 70). It was common that Tantrics always follow the 'black magic' and sacrificial rituals and the power received by such shamanism they use for exorcism, spreading terror in the society and punishing the people whom they not like (VS: 170). The *Panchamakaras* practice includes rituals related to wine, meat, urine, sex and posture (VS: 181). The sacred rite of *chakra puja* ('circle worship') involves the ritual use of the Panchamakaras (the so called 'Five ***ms***'): ***mans*** (meat), ***mina*** (fish), ***madira*** (wine), ***mudra*** (physical postures), and ***maithuna*** (sex) (cf. Parry, 1994: 256). This practice was continued by the Buddhist Vajrayanis in the 12th century (in the Gahadavala period; see chapter 3 of this book). The Tantrics performed unusual practices of necromancy and sometimes they were necrophagous as a part of the ritual.

Using special Tantric rites like Damara Tantra, many types of diseases, miseries, fear, and psycho-somatic illness were generated and used against enemies (VS: 147). It is a common perception that by terrible austerities the Tantrics acquire magical power (*siddhis*) of hypnotism, sexual attraction and longer period of copulation, and using that power victimised persons with lockjaw, insanity, epilepsy, etc. Even human sacrifice was a part of a special ritual for acquiring special powers. They have control over powers beyond the human realm of consciousness (VS; 172). The two great Vedic sages, Vishvamitra and Jamadagni (father of Parashurama) challenged the Tantric ritual of animal sacrifice and finally succeeded in stopping it (VS: 522). This challenge was a measuring scale to differentiate the Aryans from the non-Aryan tribes.

The female ascetics who follow the path of 'black magic' were known as Yoginis. They were dressed like beasts, putting even tails on their backs (VS: 188). Under the garment of *yoginis*, they often were courtesans and prostitutes (VS: 126). They were used to corrupt people through sex and alcoholic drinks (VS: 145).

The greatest sage of the 'white-form' of Tantrism had been Dattatreya, who represented a joint incarnation of the three main gods of Hinduism, viz. Brahma, Vishnu and Shiva (VS: 104). He was having the divine power to fly through the sky. Dattatreya said, "my daily work lies in Kashi; I take rest on the Sahayadri hills near its peak called Matapur or Renukapur. Daily I take a holy dip in the Ganga at Kashi. In Kalhada Kshetra I offer water to the Sun god. I ask alms around Mahalakshmi in Kolhapur, and take food in Panchalapur." (VS: 152).

Sage Shaunaka said, "I'm the composer of all the metres of the fourth section on Tantra in the *Atharva Veda*. There is a little portion of truth in its narration. To confuse and deviate the innocent masses Tantra became a bundle of falsehood and superstitions. Therefore, I feel it is immoral to use the *Atharva Veda* for professional gain" (VS: 159). This was a great challenge against the misuse and interpretation of rituals for vested interests.

9. The Antipodes: Kshatriya vs. Brahmin

Devout Hindus worship the Sun at dawn, while beseeching him to receive the power of light. The prayer, composed by the great sage

Vishvamitra, refers to the most commonly used sacred verse in honour of Sun god from the Rig Veda (3.62.10), called ***Gayatri*** *Mantra*:

> *Let us obtain the adorable splendour of the Sun; may He arouse our minds.*

The *Rig Veda* (1.164.24) describes the ***Gayatri*** as the sound of life and the way to know the cosmic order (*rita*).

Challenging the Brahmin Vashishtha, the sage Vishvamitra said, "You know that 'The Earth Canto' (*Prithvi Sukta*) of the *Atharva Veda* (12.1-69), referring to the infinite field of cosmic order (*rita*) would never be controlled by any human. ... Please leave your false ego, and try to understand the radiant integrity of *rita*. Then only the world will accept you as saviour. If you follow the opposite way, your loss will be a reality" (VS: 393). For the cause of humanity Vishvamitra had put himself into long states of penance, arduous meditation, fasting and strenuous austerities, and ultimately succeeded in acquiring the power of supreme bliss, which he used in the service of mankind (VS: 495). The prayer of *Gayatri* is a commemoration of that great achievement.

The legend says that Parashurama, to take revenge against Arjuna Karttivirya, had destroyed the Kshatriyas twenty-one times, but it is also a fact that Rama, a Kshatriya king of the Solar Dynasty, defeated him. The first fight between Vashishtha and Vishvamitra was a historical fallacy. The legend narrates that Vishvamitra defeated Vashishtha and created a separate world. As a great service to humanity he composed the most sacred and distinct prayer in the *Vedas*, called the *Gayatri*, that humbly invokes the blessing of the Sun god (VS: 12). By this prayer Vishvamitra challenged the strict rules and conservative ideas of Vashistha (cf. VS: 177-178). He started a kind of hermitage school to teach a holistic understanding of life, with subjects like yoga, law, administration, science, astronomy and health (VS: 345).

During the early stage of the Aryan civilisation, sage Vashishtha through rumours tried to establish himself as the master of the cosmic order. With the intension to humiliate he used to address Vishvamitra by the title of 'Shishnadeva' ('deity of the penis'); he however failed in his malicious intent. Society has honoured Vishvamitra by accepting his sacred metre, *Gayatri*, the most popular and respected prayer in the history of Hindu religion (VS: 41). He was honoured by the title of 'Brahmarshi' ('revelational sage having the knowledge of the cosmic order') (cf. VS: 288, also 271). He was accepted as propitiator of one among the eight clans of the Vedic period from where the Aryan society traced its descent (VS: 384). It was Vishvamitra who introduced the science of Vedic astronomy. He was so knowledgeable that he could recognise all the constellations and lunar mansions and their structural zodiacs, and was fully able to change their routes (VS: 288).

By placing Vashishtha and Vishvamitra into the categories of Brahmin and Kshatriya, respectively, and their fight on the line of caste and social groups, people defile their tradition. In fact the tradition of these two sages symbolically refers to the two phases of Aryan civilisation (VS: 329). One should note that sages are beyond the boundary of social and cultural stigma (VS: 360). The whole conflict was based on the issue of 'ego' and 'jealousy', because of the fact that Vashishtha never reached to that highest level of spiritual power overcoming Vishvamitra (cf. VS: 384). The personality of Vishvamitra symbolises humanity and forgiveness. Challenging Parashurama, the novelist conveys the message that if an eye for an eye is the strategy, then the whole world will be blind (cf. VS 459). Brahmins have been famous for their greed and lust for religious power; for money and rewards they can convert a non-Brahmin into a Brahmin and would devoid of all sense the cultural and religious norms (cf. VS: 489).

"The earliest war took place due to the conflict between two cultural leaders having different ideologies, which resulted in a great loss to the Aryan society. Sage Vashishtha proposed that his descendants should follow strict rules. He wished that only his followers (of what or whom?) should live in the country of Brahmavarta (the Aryan country). He, without hesitation, blamed the other people, calling them Shishnadeva, alleging that they were responsible for disturbing the cosmic order (cf. RgV, 7.196.4). But he should be forgiven for his attitudes, because ultimately he had accepted the noble lines provoked by sage Vishvamitra.

On the other side was Vishvamitra, who always tried to convince the Aryans that if the great contributions of the Aryan culture are to be preserved, then humiliation of the non-Aryan people should be stopped and disrespectful phrases like non-performer of *yajna*, Shishnadeva, speaker of corrupt language, etc., are not to be used for them. Opportunities should also be given to them to learn and adopt the Aryan culture and traditions (VS; 97). This was his first attempt to make the society harmonious, cohesive and common sharing in nature.

Ultimately Vashishtha apologised for his strict rules and finally accepted the path of human integration as framed-out by sage Vishvamitra, and also accepted the sacred metre of *Gayatri* as the supreme prayer. Sage Vishvamitra prays Vak Devi ('the Goddess of

Speech', also called Bharati) for the glory and prosperity of the country and of its people (RgV, 3.4.8-9; cf. VS: 386):

> O Devi Bharati, grant us the boon
> to all the humans living in Bharat [India]:
> the speech, which is blissful to all
> and also to all the intellects.
> Grant wisdom to everybody,
> the wisdom to serve others too,
> help us worship everybody living here.

10. Universal Manhood: Vishvamanusha

The main crisis that humankind faces is the crisis of 'thought-pollution', but this can easily be resolved to a certain extent with the awakening of the spirit of 'Self-realisation'. The novelist laments, "O lord! Humanity consists of many layers of meanings and messages. Get one after another layer, and find a surface of the violent and wild intentions of a beast at the place of human values" (VS: 149). No animal is more terrifying and dangerous than man (VS: 443). Remember, "if nothing in all the universe is so frail as man, nothing likewise is so divine as he!" (Arvindo, 1979: 14). The universal truth is that there exists only one cosmic order that cannot be divided, *'aditi'*; while *'diti'* is a process of desperateness. *Aditi* is infinite, *diti* is finite; both are the two faces of the same ultimate reality. Remember that chaos itself is a stage of order (RgV, 1.89.10; cf. VS: 190). The feeling of this reality can promote global humanism ("the whole world is one family", *vasudhaiva kutumbakam*), the inherent force of ecological cosmology.

The greatest contribution of the ancient Aryan culture is the manner in which to pay respect to everybody according to his/her age and relation, addressing every man as father, or brother, or cousin, or son, and every woman as sister, or daughter, or mother, or aunt... In our generation such respectable addresses have disappeared. Thanks to the new generations that try to revive the moral code of address (VS: 166).

Dhanvantari, honoured as the first Vishvamanusha, proved that to make himself Vishvamanusha he had to accept laments and repentance as his destiny. The 'self' has to be completely transformed in the service to others. He, by churning the ocean of milk, received the *amrita* (ambrosia) and presented it to the human beings. As homage to him, I offer these flowers to that Universal Man; says Trishoka Kanva (RgV, 8.45.42):

Bring that divine wealth,
Which does Vishvamanusha have.
Let's take work to get that wealth,
And have that ambrosia forever. (VS: 310; also 11).

Remember the message of the *Kathopanishad*: "The eternal seed is smaller than the atom, but it is the most powerful in comparison to any powerful force". This is comparable to the seed of the banyan tree (VS: 449).

The greatest achievement through meditation is to understand the sacred *'Om'*; it is the only eternal, without end and without beginning. The fluid of the Panchabhutas is the earth. The fluid of the earth is water. The fluid of water is the herbal juice Purusha. The fluid of Purusha is Vak. The fluid of Vak is *rita* (cosmic order). The fluid of *rita* is Soma. The fluid of Soma is Utagitha, and the fluid of Utagitha is Pranava (the cosmic sound), the immortal sacred syllable known as *'Om'* (VS: 448). This sacred word is a combination of the three seed-letters **A**, **U** and **M**, which refer to the first three sounds echoed at the creation of the universe.

Says Vishvamitra, "everybody has a right over knowledge. I already emphasised it earlier. Alas! You have presumed it your personal property. You discarded the Shudras by keeping them out of the Aryan society and called them non-Aryan! Nothing happened wrong! You think that the people following Shishnadeva have no right to live in your company. Do you think that *rita* (the cosmic order) is your personal property? Whenever you want, you can allow others to live in your community, or exile them out of it? Do you think that this is *rita*?" (VS: 392). Answering and challenging Vashishtha again, Vishvamitra described *rita* as accounted in the *Prithvi Sukta* of the *Atharva Veda* (12.1-63): 'The Cosmic Order (*rita*) is the cause, the process and the result for making the human being divine'.

11. The Message

Even in such an ancient past the *Rig Veda* (8.45.43) gave the message of the Universal Man (Vishvamanusha), who can shed new light upon humanity through the use of spiritual resources (VS: 11).

Says the *Rig Veda* (9.96.1-2), as quoted by the novelist (VS: 136):

Arise O brave fighter! Come at the front of the chariot,
Going ahead is your aim, not to turn back.
Soma always converges into the source of energy, and

provides long lasting inspiration among soldiers, and
makes people pleasant and satisfied.
Unconquerable we are for our enemies,
Uncontrollable we are for our enemies.
Our ultimate aim is the well-being of all.
Our great *yajna* will certainly be fruitful,
and make us continuously awakened.

Hypocrisy takes birth within the human mind, and to get rid of it one has to come out of the self-ego (VS: 171). Let us proceed from death to immortality; and from the darkness of ignorance to the light of wisdom (VS: 267). Vaishvanara is the 'life-breath', the essence of food and the seed of progeny. This comes as flowers in the plants and as fruits in time. In the herbs this is fluid of healing, and vapour in water which returns as cloud. ... When it comes as bliss it gives life to the organism, however if it turns to other way it sets the fire and destroys the earth. ... Let us awaken the human being by the cool-form of Vaishvanara that always exists in the corner of your superconsciousness (VS: 525).

The environmental setting is an important platform for such awakening, as "a pure and clean environment has an everlasting and deep impact on the human mind" (VS: 266). The ultimate cosmic order is the revelation of peace; this is the *dharma* (law of natural-moral order). The *dharma* of water is to flow, the *dharma* of the wind is to blow, the *dharma* of honey is sweetness; similarly the *dharma* of human life is to have peace and compassion on earth. The *Yajur Veda* (10.17.1) has put it so:

Peace in the sky, peace in the mid air.
Peace on the earth, peace in the water.
Peace in plants, peace in the forest trees.
And peace in all the divinities, peace in ultimate reality.
Peace in all things. Peace in peace.
May that peace come to us!

12. Concluding Remarks

By narrating the story of Divodasa, the ancient period legendary king of Kashi, whose stories continued even in the late Puranic period, the novelist Shivprasad Singh has done a great service to cultural understanding. Of course, no one can easily claim that the different facets of historicity and its linking connections are clearly interpreted, but with profusely cited verses from the *Rig Veda* and their contextual meanings and messages this novel is successful in its objectives. The good of the past is validated in the context of the demand of the present as shown in the idea of 'Universal Manhood' (Vishvamanusha) and ultimately the need for peace in the eras of crisis. From the point of view of the literary flow, one can easily remark that several plots are repetitive; on the other side in some instances the connection between time and incidences never coincide. However, for the student of ancient cultural history the novel is a mine of resources. The extensively cited quotations from the novel, as also citations from the Vedic texts, provide sufficient light on the complexity of traditions and their continuity. This novel is a great tribute to Kashi.

13. Basic Reference

Singh, Shivprasad 1996. *Vaishvanara* ('The Primordial Fire'). A novel in Hindi, based on ancient Varanasi. Vani Prakashan, New Delhi; referred as (VS: pp).

Note:

1. Shivprasad Singh has published three novels on Varanasi, covering successively from modern to medieval, and lastly the ancient period. These novels are respectively named *The Street Turns Yonder* (1974), *The Blue Moon* (1988), and *The Primordial Fire* (1996). Three chapters of this book: 2, 3 and 12 are taking these three novels as basic sources.

~3~

Medieval Kashi: Shivprasad Singh's *The Blue Moon*

1. Introduction: Historical Outline

The period of the 11th-12th centuries CE was a period of critical anarchy, when the whole Kashi region, including Kannauj, was suffering under Mughal invasions and internal conflicts. In 1018 Mahmud Ghazni defeated the Gurjar-Pratihar dynasty from Kannauj; but later the Prayag (Allahabad)-Kashi region came under the control of Gangeyadeva (1030-1041) and his son Karnadeva (1041-1070). The area was so much disturbed that cultural prosperity was in danger, with scholars and craftsmen leaving the region and settling in isolated parts of the hilly areas of far off territories like Kashmir, as described by the 11th century scholar Alberuni (cf. Sachau, 1910, I : 22).

By around 1090 the area between Kashi and Kannauj came under the Gahadavalas (Motichandra, 1985: 112). In the middle of the rising anarchy a great person was born, who by his bravery and strategy established again the glory of the Kashi region after a gap of about 1700 years. His name was Chandradeva, though the kingdom was founded by his father Mahichandra (*ibid.*: 113). In 1035 Nialtagin looted the city of Banaras. Again in 1194 Kutubuddin Aibak, Commander-in-Chief of Mohammad of Ghor (Ghori) invaded the city and brutally destroyed thousands of temples; the booty sent to the Ghori was loaded on 1400 camels (Sukul, 1974: 5; Singh and Rana, 2002: 36-37).

This period records some notable writings, e.g. the *Matsya Purana* (ca. the early 11th century), the *Linga Purana* (CE 1110), Lakshmidhara's *Krityakalpataru* (1125), Hemachandra's *Kumara Charita* (1184), and Damodara's *Ukti-Vyakti Prakarana* (ca. 1190), which describe the contemporary condition and glory of the city of Banaras. The descriptions tell us that the Gahadavalas were worshippers of Shiva, but also of Vishnu (Niyogi, 1959: 196). Shiva was called *Krittivasa,* and the temple of Krittivaseshvara was at the height of its glory in the 11th-12th century (Eck, 1982: 81). According to inscription sources,

Shiva, Vishnu and Surya (the Sun god) were the prominent deities to whom the king made many donations (Niyogi, 1959: 202-203). This period is taken as background by Shivprasad Singh (1928-1998) in his novel, ***The Blue Moon*** (*Nila Chanda*, now referred as **BM:**); this chapter is a critical appraisal of that novel.

2. The Canvas, and Criticism

The novelist tried to describe some vivid scenes of Kashi in the medieval period, especially when Varanasi was the capital city of Karna in ca. CE 1060 (BM: III), and was known for topophobic images as described in the writings of that period. The novelist claims that the total lifeworld of the people and character of the culture have been presented in this novel; however he has not achieved his optimal expectations.

In 1967 Shivprasad Singh had published a novel dealing with the modern lifeworld which moves around the students' struggle in Varanasi (cf. Rana Singh 1985; also chapter 12 of this book). This is the second in his three-volume set of novels on Kashi. Marching northwards (vertically) he moves from modern to medieval and finally to the ancient period. Thus, the novel *The Blue Moon* is the second in the series. His aim has been to describe the glory and downfall of the culture and society, covering a range from the downtrodden people (e.g. Doms, and Chandals) to the religiously upper group (Brahmins) with an aim to provide bare scenes (cf. BM: I-II). He claims that he envisaged the base where a group under a white mask had attempted to exploit the people through cheating (BM: II). The novelist is ambitious and biased at some places, therefore the details of negative spots were captured in an hyperbolic way. He expressed that for the last forty years he is living in Kashi, which resulted in deep experiential feelings. It is difficult to say if those feelings reached explicitly to the reality and historicity of the facts. However, in the present chapter the overall view of the novelist's perception is systematically described in the light of five aspects: metaphor and symbols, anarchism and topophobia, vividity of Kashi, face of the Ganga river, and the scene of other streams. Everywhere the comparative view of the literature of that period is cited in context.

The identity of Kashi in relation to its religious glory is portrayed well, but some incidences from the historical struggle are born in the imagination of the novelist; many of them are his own mental constructs and have no historicity. In fact, while describing 'imaginary geography' he followed a sweeping march to capture vast areas of happenings for convenient digestion. D.H. Lawrence's advice is noteworthy in this context: "Never trust the artist. Trust the tale" (cf. Reising, 1987: 165); but the *tale* is diluted by the artist Shivprasad Singh. Further, Reising's warning is appealing: "the text's actual meaning is not a position or idea articulated by an author through a text, but a struggle within the writer that the Lawrentian critic can discern by trusting the tale" (*ibid*: 166).

At some places the novelist has made great mistakes, e.g. the author of *Alexandria Quartet* (4-vols. novel) is said to be George Orwell (BM: I), while it was written by Lawrence Durrell in 1957. Kashi and Varanasi both are used as synonymous, while more commonly the first referred to the territory of the kingdom, and the latter to the city. The name of the river Varana is always misspelled as Varuna. Many modern slogans are also used without historical context, e.g. "go to hell! — "*hai hai*!" (BM: 378, 380, 537). This clearly shows the gap between the context and the happenings. But in no way are these small slips taken into consideration in the present chapter.

Of course, Shivprasad Singh claims that his novel is a place-saturated fiction; he has given more emphasis on the essence of cultural conflicts and contradictions. The novelist was able to use a setting and atmosphere for a symbolism that is blunt and rudimentary. Nonetheless, a kind of place setting is necessary for the background where the characters have to play their role, but Singh is marginally able to make a balance between these two. The present chapter throws light on the interpretation of a realistic landscape with an aim to see the geographer's "constant call to the physical reality that acts to stimulate the creative imagination" (Mallory and Simpson-Housley, 1987: xii).

3. Metaphor and Symbols

The *blue-moon* is conceived as a metaphor possessing symbolic meaning of the total lifeworld. At the end of the novel, the novelist explains it with the help of phenomenology and philosophy:

"Like this great, infinite and wide sky, there is a sky in the human mind. That no-moon night is a million times more tough, intolerable and painful to the eyes than the monthly falling earthly no-moon night. There is a courtyard in the heart of the human being; and in that courtyard is a raised platform for holy basil (*Tulasi*). In the microcosmic sky of the mind appears the *Blue Moon.* Not from false conception, nor from future foretells, but having a dip in the darkness one can see the shining *Blue Moon* in the corner of the mental courtyard; let it be as 'Eternity of Will-Power' " (BM: 645).

The symbol of darkness is a spiritual condition of time, which is to be understood by the shedding of light from the infinite (blue sky). The novelist uses the moon as a symbol of medium in this process. Above all the human cognition is the most important in the sensory interaction. Dillistone (1986: 180) says that "a *human* symbol is the highest in potential of all symbols" (Dillistone, 1986: 180); and can be used for "uniting the whole of humanity to God Himself". With this symbol-canvas, the novelist attempted to make his warp and weft of the novel.

Fire and thunder have played a major role in mythology, symbolising the dual character of human experience: heat and destruction. 'Will-power' is symbolised as thunder; the novelist says: "In times of difficulty, no power, divine or human, helps, except your own 'will-power'. It shines like a thunder in the darkness… It is always inside your own soul" (BM: 449).

"Water symbolises the whole of potentiality: it is the *tons el origo*, the source of all possible existence… Water symbolises the primal substance from which all forms come and to which they will return" (Eliade, 1979 : 188). In fact, water is considered as a symbol of the total lifeworld:

> The Matsyodari [river] was silent. The mango [*Magnifera indica*] and mahua [*Madhuca indica*] trees have clad the place. Flowering had started in the mango-trees, whose fragrance makes the whole environment different. (BM: 456)

Flowering refers to the goodness and hope in life. The colours symbolise different stages and actions of the life of a culture. In Hindu culture the landscape and colour are so combined that they reflect the lifecycle and intrinsic meanings: "Shrima said that the colour of sex is red, love — the blue moon, and their unification white. The love of Radha and Krishna makes the colour of creation" (BM: 445). Here at the first stage blue represents love, while the divine unification for the purpose of creation is symbolised with white. This denotes the cultural process that brings the human being to the fullness of cosmic connectedness. Thus, "symbols are the product of *relatedness* and *reciprocity*, just as truly as new biological life is the product of the union of male and female in sexual intercourse" (Dillistone, 1986: 212).

More specifically, the changing nature of colour symbolism shows the different states of act and unification:

> From one body to another red colour becomes deeper. From one mind to another the colour of love will be deeper. But from

> one soul to another this will be white. Is Kali really black? Is Shiva blue-and-red? Is the sky blue? Is the water of the Ganga dark? No! Not at all. All are white. Until we reach to its depth, it looks blue... (BM: 268)

The acceptance of colour symbolism in different milieus and contexts is the subject of the purview of seeing, looking and thinking which can be revealed and realised only after reaching a certain state of divine connection. Shiva, the patron deity of Varanasi, is symbolised with White, where, his face, abode, partner, garments and the beloved all converged into an invisible colour of whiteness:

> [When Shiva comes to this city in the plain] ...Shiva might not be Rudra in this shift. He would not be blue-reddish or even yellow, but White, showing softness, cleanliness and his basic affinities: White Kailash (his mountain home, *axis mundi*), White Gauri (cool mother, his wife), White the Ganga (his fluid energy), White the river, White the moon, White the snake, and White the camphor like Shiva himself — all are White. (BM: 123-124)

The glance of Shiva is then always perceived as a vision of divinity in the form of absolute unity (cf. BM: 295).

The idea of landscape refers to the physical condition as well as to the psychological make-up of an individual (*Le paysage intérieur*). With this sense the spirit of place (*genius loci*) may be projected as an organic entity. Through the unified senses of setting and sentiments the spirit of place can easily be visualised (cf. Lawrence, 1969). Space speaks, place talks; says the novelist:

> The Land also sleeps and awakens. The River too. The Earth too. Once we tried to go across the Ganga river in the early morning. The boatman said that the Ganga was still sleeping; when the Ganga sleeps, even in the cremation ground funeral pyres never lit. (BM: 114)

Several places have a sense of sentimental attachment to nature: "I feel that to be born in Bengal means to have a dip in nature" (BM: 340).

Like vision, smell also makes a place distinct, reflecting the culture and personality of the place, called as *smellscape*: "If you have visited Phul Gali, south of the Godavari, certainly you have experienced the unique smell of incense and sandal wood — a sense of the total Kashi" (BM: 296).

The black spots are also identified with the smellscape. In the Shankhudhara area, there were many Kapalikas whose rituals produced a different smell: "The inner courtyard was filled up with an obnoxious smell. Intolerable... The lamps were lightened using human skulls as cups, and human fat as oil... The participating Sadhakas were drinking wine in the skull-cups" (BM: 77, 78,79).

Sometimes, even a person represents the personality of a place. The character Rajjuk Gahadavala was that person who represented the city of Varanasi of ca. the 11th century: "Whatever good is in Kashi is also in Rajjuk, and whatever evil is in Kashi is also in its king, Kalchuri Gangeyadeva" (BM: 29). With the use of two persons as symbols, the dual personality of the city has been illustrated here. The influence of these two personalities was distinctly visualised in their respective zones of control. This can also be projected with a reference to the sense of safety (cf. BM: 34). Following the sense of humanity the novelist suggests that "If man punishes man for his mistakes, there would not be any space on this earth to live" (BM: 563).

4. Anarchy and Topophobia

It is commonly accepted that "the character of a place is conditioned by the kind of human activity that is performed there" (Lutwack, 1984: 47). During the Gahadavala period a sense of animosity was more prevalent than the humanistic sense in Kashi, as recorded in the writings of that period, e.g. Hemachandra's *Kumarapalacarita* (3.59) referred to Varanasi as a seat of thieves (*Varanasi thaganam sthanam*). A similar description is also found in Pandit Damodara's *Ukti-Vyakti Prakarana* (38.28-30), and in Kshemendra's *Avadanakalpalata* (1.22.80; 2:50.72). The defiled life of the courtesans is described in the *Vamana Purana* (3.31-45), as in Damodar Gupt's *Kuttanimattam* (735-810). In fact, Varanasi was a seat of prostitutes and brothels since the ancient period, which reached a climax in the 8-9th century CE; the glory of Varanasi was on the edge of downfall in the late Gahadavala period (Vishvakarma, 1987: 189).

Tantric rituals were transformed into left-handed black magic (*vamacaras*), and even soldiers from the royal court were involved in such activities. Such practitioners were called Kapalikas. In some of the monasteries (*mathas*), on auspicious occasions like *Chakra puja* animal sacrifices including human sacrifice were performed (BM: 80). Such seats received protection from the royal soldiers because the *Sadhakas* and soldiers both tried to instigate the participants against Chandradeva, the peaceful king of half of the territory whose palace was across the Varana: "The Kapalika math at Shankhudhara was the site where the chief soldiers of Karna instigate people against Chandradeva" (BM: 83). Day-by-day the Tantrics were increasing in number.

"They are not *sadhakas*, but instead sex-lovers and terrorists" (BM: 62). They get support with money for drink, meat, postures (*mudra*) and sex, and are involved in practising the *panchamakaras*. Moreover, even respected citizens support them and also take part in their rituals. And, taking benefit of the situation, Tantrics and participants enjoy sex and drink (BM: 63). In Bhadravana, celebrating Shakta rituals was very common (BM: 62). In fact, "the kingdom was in the foreground of Tantric rituals to deceive Kashi" (BM: 64). Sacrifices were the common act of ritual to please the goddess Nila Tara, and sometimes even human sacrifice became an essential act (BM: 80, 229).

A sect of Buddhism practising Tantrism, called Vajrayanis, dominated the territory of Rishipattan (modern Sarnath) which was formerly surrounded by a dense forest, Mahavana (BM: 53,54). "Mahavana was filled with many species of trees, and in the central part was an open plain extending from Mahadeva Kupa to Lata Bhairava and from the Varana's bank to Kapalamochana and Sangameshvara. This part was made of hard alluvial soil" (BM: 59). The common perception of the people was that it was impossible to stop easily, even at the cost of much greater loss, the corrupted forms of rituals performed in that central tract (BM: 190). In this Mahavana, "Buddhist Vajrayanis were performing their sacrifices and rituals of *panchamakaras* with the help of ***mans*** (meat), ***mina*** (fish), ***madira*** (wine), ***mudra*** (physical postures), and ***maithuna*** (sex). [Note the five, i.e. *pancha*, '***m***', that is why these are called *panchamakaras*]. These rituals create terror among the people" (BM: 197). Even today some of the Aghoris, followers of left-hand Tantrism, practice such rituals, of course not publically.

The other sect of Buddhism discarded the activities of the Vajrayanis, because "they use Buddha as a veil of the religion and together perform *panchamakara* rituals. They are the *baddha* (attached) not *Buddha* (enlightened); they are wild. They represent a modern form of Angulimala (a brutal robber and murderer) who after killing travellers would wear a garland of the corpse's fingers" (BM: 227).

During the Gahadavala period Kashi was suffering under anarchy (BM: 71); worship of Kali in the Tantric way was becoming more popular (BM: 75). This tradition promoted non-vegetarianism in the city, and "cooking meat was considered a special art worthy of pride

— how much spice and how much *ghee* (clarified butter) need to be used, only an experienced expert knows" (BM 247).

Of course, "the whole of north India was suffering under anarchy, but the worst condition was at its climax in Kashi" (BM: 224). The downfall of society and culture was reflected by the downfall of the Brahmins: "For the entertainment and relaxation of visitors, you are handling a brothel! Is this your Brahminism? Is Kashi at present unable to provide food to a Brahmin? With the lost glory of Brahminism, evil thoughts, discarding religion, and false reflection are the only professions left for you" (BM: 256, 257).

Taking benefit of being the highest in religious status, Brahmins were cheating the society: "in return for respect and honour who can give deceit except a Brahmin! Only you!" (BM: 131, 524). Moreover, antisocial elements were out-numbered and gradually walk in the night while taking shelter wherever they get place (BM: 456).

The cheating and mis-guidance of the Pandas (priests at the riverbank) were well known from the ancient times. They were, and still are, experts in cheating the customers and pilgrims through their ritual acts; the novelist writes: "You can't get the reward of the Puja until you give whatever donation the Panda is demanding. Give that and re-purchase your valuable garments...These people have taken the necklaces and the pearl-rosary of my daughter-in-law...People rarely interfere in such situations" (BM: 203). A similar situation is common in the death ritual, where *pinda* (rice-ball) offering is performed to please the manes (cf. BM: 207).

Women are mostly considered as being dependent on men. There exists a tradition of 'male chauvinism' in North India which brings either negligence or mistreatment of females (cf. Miller, 1981: 15). In a physico-cultural context the Vindhya-Narmada divide serves as a 'great divide' between the 'masculinism' of North India, and the 'feminism' of South India (*ibid*.: 24). In common perception woman is referred to as a 'riddle' (BM: 266). Theologically, the novelist mentioned: "But woman is neither the ultimate reward nor a half-part (*vama*); she is at once both" (BM: 266). After all, man cannot be in his full state of success and completeness without his wife, his half partner (cf. BM: 473).

The portrait of woman is always projected as a half-partner (*ardhamsha*) in different contexts like power (BM: 362), unity (BM: 371), vision of the soul (BM: 422), pilgrimages (BM: 422), and the meeting of Shiva and Shakti in the form of Ardhanarishvara (BM: 464). Nevertheless, most commonly woman was treated as a means of entertainment (*bhogya*). This attitude was responsible for the development of a particular class of women known as courtesans.

Following the tradition described in the *Padma Purana* (52.9) that "those who purchase girls and offer them to the temple, will go to heaven and will be king in another life, and also will get wealth", till the 6th century courtesans were given respect and on several occasions were even worshipped (BM: 543). But by the turn of the Gahadavala period the situation reversed. In this period there were four categories of prostitutes: degraded (*patita*), common (*samanya*), higher (*ucca*), and respected (*atyaucca*). There was a group of other courtesans who got their livelihood only through music and dancing but they were rare, and in a real sense they were not prostitutes (BM: 544).

These descriptions clearly reflect upon the cultural downfall of the city and the class formation in the context of gender.

5. Kashi: Vividity of its Personality

Following the spatial manifestation of sacred geometry and cosmology, the city reveals its unique personality in different perspectives, full of the vividity of milieu and meaning. In history, "metaphysical ideology based on cosmological principles had been once a dominant force shaping the cultural landscape" (Nemeth, 1987: 3). Following the morphological representation of the earth's surface, a geomantic map was followed in planning the city of Varanasi. A dual vision of the city is therefore always reflected: the appearance and the eternity together making it a unique scene (BM: 36 103). Some of the themes and aspects of this personality are presented here.

5.1. Revelation and Exposition

Light is considered as the channel coming from depression to hope. In another way, it connects earthly wisdom and the divine abode. The name Kashi means 'light' (KKh 26.67). Eck (1982: 300) describes that "the most persistent image of Kashi is light. The language of light is also the language of wisdom — 'enlightenment', 'illumination', 'vision' ...Kashi is also called *jnanasvarupa*, the 'embodiment of liberating insight' ". In the same trend, the novelist mentions:

> The meaning of Kashi is light. From time immemorial sages, saints and meditators have concentrated in lighting the flame of wisdom, which still provides the flow of love and affection to the people. The Goddess of Knowledge always keeps Kashi within her two extra arms [out of four]. (BM: 198)

Following the glory of the city described in the *Linga Purana* (cf. KKT p. 34, 58, 69; VM 179), the novelist presents the map of the cosmic mandala of Kashi:

> You don't know Kashi, Karna! The *external* form of Kashi, which occupies temples, buildings, lanes and paths, palaces, neighbourhoods, etc., Do you think that is Kashi ? With this false perception you consider yourself the king of Kashi. You have not seen the *eternal* Kashi that rests in the soul of every person. Try to understand the sheath system (*chakra*) of Kashi, the water channels:
>
> The Pingla artery is like shining fire,
> Like a dried stream but knowledgeable is Lolarka.
> Ida artery provides the light of peace.
> And Varana, washes every sin, where Vishnu sits.
> In between lies Susumna artery, Matsyodari,
> Reflecting the light to the world.

In fact, the divine king of this great city of Kashi is the innocent Shiva (*Bholenath*). The mother-queen is Annapurna and the police inspector is Kala Bhairava. Shiva lives here in many thousand forms. Parvati is the power of *kundalini* and Kala Bhairava is the inspirer of Yoga and rituals. You are only the assistant, but have not even followed the duty of a loyal devotee. (BM: 414)

Of course, one can find many unwanted spots in the city, but "the lifeworld of this eternal city, both beauty and ugliness, are not to be perceived in haste" (BM: 30). Moreover, "Like the shining skin of a brownish snake, wrapped in a cloth so fine that it can get disturbed even by breath, Kashi always tries to get separated from its materialistic environment" (BM: 30).

The cosmic territory of Kashi is protected by Devis:

> In Kedara Khanda there are three shrines of horrific Devis: Chamunda, Charmamunda and Maharunda. Other forms of the Devi like Durga, Chitragriva, Dvareshvari, Svapneshvari, etc. also have their places in this territory. The four forms of Chandi protect it from the different directions, i.e. Angareshi the west, Utareshvari the southwest, Adhahkeshi the southeast; all are well known for their terrifying personalities. (BM: 75)

The city is also considered as the abode of 56 (not 52 as referred in the novel, BM: 61) Birs who guard the city at the intersection of the

8 directions with the 7 layers (thus 8 x 7, equals to 56). This archetypal number is identical to the number of Ganeshas/ Vinayakas who performs the same duty.

Varanasi looks like a crescent moon from the other side of the Ganga, but one can only understand its beauty if one has peace in his mind. The buildings looking as a mixture of colours in the background of white — the white patches symbolise the dualistic mind that changes in time (BM: 27). Sunrise is the most fantastic vision in Kashi, "but those who have not seen the Sun throughout the year, how can they differentiate between the sunrise of Kashi or Otacamund!" (BM: 461). However, "the early rays of the sun and their reflection in the Ganga, both golden in colour, and the nearby white houses compose a scene like that of a dreamland" (BM: 28).

The struggle and competition between the two kings resulted in dividing the city into two groups:

> The whole city has been divided into two parts, i.e. Chandra Kashi, and Karna Kashi. ... Guvalpalli, Brahmapuri, and half of the neighbourhood are in favour of Karna, and the other half is in favour of Chandra. The first area has happy inhabitants, while the latter has hungry people. (BM: 166)

The conflict had badly influenced the economy and encouraged communalism: one side supports Karna, the other Chandra, however both criticise each other (BM: 183). But in spite of his prosperity and influence, Karna was not given the same high respect and honour as Bhoja was (BM: 40).

Guvalpalli (a neighbourhood of milkmen) was famous for its physical strength (BM: 225); but it was also divided into two socio-political groups. The houses of the southern part "are testimony to sufferings — everywhere hut camps, mud houses, mud walls, mud plaster, and life is as in a primitive society. But the palatial houses of the north obviously show their prosperity and better maintenance in the background" (BM: 65). Following such a sharp division, some youngsters have prepared a map of Jujhauti (neighbourhood) not in terms of physical space, but in terms of cognition (BM: 328).

The neighbourhood of Brahmapuri was the symbol of the religious glory of the city (BM: 98). Some lanes were perceived as a symbol of the city, like the Phul Gali connecting Dashashvamedha by a wooden bridge: "in the *Jatakas* Kashi was referred several times as Pushpavati. ..And, Vishveshvara, market street and Phul Gali are considered as the axial points of the symbolic triangle of Kashi" (BM: 588).

Kashi-dwellers were not so much concerned about the king, but were rather always ready to welcome any change, which would promote the mixture of so many cultures and social norms. This mixed-up of lifeworlds nowadays are called Banarasi that is known for internal contradictions. "We have one answer for all that we possess, all-in-one-mixed; that means everything is covered with algae, mud and swamp. There is neither a clear line of thought, nor a clear decision — in all the forms we are Kashi-dwellers" (BM: 134).

Whenever a temple was taken as a shelter for politics, the dwellers opposed it (BM: 386). Many non-Aryan traditions have also been accepted, e.g. Dih worship, which may be defined as an urban form of ancestral worship! (BM: 352). In fact, Dih worship is a worship of a village guardian. Moreover, some remains of the Gond culture had also emerged here (BM: 276).

Medieval Varanasi was famous for its cotton and silk cloths. A special brand like Adadhakashika (presently *addhi*) was famous for its use in summer and winter; and Kashikuttama, the finest and softest cotton cloth, was the speciality of the city (BM: 515). The latter is referred to in the *Mahaparinirvana Sutta* (5.26) when it mentions that the dead body of Lord Buddha was wrapped in this cloth. Therefore wherever the Buddhists are like in China, Korea, Cambodia, Java, Sumatra and Indonesia, merchants from this city migrated for business, and settled there" (BM: 516). The art of weaving and cloth-making goes back to the Vedic period, and only with meditation and devotion can one reach to the glory of craftsmanship (BM: 516).

The cloth business was famous during the age of Mahajanapadas (BCE 8th-6th century); loaded ships from Kashi were going as far as Europe. "The special cloth product *malmala* is so light and soft that it can flow into air even by breath. Touching that cloth gives a feeling of excitement. ... Cloths embroidered with golden lace and precious stones are exported to the European market. This shows the life-long devotion of the craftsmen" (BM: 436). "One side of the road linking Vishveshvara and Mandakini was occupied by cloth-silk merchants, and the other by the courtesans living in palatial buildings" (BM: 436).

The city was also known for artificial pearls, which were purchased by everybody for daily use or as souvenir (BM: 592).

5.2. Physical Personality

The city was formerly covered with woodlands and forests. There were five forest tracts from north to south, viz. Mahavana, Daruvana, Anandavana, Harikeshavana and Bhadravana. These are described in the KKh (cf. TS 198) and the KKT (66, 86). The name Kashi is associated with Kasha, "the name of the tall silver-flowering grass which grows wild along the riverbank" (Eck, 1982: 25-26; also Vishvakarma, 1987: 51). Anandavana was so beautiful that it attracted Parvati, who came to visit it and get relaxed (BM: 124). Bhadravana was serving as a resort for Karna's army and refugee Nats (BM: 186; also 105-109). Mahavana is mentioned by the novelist in the context of the Vajrayanis and their rituals. Shivprasad Singh has in fact not portrayed the forest landscape of the city, however it is mentioned using contextual differentiation. The water bodies are also not given due attention, except the Ganga river and the Matsyodari. Among the *kundas* (sacred ponds), only a passing reference of some is given, e.g. Gauri Kunda (BM: 303).

5.3. Temples and Divinities

According to the *Kurma Purana* (I.29-34), the three most important Shiva *lingas* in Banaras are Omkareshvara, Krittivasheshvara and Madhyameshvara. Moreover, Avimukteshvara is considered to be the primordial *linga* since ancient times (TS 166; Eck, 1982: 130). Of course, there were many temples and shrines of Shiva, Parvati, Surya (the Sun), Vishnu, Devi and the Navagrahas, but the novelist paid attention to a few selected temples and divinities.

"Avimuktesvara was the patron deity of that period. The rich devotees offer to his temple golden garments as donation from Kashi, Koshala, Panchanada, Gurjara, Karnataka, Chola, Pandeya, Anga-Banga, and Tri-Kalinga. This is a *svayambhu jyotiralinga* (self-manifested, light-reflecting *linga*) (BM: 121) ... This temple, lying along the drain linking the Varana and the Ganga in Mahavana, is unique and unparalleled" (BM: 123).

The temple of Vishveshvara was (and still is) the most sacred and famous temple. According to an inscription, king Govindachandra performed worship there (cf. *Jl. of Asiatic Soc. of Bengal*, XXXI: 123; Sukul, 1974: 178). The novelist says that Vishveshvara Temple is a unique integration of 'non-attachment to the material world' (*vairagya*) and 'attachment' (*ashakti*) to the sacred city. It is also known as 'Moksha Lakshmi Vilas' Temple (BM: 295, 301, 367). This was the most important temple along the northern route (*uttarapatha*), where pilgrims from Mathura, Rameshvaram, Kanyakumari, Kashmir, Gandhara, Kalinga, Bengal and Gurjar came for worship — all were bound up to this temple with the warp of belief and the weft of faith (BM: 295).

The architecture of the Vishveshvara temple represents the best possible integration of the Nagara and Dravida styles: "There are four pavilions and an inner sanctum. Dravidian style in some places, but on the other side a four-square plan and layers of verandas — altogether reaching to eleven... Which type of stone is used here, it is unclear!" (BM: 298).

But it had already been mentioned elsewhere that Vindhyan sandstone and redstone were used for the construction of this temple; the same stones were also used in the Khajuraho temples (BM: 302). Describing the height of the spires, the novelist says: "I don't know the height of the central spire, but it should not be less than 50 hands-size (75 ft, or 22.9 m), and the rest of the spires on the four corners record a height of about 30 hands-size (45 ft, or 13.7 m). The series of spires looks like a range of hills" (BM: 298).

Following the description of Vishveshvara as given in the *Kashi Khanda* (69-70), the novelist mentions that "the inner sanctum is the liberation space where the *jyotir linga* shines. ... But who is the feminine spirit of Shiva's mandapa? (BM: 299) ... She is Shringara Gauri, the goddess who provides wealth to her devotees" (BM: 301). Decorated shops selling items for rituals and related materials occupy the road linking Vishveshvara Temple and Mandakini (BM: 367).

Krittivaseshvara is one of the oldest temples, dating back to the 11th century, and is famous for its unique architectural beauty. The sacred *linga* in the inner sanctum faces towards the west (BM: 233). Shiva and Krittivasa were taken as synonyms in this period (Niyogi, 1959: 196; Eck, 1982: 81). Shiva is the universal and cosmic integrator, whose three most important *lingas* in Kashi are Avimukteshvara, Vishveshvara and Krittivaseshvara (BM: 233).

The temple of Nandishvara lying on the bank of the Matsyodari pond was in Nagara style, where erotic statues of divinities were exposed in the open, in a similar way as in the temples of Khajuraho (BM: 32,33). From a Gahadavala inscription, it is obvious that "a great number of regal ritual occasions in Kashi included the worship of Adi Keshava or a dip in the Ganga at the Varana confluence" (Eck, 1982: 233; cf. Niyogi, 1959: Appendix B). This shows the importance of the temple. In the temple of Adi Keshava "there is a grand statue of Vishnu in standing posture. Of course, the temple is small but the surrounding *mandapa* was so wide that many people could sit there and perform rituals and other religious deeds. ... The temple was built by the Gahadavala king Chandradeva to get the bliss of peace" (BM: 154). The glory of this temple is described in the *Matsya Purana* (185.68) and the *Vamana Purana* (3.43-50). At the junction of the two rivers, the Varana and the Ganga, lies the temple of Sangameshvara (*Linga Purana* 92.87-89) which is also visited together with Adi Keshava (BM: 154).

According to the 12th century Pandit Damodara's *Ukti-Vyakti Prakarana* (21.18-19), the temple of Karnameru was of supreme grandeur and the most beautiful temple of the period (BM: 39). This Dravidian-style temple was made of "Vindhyan sandstone and recorded the height of 50 hands-size (75 ft, or 22.9 m) (BM: 40). As symbol of the city's prosperity, glory and power, it was built as a mark of the victory of the king of Kashi over Bhoja, king of Dhara (BM: 41).

The temple of Shankukarneshvara, "located at the bank or Shankhudhara Kunda, was attached to a Kapalika monastery where some of the higher officials of Karna's royal court participate in Kapalika rituals" (BM: 76). This area lying south in the Bhadravana (BM: 111) is situated in Kedara Khanda, the southern segment of the city. "The Kapalika Math is now in ruins like a neglected site ...the inner courtyard has always been filled up with obnoxious smells — intolerable" (BM: 77).

Among the different forms of goddesses, the novelist mentioned only Shantikari Gauri who protects the city from the east and grants the boon of peace (KKh 97.17; KKT 45). "The princess Gomati is performing the Katyayini Vrata and daily pays a visit to Shantikari Gauri near Adi Keshava" (BM: 161). Sometimes the devotees think that her worship and the Katyayini Vrata are a wasteful exercise!" (BM: 236).

According to folk tales and mythology, four *yakshas* (vegetal demigods) came to Kashi with Shiva. Among them Virupaksha was well known. Infertile women worship him to get sons (BM: 66, 67). The *Linga Purana* mentions 462 temples and *tirthas* in Kashi (cf. Sukul, 1974: 165); but only a few selected ones are described in *The Blue Moon*, and many of the important ones are not mentioned.

5.4. Kashi and Its Vicinity

An area is a part of a regional system, therefore it should also be viewed accordingly. At some places the novelist has described the routes linking Kashi to other areas. There were three routes connecting Varanasi to the southern areas, and each of them was known for its special character: "the first one is the longest route, denoting a peaceful and relaxing journey. It passes through Kanyakubja, Mahoba, Khajuraho, Prayag, Kantit, Vindhyachal, Mirzapur, Chunar and finally

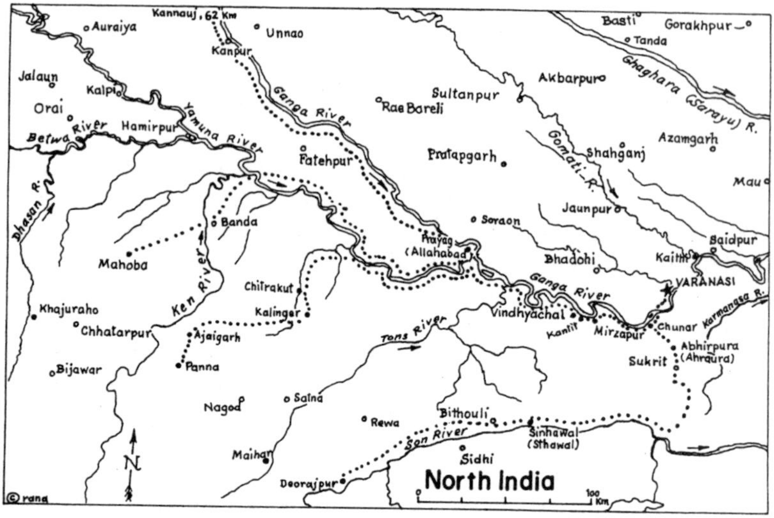

Fig. 11. Kashi and its vicinity: Medieval towns and linking routes.

Varanasi. The second route is short but tiresome; it links Panna, Kalanjar, Chitrakut, Vindhyachal, Kantit, Chunar and Varanasi. The third one is the shortest but very difficult; it is parallel to the Son river and links Bilahari, Bukhara, Deorajpur, Sinhawal, Abhirpura, Chunar and Varanasi" (BM: 23; Fig. 11). Many of these places are truly linked to the routes described according to the historical facts.

According to the novelist, the people of the Gahadavala period were familiar with the rock paintings of the Lekhania cave in Mirzapur (BM: 639). These rock paintings date back to ca. 6000 BCE (Tiwari, 1986: 112).

The greenery of the Vindhyan hills and the sanctity and wilderness of the goddess temple of Vindhyavasini, a form of Lakshmi, have been a distinct place of attraction (BM: 93). Goddess Vindhyavasini is assumed to be the elder sister of Ashthabhuja who with her eight arms protects the eight cardinal directions (BM: 94). Ashthabhuja, a form of Sarasvati, provides wealth and prosperity to her devotees; her braided hair similar to the flower of *agatsya* (*Aeschynomene grandiflora*) is tender, whitish and radiant (BM: 93,94). To visit her temple one has to climb a hundred steep steps (BM: 95). In front of Ashthabhuja, the Ganga turns and forms a half-circle, creating a unique natural scene. The third temple of this region is of Kali at Kalikhoha (BM: 94).

6. Face of the Ganga River

According to the novelist "the unity of the Ganga and Shiva is only visualised in Kashi, in the total course of the river from Gangotri (the source) to Gangasagar (meeting with the ocean). The Ganga, while wrapping Shiva in her lap, produces a murmuring sound through her currents, and always looks happy and smiling" (BM: 30). The Varanasi dwellers are well aware of this aesthetic cognition (BM: 212).

The scenic beauty of the Ganga can be viewed from the top of a tall building:

> The scene of the ghats from Adi Keshava to Kedareshvara, and the nearby whitish houses, temples, palatial buildings — all this brings the scenic beauty to its peak. The flying golden coloured flags are so attractive that the city looks like a magnetic core. The ancient sages revealed this essence of deep feeling. ... Whosoever came to this city, settled down here. Offering a single flower to the Shiva *linga* here easily gives the merit of a thousand sacrifices. ... Who can leave such an abode! (BM: 212)
>
> This scenic beauty is a new vision of understanding (BM 215).

Symbolising the lifeflow, it is said that the Ganga also flows in the inner world of consciousness. The colour of the Ganga would be perceived vividly according to the level of personal sensitivity (BM: 51). At midnight, the tender face and the soft and black hair of Ganga present a different scene (BM: 73). Boat riding on the Ganga and watching the scene gives another vision of sight and scene:

> Slowly slowly the boat was moving towards the south, and the scenic view of shining white houses and the shadow of tall palatial buildings along the bow-shaped bank of the Ganga was making everybody feel transcendent. (BM 74)
>
> Standing at Adi Keshava, one can see the curve of the Ganga like a crescent moon. It is like the god Avimukteshvara (a form of Shiva), on whose forehead rests the shining moon of the second day of the light fortnight. The light of the moon is showering nectar and coolness. The coolness of the air is like the wind coming from the Devadaru, cedar, forest of the Kailash mountain which slipped down here in the form of ghats along the Ganga to provide peace and satisfaction to the Kashi-dwellers. (BM: 154)

The reflection of the moon in the Ganga shows the rhythm of

time: "The moon is in the midst of the sky. Its shadow reflected in the Ganga looks like a hide and seek game played by the moon" (BM: 84). Moon is the symbol of coolness, peace and hope. Remember, "like the infinite sky in the universe, there also exists a sky in the human mind. ... Likewise in everybody's mind has a courtyard where lies a holy basil. No way from superstitions, and not from the false foretales about destiny, but only by a deep merge in mind one can see the radiant *Blue Moon* that is also called 'eternal will power' " (BM: 645).

The puranic sources (e.g. *Vishnu Dharmashastra* 89.1-4; *Padma Purana* 6.91; 119.12-13) glorify the sacred merit of the month of Karttika (Oct.-Nov.), which highest intensity is reached on the full-moon day, on which a high merit is achieved by taking bath in the Ganga (cf. *Hemadri Vrata* II. 137-171). On this occasion the vision of the Ganga is distinct: "wrapped in the finest blue cloth, the current of the Ganga was revealed with a sense of silence" (BM: 27). In the early morning, "after half an hour, the colour of the Ganga changed: from blue to vermilion. She, like a woman wrapped in a saffron-coloured sari, is in a hurry to meet Lord Shiva. ... The Sun has been rising" (BM: 28).

The novelist has vividly described the scene along the bank of the Ganga in the morning:

> In the early morning people go to take a holy bath in the Ganga, followed by rituals. They sit in many groups along the bank. *Tirtha-purohits* and *ghatias* under their separate umbrellas, poor Brahmins, Mahapatras, barbers, flower sellers — all come in the early morning to serve their clients. The priests, seated under their umbrellas, devote themselves to their service; their main duty is to provide all the facilities to the visitors. People fully trust them and leave their clothes, shawls and valuables, which they get back after their bath. Priests (*ghatias*) put sandal *tika* on the pilgrims' foreheads and bliss them. According to their capacity, the visitors give a donation, and finally march to continue their journey. (BM: 99)

The novelist has completely missed to mention the five famous ghats of the Gahadavala period: Adi Keshava, Vedeshvara, Kapalamochana, Trilochana and Svapneshvara (cf. Vishvakarma, 1987: 62; Figs. 12 and 13). Moreover, due attention is not given to the water *tirthas* along the Ganga as described in the *Matsya Purana* (185.60) and other several inscriptions. They are Lolarka, Dashashvamedha, Manikarnika, Bindu Madhava, and Keshava (cf. Eck, 1982: 221).

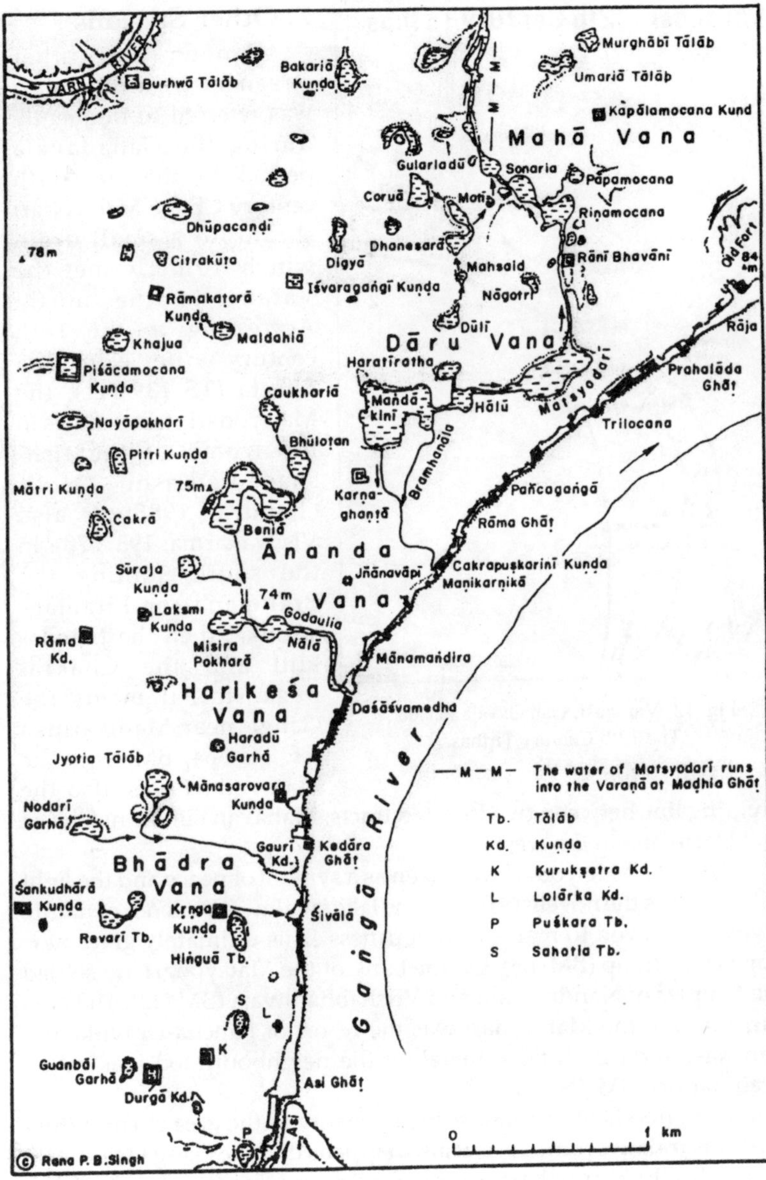

Fig. 12. Ancient water bodies, and Five Forest tracts, based on James Prinsep (1822).

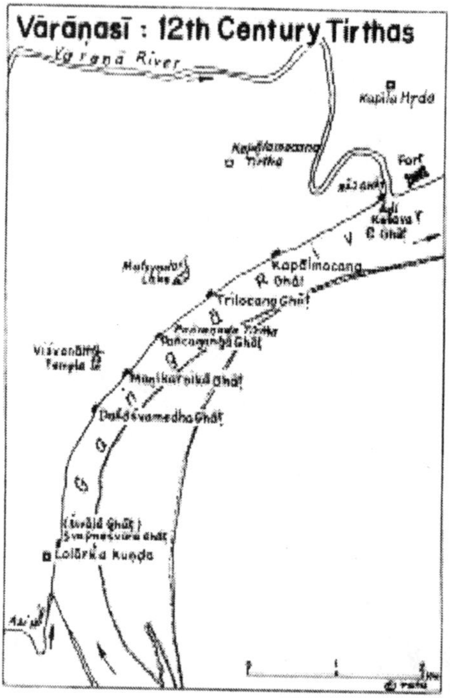

Fig. 13. Varanasi, Gahadavala Period: The 12th Century Tirthas.

7. Other Streams

Among the other streams, the Matsyodari was referred to frequently during the Gahadavala period. By the early 12th century CE the Matsyodari shrank to a small drain which formerly met the Varana to the north. According to the 16th century writer Narayana Bhatta (TS 139-141), the Matsyodari stream flows in the womb of the fish-shaped Kashi (Motichandra, 1985: 2; also Vishvakarma, 1987: 70). In the south, joining the Brahmanal or Pitamahstrotika, then the Mandakini and the Chakrapuskarini, it meets the Ganga near Manikarnika (cf. TC 364; BM: 98). The Matsyodari was also the dividing line between two forested tracts, Mahavana in the northeast and Daruvana in the west.

The lake Matsyodari was taken as a symbol of peace and the light of hope. Says the novelist: oToday the lake is calm. The silence of nature gives a rest even to man's consciousness. This ultimately gives new hope for actionp (BM: 65). On the bank of the Matsyodari are settled the temples of Nandishvara and Vrishabhadhvaja (BM: 22). The area surrounding the Matsyodari was the resort of Pancha-Dravida and Pancha-Gauda Brahmins, therefore the neighbourhood was called Brahmapuri (BM: 98).

Peak floods offer a landscape of beauty in the area surrounding the Matsyodari: osometimes it also happens that the Ganga overflows through Chakrapuskarini, and while crossing the bank of the Mandakini meets the Matsyodari with the aim of touching her beloved Nandishvara Shivap (BM: 33). Shiva himself was fond of the beauty of the overflowing Matsyodari; He describes its merit to his consort Parvati (cf. TS 141, 168; BM: 33) !

> O beloved! When the Ganga comes to meet the Matsyodari, it is a divine scene even to the gods. Taking a bath there bestows liberation from transmigration. When the Ganga comes to that place and the waters get mixed and flooded with the Varana, it is a very auspicious time indeed — a rare occasion, even for the gods.

According to a Gahadavala inscription of the 12th century, the king Govindachandra took a bath in the Ganga-Matsyodari confluence and made on this occasion a land grant to a Brahmin (Sukul, 1974: 199). The reflection of the vermilion-colour light of the sunrise on the bank of the Matsyodari is fantastic and attracts swans and ducks from everywhere (BM: 39). In fact, the best of all of nature's gifts to the city of Varanasi was the Matsyodari (BM: 32).

The Godavari river (perceived as the Ganga of Central India) was symbolically identified with the Godavari drain, which, after originating in Suraj Kunda and later meeting Lakshmi Kunda, followed the route to Dashashvamedha Ghat, where it got divided in two parts before finally meeting the Ganga. In the 11th century this stream was still visible (BM: 109), but now it has been filled up and the source area is called Godaulia.

The other two important streams, i.e. the Varana (cf. *Mahabharata, Bhisma Parva* 9.31), and the Asi (cf. *Matsya Purana*, TS 101) are only marginally described by the novelist. The Varana river is given only a passing reference (BM: 32, 71-72.). Moreover, Lolarka Kunda (cf. KKh 46.59), quite famous in that period, is also not described. These two water bodies demarcate the northern and the southern limits of the city.

8. An Epilogue: The Blue Moon hidden in clouds!

There are two ways of investigating the art of writing. Firstly, through the scale of literary criticism, where four aspects are generally considered, viz. story (*katha*), narration (*kathya*), facts (*tathya*), and the final message (*tatva*). In narrating the story the novelist has used the plot of the struggle between the two kings of Kashi during the Gahadavala period (ca. 11th century), while the landscape and the people of the city are taken as a focus of the narration; and the imaginary scenario is taken as a link to establish the factual situation. The final message is how lwill powerm(symbolised with the ***Blue Moon***), i.e. the ultimate aim of life, can be achieved. Concerning these four aspects the novelist is successful to different degrees.

Another way of investigation is to highlight the integrity among the diverse landscape together with the culture and the lifeworld of the people. In this context there are many shining spots in the novel *The Blue Moon*. Since the background is very wide and so many secondary stories are told, through contextual differentiation one can understand the literary geography of that period. But oregarding culture as a battlefield of various conflicts is, of course, an essential premise of dialecticsp (Reising, 1987: 147), the novelist has been fully successful. It is another matter if imagination supersedes the historical events. This novel should be taken as oa tool for elucidating ideas and values attached to (wilderness) landscape and naturep (cf. Olwig, 1984: xiv). This further reminds us what Lane (2003: 157) says, oTo find our way back to a greater sanity we will need to practise a new way of looking at nature: not to learn *about* her, but to learn *from* her, to see her as our mentor. To do so we will need to slow down. We will need to understand that we are but one voice in the chorus of life on Earth. We will need to quieten the voices of our own self-regarding clevernessp.

Whatever discontinuity and gaps in terms of historicity are found in the novel, these can be again compared to the contemporary texts as highlighted in the present chapter. Shivprasad Singh's common technique of telling a story is contextual differentiation. Considering this technique, in the present chapter a portrait of Varanasi has been presented with an aim to support the sense of meaning in the context of milieu (cf. Lutwack, 1984: 66).

9. Basic Reference

Singh, Shivprasad 1988. ***The Blue Moon*** (*Nila Chanda*). A novel in Hindi on medieval Kashi. Vani Prakashan, New Delhi.

~4~

Kabir's Revelation: Sahni's Vision

1. Introduction

The medieval devotional movement was related to the common people, and it attracted large masses from all the stratums of society. Ramananda and his follower Kabir (Fig. 14) initiated this movement in north India. This movement was further activated by Nanak, Raidas (Ravidas), Dadu, Daria, Palatu, Jagajivan and Shivanarain, all saints who avoided the traditional religious line of austerity, and followed the thought: "work is worship" and "service is meditation". They revolted against the taboos and ritual dogmas and reinterpreted the inside realities behind the ritual practices. Whatever they saw and experienced, they openly expressed without any fear. These saints either passed their life in Banaras or came here at some time or the other to get insight. It is therefore quite natural that their works are a true mirror of the lifeworld of the period and the city. These sages were social reformers who raised their voice against the dualistic frame of purity-pollution, Hindu-Muslim, Shaivite-Vaishnavite, Brahmin-Shudra, etc. Kabir was the leading figure amongst all. Hawley and Juergensmeyer (2004: 35) very rightly remarked that "In the whole sweep of north Indian religion there is no voice more stringent, more passionate, more confident than that of Kabir. If Hinduism has a prophet, an Amos or a Jeremiah, here he is — not in the sense that he forecast anything, but that he was ever at odds with the world around him, always ready to fling the dart of criticism in the direction of established religion". Kabir had challenged the social evils, but he was not a reactionary. In fact he was sympathetic to both Hinduism and Islam, and wished for the common well being:

> Kabir standing in the bazaar, wishes for the well-being of all.
> Never one is his close friend, nor a disparate enemy.

Fig. 14. Kabir in a posture to awaken the people.

Using satire and metaphor, Kabir attempted to disclose the cultural realities through the language of the common people, therefore Bhojpuri (now a dialect of Hindi) prevails in his works. Home and homeland were his seat and territory of meditation and learning. Doubt develops due to lack of faith and realisation: pleasure and meditation, both are possible in one's own house. Kabir never accepted the rigid Brahmanic control over Hinduism. He was confident that without rejecting that system society couldn't advance. As a challenger to dualism, he tried to make society aware of social inequality. Therefore, he was declared a revolutionary, and was rejected by the priestly community. He said about social inequality:

Higher lineage known to the world,
But repeatedly doing degraded acts

Higher-lower is an expression of doubts
The same air is there, the same waters too.
The same soil, the same potter
And the creator of the universe is the same one.

The social consciousness of Kabir and his period was taken as a plot to write the play ***Kabir Standing in the Bazaar*** (by Bhishma Sahni, 1981, in Hindi, now referred as **KS:**). Some critics argue that in Sahni's play the spiritualism of Kabir has been neglected. But this is only an academic anomaly. To understand the society of that period as perceived by Kabir is relatively more important. It would be unjustified to show Kabir's real struggle in that period without referring to the prevailing conditions (Sahni, 1981/1985: 9). This play was staged and shown on television for the first time in 1981, and later on many other occasions. The language of the play is Hindi, but to make its regional identity more alive a shade of the local dialect of Banaras, Kashika/ Bhojpuri, was often used. Kabir himself was against using a complicated or sophisticated language, such as Sanskrit: Sanskrit is a blind well, dialect is a flowing current. (KS: 83)

Kabir always preferred the dialect of the masses, and politely accepted his illiteracy (KS: 81).

Neither ink, nor paper I used,
Never used any paper at all.
The glory of all the four eras,
I described only through voice. (*Bijak-Sakhi*: 187)

Sahni attempts to present the personality of Kabir, both in the historical and the present contexts, as a fearless seeker of truth and a great leader for social awareness, who challenged religious taboos, social degradation and the inhuman behaviour of the administrators. The plot and happenings of the play both are related to Banaras; therefore the play is relevant for understanding the people and the landscape of late 15th and early 16th century.

2. Historical Context as Thought

We know very little with historical certainty about the life and family of Kabir. According to the popular tradition, Kabir (birth CE 1398 in Kashi, death 1518 in Magahar) lived during the reign of Nasiruddin Muhammad Tughlaq (1395-1412) and Sikander Lodhi (1489-1517). Hinduism was in danger in that period due to the religious fanaticism of the Muslim rulers. The Hindu religion, which had been a complete way of life and was well known for tolerance and acceptance of strange thoughts, became so weak in the face of Islam that an alternate path was much in need. The old Brahmanic taboos and rituals were challenged by Islam. This resulted in dividing the Hindu religion into various sects. In fact, there was no such religion as Hinduism, rather each sect had its own faith and tradition. In this situation of doubts and fanaticism, a new light came from Smarta scholars (Dwivedi, 1971: 171). These scholars had given emphasis to new ways of rituals and religious practices, but this resulted again in traditionalism and fanaticism (Motichandra, 1985: 189). Ramananda (1299-1410) and his followers at Banaras started the first real revolution against these social evils. It is a question of controversy whether Kabir was a disciple of Ramananda! (Motichandra, 1985: 190). While giving the names of his contemporary spiritual teachers, Kabir referred to the names of Gorakh, Bharthari (Bhritahari), Gopichand, Namadev and Jaidev, but never Ramananda (Gupta, 1968: 5). According to a common belief Kabir was considered to be a Muslim weaver (*Julaha*), but later in his life he left this occupation. Towards the end of his life he settled at Magahar, Basti District, which was considered to be an unholy area, and passed his last breath there. He strongly believed that it is devotion and faith, which help in attaining revelation, not the place (*ibid:* 28). Kabir says (*Bijak* 28.103, cf. Singh and Hess, 1977: 28):

> So much for your faith in Rama
> What's Kashi? Magahar? Barren grounds,
> When Rama rules in your heart.
> If you give up the ghost in Kashi,
> is there some debt
> on the Lord's part?

In this reformist tradition Kabir was considered as the most influential saint of the period. But in spite of being a promoter of equalitarianism, he did not favour the complete annihilation of the caste system (Hussain, 1959: 14). He was a great challenger, and "until now no such writer has yet been born using the highest level of satire like that of Kabir" (Dwivedi, 1971: 164). His influence reached up to Punjab, Gujarat and Bengal. In fact, the religious idea of the *Din-e-Ilahi* proposed by the Mughal emperor Akbar (CE 1556-1605), to integrate the best parts from Hinduism and Islam, was based on Kabir's teachings (Tarachand, 1963: 165).

But it would be a misinterpretation to consider Kabir as an integrator of the Islamic and the Hindu faiths. He never tried to compromise with any social evil from whichever root it might come. He was a highly conscious reformer who would place humanity at its glorious place through the path of love and kindness. He followed the *Narada Bhakti Sutra* (69) teaching that "a devotee makes the place holy, not the rituals or traditions" (cf. Upadhyay, 1986: 289). Moreover, Kabir gave their due importance to saints and sages and challenged the superstitions taught by Brahmins (cf. Das, 1970: p. 76: 27). Kabir insisted that by faith and self-realisation one can experience Kashi in his own body, while the outer appearance is a false notion (cf. Das, 1970, p. 35: 10, p. 161: 377, p. 251: 206).

His ideas were considered by some as an attack on Islam, therefore Sikandar Lodhi called Kabir and asked for an explanation at Jaunpur in 1495 (Motichandra, 1987: 191). Here Sahni has failed to refer to the correct place as per historical facts, as according to him Lodhi visited Banaras and discussed with Kabir there (Sahni, 92). Sahni again did not refer to the place of Sheikh Takki (*ibid:* 97, 102), who was in fact living at Jhusi, across the Yamuna at Prayag (Allahabad), where Kabir met him to have his blessing for driving away the religious illusions among Hindus and Muslims (Motichandra, 1985: 191).

In the period of Lodhi the city of Banaras suffered from two different evils: on one side the cruelty and power of the Muslim administrators oppressed the Hindus, and on the other side fanatic Brahmin priests misguided the innocent people for their own selfish benefit. Thus, the whole city became a hell (*ibid.*), and the dwellers had to tolerate patiently every kind of evil deed and action (Upadhyay, 1986: 290). In this purview, Sahni's play presents vivid accounts of the social strata, the pitfall of religion and the condition of the monasteries. He presents a whole picture of religion and power, pilgrimage, the struggle for understanding and finally Kabir's revelation of the ultimate reality — altogether encircled in and around the city of Banaras.

3. Social Strata

The Hindu society is religiously structured in a hierarchy of lower and higher, and pure and impure. Brahmins are ranked on the top of the hierarchy. Of course, all are known as Hindu, but they are compartmentalised into several sects and paths. It is not easy to understand. Even within the Brahmin caste itself there are more than a hundred sub-castes, which are again sub-divided into many more (KS: 25-26). The Gaur claim that they are the superior-most among all the 108 sub-castes of Brahmins (KS: 63). Sometimes these sub-divisions are clearly manifested through the marks on the forehead. The number of lines does indicate the symbol and tradition of the sect (KS: 26). One line mark on the forehead refers to the conception of one supreme entity or absolute (*Brahman*), while two lines refer to an absolute plus a life organism (*Jiva*), and three lines add nature (*Prakriti*). In this perception Brahman is the supra-cosmic reality and the other two are its manifestations. It is comparable to the *Bhagavada Gita*'s lines (VIII. 3): "Brahman (or the Absolute) is the indestructible, the Supreme (higher than all else), the essential nature is called the self. Karma is the name given to the creative force that brings beings into existence" (Radhakrishnan, 1971: 227).

Since Brahmins were the makers of religious law, for them there was no untouchability or defilement. Using a metaphor, Sahni expressed how Kabir was an illegal child of a Brahmin but later the society never recognised him (KS: 20). To maintain their position of superiority, the Brahmins avoided the routes followed by untouchables (KS: 47). And when any untouchable passed on their way, they cleaned it by pouring Ganga water (KS: 28). Through a character of the play, a Mahant, the chief of a monastery, Sahni conveys how priests and ascetics maintain hierarchy in society, and while maintaining it they follow the principle of 'might is right'. For those having the power of dominance, the caste factor never is as an obstacle in the way (KS: 27).

When the *varna* system was introduced it was based on occupation, but as it took the shape of caste identity, it became the destiny of man's birth. This belief is so strong that the social stratification completely depends on it. Using a strong satire Kabir challenged this notion; he used the weapon of devotion to humanity against social evils. He asked (KS: 101):

> If by birth you are a Brahmin,
> Why did you not came with a *tika*
> On your forehead from the womb.
> If by birth you are a Muslim,
> Why did you not came with a *khatna* from the womb.

He further explained that by birth everybody is a human being, it is the social norms and beliefs which give him a notion of social belongingness. While challenging a Brahmin, Kabir illustrated the equality of people (KS: 64):

> Same blood, same urine-stool, skin, anus,
> From a human being all are born,
> Why one Brahmin, the other Shudra.

He raised this question amongst the *Sadhus*, who ultimately failed to answer it or had to accept his answer. With his strong faith in humanistic equalitarianism he realised his limits as well as that of his companions. The oldest tales portray Kabir and Raidas as spiritual brothers by making them both pupils of Ramananda (cf. Hawley and Juergensmeyer, 2004: 45). It is further narrated that both the saints were born to the nearby settlements, i.e. Kabir in Lahartara and Raidas in Manduadih. Raidas, the cobbler saint, says:

> My caste is low, so is my work
> low are my traditions.
> But the Lord has given a high seat
> to this lowly man, so says the cobbler Raidas. (KS: 55).

Further:

> He who becomes pure through love of the Lord
> Exalts himself and his family as well. [AG: 29]

And,

> Oh well born of Banaras, I too am born well known;
> My labour is with leather. But my heart can boast the Lord.
> (AG: 38]. (Both, Hawley and Juergensmeyer, 2004: 25)

Kabir tried to unite the *dalits* (downtrodden) and untouchables, therefore cobblers, weavers, sweepers and beggars became his followers. He taught this low society not to suffer any inferiority complex. Of course, his adopted father Nura tried to convince him about the old tradition to follow his own occupation and not to revolt: "If you are the son of a Julaha, live like a Julaha. Why do you come into conflict with people and waste time in convincing others!" (KS: 14). Moreover, his adopted mother too threatened him in this context: "Those having power are always without kindness. Dear son! Try to understand your status. Don't try to react to others, they are to be pitied for giving false statements" (KS: 21). But it was not possible for Kabir to stop his eternal wish and will for challenge. He worried about the silence of Hindu or Muslim priests about his serious questions (KS: 22). He felt it is beyond his capacity to stop himself because the voice of revolution came from his heart, soul and mind (KS: 64).

When Lodhi asked Kabir why he was dressed as a beggar, Kabir answered "this is the uniqueness of the Julahas, who weave clothes for others while they personally wear cheap or ruined clothes" (KS: 98). Since work is worship, any occupation may be respected. It is not that fate is responsible for that.

4. Defiled Hindus and Muslims

During the 15th century Banaras was being crushed between fanatic Hinduism and cruel Islam. Kabir realised that there was no religious tradition that could reduce the gap between the two religions, rather each tradition encourages conflict and tension and treats the other as an enemy (KS: 65). The misinterpretation of religious epics provides a strong base in this respect. Kabir challenged both Hindus and Muslims (KS: 17):

> Saints, I've seen both the ways.
> Hindus and Muslims don't want discipline,
> they want tasty food.
> The Hindu keeps the eleventh-day fast
> with a bowl of chestnuts and milk.
> He curbs his grain but not his brain
> and breaks his fast with meat.
> The Turk prays daily, fasts once a year,
> and crows, "God! God!" like a cock.
> What heaven is reserved for people
> who kill chickens in the dark?
> Turk's compassion, Hindu's kindness:
> for these, they've lost desire.
> One kills with a chop, one lets the blood drop,
> in both houses burns the same fire.
> Hindus and Muslims have one way,
> the Guru's made it clear
> Rama nowhere, Khuda nowhere —
> So says Kabir.
> (*Bijak* 4.10; Singh & Hess, 1977: 10).

About the ritual sacrifice and fasting of the Muslims, Kabir says (*Bijak* 49.15-18; KS: 17):

> Fasting in the day but killing cows in the night
> Killing and worshipping together, how thy Lord be blissful.
> Again he asked satirically:
> With stone and bricks a mosque is made
> From the top the Mullah calls loudly Allah-ho-Akbar there.
> Has God become deaf?

Kabir challenged the Hindus who with their variety of complex rituals want to please God (KS: 44,65) :

Neither God is pleased with austerity, nor meditation,
And neither with torturing the body.
Neither God is pleased with sacred bath or clothing,
And neither even by controlling the five sensitive organs.
Keep kindness, help others, and go far from worldly affairs,
Let your own soul lie everywhere — then will you meet God!

Kabir never compromised with fanaticism, whether propounded by Muslims or Hindus. He asked how it could be possible that, both treating each other as enemy, they would compromise for the cause of humanity. It would only be possible when they would leave their fanatic and sectarian line of thought and action. Brahmins avoided even touching the shadow of Kabir, Muslims felt that only Muslims were their brothers; if both of them considered him lapsed, then who will serve the poor masses? (KS: 85). Kabir raised his voiced against such social evils through the process of mass awakening and self-realisation. All this is still of much relevance in the modern cosmopolitan society of Banaras.

In spite of threats, Kabir never cared for the mighty power of Lodhi, therefore he was tortured many times. But he never stopped his voice; he said (*Bijak* 25.83; Singh & Hess, 1977:26):

They're morons, mindless fools
who don't known Rama in every breath.
You rampage in, knock down a cow,
cut her throat and take her life.
You turn a living soul to a corpse
and call it a holy rite.
You think the meat is pure?
Ask the one who made it.
Meat is born of blood and seed,
it's not pure when you eat it.
Fool! You say, "It's not our sin,
but our forefathers' preaching".
The blood they shed is on your head
who taught you such a teaching.
The hair is white that once was black,
but the heart's as black as before.
Why pray and shout from the minarets
with corpses at the mosque door?
Pandits read *Puranas*, *Vedas*.

Mullas learn Muhammad's faith.
Kabir says, both go straight to hell
if they don't know Rama in every breath.

5. The Mahant

The *mahants* (chiefs of a monastery) are leaders of particular sects or monasteries. Still, they keep quarreling with one another, which sometimes may turn into struggles and collisions. When the *mahant* travels on a chariot, no one should be on his way, otherwise his assistants will beat them. This happened to Kabir, who was ultimately beaten while he attempted to save an innocent poor child from the curse of the *mahant* (KS: 12). When their processions were going to start no person from a low caste was allowed to stand nearby (KS: 28).

A full-page description of a *mahant*'s procession (KS: 29) has been written by Sahni with vividity and minor details: his followers would drink *charanamrit* (sanctified water taken from the feet of the *mahant*); they poured this water on their head and offered flowers at his feet. The *mahant* was considered as a representative of God.

The *mahant* usually rode on a silver or golden palanquin, and took food in silver or golden utensils. His lavish and royal life-style can be guessed by knowing that he possessed 115 elephants. "One follower said, Look! His eyes have divine light — this symbolises his knowledge of the ultimate reality, the supreme Brahman; see his forehead — how shining it is! ... We heard that the *mahant* can copulate with hundreds of women one by one without discharge. One can imagine the power he has acquired for such a control" (KS: 30). Using satire, the play-writer exposed the false perception of meditation as related to the power of sexuality, which is still a common belief among religious Hindus.

Kabir criticised this *mahant*. He asked: "O Maharaj, welcome to Kashi! Let me know how many days there will be theft, stealing and snatching in Kashi. (The period you will stay here, you are bound to do these acts). From where did you got this long whip which you use in the name of God to torture innocent people" (KS: 63). They would use this whip to beat innocent people on the back, as they inhumanly tortured the boy who had committed the crime of standing aside the route of the *mahant*'s procession (KS: 67). With such incidences life became hell in the city.

Kabir had to tolerate the bad consequences of the *mahant*'s curses. His opponents threw Kabir into the Ganga with the intention to kill him, but somehow he escaped (KS: 72). After this, he had to suffer several attempts on his life.

6. Religion, Status and Power

When talking about the prosperity and growth of religion, the play-writer shows the role of power (KS: 36-37):

> Kotwal: Service to religion can't flourish only by philosophy and preaching. In the name of religion many kingdoms were established, and under their patronship religion flourished smoothly. The sword of royalty serves the cause of religion. These are the secret facts of philosophy.
>
> ~~~~~~~
>
> Mullas are usually sentimental, and because of these sentiments they lose their dignity; while officers are never sentimental. They always use their mind and sense of judgement. This is the big difference between them. Officers always use their skill. Thinkers and sentimental people never win the game. This too is a secret fact.

The power always uses its resources to control religion. Therefore punishment has not to be given without full understanding of the situation.

> Kotwal: It is not necessary to punish Kabir, in fact it is more important to create terror amidst his pupils. If we punish Kabir, he would get the sympathy of the people. This is a tactful strategy to rule. (KS: 41).

Many of the reformers of the period became supporters of the king with a view to get recognition and monetary gains, but Kabir completely rejected this path, based on personal greed and mis-guidance of his own people (KS: 83). Kabir had never given importance to any group of society, be they priests or even kings, and never feared anyone in spite of the suggestions that many gave him (KS: 86).

The relation between the state's power and religious adherence was narrated in a debate between Sikandar Lodhi and Kabir (KS: 99-100):

> Sikandar: Fakirs get blessings from Allah
> and pray for other's well-being…
> Oh ! You are not a professional fakir!
> … Nowadays even fakirism is a profession…
> surprisingly, you have some other
> profession and fakirism too.

Kabir : But, what do you think about fakirism —
Is that essentially a profession?
Sikandar: Is your fakirism different from others!
Kabir: In my fakirism, there is no need to leave house
and occupation. In my view all the work is God's work.
Sikandar: ...How can every profession be the service of
God? Let me know, how is weaving God's work? ...
We fight wars — is that also God's work?
Kabir: No war is God's work. To serve humanity,
to give it joy and peace is God's work in a true sense.

~~~~~~~~

Kabir: I am the servant of Khuda (God). My religion is to love
human beings, and this is the worship of Khuda.

Kabir believed in the omnipotence of the Almighty. He realised that religious acts are not necessarily service to God. Fasting and prayers, *puja* and muttering the names of God, performing vows, as well as festivals, are all religious acts (KS: 101). He raised his voice by awakening that service to humanity, is service to the cause of the Almighty as a servant. Let a man first serve a man!

7. Kashi: Centre of Pilgrimage

In historical context and religious tradition, Banaras is considered to be the cultural capital of the Hindus and their most sacred site. Kabir's mother told him that Banaras is a citadel of religion, where at every step lies a sacred shrine or even mosque (KS: 23). It was considered that any voice raised in this city would influence the whole country (KS: 40). The city was unique. The king of the city was Hindu but the Kotwal (chief of the police) was Muslim (KS: 40, 86). While talking about Banaras, at one place Sahni failed to give the correct number of *ghats;* he wrote that there were two hundred lanes and one hundred *ghats* (KS: 52). This is a hyperbolic expression. Among the most sacred *ghats,* the five most commonly referred to are Adi Keshava, Panchaganga, Manikarnika, Dashashvamedha and Asi (Fig. 15). The play-writer has given due credit to the folk history about how Kabir received the guru's blessings from Ramananda on the steps of Panchaganga Ghat. When Ramananda was going to take a sacred bath in the Ganga in the early morning, he stepped on Kabir's body. Kabir considered this as the rite of initiation (KS: 53).
~~~~~~~~

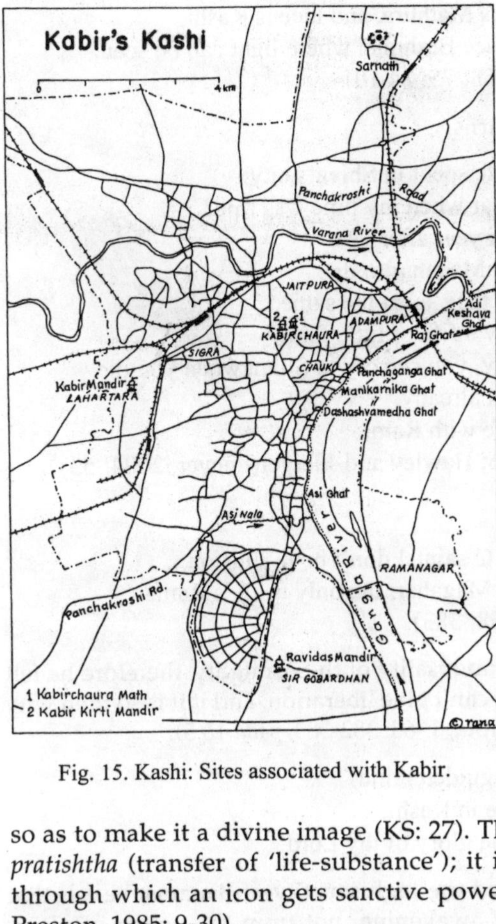

Fig. 15. Kashi: Sites associated with Kabir.

The history of icon making among the Muslims goes back to the medieval period; Muslims are the manufacturers of Hindu icons and statues. Most of them were formerly Hindus who later converted to Islam, but they continued to practice their craftsmanship. In many other places, including Banaras, there are Brahmin icon-makers (Saraswati, 1975: 30). To purify the icons, as being polluted by the touch of Muslims, a ritual is performed at the time of their installation, including sprinkling of the Ganga's holy water; by this process life is transferred to the icon so as to make it a divine image (KS: 27). This ritual is called *prana-pratishtha* (transfer of 'life-substance'); it is a highly sacred ritual through which an icon gets sanctive power and eternal breath (cf. Preston, 1985: 9-30).

A centre of pilgrimage certainly has a distinct sense, which can be perceived through different sensuous attributes like smell and sound. Near the temples the smell of *dhup* (aroma chips), flowers, incense sticks, etc., together create a *smellscape*; also, the different sounds from bells, conch shells, and drums, etc., compose another scape, i.e., a *soundscape*. One can perceive these from the early morning (cf. KS: 24, 27, 57, 62).

By awakening the inner soul one can experience the spirit of a sacred place within one's own body through sensuous and emotive perceptions. This idea was fully raised by Kabir:

For Kabir mind is Mathura, and face is Kashi,
Body's holes to see Brahman where light can be seen.
(Gupta, 1968: 75: 24.10)

Moreover, Kabir warns:

I squandered a life spent in Shiva's city:
moved to Magahar when my time was ripe?
Penance in Kashi year after year
And here I am in Magahar to die.
Kashi, Magahar: they seem the same.
Which can rectify a fife of little faith?
In Kashi, they say, you can cry to Shiva when you die.
And Kabir? Dead already.
He's enjoying life with Ram.
(KG *pad* 46; Hawley and Juergensmeyer, 2004: 53)

Again,

Says Kabir, hear O saints! don't be in illusion.
Like Kashi, so is Magahar; the only truth is Rama.
(Gupta, 1968: 383).

Kabir realised the universality of the Almighty, therefore he felt that death in Kashi alone can't give liberation, and if it is so then why not the other places? (Gupta, 1968: 382-383, *pada* 16.5):

People are of misguided mind!
If Kabir has to die in Kashi,
then where lies the glory of thy Lord.

Kabir also questioned the high sanctity of Banaras; he felt that sanctity comes from self-awakening, not from the power of place. Banaras is the greatest seat of learning; certainly it is a resort of enlightened gurus but one is not restricted to living there!

Says Kabir, Guru resides in Banaras
and the disciple near the coast,
one can't forget in spite of will
who received the merit of the revelation.
(Gupta, 1968 : 113, *Sakhi* 44.2)

Through experience and direct perception, Kabir was convinced that real worship and austerity could be performed at one's own place of residence, whichever this would be. Yoga, telling of sacred beads, chanting mantras and penance — all should be performed there. One's own home is the seat of real meditation (KS: 69).

8. Struggle for Understanding

Having a firm determination and hope for mass awakening, Kabir never tried to follow the mild path of acceptance or adjustment. As a revolutionary and reformer, he presented an example to the society, at the cost of losing his own house (i.e., his ego), and tolerated all kinds of tortures. He loudly raised his message (KS: 87-88):

> Kabir stands in the bazaar,
> with fire-stick in his hands.
> Those could set fire to their own house first
> They are welcomed to accompany me.
>
> ~~~~~~~
>
> I've set on fire my house, having fire-stick in my hands
> Now I'll set ablaze the houses of those who'd follow me.

His companion, Raidas, replied jokingly that —

> Ah! How can you set on fire my house?
> I have no shelter at all;
> when there is nothing what can you burn?

Usually, when a new movement starts against the established tradition, its leaders have to face obstacles from different sides, but awareness can help to succeed. Kabir was acquainted with this (KS: 45):

> Kabir : We should make a meeting all together. The *kotwal* is willing to stop our voice but we would not be silent. Even the *pandas* and *mullahs* also want us to be silent. Not at all, Raidas! Now we will sing in groups from one street to another, give discourses in one place and another and awaken the masses.

For these marches and to attract more people Kabir proposed to have *bhandaras* (group feasts), which have a historical tradition in Banaras. Sahni (KS: 89) gives a full glimpse of the *bhandara*:

> Kotwal : What is that *bhandara* ?
> Kayasth : Everybody will feast together in a group, e.g. cobblers, shoe-repairers, barbers — Hindus and Muslims — all together.
> Kotwal : What will happen then?

> Kayasth : Religious traditions will be broken. The laws of distinction between high and low caste will be condemned. I heard that this disease has not yet touched Kashi, but it has already spread over in other parts of the country; also, the wicked and the downtrodden are coming close to each other.

Such *bhandaras* are open for all without any sense of social hierarchy or discrimination (KS: 94). Those who realise the purpose certainly join to serve human beings.

In such a long path of understanding and struggle, sometimes it is quite natural that Kabir may also become disappointed and lose confidence in his movement. One such example was when his mother wanted that his son should lead a peaceful life (KS: 24).

> Kabir said:
> ...Everybody thinks that I am a loafer, always making trouble for others, my mother too. When will my wandering stop, my Lord! Should I again return to the forest? I don't want peace, I want a beam of light in this darkness. Every time a question raises in my mind that if my march is false, then what is the truth? I too am your servant, my Lord! Let me know the site of my final retreat?
> Wandering from one hill to another, I lost my eyes with weeping.
> Still I couldn't find that herb that saves my life.
> (Gupta, 1968, p. 19:40).
>
> Most part of the world is pleasant,
> enjoying drink and be merry
> The only pity is Kabir, he always arouses and weeps.
> (*ibid*, p. 20:45).

Kabir never blamed people when they deviated from the right path, as they are ignorant and pitiable. Therefore, Kabir prays to the Almighty that they should get divine light.

9. Kabir's Revelation

Kabir emphasised the universal brotherhood and wanted to understand it through the path of love. Even Mullahs were impressed by his revelation as "he may be saying the plain truth with deep experiences, therefore whenever he spoke people were attracted to hear him in silence, whatever their status — high or low" (KS: 35).

Whatever religious acts or rituals one may perform, one cannot understand the Almighty because these are deviant acts (p. 38). All the paths merge into to the path of love, either Hinduism or Islam; it is only for our convenience to label them under disparate identities and belonging (p. 39). Kabir explained:

> For conversation we make two:
> this *namaz*, that *puja*;
> this Shiva, that Muhammad,
> this Brahma, that Adam,
> this a Hindu, that a Turk —
> but all live on one earth.
> *Vedas*, *Quran*, all those books,
> those Mullahs and those Purohits —
> So many names, so many paths,
> but all the pots are of one clay.
> Kabir says nobody can find Rama,
> both sides are lost in schism.
> One slaughters goats, one slaughters cows;
> they squander their birth in *-isms*.
> (*Bijak* 3.30)

Kabir opposed reading many texts to acquire wisdom, or knowledge as ordained in the religious texts; he rather felt that through the realisation of love one could be a real scholar. The real worship of God is to love him (KS: 44):

> Through reading so many texts
> no one becomes a scholar.
> Only those who realised the lover
> became the real scholars. (Gupta, 1968: p. 65, 19.4).

But to remove illusion, there is the need of a guru who can keep the devotee on the right track through his blessings and guidance. If one has faith and confidence, no action can disturb him (KS: 67):

> Those who believe in the guru and have his blessings
> To those even the troubles cannot trouble;
> they will never go astray.

Kabir always used to explain that the Almighty is infinite and he cannot be realised through the ordained and dogmatic rules and rites of religion or through rituals (KS: 102; Gupta, 1968, p. 347,8.13):

Thy Lord is Infinite, Hindus and Muslims are not different to me.
Neither do I *puja* nor *namaz*, in my heart I pray to the Almighty,
Neither go I to *haj* or *tirtha*, why follow the left-over.
Says Kabir, now my illusions vanished,
my heart loves the Supreme Spirit.

The search for God is an eternal quest and insightful process; the play ends with Kabir's provocation in this context (KS: 55, 67 and 103):

Where are you searching me, I'm near to you,
Neither in temple, nor in mosque, Kaba or Kailash,
Neither in rituals and *puja*, nor in yoga or asceticism.
A searcher can find me easily within an instant of search.
Says Kabir, hear O pious friends!
Thy Lord is in every instant of breath.

10. Concluding Remarks

Kabir and Banaras were an integral part of the social revolution that took place in the 15th-16th century. His poems and sayings clearly reveal the defiled condition of society during that period; moreover, he took the lead to awaken the innocent and downtrodden. Like the Buddha (BCE 563-483), who had given his first sermon at Sarnath in Banaras (ca. 528 BCE), Kabir too respectfully accepted untouchables and strived for equality. His message reminds us of the following lines of the *Bhagavad Gita* (IX. 32): "For those who take refuge in Me, O Arjuna, though they are lowly born, women, Vaisyas, as well as Shudras, they also attain to the highest goal" (Radhakrishnan, 1971: 252). Kabir proved this and gave a message of love to all by following a tradition of 'spantaneity' (*sahaj*), as expressed by him (cf. Hawley and Juergensmeyer, 2004: 53):

Kabir:
The instrument is still,
Its strings snapped.
What can the poor thing do?
Its player's no longer
there. (KG Sakhi 16.1)

~~~~~~~

Kabir:
My mind was soothed
When I found the boundless knowledge,
~~~~~~~

And the fires
 that scorch the world
To me are water cool. (KG Sakhi 17.1)

11. Basic References

Sahni, Bhisma 1985. ***Kabir Standing in the Bazaar*** (*Kabira khara Bazaar me*). A play in Hindi. Raj Kamal Publ., Delhi. Orig. ed. 1981.

Bijaka (Kabirchaura reading, in Hindi), eds. Ganga Saran Shastri, 1982. Kabir Bani Publ., Varanasi.

~5~

Tulasi's Vision of the Lifeworld in the Middle Ages

1. Introduction

Tulasi (CE 1547-1623; Fig. 16) is considered to be an incarnation of the great Sanskrit poet who wrote Rama's story, Valmiki. In fact, through Tulasi's writings Rama's story becomes part of Hindu culture as an ideal scale of reference for the masses. As the greatest among all the *bhakti* (devotional) poets, Tulasi followed the devotional philosophy of that tradition and promoted a line of movement for the revival of Hinduism; he is thus considered to be a great synthesiser. This idea he developed through integrating the Shaiva and Vaishnava traditions of *bhakti*. Tulasi's first acquaintance with Banaras goes back to his childhood, when at the age of twelve he came to Panchaganga Ghat where he got his education under Shesha Shanatana. According to folk and local traditions, he returned to his home in CE 1573 after staying in Banaras about fifteen years. When Tulasi left his home in 1582 to become an ascetic he again came to Kashi, and from there he made pilgrimages to Chitrakut, Prayag (Allahabad), Vrindavan and Ayodhya. He finally settled in Kashi for the rest of his life, where he completed almost all his works. Therefore, vivid pictures of the lifeworld of Varanasi have been presented in his writings. Following the middle path of *bhakti*, similar to the Buddha, he justified his synthesis against the already existing thesis of Hinduism and its parallel antithesis of Islam.

The basic idea of *bhakti* was started in north India by Ramanuja (CE 1016-1137), but its base as an integrating link between 'traditional-Puranic' and 'local culture' was initiated by Ramananda (CE 1299-1411). Other contemporary *bhaktas* were Nanak (1469-1539), Vallabhacharya (1479-1531) and Kabir (1398-1518). Tulasi was well acquainted with the fact that bare criticism and the teachings of *nirguna* (formless God) could not inspire the common people; it was already known that Kabir was not successful up to his expectations. With this

Fig. 16. Tulasi completing the *Ramacharitamanasa* at Bhadaini Ghat.

realisation Tulasi advocated the Rama *bhakti* tradition. Kabir criticised without nuances the Puranic ritual traditions, while Tulasi propounded a thought based on the earlier existing tradition. As a synthesiser, Tulasi felt that Rama is the supreme Lord worshipped even by the patron deity of Kashi, Lord Shiva. But again, reciprocally Rama worships Shiva for various purposes. Some scholars misinterpret this as a dualistic approach; in fact, realising the defiled condition of society, Tulasi initiated a popular form of bhakti that integrated different sects and sections of society, and ultimately succeeded in his appeal. In this perspective Tulasi presented the multi-dimensional personality of the city, but he did not miss narrating the inside negative realities of the society, like corruption and loss of faith. Tarachand (1963:178) has rightly remarked that "Tulasi is like a natural spring in the hill, water of which provides relief to human beings of the plain".

Discarding Sanskrit, the elite's language, Tulasi wrote in the popular dialects of Avadhi and even Braj. For this pioneering task he struggled against conservative forces, and he even had to endure the theft of his manuscript of the *Ramacharitamanasa*. He was also harassed by the Pushtimargi Gosains living around Gopal Mandir, and as a result he had to change his residence from there to Bhadaini under the shelter of Raja Todarmala. But ultimately the Banaras dwellers gave him their final note of acceptance. Commenting on Tulasi as a poet and religious reformer, George Grierson (1903: 399) remarked: "Tulasi is to be placed among the three or four great literary giants of the world. In northern India, he has no comparison. His *Ramacharitamanasa* is as popular as the *Bible* in England".

In the present chapter Tulasi's feelings and expressions while residing in Varanasi are highlighted, with emphasis on the then lifeworld of his times in the city.

2. Historical Context

The life span of Tulasi spread over the reign of two Mughal Kings —Akbar (1556-1605), and Jahangir (1605-1627). According to historical sources, it is believed that in 1194 Kutubuddin Aibek demolished the Vishveshvara, Krittivasheshvara and Avimukteshvara temples, but in spite of their reconstruction, they were again destroyed in 1447. Later in 1585 Narayana Bhatta, under the protection of Todarmala, the revenue minister of Akbar, reconstructed the temple of Vishveshvara/ Vishvanatha. (After Tulasi's lifetime, it was again demolished in December 1669 by order of the Mughal king Aurangzeb; Ahilyabai Holkar constructed the present temple in 1776-77).

When Tulasi came to Kashi and attempted to preach Rama *bhakti*, there was a strong opposition, which he overcame by presenting the reciprocal worship between Rama and Shiva. In his *Kavitavali* (VI. 48), he says:

> Tulasi ! Why give undue weight to others,
> If Lord Rama is protector, who shall destroy you !

Tulasi had realised the religious importance of Kashi, and therefore tolerated the mis-happenings. It was his belief that whatever troubles may be there, one has not to leave Kashi as it possesses special merit; in fact, "never troubles trouble till trouble troubles you". His strong sense of attachment to Kashi led to his final settlement in the city, which he expressed in the *Ramacharitamanasa* (IV Soratha 1); the same verse appears in his *Dohavali* (237):

Liberation giver, mine of knowledge,
        and remover of sins,
Where Lord Shiva and Parvati reside;
        why not live in Kashi!

Moreover, writing in the folk language (Avadhi and Braj) was also a source of problems for him, but at the end he established his worth with the recommendation of the then greatest Sanskrit scholar of Kashi, Madhusudan Saraṣvati (1540-1623), who was living at Chausatthi Ghat; he wrote in praise of Tulasi (cf. Kaviraj, 1965: 38) :

In this Kashi —'the forest of bliss',
Tulasi is like a moving holy basil (*tulasi*).
His garden of poetry is so grand,
Where Rama always circles like a black wasp.

During the 15th century the culture and the people of Kashi faced serious attacks, but in the late 16th century a better era arrived under the reign of Akbar, a liberal king who protected Hindu traditions. This helped to create a strong base for traditional beliefs. In fact, due "to a diffuse, individualistic system, putting stress, on the one hand, on concrete ritual acts of worship of the physical, symbolic representations of divine persons and forces, and on the other hand, on broad, speculative, and free thinking about eternal questions of right morality, and the nature of the universe" (Cohn, 1971: 67), Hinduism was on the verge of disaster. In this context, Kabir took the lead to provide a path, but succeeded only marginally, while Tulasi achieved much better results. There is no doubt that Tulasi was disturbed by the degraded state of society, as he mentioned it in many places. Tulasi felt that such happenings were due to some inauspicious moment of time, as the shadow of Saturn fell on the Pisces constellation (*Kavitavali* VII. 177):

The hideous Dark Age is
        the one root of these troubles;
And in it Saturn rests on Pisces
        as do scabs rest on leprosy,
The *Vedas* and religion flee afar
        Kings are but thieves on earth
And holy ones, seeing
        sins grow fat, are downcast.

It has been noted that two astronomical events occurred which cast their dark shadows over Varanasi and brought disease and pestilence (Allchin, 1964: 35); as alluded in *Kavitavali* (VII 170):

> In the universal Master's score of years
> great trouble has come upon Banaras,
> Do not enquire regarding
> the condition of the city of Shiva!
> Yet, Tulasi, what can one say? knowing how
> he granted a boon to the demon Vrisha,
> And how he put aside the nectar
> so as to drink the poison.

A very bad astrological configuration ocurred during this period, viz. the 21st cycle of Rudra (CE 1599-1619), together with the conjunction of Saturn with Pisces in CE 1612. Again in CE 1616 pestilence broke out in Varanasi and Tulasi's health seems to have broken, he mentioned his physical infirmity in his later poems, e.g., in the *Kavitavali*, the *Dohavali* and the *Hanuman Bahuka*. In these poems he refers to personal afflictions like pain in the feet, stomach, head and even general sickness of the body (Allchin, 1964: 35). Finally, another epidemic emptied the city in 1623; according to popular belief Tulasi died during this plague (Motichandra, 1985: 199).

As claimed by folk history, Abdul-ur-Rahim Khan-Khana, the Suba Chief of Jaunpur (1589-1591), was Tulasi's personal friend. Since Rahim himself was a devotee of Krishna, in spite of being a follower of Islam and a Muslim by birth, it was quite natural that they maintained close ties. Influenced by Tulasi, Rahim too described the glory of Krishna in the local dialect (Motichandra, 1985: 207).

As a religious reformer promoting *bhakti*, Tulasi had three main objectives in mind: to maintain and continue the age-old tradition of Hinduism, to keep the *shudras* in its fold, as they were converting to Islam in large numbers, and to preach an easy way to get liberation (Chaube and Srivastava, 1979: 391).

3. The Territory of Kashi

The outer limit of the territory of Kashi is still demarcated by the Panchakroshi route; the name 'Panchakroshi' refers to a radius of five *kroshas* (11 miles/ 17.6 km) extending from the temple of Madhyameshvara (in the north-central part of the city, called Daraganj) to Delhi Vinayaka in the west, as mentioned in the *Padma Purana* (cf. *Tristhalisetu*

100). Even during the days of Tulasi this was the established outer limit (*Kavitavali* VII 172; Allchin, 1964:199):

> Knowing the eleven-miles circuit of the city
> To be a store of merit and highest good for any one.

This area is further comparable to the one described in the *Kashi Rahasya* (KR. 9.11); it is again referred as "the merit-giving holy territory" (*Vinaya-Patrika* 22.5).

Following the *Kashi Khanda* (74.45-46a), which refers to the special merit of the inner sanctum (*antargriha*) around Vishvanatha, Tulasi mentioned its glory in his *Vinaya-Patrika* (22.3). He also mentioned *Anandavana* ('the forest of bliss'), a forest-clad zone, which was famous for the great temple of Vishnu under the name of Bindu Madhava (*Vinaya-Patrika*, VP) :

> Giving joy, giving comfort, granting vows,
> dispassionate, unsustainable, entire,
> disporting in the lanes of Kashi,
> the forest of delight. (VP 49.8)
>
> ~~~~~~~
>
> Cloud of all joys, making pure Kashi —
> the forest of delight,
> Bindu Madhava is the despoiler of
> misfortunes arising from duality. (VP 61.1)

These verses are comparable to some passages in the Puranic literature like the *Kashi Rahasya* (14.39), the *Kashi Khanda* (39.74), and the *Linga Purana* (1.91.76).

Tulasi did not mention the outer territorial limits, the circumambulation routes which delimit the city's boundaries, such as the Nagar Pradakshina, a city pilgrimage route (*Matsya Purana* 183.61-62; 184.40-1; *Tirtha Vivechana Kanda* 39), and the three divisions of Kashi with their respective patron deities: Omkareshvara (*Kurma Purana* I 30.4, 5, 8), Vishveshvara (*Kashi Khanda* 74.45-69), and Kedareshvara (*Kashi Kedara Mahatmya* 29.38). Perhaps these sacred journey routes were not so popular during Tulasi's time.

4. The Glory of Kashi

In the *Vinaya-Patrika* (22) Tulasi presented a hymn to Kashi which vividly accounts all her important shrines, holy places and related images. Using a metaphor, the city has been conceived as a 'wish-granting divine cow' (*Kamadhenu*) in this era of falsehood / darkness (*Kali Yuga*) (cf. Allchin, 1966: 95).

Serve with love all your life through Kashi,
the Wishing-Cow of this *Kali Yuga*.
It banishes woe, affliction, sin, disease
and amasses all things auspicious. (1)

Her comely feet are its boundaries on all four sides
Worshipped by the inhabitants of the heavenly city,
Her radiant limbs are its hallowed pilgrimage-spots
Her hairs are its Shiva Lingas, countless and indestructible. (2)

Her excellent udders are its habitations
Her nipples are the four fruits (stages) of life
Her calves are the believers in the *Vedas*,
Her dewlaps is the shining Varana river,
the Asi river is as if her tail. (3)

Her horns are Dandapani and Bhairava with stave in hand
Herewith she intimidates the evil whose minds are set on filth
Lolarka and Trilochana are her eyes.
Karnaghanta is her neck-bell. (4)

Manikarnika is her moon-face beautiful
and the joy of the gods' river is the beauty of her countenance
Her greatness is the Panchakroshi
replete with one's own and others good. (5)

Vishvanatha with compassionate mind cares for her,
and Parvati ever cherishes,
The eight accomplishments, Sachi and Sharda
worship her and Rama tends her. (6)

The 'Five-Lettered mantra' is her five vital breaths
Bindu Madhava is her joy, and the Panchaganga is the five products.
The two letters of Rama's name imitating the universe
'Ra-' like *Brahman* and 'Ma-' the *atman*. (7)

The good and evil deeds of the hosts of beings
who die there are as the grass she chews.
Producing the purifying milk of highest salvation
which does indifferent to Maya long for. (8)

The Puranas tell that Keshava made it with his own hands
endowed with every art, Tulasi if you would be happy,
Dwell in Shiva's city repeating the name of Rama. (9)

In this hymn fourteen sacred sites and water bodies are referred to — they are the sites which bestow more religious merit, and which are fully described in the Puranic literature; they are presented in Table 1 and references of the main Puranic sources are given.

Table 1. **Varanasi: Shrines and rivers mentioned in Tulasi's writings** (Fig. 17)

Sacred attribute	*Puranic source*	*Description*
Asi river	KKh 46.60	City's southern edge, known as *Ida* in the mystical representation of the body (KKh 5.25)
Bindu Madhava	KKh 60.61, MP 185.68-69	The grand Vishnu temple at Panchaganga Ghat, destroyed by Aurangzeb in 1669.
Dandapani	KKh 32	The terrifying form of Shiva who serves as administrative chief of the city.
Ganga river	KKh 53.43, and KKT 31	The holiest river of India, the eastern edge of the city.
Kala Bhairava	KKh 31	'Lord of Time', a terrifying form of Shiva who oversees the city.
Karnaghanta	UvP 21.18-19	A lofty temple denoting the glory of the Gahadavala dynasty.
Lolarka Kunda	KKh 46.48, VmP 3.40	A tank related to the Sun god, marking the southern limit.
Manikarnika Ghat	KKh 26.66,67	The greatest cremation site, formerly related to Vishnu.
Panchaganga Ghat	KKh 59	One of the five more important ghats, where five rivers meet.
Parvati/ Annapurna	KKh 61.123-38	The patron goddess who provides food, Shiva's wife.
Panchakroshi	KKh 26.80, 114; 54.44	Five *krosha* (11 miles/ 17.6 km), circular limit of Kashi.
Trilochana Ghat	KKh 75, 76	One of the great ghats at the Ganga, referring to the three-eyed form of Shiva
Varana river	TS 141, 168, JU 1-2	The northern edge, known as *Pingala* in the mystical representation of the body (KKh 5.25)
Vishvanatha	SK 10.9.93	The patron deity of the city, a form of Shiva as 'the Lord of the Universe'.

(KKh, *Kashi Khanda* of SK. SK, *Skanda Purana*. MP, *Matsya Purana*. KKT, *Krityakalpataru*. VmP, *Vamana Purana*. TS, *Tristhalisetu*. JU, *Jabala Upanishad*. UvP. *Ukti-Vyakti Prakarana* by Pandit Damodara Sharma (written in ca. 1190).

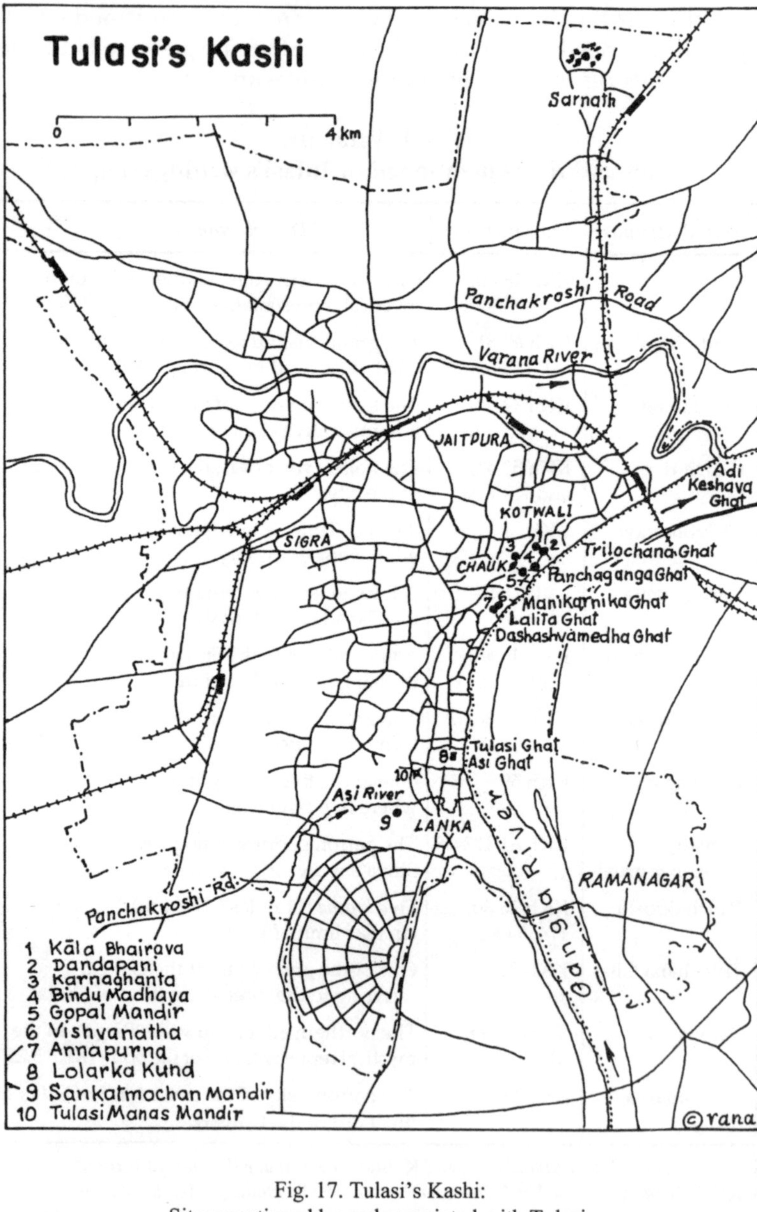

Fig. 17. Tulasi's Kashi:
Sites mentioned by and associated with Tulasi.

At different places in the *Vinaya-Patrika* Kashi is presented as the city of liberation from transmigration (VP 3.3; 7.4), Shiva's own city (4.3; 8.3), the abode of Shiva and Parvati (6.1), and the city having a heavenly river which can wash away any sin (19.3).

In the *Kavitavali* (VII. 172), the glory of Banaras/ Varanasi has been represented with symbols and metaphors (cf. Allchin, 1964:198).

The greatness of Banaras is framed
in the world and in the *Vedas*,
Its inhabitants are rich ones,
the man as if the Lord, the woman as the Mother.
Its *kotwal* is the Lord of Time, Kala Bhairava,
its judge the staff-bearer, Dandapani,
And ones such as Ganesha are
its unlimited and unequalled councillors.

The terrifying form of Shiva, i.e. Bhairava, has always been worshipped in Banaras. Tulasi has given due attention to Him; Tulasi praises Him in this way (*Kavitavali* VII.152.1-2):

Lord of ghosts, fear-expelling, terrible,
placer of fears and bearer of the earth,
Radiant as the Sun, and blessed one
adorned with ashes and covered by a great snake.

In the hymn to Annapurna ('plenitude of food'), Tulasi sings the glories of the goddess, who is a form of Parvati, Shiva's consort. Believing in fate and miraculous bliss, the poet felt that without her blessings one cannot get food (*Kavitavali* VII.148, cf. Allchin, 1964: 189):

The covetous crave
the wretched whine from door to door,
With squalid looks and mind
that cannot drive away anxiety;
Seeking for funeral food or that
of wedding or of any other festival,
They wander wildly, questioning
at each note of drum or Clarion;
Thirsting — yet they find not water,
hungered — yet finding not four husks,
Dreaming of a mountain of food
when there are not even lentils;

Man must remain a facade of sorrows
weighed down by a load of grief,
So long as the goddess Annapurna, plenitude of food,
does not melt with compassion.

The temple of Bindu Madhava has been given special attention by the poet, as he lived for a long period at Panchaganga Ghat where the temple stood; he described Vishnu's icon, the minute details of the temple and the adjacent landscape (*Vinaya-Patrika* 61-63; cf. Allchin, 1966: 129-132):

To his lotus-feet, Brahma, Shiva, Sanak,
and his sons, Shukadeva,
Shesha and the hosts of sages
in the form of bees ever resort. 61.1
~~~~~~~~
Treasury of knowledge, pure knowledge
dispassion and lordship;
Generous bestower of the *eight** accomplishments,
Das Tulasi is caught by the serpent
of existence and is exceeding downcast,
O protect him Shri Rama,
whose vehicle is the serpent-consuming eagle! 61.9

The lovely anklets are of gold, gem-studded,
giving comfort to the devotee,
As if Hari had taken varied forms
within the heart of Shiva,
had built a choice temple and dwelt there. 62.4

Hundreds of Sarasvatis, Sheshas and Vedas
meeting together cannot tell the praise of that brilliance
How then can dull-wit Tulasi Das,
given to the dualities of existence, sing them? 62.13

On his right hand — a mine of beauty,
graciousness and virtue-is the Ocean's Daughter.
intent upon the worship of his feet
She whose compassionate glance Shiva,
Brahma, sages, men, gods and demons *all* desire. 63.8

* The eight forms of *siddhis*.
~~~~~~~~

> The terrors of existence for Tulasi Das
> will pass away when his mind is
> ensnared by this beauteous image,
> Otherwise he will wander aimlessly
> for countless births,
> wretched, filthy and without comfort! 63.9

Following the Puranic tradition, Tulasi wrote many poems in praise of Hanuman (the monkey god, assistant of Rama) (*Vinaya-Patrika* 25-36). He presents Hanuman successively as an incarnation of Rudra (VP 25.3-a), an incarnation of Kapalika-Shiva (26.I-b), Shiva in the form of monkey (27. I-a), and as a form of Trident-holder Shiva (29.5-b) (cf. Keul, 2002). These forms firmly establish Hanuman's association with Shiva. According to the *Shiva Purana* (3.20. 3-7), he is born from Shiva:

> One day Shiva saw the Mohini form of Vishnu. He was struck by Kama's arrows and let his seed fall. The Seven Sages put the seed in a pot and they infused it into the daughter of Gautama through her ear. In time, Hanuman, the monkey-god, was born of it. (Cf. O' Flaherty, 1973: 228)

It is believed that Tulasi established twelve temples of Hanuman in Varanasi, with the support of twelve thousand rupees that he received as a donation from the astrologer Pt. Ganga Ram. The temples are respectively located at Hanuman Phatak, Vriddhakal, Rajmandir, Panchaganga, Karnaghanta, Nichibagh, Manikarnika, Mir Ghat, Hanuman Ghat, Bhadaini, Tulasi Ghat and Sankatamochan (Bharati, 1986: 175, also Singh and Rana, 2000: 182-184, Fig. 18). Hanuman is considered to be the greatest devotee of Rama, therefore His worship will help to please Rama. According to the *Shiva Purana* (2.1.2.1.55; 3.1-59; 4.1-76; 5.1-20) "as a remedy to Narada's suffering Vishnu gave him the face of a monkey. After he failed in his aim due to his monkey face, Narada cursed Vishnu to take birth as a man (Rama), to have a monkey as his ally (Hanuman), and to suffer for the sake of a woman (Sita)" (cf. O' Flaherty, 1973: 196).

With the Puranic tradition in mind Tulasi popularised Hanuman's worship through many hymns (VP 25-36; *Kavitavali* VII. 176, cf. Allchin, 1964: 201). Tulasi feels that only Hanuman could protect from the misfortunes of Varanasi/ Banaras (*Kavitavali* VII. 176):

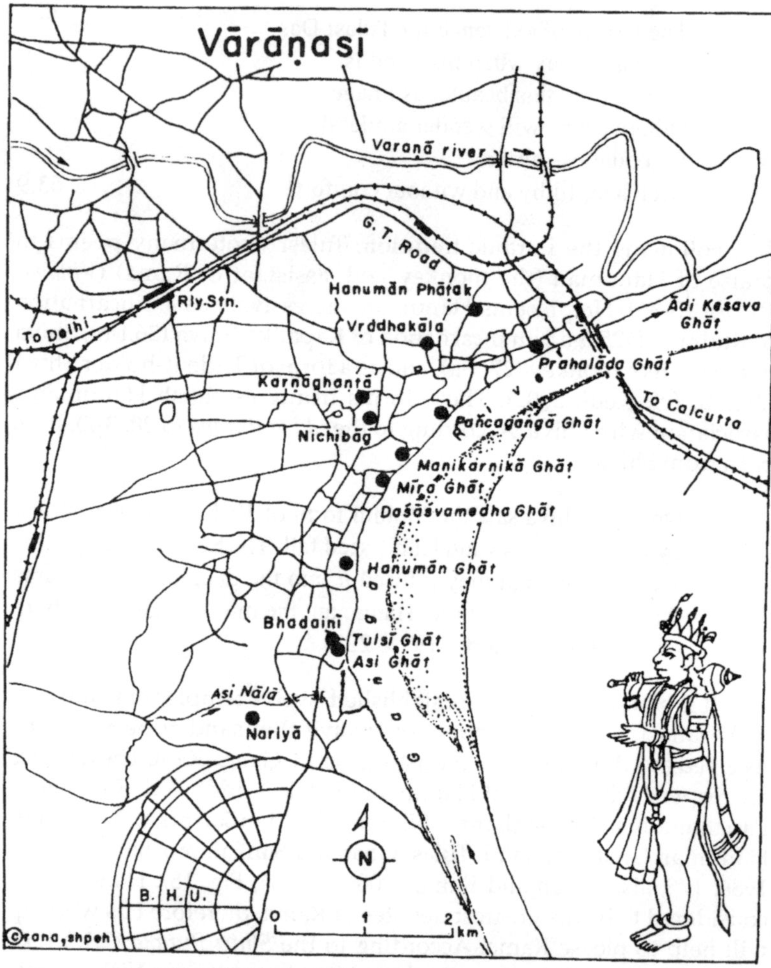

Fig. 18. Varanasi: Tulasi's Hanuman temples.

Gods shows no clemency,
and kings no tenderheartedness,
And even now misfortunes
increase within Banaras;
Protect then, king of Raghu's line,
protect O Monkey Lord — Rama's messenger,
For whenever Rama's affairs went wrong,
it was you who set them straight again.

According to oral tradition and historical sources Tulasi stayed for a shorter or longer period at six sacred sites: Panchaganga Ghat, when he got education there during his childhood; Hanuman Phatak, the first place where he stayed after becoming an ascetic; Gopal Mandir, where most parts of the *Vinaya-Patrika* were completed; Bhadaini-Asi Ghat, where he lived after leaving Gopal Mandir, and where he established a Hanuman temple; Prahlad Ghat, where he lived for some time with his friend Pt. Gangaram; and Sankatmochan, where he lived in isolation for sometime and established a Hanuman temple (the most popular Hanuman temple in Banaras today).

5. Defiled Kashi

During the last phase of his life Tulasi very much resented the defiled condition of Kashi (*Kavitavali* VII. 171. 5-8; cf. Allchin, 1966: 199):

> The offences there committed are
> the deceptions of the Kali Yuga, how else
> Should these fools not realise
> that here the Lord of Ghosts is King!
> Now tricksters flower, bear fruit and spread
> while holy ones at every instant perish,
> As the saying goes, the lamps eat up the *ghee,*
> tomorrow they'll beat the winnowing fan.

During the late 16th century the citizens lost the practice of Puranic rituals and accepted materialistic celebrations. Leaving the paths preached by the *Vedas* and the *Puranas,* they followed their own paths for economic gain. Even the main ideas of Hindu *dharma* were challenged, ultimately causing the decay of the social order, which in turn lead to sufferings, doubts, poverty, hunger, etc. — altogether it was a curse for the people (*Kavitavali* VII. 83-85). The will and devotion to understand puranic scriptures had lost motivation (*ibid.* VII. 104-109). Taking benefit of the Hindus' religious feelings many false saints started flourishing and asceticism became a profession. In fact, they were leading dual personalities — saints in appearance, worldly men in practice. At that time many Brahmins also started begging alms and lost any sense of respect. Altogether this resulted in the development of a culture of terror (*Kavitavali* VII. 171, 174-176; *Dohavali* 239). Tulasi fully exposed in his writings his own experiences with pestilence and the afflictions of his later life (Allchin, 1966: 35). The last misfortune last misfortune was his death due to epidemics in 1623. As a *bhakta*, he pleaded his appeal to Lord Vishvanatha to be kind and save his own city of his own curse (*Dohavali* 240):

> Lord Vishvanatha ! You started destruction
> in your own city,
> I pray to our Lord for escape
> on behalf of the whole city.

Tulasi lamented the defiled condition of Kashi and was surprised that because of the grip of Kali Yuga everyone has to suffer (*Kavitavali* VII, 182.5-8):

> Home of the Goddess and the God, home of the Ganga,
> dwelling-place of saints and excellent sages,
> Wiping away at a glance the
> ill-fates written on the foreheads of the evil,
> Tulasi laments for every one
> O compassionate Rama,
> Such is the sad condition of Kashi brought about
> by the terrible Kali Yuga.

Tulasi continued (*Kavitavali* VII, 183.1-4):

> This darkest of ages has destroyed
> the lines of caste, the stages of life:
> All that is proper has been tossed aside
> like a bundle thrown to the ground.
>
> Shiva is angry:
> his anger is seen in the plague.
> The Master is angry:
> daily poverty doubles.
> (cf. Hawley and Juergensmeyer, 2004: 173):

The social condition of Kashi was so bad that even daily life was in danger (*Dohavali* 239):

> In the day time thugs cheat,
> and after dusk the thieves.
> Therefore, O Lord Shiva ! be kind
> to provide me escape in Kashi.

Tulasi ultimately reached to the conclusion that one can get relief only by uttering the name of Rama; His name is *Kamadhenu* (wish-giving divine cow), and *Kalpataru* (wish-giving divine tree) (*Kavitavali* VII. 178); but the cow is at present under the grip of a butcher (*Kavitavali* VII. 181.8; Allchin, 1964: 203):

For the Kali Yuga like some butcher
is slaying Kashi, the wish-granting cow!

But Tulasi keeps hope, and thinks that all these bad happenings are the products of bad times, however a future auspicious time will restore the glory of Kashi (*Kavitavali* VII. 179.3-4).

In Kashi as many such thorns as there be
have gained the fruits of their actions,
and are glutted,
Today, tomorrow or in two or three day's time.
having licked the Diwali lamps.
snake-like they'll go their ways.

6. Concluding Remarks

Tulasi's works reveal the twofold aspect of the Kashi of that time (late 16th-early 17th century), i.e. on one side the glory and heritage of the city, inhabited by prestigious scholars, brimming with sacred sites and bathed by the Ganga, and on the other the negative utopia of the time materialising in so many social evils. Conscious of this, he never failed to criticise the bad traditions, but he also provided a new rational path to the people, in purview of the need of time, through the integration of Rama (an incarnation of Vishnu) and Shiva. Tulasi's *Hari Shankari hymn* of the *Vinaya-Patrika* (49) is his best achievement. The first line of each metre praises Rama/ Vishnu and the second Shiva; thus the beauty of this magnificent nine-metre hymn composition: (VP 49)

Burner of the forest of the demons,
full of virtues, Govinda
Joy-giver of Nanda and his family, imperishable;
Shambhu, Rudra, Shiva, Shankar, terrible,
horrid of fierce brilliance, a mass of anger. (1)

This sweet prayer-string of the Names
of Hari and Shankar
drives away duality's woes, and is a mine of bliss.

It resembles a stairway to the worlds
of Shiva and Vishnu, for all time,
declares Tulasi Das with clear utterance. (9)

Tulasi vividly presents both faces of Kashi — the glorious merits and the defiled conditions. Tulasi trod the middle path once again after Buddha in the history of Hindu revivalism, and he spoke with the language of the common people.

In view of Tulasi's writings, one can justify the importance of literary sources in weaving out the social history of the city of Varanasi. The idea of *bhakti* should also be examined in the context of symbols, metaphors and milieu within the perspectives of time, text, context and the lifeworld; only then the real condition can be understood fully.

7. Basic References

Allchin, F.R. ed. 1964. ***Kavitavali.*** English trans. with critical introduction. A.S. Barnes & Co, Inc. New York.

Allchin, F.R. ed. 1966. ***Vinaya-Patrika*** (The Petition to Rama). English translation with introduction, notes and glossary. George Allen & Unwin Ltd., London.

Dohavali by Tulasi Das, ed. H.P. Poddar 1984. In Hindi. Gita Press, Gorakhpur.

Kavitavali by Tulasi Das, ed. H.P. Poddar 1985. In Hindi. Gita Press, Gorakhpur.

Ramacharitamanasa by Tulasi Das, ed. H.P. Poddar 1984. In Hindi. Gita Press, Gorakhpur.

Vinaya-Patrika by Tulasi Das, ed. H.P. Poddar 1985. In Hindi. Gita Press, Gorakhpur.

~6~

On Banaras: Ghalib's *The Lamp of the Temple*

1. Introduction

The original name of Ghalib was Asadullah Beg Khan, and 'Asad' and 'Ghalib' were his pseudonyms. He was born at Agra on 27 December 1797 and died at Delhi on 15 February 1869. He wrote twelve books of poems and writings in Urdu, four in Persian and many other collections. His most famous book of Urdu poetry is the *Diwane-i-Ghailib*. Ghalib, considered as one of the greatest poets of Urdu and Persian literature, was greatest among all in crafting symbols, metaphors and words, altogether to make the poetry a continuous flow of feelings, experiences and thought. Those writers who supported the common human masses influenced him. Being a Muslim-Sufi by belief, he was against casteism and religious taboos, therefore he used to think of himself as a follower of universalism and humanism. Says Russell (2000: 115), "About a century before Ghalib began to write, Urdu had become the accepted medium of poetry, but Ghalib was one of those who regretted this change and continued to write in Persian as well as in the new medium. If his language had been English, he would have been recognised all over the world as a great poet long ago". In his famous couplet, Ghalib says: " *I'm the renowned Ghalib; don't ask of my name and fame. I'm both Asadullah and Asadullah's man*". That, is my name is Asadullah, and my allegiance is to Asadullah, 'The Lion of God' — a title of Ali, cousin and son-in-law of the Prophet Muhammad, and the object of Ghalib's special reverence (Fig. 19).

Ghalib wrote both in Persian and in Urdu, and what he had to say was often beyond the imaginative reach of the men of his days. Readers today, however, are able to relate to his words and meaning, and comprehend. Ghalib's remarkably modern thoughts and philosophy were far more meaningful than those of his contemporaries. Ghalib prophesied the fate of his poetry when he wrote:

Fig. 19. Mirza Asadullah Khan Ghalib.

Today none buys my verse's wine
that it may grow in age,
To make the senses reel in many
a drinker to come,
My star rose highest in the
firmament before my birth,
My poetry will win the world's
acclaim when I am gone.

His confidence has proved to be well founded (cf. Russell and Islam, 1994: 28). He further added:

> I do not long for people's praise;
> I seek no one's reward,
> And if they say my verses have
> No meaning, be it so.

In the context of his case for pension in the Calcutta High Court, he started his journey for Calcutta (now called Kolkata) in August 1826 from Delhi and *en-route* he visited Lucknow, Kanpur, Banda, Modha, Chillatara and Allahabad. In August-September 1827 he reached Banaras and stayed there for over four months (Nayyar, 1969: 134-135). But if Ghalib did not achieve the purpose for which he set out for Calcutta in 1826, he gained greatly in other ways. The experience of such a long and arduous journey was itself an exciting and interesting one for him. Large parts of the journey were over unmetalled roads; part of the way he travelled by river; and the final stage, from Banaras to Calcutta, he did on horseback. The journey brought him in personal contact with men of letters in all the important centres along his route, and he continued to maintain this contact by letter in the years to come (Russell and Islam, 1994: 47).

Mirza Ghalib came to Banaras while he was sick, but the weather and natural beauty of the city helped him to relax and get healthy. He stayed for a few days in the Sarai of Navarangabad (Aurangabad), with an old woman, and later shifted to the palace of Mirza Gulam Ahmad.

During his four-month stay in Banaras, Ghalib developed a high sense of attachment (topophilia) to this great place, and insightfully experienced the *genius loci* of the place, which are profusely reflected in his poetry. The Hindu rituals and festive acts attracted him so much that he wrote to his friend Mohammad Ali Khan: "This city (*Banaras*) is so beautiful and lovely that even a stranger misses counting his sufferings. If I would have no fear of religious contempt and criticism from my enemies, I would have left my religion and used to count beads, bear sacred threads, put a mark on the forehead and in this way I would have passed my life on the bank of the Ganga" (Nayyar, 1969:135). On December 31, 1860, he replies to a letter which his friend Sayyah had written him from Banaras:

> My friend, I like Banaras: it is a fine city. I have written a poem in praise of it called '*The Lamp of the Temple*'. It is in my volume

> of Persian verse. Have a look at it... You have written an account of your journey from Lucknow to Banaras, and I'm expecting you to go on with it. I am very fond of travelling and sight-seeing... Oh well, if I cannot travel, never mind. I will content myself with the thought that 'To hear of pleasure is to experience half of it', and will think of Sayyah's account as itself a journey. (Russell and Islam, 1994: 246)

Even forty years after of his visit to Banaras Ghalib remembered the city with great respect and love. In a letter to his student Miyan-Dad Khan Sayyah he wrote "Oh ! Banaras is a unique city. What to say more about! When is such city born? At the end of my life I visited the city. If I had been young, then I would have settled there and left Delhi" (*ibid*). In fact, he might have seen the fantastic view of the meeting of the sky and the Ganga at dawn, when the city-edge of the river looks like a garland of oil lamps; while in the morning the reflection of sunlight on the *ghats* and their shades in the Ganga is another scenic beauty (Gupta, 1984: 22). With this view in mind Ghalib wrote a poem of 108 stanzas in Persian called ***'The Lamp of the Temple'*** (*Chiragh-e-Dair*), of which 69 stanzas directly narrate his feelings for Banaras. Even poets earlier to him also wrote poems describing the glory of Banaras, about whom sometimes he refers. In this context one stanza by Sheikh Ali Hazim (1697-1766; he passed thirty two years of his life in Banaras and died there) is popularly cited in Banaras:

> I won't leave Banaras for anywhere else,
> As it's a house of realising universalism.
> In fact, each and every Brahmin boy,
> Looks like Rama and Lakshmana here.

2. The Feelings

Out of 108 stanzas of Ghalib's *The Lamp of the Temple*, 69 which deal Banaras are translated here and their original numbers are given (based on Nayyar, 1969: 136-150).

> In my imagination, there's a city full of flowers,
> Where always lives spring — the most loveable city. (21)
>
> It is such a city, which Delhi has to praise
> It comes to circumambulate this city. (22)
>
> When eyes see this city, visioned it like spring,
> As they perceive innumerable scenes of beauty. (23)

Those writers who praise the city of Kashi
Their works got the merit of heavenly bliss. (24)

From the evil eye, may God in his greatness
save Banaras as it is a grove in paradise. (25)

Praising Banaras someone said — it's like China
Thereafter on its forehead the Ganga turned into a curve. (26)

Banaras is a beautiful, attractive painting
And Delhi has always to worship it. (27)

Perhaps Delhi had seen Banaras in a dream
And got water in its mouth with greed, flowing now as a canal. (28)

It's wrong to say: Delhi's jealous of Banaras
It's no wonder Delhi wants to be like Banaras. (29)

Hindus believing in pilgrimages
Always worship and praise Kashi since time past. (30)

Those who die in this grand city of Kashi
Get liberation from transmigration. (31)

Such persons' wishes and wills flourish
And they become immortal after death. (32)

Banaras gives peace and relaxation to souls
And cleans all the sufferings of the heart. (33)

There's no wonder that even the departed soul
Never wishes to leave this city. (34)

O ignorant people! Come and see —
The great heavenly nymphs of Banaras. (35)

See body-less souls! These icons are without water and mud,
It means heavenly nymphs are soul from head to foot. (36)

Their faces are like light as the flowers' sweet smell
And pious from head to foot like the pure soul. (37)

Even thorns and grasses are like flowers in Banaras
Moreover, even a particle of dust is full of soul. (38)

In this transforming world, Banaras' glory and beauty
Are protected from all the changes that time brought. (39)

Either be spring, or cold or summer season
Banaras' environment presents heavenly glory in all. (40)

All the springs of the world came to Kashi
To pass the cold and summer pleasantly here. (41)

Although even autumn has the quality of sandalwood
Yet it always opens its wing to complete its cycle here. (42)

In the city of gardens, Banaras, to get popularity
Even spring use to wear a sacred thread of flowers. (43)

If Banaras has not kept the mark on the forehead
Then from where does the red light of sunrise come. (44)

Even a handful mud here equals a sacred fire-pit
And each thorn in the greenery is like a heaven. (45)

Banaras is the capital of the icon-worshippers
And the site of pilgrimage for devout people. (46)

This city is a worship-place for conch-shell user Hindus
And the greatest seat of pilgrimage of Hindustan. (47)

The courtesans have the dazzling beauty of the Tur-hills,
a divine brightness from head to toe.
May this radiance be safe from the evil eye! (48)

Their waists are tender but their hearts are passionate.
They may look innocent but they are clever too
and skilled in the business of love. (49)

Their smiles enrapture the heart and their beauty
would cause even spring roses to blush with envy. (50)

Their graceful movements and the delicacy
of their gait make flowers bloom in their footsteps. (51)

Courtesans' tender mood is much tenderer than pearls,
More speedy than running blood in coquettish lovers. (52)

These courtesans when walking with sweet strides
Paintings develop on the ground and enslave the visitors. (53)

By charming gestures they win heart and minds of lovers
On bed they're like spring, and in lover's lap like *Id*. (54)

Their scorching looks like the idolatrous Brahmin dumb.
They contrive to make their faces glow
like lamps beside the Ganga. (55)

When they go down to the riverside a whole garden seems
to spring up around them and a myriad lights shine. (56)

The heavenly nymphs when bathing in the Ganga water
Pay respect and homage to the holy water-current. (57)

Like long strides of doom's day these courtesans walk
With their eyebrow throw arrows on their lovers' heart. (58)

Their glancing produces flame of love in the heart
And their meetings give satisfaction and joy. (59)

Every ripple they make as they bathe
seems to reflect their grace.
Their merriment brings joy to the river's current. (60)

They produce agitation in the body of water
Where many lovers like fish toss out in agony. (61)

The Ganga stands in zeal with open lap,
Aiming to receive these beautiful courtesans. (62)

In presence of their shiny gestures and beauty
Even pearls enter in their shell and feel shy. (63)

It seems that Banaras is a beloved for those
Who has the Ganga as mirror in her hand for day and night? (64)

The face of heavenly nymphs turns
the sun into a mirror in the sky,
So as to see her reflection in this mirror. (65)

O grand, wonderful beauty! What unalloyed loveliness!
The shadow of Banaras is dancing in the mirror of the sun. (66)

The city is a garden of grand peaceful greenery
Where springs always live —
this is a story told throughout the world. (67)

When Banaras views its reflection in the Ganga,
It becomes a symbol of beauty in itself. (68)

Reflection of the City's turned to a radiant symbol
The fear of evil eye lost without any care. (69)

There in no such grand painted place even in China
There is no other comparable city to Banaras. (70)

There're everywhere red-flower trees in forests,
Even in fields and gardens always lives spring. (71)

One night I asked a distinguished scholar of the city,
Who knows the mysteries of evils in the world and sky. (72)

He told me to see what are lost from the world —
Piety, loyalty, love, kindness and courtesy — all! (73)

In the place of religion only its name remained,
Nothing left except cheating and deceit everywhere. (74)

Fathers are thirsty for their son's blood,
And, son's are enemies to their fathers. (75)

Brothers fighting to one another now,
Companionship and love loosening day by day. (76)

These are the signs of cosmic dissolution,
But still why not that is appearing soon? (77)

At any time the conch shell of dissolution can blow
And who has stopped the dissolution yet? (78)

He smiled and answered, indicating Kashi, that —
This city has stopped dissolution till now. (79)

The truth lies somewhere there,
Even the Lord doesn't want to destroy it. (80)

The glory of Banaras is the greatest of all,
Even our dream can't reach to its height and prestige. (81)

O! diverted from the line of tradition! Ghalib —
You have fallen down in your own eyes and others' too! (82)

You are now alien even for friends and relatives,
You became lunatic while living and loving this city. (83)

How you take all this?: Like a mad man,
We feel pity and are sorry for you and your heart. (84)

Why are you searching beautiful scenes in the garden,
See your own heart and enjoy those scenes inside. (85)

If yours manic love is true, only left half-a-footstep
Between Kashi and Kashan [in Iraq];
for a skillful man no troubles trouble him. (86)

~~~~~~~

If you stay in Kashi, how would you reach your goal?
O Ghalib! What're you doing there — leaving your goal aside! (89)

Remember such views never grace your personality,
Kindly continue your work (your tour to Calcutta). (90)

In Kashi for a moment remember your own homeland
Even in this city of heaven, think of your own home too! (91)
~~~~~~~

In these stanzas the natural beauty and landscape are not properly highlighted. Since the medieval period of Urdu poetry, there was a lack of such naturalistic descriptions; moreover when Ghalib reached Banaras the season of the famous *langara* mango (*Magnifera indica*) was over, therefore he did not describe it in spite of being his most favourite fruit. Ghalib's love of mangoes alone was enough reason for loving a place, like Kolkata (cf. Russell and Islam, 1994: 48). He was extremely fond of mangoes and pretty women; together they made Kolkata a special place for him. His attraction to the beautiful courtesans of Banaras indicates the importance given to the local women. But he was intent to follow the Sufi tradition, as a Fakir (Muslim saint). He says:

> Within the face of Fakir, myself Ghalib
> Try to see the scenes and actions of the world.

3. Remarks

The sensitivity of the Banaras-dwellers was exposed in Ghalib's stanzas in at least three ways — the fantastic scenes, the religious tradition, and the degraded situation. Ghalib's visit took place during the reign of Uditya Narain Singh (CE 1795-1835), the king of the Banaras State. Ghalib never encouraged negativism; he felt that everywhere there are dark spots but also some rays of light, whatsoever may be — city or man. This thought is seen in the *Chiragh-e-Dair*, where he said:

> Ghalib ! Don't be upset if some calls you bad,
> Is there somebody to whom everybody says good!
> I know the inside reality of heaven,
> To please the mind, this mirage is good medicine.

Ghalib seems to have lived in a unique state of trance during his four-month stay in the city. His description of Banaras is an excellent example of the secular spirit, which is the life-breath of India as a nation (cf. Tripathi, in *NGJI* 1990: 145). He was well aware of the spiritual insights and the beauty of the city, and also of the downward trend of the society during his times— the period referred to as a transitional phase — and he presents both faces in his poem. Some of his verses remind us of similar ones of the English poet Matthew Arnold (1822-1888), who was his contemporary:

> Wandering between two worlds, one dead,
> The other powerless to be born.
> (*The Grande Chartreuse*, 85)

4. Basic References

Ghalib, Mirza 1827. ***Chiragh-e-Dair*** (*The Lamp of the Temple*), 108 Stanzas in Persian. Translated and written in Devanagari (Hindi) script by Nayyar 1969: pp. 136-150; also in Mukherji, ed. 1978: 169-173.

Mukherji, Vishwanath, ed. 1978. *This is Banaras,* in Hindi. Thalua Club, Varanasi.

Nayyar, H.C., ed. 1969. *Ghalib Gaurav* (an anthology of poetry and prose of Mirza Ghalib), in Hindi. Banaras Hindu University, Varanasi.

~7~

Images in the Late 19th Century: Bhartendu's *The Love-lorn Female Ascetic*

1. Introduction

The phenomenological approach has been applied to describe the lived-world of everyday experiences as given in Bhartendu Harishchandra's *Premajogini*, a play that describes the places and the people of Banaras in the late 19th century. The philosophic frame, the setting and spots, positive and negative issues of references, and finally the phenomenological search for further work on Banaras — its merits and demerits, all are presented in this chapter.

In the frame of perceiving landscape and people, two perspectives emerge: a place as a hostile and alien site, keeping man away from his human potential; and a place as the true home (cf. Lutwack, 1984: 3). Among the two, the former refers to *placelessness* and the latter to *placefulness*. In a different way, this may be interpreted respectively as an aversion (*topophobia*) and a strong affection (*topophilia*) to a place. Relph (1986: 27) mentions: "Belonging to a place, feeling part of it, gives many people a positive sensation of security, yet for others it may be oppressive and restrictive". Bhartendu describes both these qualities of the spirit of a place (*genius loci*). The real Kashi/ Banaras/ Varanasi lies in the hearts and minds of many dwellers, who enjoy life with delight, *joie de vivre*, carefreeness and headstrongness (*mauj*, *masti* and *akhkharpan*), as in those who still cherish old ways and traditions, while also making their minds to accommodate with the coming 'New Kashi'. This dialectical view combines traditional continuity and acceptance of modernity. In most of Bhartendu's writings such expressions are prevalent.

2. Bhartendu Harishchandra: an Introduction

Harishchandra (Fig. 20) was born on 9 September 1850 in Banaras as the eldest son of Gopalachandra, himself a renowned poet of that time. His father died when Bhartendu was only fourteen years old.

Fig. 20. Bhartendu Harishchandra.

And he himself passed away on 6 January 1885, at the age of only thirty-five. During this short span of life he wrote forty-one literary works, twenty-six plays and thirty-five essays, all in Hindi. Besides these, he also wrote in Urdu, and some works in Marathi.

He was born during the climax of the British colonial regime, but he was commited to India's independence, and wanted Hindi to be established as the national language. Writing in such a crucial period of time, he had to tolerate criticism from two sides — the British government and social reactionaries (Sharma, 1966: 13). However, later on he was recognised as the father of modern Hindi and also as the pioneer of Hindi plays. Among his works, ***Premajogini*** (*'Love-lorn Female Ascetic'*, from now on referred as **PY**:) is the only major work that describes the landscape of Banaras — both the positive and negative aspects. It was first published in 1875 with the title 'Kashi's Painting' or 'A Couple of Good and Bad Photographs'. The play *Premajogini* is an outcome of the 'critique for all manner of autocracy in social matters', in fact, it is a document representing historical reconstruction of the social reality (cf. Dalmia, 1997: 128). Furthermore, in his following play, *Satya Harishchandra* (1876), the glory of Kashi was also narrated in contextual descriptions.

In this chapter, *Premajogini* is taken as the basic text while portraying the landscape and people of Banaras, but descriptions of Kashi as given in *Satya Harishchandra* have also been discussed wherever needed. *Premajogini* has been divided into four parts, excluding the introductory part. Part one deals with the condition of a temple, endowed with two different sides: spirituality and corruption. In the common conversations, the writer exposed his own personality with self-criticism as satire for the dwellers, and narrates the lived experiences of the people attached to a temple. In the second part the negative aspects of the culture and personality of the Banaras-dwellers are described, using the representative characters of a broker, a ghat-priest, a shopkeeper, bards and a common man. Dalmia (1977: 303) says that "he was aware that there was no precedence for the form he was creating in the older tradition and, in choosing the word 'photograph', he both indicated the modem character of his undertaking — he was considered a good amateur photographer — as well as the reality of the individual in social situations that the photograph as a medium sought to capture and hold fast".

In a lengthy poem various issues of topophobic scenes are disclosed with typical examples of incidences. Some scenes of the railway station of Mughalsarai are showed in part three: sweet-sellers, toy-sellers, coolies, peons, a stranger and a broker meet together, and the placefulness quality of Kashi is vividly accounted with a reference to history. The cheating culture of brokers is narrated, with full view of their perception and images. The fourth part is a reflection upon the Brahmins' manipulative strategy in performing rituals and how they escape themselves with the power of religious dogmas. Thus, this play provides a full glimpse of the negative and positive aspects of the landscape. When in 1874 Harishchandra started writing PY, he "began first with a vivid sketch of life inside the temple, the conversation between the various kinds of attendants, the one responsible for *kirtan*, the Jhapatiya, the lunger, who whipped back the throngs of *bhaktas* when they surged forward during the course of *darshan*, the water carrier and Vaishnavas from Kashi, Gujarat and Multan — the mundane everyday life of the temple and its inhabitants" (Dalmia, 1997: 365). Of course, PY is an unorganised play, in fact "it is completely a realistic and innovative effort of which only Bhartendu had the courage to depict the bad impact of colonialism and the deteriorating Hindu culture" (Sharma, 1966: 102).

With its unique historico-cultural background and sense of its own individuality, every place has the images of topophilic and topophobic natures. Both mostly depend upon the context and meaning, to be especially highlighted with non-verbal communication. With interpretation of texts and visualisation of the places mentioned in these texts, the place identity was looked into the frame of its three components — distinctiveness, continuity, and transformation. Of course, one can emotionally claim that "*Premajogini* is obviously written by a crazy man, and only a crazy man could understand it". But there is scope for more rational and balanced thought over this statement. The above narration arose with be observation that many dwellers love the city (inside feelings), and many other dwellers hate it (outside reflections). This love/hate relationship is very much a part of the attitudes and spatial contexts in temporal perspectives.

It is too easy to criticise the negative side of Banaras and then say nothing more. It is obviously ugly, confusing, and unpleasant. Yet it seems to be a basic context for activity and convenience, and it fits into the way of life people have lived in Kashi for long. The city was famous as a *thaganam sthanam* ('an abode of thieves'), as mentioned in a 12th century text (cf. Singh, 1985: 301). The playwriter was very much in favour of visual and personal experience of the landscape, rather than getting knowledge only through books. The first expression in the above play refers this view:

> To sit and visit the scenes of the country,
> This mystery is seen only in books. (PY: 320).

Therefore, it is quite fitting to highlight the visual impressions of the spots and places described by Harishchandra with the help of field observations (cf. Fig. 21).

3. Topophilia

The term 'topophilia' includes all the humans' bad affective ties with their material environment, thus it presents vivid and concrete personal experiences as a bond between people and place (Tuan, 1974: 93, 94). It, therefore, refers sensitivity to the spirit of one's place (*genius loci*). With this spirit it has two reflections — behavioural, lived experiences of an individual but reflecting the worldview through the common eyes; *placefulness* indicating love and affection to a place and people. It is notable that, "places are neither good nor bad in themselves but in the value attached to them, and literature is one of the agencies involved in attaching values to places" (Lutwack, 1984: 35). Moreover, "the character of a place is conditioned by the kind of human activity that is performed there" (*ibid:* 47). We can compare this with William Shakespeare's poem (*Hamlet* II. ii. 259):

> There is nothing either good or bad,
> but thinking makes it so.

Bhartendu expressed that the spirit of place has a distinct beauty in its environmental setting and religious ethos. To a stranger, a knowledgeable resident, Sudhakar expresses (PY: 337):

> The changed name of Kashi is Varanasi, where the motherly goddess Ganga flows in an arc-like shape on its three sides, as if willing to put Shiva's affectionate Kashi in her lap. Furthermore, while touching it with her sacred water she also wishes to make

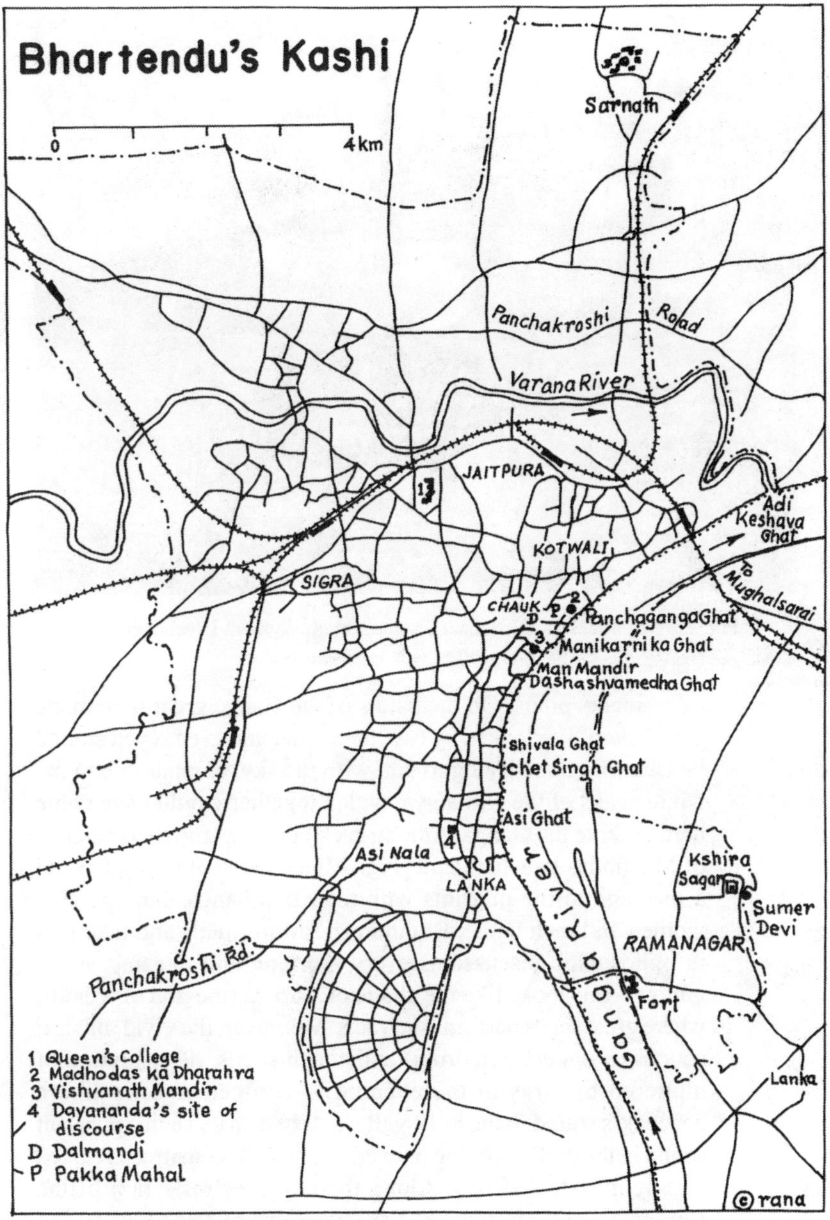

Fig. 21. Varanasi: Sites referred to by Bhartendu Harishchandra.

Fig. 22. Madhodas ka Dharahara (Aurangzeb mosque) at Panchaganga, a view in the late 19th century.

its residents pious. On the banks of the Ganga great men made grand *ghats* overlooked by two, three, four and even seven storied houses which are trying to talk with the sky, comparable to the white peaks of the Himalaya, which together would have come here to serve the Ganga. Among such buildings the two minarets of Madhodas ka Dharahara [Fig. 22] appear as if trying to send a message to the pilgrims with their two hands. Innumerable women and men bathe; Brahmins perform rituals and take part in philosophic discussions every morning and evening at the *ghats* — this looks like the abode of Kubera (the god of wealth) where great sages perform such acts. Moreover, the vivid musical sounds of *nagadas* (a drum) and conch-shells, the vibration of muttered mantras in the evening — altogether echo like a peacock's sound in the hilly-valleys. If one hears such a pleasant sound in the early morning or evening, he will be so much relaxed that he may feel sleepy. Along the river, the reflection of the sunlight in the morning and the shadows of the *ghats* in the evening are always fantastic and unparalleled.

Fig. 23. The great bull of Shiva, Nandi, in the Jnanavapi compound, a view in the late 19th century.

The most ancient name of the city Varanasi is Kashi, which comes from Kasha, the name of an ancient king. It is also called Kashya, the luminous one, "because that light, which is the unspeakable Shiva, shines here, let its other name be called Kashi" (*Kashi Khanda* 26.67; see Eck, 1982: 26). The name Varanasi refers to the holy land between the two rivers, the Varana in the north and the Asi in the south (cf. *Matsya Purana* 184: 40-41; *Mahabharata, Bhishma Parva* 6.10.30: 338). The name Banaras is a synonymous form of the Pali version of the name Banaras, and now this name has been revived as the popular name of the city.

Both at the sunrise and the sunset one can see ravishing reflections of light in the Ganga. In the morning the reflection of the sun's light on the Ganga-water alomg the *ghats*, and in the evening the shadow of the *ghats* on the surface of the Ganga make a spectacular view. This is a unique scene in this city. This feeling is only possible after "seeing, thinking and describing" (cf. Relph, 1984: 212; also Relph, 1985); since understanding all the features of the world encountered visually is only possible with the closed sensible reality (*ibid:* 213).

About the relation of things to a place, Cassirer (1952: 92) rightly puts, "it is never purely external and accidental; the place is itself a part of the thing's being and the place confers very specific inner ties upon the thing". This sort of experience is possible only after visiting the specific sites of the city landscape of Kashi, "where after visiting the observatory at Man Mandir, the ancient remains from the Dhamek at Sarnath, the great sacred bull in the Vishvanatha temple [Fig. 23] and its golden summit, the temple made by Chet Singh across the Ganga, the *haveli* of Kashamirimal, the architecture of Queen's College, and the high rising minarets of Madhodas ka Dharahara, any outsider becomes astonished" (PY: 340).

Banaras has several distinct environments "where certain relationships evolve not only between men and men, but between men and the forces of nature" (cf. Jackson, 1970: 76). Throughout history, this harmonious relationship has resulted in attractring people from different parts of the country to settle down in this city, "where people from different parts of India, e.g. Dravida, Magadha, Kanyakubja, Maharashtra, Bengal, Punjab, Gujarat, etc., all together have mixed up and engaged in their distinct occupations (Fig. 24). Their neighbourhoods reflect their original identity symbolised with the cultural grouping. In Bengalitola, one can visualise Dhaka, in Lahoritola one can search Amritsar, and in Brahmaghat one feels as if in Poona" (PY: 341).

With the help of spatial pattern of the socio-religious landscape of Varanasi, referring to localisation and segregation of various peoples from many parts of the country, its ethnic diversity can easily be highlighted. These distinct pockets are represented with specific shrines and temples, which are looked after by priests belonging to the families connected with the original site. Moreover, in those areas one can hear the different languages of India, like Bengali, Punjabi, Sindhi, Marathi, Gujarati, Marwari, and even Dravidian languages like Tamil, Telugu and Kannada.

Throughout history the city of Varanasi has been a great seat of thinkers, philosophers and scholars. It is like a mine having many treasures: "Although many great scholars passed away, there are still several of equal status one can meet", (PY: 343). At the end of the narration a resident of Kashi, Sudhakar says, "How can I describe Kashi! Kashi is the only *Kashi*! There is no city like Kashi in the three realms. You can see it, and realise it; but it is useless to talk much about it" (PY: 342).

Among all the places and scenes of landscape beauty, the view of the riverfront of the city becomes unique with the northerly flow of the holiest and sacredmost river of India, the Ganga. This river has not been given prominence in *Premajogini*, but in his next play, *Satya Harishcandra*, SH (1875) the Ganga has been described vividly, with deep and religious emotions:

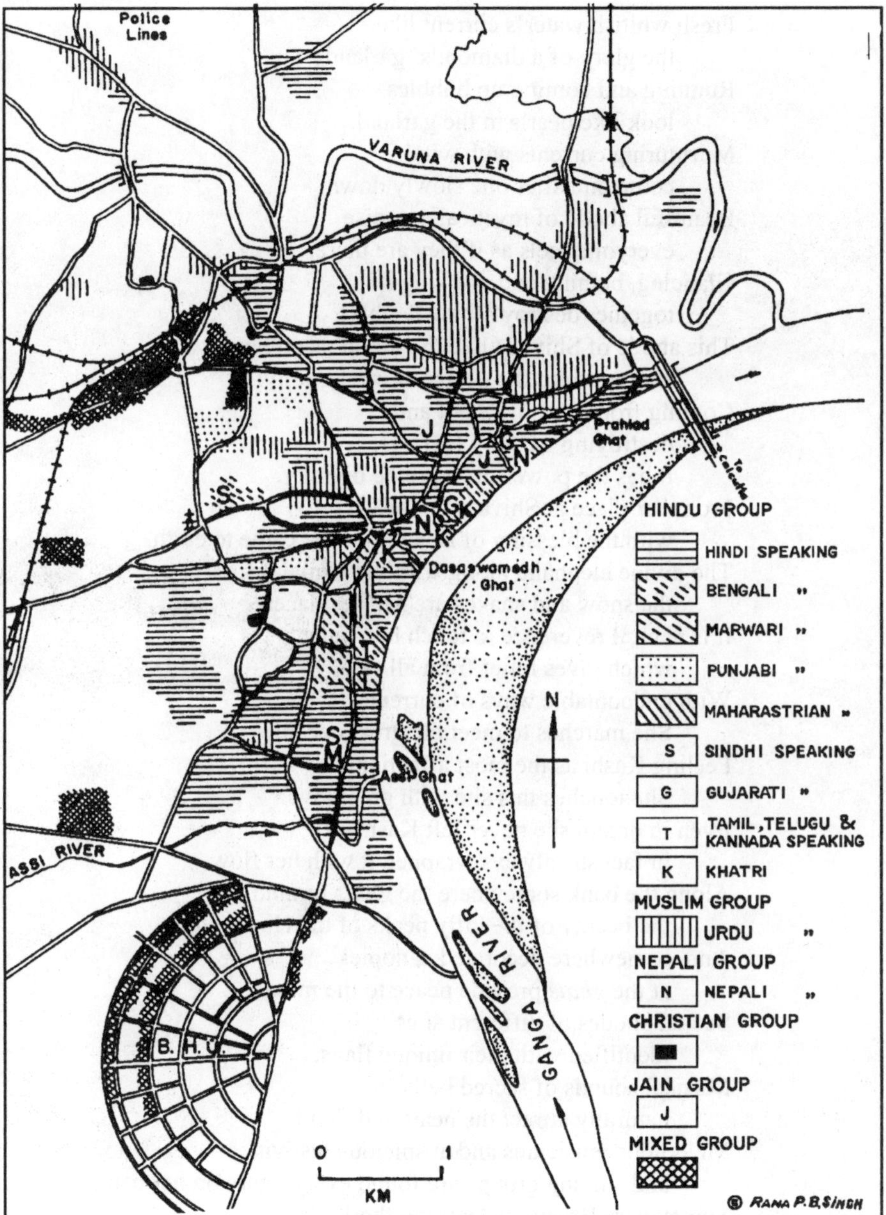

Fig. 24. Varanasi: Socio-cultural space.

Fresh whitish water's current like
    the glory of a diamonds' garland
Running and coming up bubbles
    look like pearls in the garland.
Murmuring currents with wind
    come one after one slowly down.
Beautiful abode of mystical paradise
    everyone feels as if they are there.
Glancing, bathing and drinking it
    together destroy all the doubts.
This abode of Shiva is like the moon's coolness
    and provides the nectar of immortality.
Coming from Brahma's pot and
    destroying worldly feelings,
    it has the power of Supreme divinity.
From her place at Shiva's forehead
    with the blessing of Bhagirath, she came to earth.
The divine elephant, along with the Himalaya,
    the snow and snakes are her necklaces.
It is natural reverence to touch her water
    which gives relief from all sins.
With uncountable ways of currents
    She marches to meet the great ocean.
Feeling Kashi as the most affectionate
    She touches this site with great love.
Even in dream she never left Kashi,
    in fact she always wrapped it with her flow.
Along the bank somewhere the *ghats* remind
    the beauty of the lofty peaks of the Himalaya.
And, somewhere decorated canopies
    at the *ghats* provide peace to the mind.
Sacred abodes of different sites
    identified with their unique flags.
Musical sounds of sacred bells
    naturally attract the heart and mind.
Melodious musicians and auspicious festivities
    and singing groups are found everywhere on her bank.
Somewhere Brahmins learning the *Vedas*
    and somewhere Yogis practising meditation.

Somewhere charming girls take bath
    and play with their friends in the water.
Comparable to pearls meeting lotuses —
    one after one, and coming out of water.
These beauties while rubbing their faces in the water
    present an excellent scene of attraction.
The cloudy spots on the moon are
    comparable to the flourishing lotus flowers.
The reflection of the beauties in the river
    reminds the moon's shadow in the water.
The reflection of faces as lotus and flourishing lily
    attract the mind and the soul for ever.
Wherever the sight reaches here and there,
    it also rests at a point to see the fantasy.
It is beyond the scope of description —
    the glory and beauty of the Ganga, says Harishchandra.

The content of *Satya Harishchandra* is based on Puranic sources, especially as described in the *Markandeya Purana* (VIII). But Bhartendu did not take care of the historicity of the place, but rather described the emotional feelings and bonds of the people living in this city. This perceptive sense can easily be applied for any other holy city of India. He has neither tried to describe the glory of Varanasi in the Puranic era nor in the present time. In fact, in his narration he especially highlights the dwellers' feelings and the spirit of place (cf. Rudra, 1973: 48). Such ways of describing a city have been very popular in the Sanskrit literature, with the use of hyperbolic expressions, similes and metaphors (*ibid.* 46). This can also be seen in PY (p. 337-338).

Bhartendu has missed to describe the patron deity of the city, Lord Shiva. According to mythological metaphoric expressions, this city is established on the 'trident' (*trishula*) of Shiva. This three-fork spear-like weapon represents various symbols related to the number three: the three realms; the three original sacred abodes of Shiva and their respective zones, i.e. Omkareshvara in the north, Visheshvara in the centre, and Kedareshvara in the south; and the three basic qualities of nature, i.e. purity (*sattva*), passion (*rajas*), and dullness (*tamas*). Having these sacred qualities, Shiva is considered as the 'Lord of the Great Time' (*Mahakala*) whose identity expands from 'life' to 'death' (cf. Singh, 1986: 303, 310).

4. Topophobia

Hermeneutics and phenomenology both assume a close tie between the person and the world; "both are our pre-reflective experience and our critically self-reflexive knowing" (Mugerauer, 1984: 241). This can fully be exemplified with the description of a place from the points of view of its inside realities and of its outside reflections; of course within limits of the two of these edges there also appear overlapping among 'doing', 'saying' and 'knowing'.

About the averted description of Bhartendu, it has been commented that he was fond of 'self-praise' and egoism, and that he was far from reality. In the introductory part of *Premajogini,* he described himself as a great personality; indeed the impresario says:

> ...Our esteemed brother, kind hearted like father, friend and son, the only statue of love, the only resort of truth, the only character of generosity, the only well-wisher of India, the only father of Hindi, the only pioneer of Hindi plays — Harishchandra is indeed unhappy! ...Your motto is 'whatever sufferings may be, accept them as happiness'." (PY: 322-323)

Such statements are not the negative part of his literary creativity; he rather follows the tradition of using such expressions in Sanskrit and Urdu (Rudra, 1973: 57). The three qualities of nature used in Indian thought (goodness, passion, and dullness) are described according to context and milieu. Through one of his characters (who represents him) Harishchandra says:

> Ramachandra: Look! These two fellows (indicating Dhandas and Banitadas) — both are wicked. I heard their talk from outside the door. They are talking about women and sex for hours.
>
> Balmukund: This world is full of mystery. Here someone talks something and others talk something else. To what extent can you waste time thinking about them. (PY: 330)

Bhartendu's lived experiences are, of course, personal but they are deeply rooted in the psychological realm of the common people. Such "intimate experiences are difficult but not impossible to express. They may be personal, and deeply felt, but they are not necessarily solipsistic or eccentric" (Tuan, 1977: 147) This has been taken as a challenge by Bhartendu, and he succeeded in disclosing many intricacies of the inside extremities. These descriptions need to be taken as a critical diagnosis of a psychological disordering in such a religious place.

In the beginning of the performance, Harishchandra expressed that this play is an attempt to show a glimpse of the Kali Yuga, the era of falsehood, and by turn which also represent his own personality and the existing culture:

> This play is quite fitting to represent the age of falsehood, and also reflecting the writer's personality. This play will provide a good sample of the present cultural crises and additionally a combination of the *old* and *new* traditions. (PY: 324)

The first part of PY presents vivid accounts of different people associated with a temple. Disclosing the inside realities, the pitfalls of Vaishnavism were badly criticised (Sharma, 1966: 49). As a place of worship and spirituality, people profoundly revere the temple, while its attendants and caretakers are considering the place as a site of enjoyment, relaxation and easiness. In the course of conversation, one attendant speaks about offering a woman or even someone's wife to satisfy the priest of the temple (Maharaj):

> Banitadas : On the face of Maharaj, by their own will all women use to tumble down to get religious merit; why should I send somebody!
>
> Dhandas : O Guru! The fate of these priests is quite bright; they plunder wealth, and enjoy sex too.
>
> ~ ~ ~ ~ ~ ~ ~ ~
>
> Dhandas: And, Guru! Due to such fellows four kinds of people feel relaxed: firstly, the bards; secondly, all the attendants; thirdly, the recluses; and fourthly, the prostitutes.
>
> Banitadas: Nothing left to talk about them. Living in a temple is like living in paradise; you get good food, garments — thus avoiding to wear rough clothes, as you get very soft and good clothes, using scent, fragrance and costumes, chewing saffron-mixed betel, getting served by attendants, and above all enjoying the extreme pleasure [of sex]. (PY: 329)

It is a common belief among the people that Annapurna (the goddess providing food to everybody) will certainly provide food to the Kashi-dwellers: "(Kashi) — here even blind, crippled, handicapped, fools, indolent, and lazy fellows do receive food and cloth with the blessing of the mother goddess Annapurna" (PY: 338). At another place, the same theme is narrated in a poetic way:

> Hungry belly no one sleeps,
> Kashi is like this. (PY: 332)

Using a semiotic approach with its three components, i.e. the sign vehicle, the designation, and the interpretant that narrate environmental meaning (cf. Rapoport, 1983: 36-38), Bhartendu's imagination and expressions about Kashi can be highlighted. An experienced and knowledgeable outsider has strange feelings, but the bare truth is the most strange, says George G.L. Byron (1788-1828):

> 'Tis strange — but true; for truth is always strange;
> Stranger than fiction. (cf. *Don Juan* XIV. ci)

Analysing PY, Dalmia (1997: 304) observes: "The city as a whole, just as the *nayak*, hero, of the play, clearly has two sides, the exalted and the seamy. We are first presented with the seamy, with the view from below. The scenario resembles that of John Gay's *Beggar's Opera* or indeed Brecht's *Dreigroschenoper*. In any case, with the exception of the *nayak*, Babu Ramchandra, and his *musahib* or agent Sudhdkar, the characters in the play consist almost in their entirety of the rogues and charlatans of the city. For all their roguishness, they are presented with a vigour, vitality and gaiety which is as irresistible as it is irrepressible". In a lengthy poem, Bhartendu expressed through the words of a stranger (*pardeshi*) the good and bad qualities (topophilia, topophobia) of Kashi, which fully disclose the real picture of the city at that time (Sharma, 1975: 53); similar scene can easily be seen even today (PY: 333-334, cf. Schilder and Callewaert, 2000: 71):

> Look at your Kashi, O people!
> Look at your Kashi!
> City of the Lord of the universe, Vishveshvara,
> the Indestructible Lord.
> Half Kashi is an abode of bards,
> inn-keepers, Brahmins, ascetics,
> The other half is occupied by prostitutes,
> widows and distinguished courtesans.
> Full of idle loafers, cannabis addicts, unreliables,
> scoundrels, sweepers, and thieves.
> Indolent, liars, rogues, and the defamed
> having no concern for anything.
> They never do their duties,
> plainly ridiculing others,
> Taunting you if you work,
> ruining their own worthiness.
> All the rich men are liars, censors

and worshippers of treachery.
Cowards living on recommendation,
stupid, but preaching high morals.
Filthy alleys full of garbage,
rotting waste of leatherworkers.
The foul smell from water-taps,
Eighty-four hells making you vomit.
Barking and aggressive dogs in Kashi,
roaming bullocks destroying roads.
Leaping monkeys from balconies,
like men jumping from high.
On the ghats, ghat-priests exploit you,
strangling a rope around the neck.
With false pretenses ghat-priests cheat,
taking even your clothes and beds.
Beggars trailing behind you cheat,
speaking like big givers.
In the temple priests cheat,
making a joke of religious acts.
While shopping brokers cheat,
snaring you to deceive.
During purchase shop-keepers rob,
while offering gifts of goods.
After a theft even the police cheat,
by friendly talk and false assurance.
In the court, the lawyers and judges cheat,
stripping you naked and helpless.
Roaming pickpockets swindle
and snatch your valuables anywhere.
Going to jail without remorse at all,
Like a naked dancing-girl without shame.
Visit to officers and giving them bribes,
is a pleasant common routine.
While gifting to temple feel fever,
become disappoint and unhappy.
In the home wife and children hungry,
but serving others like slave.
The bards in brothel lane are worshipped
by them like their mother's sisters.

Taking good food and drinks from others,
    for this they roam since morning,
But at their own father's funeral ceremony,
    serve food-remains to the Brahmins.
Their outer behaviour looks pure,
    but wealth is the end of their lives.
With their extravagant habits,
    all the properties are mortgaged.
Hearing erotic stories with devotion,
    swallowed like divine nectar.
While trying to mutter Rama's name,
    they feel coughing in their throat.
Look at your Kashi, O friends!
    Look at your Kashi !!

The description above of cultural setting and symbolism of city life may be considered as blunt and rudimentary. The same claim was made against Thomas Hardy, who has been considered one of the greatest writers of 'place-saturated fiction' (cf. Van Ghent, 1953: 203). Remember what Edward Said (1978: 168) said about the formation of such images: "Every pilgrim sees things his own way, but there are limits to what a pilgrimage can be for, to what shape and form it can take, to what truths it reveals". Here too this question still remains unanswered that to what extent his use of place is too blunt and rudimentary! This comment can easily be challenged with the personality of a conscious intellectual, like Sudhakar who laments amazingly:

> Oh! Why has this city to face such situations, citizens are fools and never think about the future! Leaving aside this foolishness, they hardly know anything! How can one think of prosperity of this city! Except foolishness they don't have any other skill! Without any cause they abuse everybody. Taunting on others is their great motto. Whatever right or wrong comes into their mind, they discuss it loudly. They neither want to read, or to learn! Oh! When will God liberate them? (PY: 336)

The city of Varanasi was perceived as a refuge for sinners even in the Puranic literature (Singh, 1985: 310). This is an extraordinary cultural notion about this holy city. But the city is so pious and holy that it can give liberation from transmigration to even the wickedest among the wicked: "Says the *Kashi Khanda* 'those who have no refuge at all can get salvation in Varanasi' " (PY: 347). The original passage of the *Kashi Khanda* (26.136) mentions:

> Even after committing heinous sins, if one comes to Kashi in due course and casts off his body, he attains me alone with my favour.

The highest form of spiritual power rooted in this city can be narrated in a different way by the use of satire. Chaudhuri cites a Sanskrit couplet based on Wilson's translation from the *Vishnu Purana* (cf. V. 34):

> For those who are ignorant of the revealed scriptures and the sacred traditions, who have abandoned purity and proper conduct, and for those who have nowhere else to go, for them Benares [Banaras] is the refuge. (Chaudhuri, 1979: 172)

Chaudhuri's viewpoint is comparable to Ramanujan's, who said (1973: 27), "Religions set apart certain times and places as specially sacred: rituals and worship are performed at appointed times, pilgrimages are undertaken to well known holy places. There is a holy map as well as a holy calendar. If you die in Benares (Banaras), sinner though you are, you will go straight to heaven". He cited the following couplet by the medieval saint Dasimayya which represents the contempt of the saint for all the sacred places and sacred times:

> To the utterly one with Shiva
> There's no dawn, no new moon,
> no noonday, nor equinoxes, nor sunsets,
> nor full moons;
> his front yard is the true Benares,
> O Ramanatha.

Pitiful places, people and cultures as described by Bhartendu should be taken sympathetically in the way T.S. Eliot (1888-1965) has put it:

> To make an end is to make a beginning
> The end is where we start from.

At several other places, Bhartendu has described various aspects of Kashi. The extremely hot weather of Kashi in summer is described in *Harishchandra Magazine* (May 1874):

> Don't ask about the rocky-like city, Kashi, where all houses changed into brick-boxes. The roof-stones do not get cooled

> throughout the night even with the cool rays of the moon. If one places his face near a window, one will think he is near a boa-breath or an ironsmith's bellows. Although the hot rays of the sun do not reach the lanes below, yet with the heat of the upper roofs the lower houses also become so hot and moist that only youthful lovers can stay there, for whom even this hot sun will look as the moon of the cold season. In this area even a baby bird cannot get shelter in this season. (cited in Sharma, 1962: 67).

This feature of extreme condition does illustrate a single aspect of the actual situation, which sometime becomes intolerable. This can be especially realised in the Pakka Mahal area, the most congested and ancient part of the city. To understand the seasonal rhythms and the feelings of people living therein, one has to know these distinct conditions of the environment.

Through Bhartendu's narration in the *Kavi Vachan Sudha* (*Ashadha* Shukla 15, Samvata 1928, i.e. 1871), one can realise how the civic conditions of the city of Kashi degraded under British rule. Using satire, he described the state of Kashi, which can easily be seen here and there even today:

> Lanes are never cleaned... Lanes became muddy due to water logging, and fermented mangoes produce an intolerable smell... Anglo-Indians dry their clothes on the bind strings in the streets... Those who are constructing or repairing their houses throw the waste materials in the street... By providing shelter to cows and buffaloes, people obstruct the way... Many people believe that the limit of the municipality is up to the line where horse-carriages can reach... Prostitutes are slowly spreading over the areas of common householders and ... the number of wine shops is increasing... It shows how the government is looking at every piece of space with equanimity. (Sharma, 1979: 338)

Some common expressions of the Kashi dwellers are related to their distinct unstable mental state. The dwellers are famous to worship several gods together (*bahudevapujaka*), which reflects a distinct unstable mental state, i.e. a polytheistic character what Max Müller called *kathenotheism* (Eck, 1982: 40). Watching sideshows and following the dominating mood are common habits. Bhartendu was deeply influenced by the culture and society of Kashi; it is with this deep-rooted feeling that he expressed: "Banarasi people are like a waxen nose, you can divert them wherever you want... Not only Banaras, even other cities have a similar character" (Sharma, 1975: 333). Moreover, at many places he criticised the evil part of the Hindu religion, with the intention of making people aware of such deeds. He felt that only after such awareness and realisation, an innovative thought with practical solutions might be sought.

Any visitor coming to this city can experience its negative features as described by Bhartendu. It would not be a surprise, as "the best surprise is no surprise" (cf. Rapoport, 1983: 53). Since everyday experiences record such happenings, it is not a subject of 'surprise'. Bhartendu's dialectic glimpses record cries, but at the other end also a wit of happiness, humour, repartees and satire, which together help to understand the Banarasi culture (Sharma, 1975: 54). Of course, Harishchandra has badly criticised the temple life and the rituals performed therein, moreover "he made known his low opinion of some of the *bhaktas*, devotees, who congregated there. He was aware that they regarded him and his ways as alienating and, possibly, as influenced by Christianity; in short as being of a suspiciously critical, reformist nature. Yet, he was one of them and viewed himself as one of them. His critique, when it came, came from within the ranks" (Dalmia, 1997: 366). Topophilia and topophobia come together everywhere, and one can get an experience of the various place-scapes through a non-verbal communicative approach, especially through various spatio-temporal forms of place-scapes like visionscape, soundscape, smellscape, imagescape, faithscape, etc. (cf. Porteous, 1985). Such study will lead to a further step in 'sensuous geography'.

5. Reaction on Colonialism: Contextuality

Under the British colonial regime in the 19th century, the society reached the state of being subservient to the British Empire. In March 1857 the first sign of open discontent was recorded among the armies. Due to the speedy rise of prices and disturbances here and there, the authorities perceived civil disobedience. Rebellion was spreading throughout north India, and the revolution of independence was also in stream (cf. Sukul, 1974: 283-85). In such a circumstance, it was natural to take a lead for re-vitalising the normal values and ethos of Indian culture. Bhartendu took an active part in the renaissance of that period. His earlier plays provide a sound background for revivalism, but his later plays very openly exposed the worst conditions of the culture and people. He openly described the degraded situation; he reached the climax in his later play, *Andher Nagari* ('the Dark City') written in 1881. The Brahmins, known as protectors of Hindu religion and practices, became so corrupted that they were prepared to sell all their morals for money, with the motto that "since money is everything, everything is justified to get money". In *Andher Nagari* (cf. Sahai, 1905: 196), the caste-seller ('satire for a Brahmin') says:

> For a caste, another caste; for each rupee a caste. Give me a rupee, I will change you to my caste. For some rupees I will convert a washerman into a Brahmin, and a Brahmin into a washerman. For a rupee, whatever you ask I can arrange. For a rupee I can change falsehood into truth, a Brahmin into a Muslim, for a rupee a Hindu into a butcher; for a rupee I can sell the *dharma* and the prestige. For a rupee I can witness in favour of falsehood, for a rupee I can accept sin as religious merit, for a rupee I can accept degraded people as our ancestors; all — the Vedas, the *dharma*, ancestry, morals, truthfulness, prestige, etc. are on sale for a rupee. I am giving you such invaluables per rupee per *seer* [a little less than a kg]!

When Bhartendu was nineteen years old, he took an active part in the discussions with Dayanand Sarasvati (1824-1883), the founder of the *Arya Samaj* (a re-vitalised form of Vedic Hinduism), when he visited Varanasi in 1869. Such discussions inspired him to speak very boldly against the degraded socio-cultural conditions of that period. Taking the benefit of simile and metaphors, he deeply criticised the British rule and its corrupt policies, which very few persons dared to do at the time. Again in his *Andher Nagari,* he described the scenes of 'a dark city' (Sahai, 1905: 197):

> In the dark city, the foolish ruler,
>   Vegetables per seer per rupee and the sweet too.
> All are equal — defamed and distinguished,
>   Equal treatment for the bards and the priests.
> No consideration for family morals, nor castes,
>   All are looking to one another equally alike.
> The prostitutes and the wives are treated equally,
>   And, equated cows and goats similarly.
> Worthy people wandering here and there,
>   while the deceitful and indolent are respected.
> Apparently civilised, but internally cheater,
>   Their voice has weight in the ruler's meetings.
> In the presence of the swindler, no one dares,
>   whatever others tell, they never use to care.

In such an environment, how was it possible to describe only the glory of the city? With a rational thought and with a view to preserving the invisible qualities, he painted the spots along with the colourful scenes. Simply and openly, he described and disclosed the fallen and ruined aspects of the colonial culture making it fully naked (Sharma, 1975: 131). It seems as if he had followed Descartes' dictum that "doubt is the only correct method of cognition" (*De omnibus dubitandum*), rather than accepting St. Anselm's proposition that "faith is the basis of knowledge" (*Credo ut intelligam*). Descartes' dictum gave him the courage to develop a sense of critical appraisal. Only with this spirit can Bhartendu's description of Banaras be rationally judged. His writings should be properly explained through a phenomenological approach that seeks to return to the original and direct experiences. Heidegger (1927: 67) expressed that this approach is not one of the perceptual cognitions, "rather that kind of concern which manipulates things and puts them to use" — the "own form of knowing". Reaction to our existence is just an essential, as existence means *shared* experience in time (cf. Jackson, 1970: 147).

6. An Epilogue

Dalmia (1997: 308) rightly remarked that, "It is perhaps no coincidence that Harishchandra did not complete the play [PY]. In retrospect, the social vignettes provided in the play seem precocious for their times, and thus almost destined to remain unique". Like John Ruskin's (1819-1900) enormous literary output (see Cosgrave 1979), Bhartendu's literary works, composed within his very short span of life, are significant in terms of quantity as well as in their ambition to awake socio-cultural consciousness. His power of imagination, his reflection on colonialism and his aim of a renaissance were of great merit, and are still valid in different contexts. Using literary skill of contextual differentiation, he presents his words, symbols, and metaphors in the cultural milieus of his time, helping to understand the cultural scene of the late 19th century. He was trying to create a movement of self-awakening so that society would be aware of its own pitfalls. He has been really a light on the path in preserving humanism, i.e. a justified sense of action what Relph (1981: 19-21) called 'environmental humility'.

7. Basic References

Harishchandra, Bhartendu 1875. ***Premajogini***. In, *Bhartendu Granthavali* Vol. I, ed. Brajaratnadas. Kashi Nagaripracharini Sabha, Kashi : 319-354.

— 1876. *Satya Harishchandra*. A play in Hindi.

— 1881. *Andher Nagari*. A play in Hindi.

'Rudra', Shivprasad Mishra ed. 1973. *Bhartendu's Satya Harishchandra*. Nagaripracharini Sabha, Kashi/ Varanasi (in Hindi).

Sahai, Shivnandan 1905. *Harishchandra* (in Hindi). Hindi Samiti, U. P. Government, Lucknow. Reprinted 1975.

~8~

The Images in the 19th-Early 20th Centuries: Rudra's *The Flowing Ganga*

1. Introduction

Rudra's novel ***The Flowing Ganga*** (***Bahti Ganga,*** referred as **FG:**) presents openness and humility together in describing the social world of the 19th-early 20th century Kashi/ Banaras. While narrating the sociology of place in time, of course with no bias or intention, Rudra examined various issues related to ethnic pluralism on the scale of historical events. In this novel, within its 'contextual environment' the place has been contemplated as people, and people as place, which together form a 'spirit of place' (*genius loci*). Following this analogy, specific attention is thus not given to describe the landscape and its associated processes of social formation, but rather characters are the major consideration; thus Rudra's work does not fit into Durrell's scale.

The period of Rudra's descriptions that link to his canvas, characters and culture represents the continuty of offshoots of the preceding time. Like other important centres in the Ganga valley, it is known that the early 18th century Banaras was a *'mughalising city'*, owing much to the cultural patterns established first by the Mughals and then fostered by the Nawab of Awadh's court. but after the decline of the Mughal empire in the following early 19th century, three power groups emerged in the city. They were represented by the local Rajput/ Bhumihar dynasty, the merchant-bankers, and the 'Gosains' — 'merchant trader-soldiers'. The political and economic power of these groups was deeply interrelated with 'cultural patronage' (cf. Freitag, 1989: 9). These power-holding groups played a crucial role in 'reinventing' a Hindu tradition which could cope with their own interests. The relationship between the Nawab and the Bhumihar king of Banaras was chacterised by several ups and downs. In 1910-11, the final decision to reinvest the king with the powers which previously had been partial, was removed by the king's capacity to keep "conservative Hinduism at Banaras" on the British side (cf. Freitag, 1989: 11). This period recorded several scences of turmoil and tensions as narrated by Rudra.

2. Rudra's Novel: an Introduction

This book-length collection of stories, or novel, entitled *The Flowing Ganga,* has been presented by Shivprasad Mishra 'Rudra' Kashikeya (1911-1970). It was first published in 1963, and the second edition in 1967, which was followed by several reprints, including an English translation (1997).

Rudra was amazed with the enthusiastic response to the first edition of *The Flowing Ganga,* because "in Hindi literature, criticism is made not of the work but of the personality of the writer, where his belonging to a group is given special consideration" (FG: 7). In fact, the writer was not associated to any *'-ism'* or any such other group (*ibid.*). Not following the common tradition of narrating independent incidents as separate stories, or chains of incidents in the form of a novel, the writer has produced this work as a connecting chain between a 'series of interconnected stories' set into the frame of a novel. Therefore, he humbly suggested that the readers interpret the work however they would like to.

Rudra raised the question: "Is it a necessary task to first fit the work into a frame of literary type?" This is a pure structural perspective. He followed the dictum that "the styles are not the mother of literature, rather literature is the mother of styles" (FG: 8). The discussion on this issue should be according to *argumentum ad ram.* Voltaire's (1694-1778) maxim that *Tout est pour le mieux dans le meilleur des mondes possibles* ('all is for the best in the best possible world') is to be applied in this writing of Rudra where each of the stories is fitted into the best possible way of the cultural context. In this context Rudra cited an Urdu poem (FG: 8):

> The excellency lies in the contents of the story
> Whom is to be praised — the writer or his creativity?

Rudra's imagination was not, of course, geographical, his concern was more for the common man and the struggles of man's existence. With individual commitment and historical understanding, he tried to paint with authenticity a portrait of the social world (compare Cosgrave, 1979: 62). For this purpose he took the help of folk tales, oral histories and epics, and sometimes even of historical documents to justify the connecting chain of incidents.

Banaras has been famous for two opposite kinds of men — the sages, and the loafers. Therefore, one must highlight different types of men and environment before trying to present an appropriate picture, which ultimately makes this city unique (cf. Golledge, 1985: 115). Rudra is successful in describing these two models. The distinct places, people, and characters are vividly presented, and ultimately the work ends with the message of revolution against social evils.

The collection consist of seventeen independent stories, but interrelated sequentially in historicity and contents. They are: 1 Let us sing the praises of Ganesha, 2 Howdah on the horse, and saddle on the elephant, 3 Nagar's boat is going to Kalapani, 4 My husband's bedstead is on a spike, 5 Come to me, come to me, 6 Allah, how grand is thy mosque! 7 In every pore, a thunderbolt of power, 8 Shivnath Singh and Bahadur Singh, what a pair, 9 This is where my nose-ring got lost, 10 This mortal body for Rama, 11 On this side the Ganga, on the other the Yamuna, 12 The drowsiness of *Chaitra* dulls the spirit, 13 Early sow, early mow, 14 Let us be in good spirits during heart-griefs, 15 Women, you are meant for reverence, 16 Divine sayings never fail, and 17 All became red. Out of the seventeen, thirteen stories were translated into English along with introduction, comments and postscripts by Golding (1997); however the translation slipped down many passages of the original stories. In this chapter the original Hindi text is taken as a basic source. The contents of these stories can be grouped under six themes highlighting the personality of Banaras, as presented below; the rest of the narration, dealing with society, culture and on-going activities is not taken into consideration. In the present analysis, contextually relevant sources are also illustrated.

3. A Unique City

Any perceptive expression has two dimensions — insideness and outsideness. The dimension of outsideness has been expressed through the character of a British military officer, Major Bukley, who wrote a letter to his fiancé in September 1858, in which he described the peculiarities of Banaras:

> It is a peculiar city; it is one of the most ancient. The sentimental feelings that Muslims have for Mecca, Jews for Palestine and Christians for Jerusalem or Rome, Hindus have for this city, which they regard with full respect and reverence. One of my civilian friends said that citizens of this city are quite turbulent. They just smile about serious matters, but fight to death over

> very small things (FG: 61). ... Here one thing is quite notable: that the lanes are very narrow, very dirty and circuitous (FG: 61-62). ... As I've said earlier, this country is quite strange, and that is doubly true of Benares [Banaras]! (FG: 62)

This description presents an inter-mixture of outside purview and inside experiences gained through native feelings. The religious glory of Banaras is well known; in fact, it is the cultural capital of India, where various sub-cultures of the country are represented by the immigrants from different parts. They all mixed together and formed a unique culture, known as Banarasi, a synonym for 'delight, joie de vivre, and carefreeness'. It is through this peculiar quality that the Banaras dwellers take serious matters very lightly and become serious over small issues. Their feelings for the traditional king were very high in their heart and soul:

> Another strange thing about this city is that in spite of our rule, another person is recognised as the king by the common masses" (FG: 63). ... Whenever people see the king, they loudly raise their voice, *Har Har Mahadeva*, Hail to the great Lord Shiva. (FG: 145)

In spite of narrow lanes and structurally compact neighbourhoods, people are not very well acquainted to each other because they are busy in their own businesses, and they are rather little conscious about their social relations and their mutual cohesiveness. To cite an example: "Chaukhamba is a very big neighbourhood. But in spite of living in the same locality, people are not acquainted to each other. Their homes are not closed to one another in mental space" (FG: 138).

There are numerous cults and sects followed by saints and ascetics; among them the philosophy of wandering is most popular. One *sadhu* (ascetic), while describing his identity, cites Kabir:

> A *sadhu* is like running water,
> Never merged into the sea.
> Being stationary at a place, he turns into stone,
> Or otherwise into a miserable pond. (FG: 142)

Smoking intoxicants is common among *sadhus*; it is the only way of relaxation according to Tantric ethics. Among such items, *bhang* (*Cannabis indica*) — dried leaves of hemp, and *ganja* (*Cannabis sativa*), another narcotic and intoxicating preparation from leaves and buds of hemp, are common (FG: 142). These *sadhus* are also known for giving spiritual discourses, especially after having smoked; but citizens never appreciate such talks. On such an occasion, a Banaras dweller says:

> Oh! Don't preach us about knowledge. I have seen many parrot-*sadhus* like you! How would a real *sadhu* be like you? (FG: 142).

Sometimes Rudra was confused with the spatial affinity and distance factor in the description of landscapes. One such example will be cited: while describing the Sankatamochan temple (lying in the southern part, across the Asi stream), he mentions the locality of Ramapura, that according to him was inhabited by turbulent Doms who would get subsistence through theft and robbery by means of bow and arrows, and this even during the day hours. This information has no historical reality at all (FG: 73). Moreover, his description of the landscape surrounding the temple is not correct; in the 18-19th century it was not covered with dense forest as resort of wild animals, big snakes and scorpions (*ibid*).

4. The City of Gundas

The word *gunda* is a corrupted form of the Arabian word *'gundah'*, meaning a hoodlum or rogue. According to historical sources, during the rule of Balwant Singh (CE 1738-1770) crime steadily increased, reaching a climax under the rule of Chet Singh (CE 1770-1781) (see Motichandra, 1962: 265; 294). Rudra got the inspiration to write about them from the short story *Gunda* written by the (late) great Hindi laureate Jaishankar Prasad (published in *Hamsh* "Kashi Anka", ed. Premchand, 1933); who wrote:

> In the late 18th century, to oppose socio-political power, characterised by a corrupt jury system the disappointed and discarded Kashi-dwellers took a step to form a new cult of society. The cult's religion was bravery. To die on one's word, to seize one's livelihood with courage, to avoid using weapons on wounded enemies and on the cowards who beg for mercy, to render help to the suppressed poor of the society, and to live each moment as if it might be one's last was the cult's creed. The citizens of Kashi called this group '*Gunda*'. (see Chaturvedi, 1984: 57)

In folk-tales and oral histories the names of Bhangar Bhikshuk, his disciple Dataram Nagar and their associates, and later on Shivnath Singh and Bahadur Singh were frequently mentioned. In three stories Rudra described the social world of these *gundas* and also their status in society. Of course, he did not describe the places where *gundas* used to live, but folk-histories tell us that three specific areas were well identified: Harahasarai, Piyari, and Jatanbar. According to a folk song these *muhallas* (neighbourhoods) are the resort of *gundas* (*Eh tino gundan ka ghar*). These neighbourhoods were associated with the *gundas* of three castes — the Muslims, the Rajputs, and the Yadavs (Ahirs). Still today these areas have a similar reputation. Rudra writes, "with the fall of Chet Singh, Kashi was falling asleep, but its wicked sons, known as *gundas*, became conscious and took a vow of hatred against foreign rule. Among such people Dataram Nagar and Bhangar Bhikshuk were particularly notable" (FG: 23).

The dates mentioned by Rudra are mistaken (FG: 23). In fact, Warren Hastings visited Banaras for the first time in 1773 and ultimately had to flee; but in 1781 he plundered the city. The two *gundas*, Dataram Nagar and Bhangar Bhikshuk, were associated to the case of 'the barrel explosion' in 1852 (Motichandra, 1962: 378).

The increasing influence of the *gundas* during the early 19th century responded to the demand of the times. Of course, once the common man admitted the fact that even by change of rule the major problem related to social oppression will continue, they tried to adjust accordingly with a view to following the Hindu philosophy of tolerance. But there were many others who revolted against the situation, completely rejecting the suffocating foreign rule with the motto: "let's live and die for our own homeland"; these persons were known as *gundas*, but they were respected by the society.

> Bhangar Bhikshuk was the true symbol of bravery for Kashi dwellers. Dataram Nagar and Bhangar Bhikshuk were considered as the pair of divine brothers, Rama and Lakshmana. (FG: 33)

The *gundas* were never proud of their acts. When the East India Company ordered the capture of Bhangar Bhikshuk, it was not an easy task, because he was very popular and the majority of the people supported him. With his bravery and impressive gestures he walked without fear and smiled with the sense of victory; Rudra remarked that "the sweet smile of victory on a man's lips makes him divine, but the same smile on a woman's lips turns her into a prostitute" (FG: 34). Moreover, they never felt sorry for their bad deeds either. When Nagar was given imprisonment for life (on the Andaman Islands, known as *Kalapani*) "after reviewing the bad and good aspects of the life, Nagar felt that his life was full of meaning (*sarthak*); he was satisfied" (FG: 29).

Some of the folk songs presented in the book, *Kajari*, are full of anecdotes and seasonal beauty, and they provide details of the emotions, moods and life of Nagar. His imprisonment, about which still today the folk-singers use to sing, is expressed sympathetically:

O Rama! Nagar's boat is going Kalapani, *Re* Hari!
Everybody else's boats go to Kashi and Visheshvar, O Rama!
Only Nagar's boat is going Kalapani, *Re* Hari!
Again and again forbidding you, Gunda Nagar, O Rama!
For god's sake don't use knife and dagger, *Re* Hari!
At home mother and sisters are weeping, O Rama!
On the bedstead is weeping your wife, *Re* Hari!
On the wall pegs are weeping Nagar's shield and sword, O Rama!
And your rifle is crying in a house-corner, *Re* Hari!
In the route your companions are weeping, O Rama!
At Narghat (Mirzapur) is weeping a whore, *Re* Hari!
(FG: 30; see *Hamsh* 1933: 43-44)

The climax of emotion is reached when his beloved accuses herself for not meeting him even once in her lifetime:

If I had known, Nagar, that you'd go Kalapani, O Rama!
Certainly I would've come to you as bride,
without *gavana* *, *Re* Hari!

Under the rule of Uditya Narayan Singh (1795-1835) a strong protest against British rule happened on the 13th of January 1799. The armies of the kingdom of Kashi were supporting Wazir Ali, an exiled contender for the throne of Awadh, who killed the British Magistrate of Banaras, but received a little active support in the city (cf. Bayly, 1983: 319). Among the great soldiers, the names of two *gundas* were remembered with respect; they fought together with their group against five hundred British soldiers and killed them on the spot. To commemorate the site of this heroic deed, a raised platform (*chaura*) was constructed. Their story has been presented by Rudra (FG: 77-82) composed in a form of a famous folk-song (*lavani*) which describes their bravery (FG: 77); the *lavani* in its full form is given here (Mukherji, 1978: 67):

With two hundred soldiers came a peon,
In all the streets and lanes stopped the passage.
Mirza Panchu took his vow with the *Quran* in hand,
Calling the Prophet in between, and convinced himself.
Let's go to court and leave the State's struggle,
Fought in the front, and never shown their back,

* *Gavana*, the ceremony when the bride goes to her husband's house for the first time after marriage.

Shivanath Singh and Bahadur Singh, what a great pair!
They're stronger than any fighter in the front,
Got wounded only after cannonading thirty bullets.
The *subedar* ordered smilingly to have them beheaded,
Stood up Shivnath-Bahadur and killed the soldiers.

It is notable that *gundas*, in spite of their anti-social activities, were also leaders in the revolt against British rule. Moreover, they were always ready to help the opressed. For these unique deeds, society always respected them.

5. Seasonal folk-songs

In classical vernacular literature, a particular folk-song has been prescribed for each month; in fact, they form a "well-regulated idiosyncrasy, consisting of reactions well-attuned to the stimuli of the external milieu" (Zimmerman, 1980: 106). Among such songs of the twelve months (*barahmasa*), each one refers to different emotions, moods and contexts, resulting in befitting socio-environmental conditions (see Wadley, 1983; Vaudeville, 1986). In Banaras half a dozen popular folk music styles are common, e.g. *Kajali, Chaiti, Holi, Birha, Qawwali* and *Ghazal*. Among them three stand for different seasons like the rains, early and late spring, respectively (Kumar, 1984: 9). Throughout the year the *Ramayana* is sung in the above-mentioned three seasonal styles. Additionally, another style, *Lavani*, is also sung, either based on historical events or on current happenings. One of the variations is a refrain of "Ho Rama" for *Chaiti* and "Re Hari" for *Kajali*, but sometimes both refrains are mixed alternatively.

Among such seasonal songs Rudra has presented examples of *Chaiti* and *Kajali*. One very common *Kajali* is related to a historical event — the imprisonment of Nagar, already mentioned earlier. Another most popular *Chaiti* is related to the conditions of nature and their related human emotions. It is well known that sleep in *Chaitra* (March-April) is particularly relaxing and makes a person lazy (FG: 17). One of the *Chaitis*, that the female singer Rasulanbai made very popular, is:

In the presence of my husband,
    don't throw marigold, it hurts my heart.
Unkind my husband, never cares for compassion,
    and attacks me in a wink of the eyes.
The drowsiness of *Chaitra*
    dulls the spirit, o Rama...

Another example of *Chaiti* may also be cited (FG: 94):

> Right here my nose-ring got lost, Ho Rama
> Whom can I ask about it?
> Should I ask mother-in-law, or sister-in-law!
> I'll feel embarrassed if I ask brother-in-law,
> Whom can I ask about it? Ho Rama.

Lavanis are mostly the expression of historical events and contextual conditions. One of the popular *lavanis* records the incident when Warren Hastings, the British Governor General, had to flee from Banaras in 1773 (FG: 21; Motichandra, 1962: 284):

> A howdah on the horse and a saddle on the elephant,
> Look! How quickly fled Warren Hastings.

Another popular *lavani* describing the bravery of the two *gundas* has already been mentioned.

6. Budhva Mangal: a unique celebration

Among the celebrations that have been forgotten, the Budhva Mangal ('the old Tuesday') is noteworthy (cf. Fig. 25). Although it was introduced sometime in the late 16th century (Sukul, 1974: 258), it was Mir Rustam Ali, enthroned by Balwant Singh in 1738, who revived and organised it in a proper way (Motichandra, 1962: 251; *Hamsh* 1933: 44). Rustam Ali was respectfully mentioned in a popular folk song of Holi (Sukul, 1974: 274; Motichandra, 1962: 252):

> Where has gone our Holi player!
> Our great soldier! Rustam Ali?

This festival reached its climax during the rule of Ishwari Prasad Narain Singh (1835-1839). Bhartendu Harishchandra (1850-1885), the father of modern Hindi literature and theatre, took an active part in it. Due to a drastic rise of prices and capital loss by the weavers and merchants it was not celebrated in 1884, however it continued in the following years. Again, it was not celebrated during 1920-23, but was restarted in 1924. The growing involvement of loafers reached a height in 1935-36, and as a result this celebration was stopped in 1938 (cf. Motichandra, 1962: 408). But it was again celebrated in 1949 to commemorate India's victory in the struggle for independence. This festival has been vividly described by the sociologist-poet Narsi Patel in his poem 'Carnival in Banaras'; two stanzas describing the dancers and the ethos of the festival are worth citing (Patel, 1977: 2, 12):

Fig. 25. A scene of the Budhva Mangal (after James Prinsep, 1833).

Look at those dancers
balance their heavy breasts
on a tightening torso
from one equilibrium to the next.
The rhythmic feet with serpentine heads
weave a tapestry of life forms
not quite different from the mundane
and yet so distinct
while the Ganga smiles away. (2)
Let them know, let them think
I murmur and turn my back to leave
let them know I hope they know
they better know
that rite here in this pilgrim city.
Yuwa (*Budhwa*)-Mangal was a revolt of man
against Religion
against Death
against the cavernous Universe! (12)

The Budhva Mangal was celebrated for three consecutive days starting on the first Tuesday after Holi, the festival of colours (Phalguna

Fig. 26. Chet Singh Fort and Ghat, in the left side bank of the Ganga river, in the early 19th century.

Purnima, February-March). The first day was called Mangal ('auspiciousness'), the second day Dangal ('wrestling'), and the third Jhilanga ('music and dance competition on boats'). This festival was famous for its musical meetings (*mehfils*) on hundreds of decorated boats (*bajras*) along the bank of the Ganga. The festival was performed each day in one of three areas successively: from Dashashvamedha Ghat to Sindhia Ghat, at Dashashvamedha Ghat linking Chet Singh Ghat, and at the bank of Ramanagar fort (cf. Figs. 26 and 27). The transitional season provided an opportunity for singing the local folk songs of *chaiti* and *kajali*, sometimes with the tunes of Holi (see Kumar, 1986: 160-164). By the initiative and support of the Department of Culture and the Department of Tourism, Government of Uttar Pradesh, the tradition of Burhva Mangal has been revived recently (since 1996); it is celebrated again as modern carnival, of course with an intention to attract tourists, mostly from abroad. It has been organised at the raised platform at Rajendra Prasad Ghat. The celebration starts with classical Shenai music, classical songs, folk songs of the Banaras region, and ends with a poets' assembly full of laughter and jokes, fooling each other by flirting. Due to a difference between the two departments, recently (16 March 2004) the Budhva Mangal was celebrated at Assi

Ghat along the riverfront, and was attended by the king of Banaras, HH Anant Narayan Singh. The major change in the present celebration was the absence of house-boats and musical competition. However the traditional drink, *thandhai*, was served to the public. This was an attempt to revive the old tradition in a new manner.

One of Rudra's characters remembers the beauty and the height of glory of that festival. Harishchandra published an article about this festival in a monthly Hindi magazine, *Kavi Vachan Sudha*, in 1875, which Rudra has cited (FG: 116):

> There was an unprecedented happening in the celebration to the last Budhva Mangal...It was the day of the festival, when suddenly a speedily blowing wind dispersed all the preparations. It became nearly impossible for the boats to reach Ramanagar. The yacht of the king of Vijayanagaram was stuck at this [left] side of the bank. Soon this news reached Kashiraj [the king of Kashi], and he ordered to get the help of his tusker elephants. Afterwards many naked tuskers delightfully entered into the Ganga. Some pulled with their tusks, while some butted with their heads or face. And some tuskers used their trunk to pull the rope attached to the boat. The whole scene was fantastic, and worth of being memorised only after seeing it, not through acquaintance by writings.

Fig. 27. Ramanagar Fort, in the other side of the Ganga river, in the late 18th century (after Thomas and William Daniell, 1795).

These festivities were lost in time, however they have been now revived in a different form, especially to promote cultural tourism by the Departments of Culture and Tourism, State Government of Uttar Pradesh (U.P.). Since the Banaras dwellers are very busy earning their bread-and-butter, leisure time is also becoming a rare comodity. But still there are enough events and occasions which satisfy their appetite for watching side-shows (FG: 36).

7. Typical Lived-world Experiences

Out of the seventeen stories, six describe the philosophic background and practical reasoning of some of the traditions of society. Those who are involved with practising Hinduism can easily realise that these stories are the mirror of life, beliefs and customs. Hindus mostly believe in fate, chance and gods' will; whatever is happening, right or wrong, is the gods' will. This is a dilemma that idealism only cannot give the way for survival. In the story 'Early sow, early mow' (13), a rich lady and an old fellow are talking on the issue of ideals in Hindu philosophy (FG: 121) :

> Well! Don't you like ideals?
> ...in fact, ideals are dead. As a mother monkey carries her dead baby until it falls down in parts, you Hindu people also carry the corpse of ideals.

In spite of such feelings among the elite, the common people certainly believe in fate (FG: 118):

> If fate is right
> You would also be quiet
> Be silent, look there
> Who's coming to conciliate.

The common perception of Hindu religion is that the human body is mortal and meant only to serve the Lord. If somebody wants to spoil his body due to distress and disappointment, a warning is given (FG: 98):

> Why are you disappointed with life, so much?
> Why are you prepared to immerse and die?

Since death is the ultimate reality, it is to be taken in good spirit (FG: 99):

> Since death is certain one day!
> Why am I not able to sleep all night.

No love, no life. George Byron (1788-1824) describes hideousness by the "dying embers of an altar-place" fire (see Lutwack, 1984 : 188):

> No love was left;
> All earth was but one thought —
> and that was death.

Sometimes, in the hope for a good future, life passes smoothly but unbelievable (FG: 99):

> Without you, my lover, I'm still alive,
> But I can't believe how I've managed.

Suffering is also taken as God's will; it is the toughest task to pass one's life in sufferings. But an aged and experienced lady challenged this:

> You're completely wrong! The easiest task is to die sadly even in happiness; and the hardest task is to lead a life happily in sadness. (FG: 99)

A city of high religious status has naturally a philosophic and emotional attitude with reference to love affairs. It is a popular saying: "How can one leave apart the love developed in childhood?". Touching movements are always remebered through the memorable events and feelings. While passing her life in the hope of meeting her beloved, Amiran reached to the end, and sung (FG: 58):

> What should I do now my friend?
> Which co-wife delays him from coming to me?

but ultimately, before her death:

> He came, he came, he came…!

A hut is taken as a metaphor for life, the Ganga for the good, and the Yamuna for the bad. The hut stands between these two currents, on a bank now here one must search for a way to establish a stable life. The question can be solved to a certain extent by the remembrance of the lover (FG: 110):

> On this side the Ganga, on the other the Yamuna,
> In the middle, a hut is built.
> How will my days pass? Tell me what to do.

Rumour about women and watching women's performances are very common social traditions. In fact, people show more interest in seeing famous men and defamed women (FG: 96). Among the poor and illiterate people the tradition of *purdah* (veil) is so strong that the women were never able to express even a little wish, and never saw their husbands face-to-face (FG: 129). If a person has left home for ascetic and meditation practices, he has to strictly maintain celibacy, considering sex as the most sensitive obstacle on this path; moreover, once sex is renounced, it is never to be accepted again — this rule has to be followed strictly (FG: 39); the ascetics and mendicants try to follow it.

It is a common belief that the wife of a king, a prince or a zamindar, whatever her caste at birth, takes the caste of her husband. But the common people, in spite of accepting such happenings, see the bride through different eyes. Rudra has described the perplexing situation that happened with the second wife of Balwant Singh (story 1). According to historical evidences Panna (a Rajput by caste) was at first a mistress and later a wife of Balwant Singh, a Bhumihar king (Motichandra, 1962: 266, 268). Rudra writes that when Panna gave birth to her first son, relatives and cousins of the king loudly ordered the drummer: "Stop your drumming. Praise is not warranted on the birth of a bastard" (FG: 10). The king was amazed, and he lamented: "Only I was ignorant of the social rule that even the son of a married women could also be called a 'bastard'." His friend and advisor replied: "Not in the eyes of God, but certainly in the eyes of society" (FG: 11). Here the description clearly suggests the predominance of Brahmanic traditions even over the royal families. Ultimately Panna challenged the powers of masculinity, rule and kingdom: "Be silent! Let me see how long your people will keep sacrificing the heart and pride of a woman for the sake of politics?" (FG: 13). She further challenged the dignity of rule very loudly (R 13):

> ... I will not be scared. Your politics can stop the official honours on the birth of the prince; but neither you nor your rule can stop a mother singing auspicious songs on the occasion of the birth of her son; even your kith and kin can't stop it. Did you understand? I will certainly sing auspicious songs. Call your cousin and let them try to stop me!

And, finally Panna alone started to pound her chest and sing as if crazy.

8. Red as Symbol: Revolution

As selfishness is now common in Indian society, whatever *-ism* may be will be interpreted with the language of individuality, especially so the elite, who is more expert in discourses than in practice. The son of a lord, Lallan, is an example of such a character. After a discussion with Lallan, Sudha, the wife of his driver, explains:

> In my opinion there is no basic difference between the mind sets of bourgeois and proletariat. In the former there is an excess of emotional attachment, while in the latter to the intellect. The former becomes greasy with excess of selfishness, while the other dries due to the reaction of revenge. Therefore, in spite of your proletariat background, you take more interest in discussion and neglect to care this dying baby.

Lallan realised the bare truth that was like a slap on his cheek. He replied suddenly: "I am going to call the doctor" (FG: 152).

This condition is common in Banaras, where modern thoughts are flourishing either parallel to or along with age-old traditions, sometimes with adjustment and sometimes reactions. But at least one should awaken them to challenge, without even looking at the consequences.

On the death of her son, motherly sentiments and revenge against her husband, for the sake of whom she spoiled her life, distressed Sudha. Seeing her husband Jhingur enjoying the musical *mehfil* (performance) of Seth, she completely left the dead baby unattended, and rebuked both Jhingur and Seth. She cried:

> Leave me, O *chandal* [Seth]! Are all the happiness of such performances meant only for you people? Those who tolerated injustice and tortures throughout their life without whispering a word, whose lives became darkened in the thrust of love — do they not have the right to enjoy such musical meetings? Those who are farmers, labourers, and coolies — are such *mehfils* not meant for them? Those who always live in scarcity, not getting even the minimum of food and cloth, who are not carrying false notion of prestige and never openly enjoy the pleasures of life, to whom you rich people call 'middle class' — let me know, are they not born to enjoy such *mehfils* ? Do answer me, O treacherous! Speak! Are the fragrance and colourful roses meant only for you, and the thorny bushes for we poor! I will set fire to your *mehfil*!
>
> ...Sudha set on fire the silk curtains on the wall" (FG: 157).

But as a true servant Jhingur had to follow the norms and taboos of society, therefore he attacked Sudha with a hammer and broke her head, which stated bleeding. Jhingur saw that the whole environment had become reddish: the red sunrise, the red vermilion in Sudha's forehead, the red roses, the red fire, the red blood, and the red turbans of policemen (cf. ibid.: 157). He saw by his red eyes that the whole scene was looking like a reddish sea.

> Lallen asked, what have you done?
> Weeping, Jhingur replied while indicating the corpse of Sudha (his wife): 'All has turned red!' (FG: 158)

Altogether, the red as symbol for six aspects indicates the six most important part of the Hindu social life, especially in urban area. Respectively, they are signs of new vigour, husband-wife relationship, better future, challenge to traditions, sacrifice for preserving truth, and the corrupt administration. This clearly indicates that in spite of several disappointing issues in the social world, there are enough seeds for revolution. While ending with the last paragraph above *The Flowing Ganga* met with the ocean of thought and practice. It has given a message that man is a creature of time in terms of existence and continuity, but he always faces the processes and conditions of transformation and adjustment. In fact, he had "liberated himself from the constraining beliefs of conventional society and grasped the potentials of new *transformations*" (Gold, 1984: 377).

9. An Epilogue

Of course, Rudra did not write *The Flowing Ganga* with the intention of making a novel, but by connecting a series of stories, vivid accounts of the people, and the society and culture of the 18th-mid 19th century, he has described the implicit realities of Banaras. In most of the cases, it has been observed that "societal controls so constrained individual human behaviours that they were impossible to explain outside of the general social context" (Golledge, 1985: 114). The distinction and speciality of 'the social world of that period were reflected through the *genre de vie* in historical perspective' (cf. *ibid.*), and resulted in giving a symbolic power to the landscape.

The Flowing Ganga gives emphasis on the cultural meaning and the experiences of place and people; the expression of environmental mood and ethics is of superb quality, putting in parallel the changing rythmic scenes of Banaras with folk songs of the city. So many visible, and even invisible milieus too, formed a system of regulating the social world which resulted in making this city unique, a place where both extremes, good and bad, flow parallel as well as together. With *The Flowing Ganga* Rudra has attempted to build up a specific 'regional image' based on the folk and oral historical traditions rooted in local culture; and he has succeeded to a large extent. Through their vividity and connections, all the stories project the 'local colour' as a complex system of cultural webs (cf. Silk and Silk, 1985: 189).

10. Basic References

'Rudra' Shivprasad Mishra 1967. ***The Flowing Ganga*** (*Bahti Ganga*). In Hindi. Radhakrshna Publ., Delhi.

Golding, Paul R. 1997. *Tales of Banaras. The Flowing Ganges*. (With Virendra Singh). Book Faith India, Delhi [Pilgrims Book House, Varanasi]. (Introduction, commentary and English translation of 13 of the original 17 stories of Rudra's *The Flowing Ganga*).

~9~

THE SURREALIST CITY: RAJA RAO'S *The Serpent and the Rope*

1. Background and Exposition

Arguably, Raja Rao (1908-2002) is the most brilliant master of Indo-English writing. Inarguably, he is the only true philosopher-novelist of Indian literature in English, whose works are deeply rooted in Brahmanism and Hinduism. Rao's semi-autobiographical novel, ***The Serpent and the Rope*** (1960, here after referred as **SR:**), is the story of a search for spiritual truth in Europe and India. In quest of the spirit his search brought him to Banaras (Benares, as commonly spelt in the West and also by the novelist), where he deeply submerged into Shankara's philosophy. This novel established him as one of the finest Indian stylists. "Writing is my dharma", he once said. Raja Rao was an *expatriate,* who lived and worked away from home; he nevertheless always kept the spirit of India's spirituality and rich traditions alive — expressing the eternity of his homeland, in contrast to the West.

Raja Rao (Fig. 28) was born on 8 November 1908 in Hassan, in the state of Karnataka in south India, into a well-known Brahman family. His native language was Kanarese, but he received his post-graduate education in France, and all his publications in book form have been in English. Rao has been always concerned with language and consciousness. In the foreword to his classic *Kanthapura* (1938) he admits the difficulties in using in "a language that is not one's own the spirit that is one's own", and conveying "the various shades and omissions of certain thought-movement that looks maltreated in an alien language".

Raja Rao, from the outset, is set upon exploring the many ways to truth. He studied at the Muslim University of Aligarh, and after taking a degree from Madras University, at the age of nineteen he left India for the International University of Montpelier and the Sorbonne in Paris, where he gave himself to a study of Christian theology — jumping into Western civilisation at the deep end. At that time French

Fig. 28. Raja Rao

culture was under the leadership of Valéry and Gide, and Raja Rao's first stories were written in French. He then turned to English, but with the proviso "I will not write like the English, I can only write like an Indian". But throughout his life 'literature' as such has been for him a tool in the service of a deeper spiritual quest for truth. In 1931 he married a French academic, Camille Mouly. He depicted the later breakdown of their marriage in *The Serpent and the Rope*.

When his marriage broke in 1939, Rao returned to India and began his first period of residence in an ashram. During the Second World, he travelled widely in India in search for his spiritual heritage, and in 1942 he was active in an underground movement against the British.

Rao's involvement in the nationalist movement is reflected in his first two books. The novel *Kanthapura* (1938) was an account of the impact of Gandhi's teaching of non-violent resistance against the British. The story is seen from the perspective of a small Mysore village in South India. Rao lends the style and structure from Indian vernacular tales and folk-epics.

After World War II, Rao spent much of his time in France and travelling throughout the world. He visited America in 1950 and later spent some more time living in an ashram in India. In 1965 he again married an actress, Katherine Jones. From 1965 to his last breath in 2002 Rao lectured on Indian philosophy and literature at the University of Texas, Austin. Raja Rao is exceptional in the depth of his understanding of both Eastern and Western civilisations — a major theme in all his works, from *The Serpent and the Rope* (1960, which received India's highest literary Sahitya Academy award) to his most recent novel *The Chessmaster and his Moves* (1988). In his latter novel, in 1988 he received the prestigious Neustadt International Prize for Literature. Several Neustadt Laureates have received also the Nobel Prize in literature, among them were Gabriel García Márquez, Czeslaw Milosz, and Octavio Paz.

Nobel Laureate Czeslaw Milosz (in *'To Raja Rao'*, Berkeley, 1969), honoured Raja Rao in a poem:

> I hear you saying that liberation is possible
> and that Socratic wisdom
> is identical with your guru's.
> No, Raja, I must start from what I am.
>
> I am those monsters which visit my dreams
> and reveal to me my hidden essence.
>
> If I am sick, there is no proof whatsoever
> that man is a healthy creature.
> Greece had to lose, her pure consciousness
> had to make our agony only more acute.
> We needed God loving us in our weakness
> and not in the glory of beatitude.
>
> No help, Raja, my part is agony,
> struggle, abjection, self-love, and self-hate,
> prayer for the Kingdom
> and reading Pascal.

The Serpent and the Rope was written after a long silence in which Rao returned to India. He renewed connection with his roots in the modern rendering of the *Mahabharata* legend of Satyavan and Savitri. While searching for his roots he returned to Banaras and found the dilemma of life, where the contrast of an illusory mirage and the hard realities of life flow together. The work also dramatised the relationships between Indian and Western culture. Ramaswamy, the hero, a young Brahmin studying in France, is married to a French college teacher, Madeleine, who sees her husband first as a guru. As the hero struggles with commitments imposed on him by his Hindu family, his wife becomes a Buddhist in her spiritual quest and renounces wordly desires. She leaves her husband to find his own true self. In the book the serpent symbolises illusion, and reality is symbolised by the rope, as in the well known image of Shiva.

After his first trip to Europe, at the age of twenty-two Raja Rao visited Banaras with his stepmother and had his first impression of the city during the early 1930s (SR: 9). The first contact with the worldview of Banaras started with the teaching of his grandfather Kittanna when he returned home from a pilgrimage to Banaras (SR: 21). Later in the course of realisation and understanding, the novelist's sensitivity to Banaras expressed as — "*Shivoham, Shivoham,* I am Shiva" (*ibid.*). The sense of understanding the eternity of Indian culture was developed in Rao's mind since childhood as he "was born a Brahmin — that is, devoted to Truth and all that ... Brahmin is he who knows Brahman, etc., etc..." (SR: 5).

The description of the spirit of place in Banaras is an outcome of the feelings and the search towards the vitality of India, "where the past and the present are for ever knit into one whole experience going down the Ganges; who could not imagine the compassionate One Himself coming down the footpath, by the Saraju, to wash the mendicant bowl? — and so for me time and space had very relative importance" (SR: 19). His novel *The Serpent and the Rope* (1960) is a highly acclaimed work which "portrays the meeting of East and West on the most intimate plane..." Describing Banaras as a plot for this meeting Rao called it a 'surrealist city' (SR: 11): "...where reality starts and where illusion ends; whether the Brahmins of Benares are like the crows asking for funeral rice-balls, saying 'Caw caw'; or like the Sadhus by their fires, lost in such beautiful magnanimity, as though love were not something one gave to another, but what one gave to oneself" (SR: 12). This sense of eternity has been elaborated in the *Kashi Rahasya* of the *Brahmavaivarta Purana* (II.13.39), which states that "in Kashi every time some creation is in action, and ultimately everything has to emerge in Kashi".

From the historical past Banaras has been a resort of intellectuals (Bhatta); among them two were most influential: Lakshmidhara (early 12th century), and Narayan Bhatta (16th century) who wrote well known digests of Puranic verses, i.e. *Krityakalpataru*, and *Tristhalisetu*, respectively. Everywhere one can find Sanskrit scholars who follow that tradition, therefore it is remarked that Banaras is filled with Bhattas (SR: 304).

The city of Banaras is called Avimukta ('never forsaken' by Shiva), because it is that divine seat where male (*Purusha*, Shiva) and female (*Shakti*, Durga) energies meet and form the supreme bliss from where comes creation — Ardhanarishvara (Fig. 29). Following this perception, it is traditionally believed that newly married couples may come to this city and pay their homage to Shiva and Durga to receive the bliss of completeness. Metaphorically, in the marriage ritual, the bride is representing Durga, and only after the ritual performance she would be the real bride. It is in this sense that it is said that "all brides be Benares born" (SR: 50). The novelist at the end of the novel gives a clear exposition of this tradition (SR: 406):

Fig. 29. Ardhanarishvara, a sketch based on an old painting (after W. J. Wilkins, 1882).

> Marriages are made in Heaven, they say, don't they? Sometimes they are made on earth. ... I will tell you what: marriages are made in Benares.

But for the Westerners Banaras represents a scene of the odd and odorous, which is perceived according to an individual's level of environmental sensitivity, and is especially related to pollution for which the city is also known. The novelist writes: "Of Benares all I know is the bits of floating human flesh and the pyres of the dead, and that the Ganges water when chemically examined shows no bacteria. We Europeans are not yet holy enough to have crypts with no bacteria" (SR: 39).

Banaras always presents two purviews of 'perceptual-reflection', which may be termed as the 'divine-world' and the 'lived-world'. The former refers to the cosmological imprint and the divinity imposed on the cityscape, and the latter identifies the cultures, especially of the current contexts. Raja Rao has given more attention towards the first purview, but with contextual differentiation and sensitivity he has also presented the second purview according to the needs of expression.

2. The Ganga and Eternity

The Ganga, the patron deity Shiva, and the sacred territory of Kashi, altogether form the Cosmic Trinity of this great city. The *Kashi Khanda* (35.10) lucidly expressed this:

> The Ganga, Shiva, and Kashi :
> where this Trinity is watchful,
> no wonder here is found the grace
> that leads one on to salvation.

Citing Damodara Sharma (a 12th century poet), the novelist expresses the sacred power of the Ganga:

> O Holy Ganga, Mother Ganga, thou art purity
> itself, coming down from Shiva's hair. (SR: 12)

The Ganga is considered as a mental state which can be perceived and reflected anywhere when a person can realise it, therefore it is reffered to as inner truth; in fact, the Ganga represents the totality and vitality of Indian culture. Says Raja Rao (SR: 376): "My India I carried wheresoever I went. But not to see the Ganges, not to dip into her again and again. ...No, the Ganges was an inner truth to me, an assurance, the origin and the end of my Brahminic tradition". This is comparable to Singh's remark that, "The whole Hindu lifecycle is related with ritual purification by water, especially of the Ganga; in fact, the concept of 'life-flow' may be especially represented with 'water-flow' ". One such explicit expression can be made with the concept of Gangaisation — a process of spatial transposition and perception in which many rivers or water bodies are conceived as being the Ganga during sacred baths and other auspicious events" (Singh, 1985: 304, and 1987: 316; also Buttimer, 1985: 266).

The above realisation has again been exposed metaphorically: "I had risen from the Ganges, and saw the luminous world, my home" (SR: 403). The idea of creation attached here is comparable to the following verses of the *Katha Upanishad* (IV. 6): "He who was born of old was born of water". The word 'luminous' in the above-quoted sentence is further to be taken as a symbol of sound and water-flow. Having a glance of 'the luminous world', and 'my home' in the Ganga, reminds us of the restoring quality of the river as narrated in the epic history of the great mythological war, the *Mahabharata* (XIV, ca. 10th century BCE): "at the end of the great war Vyasa, the legendary author of the epic, calls the slain armies from the depths of the river for a final reunion and 'free from all animosity and pride, anger and jealousy and purged of every sin, the heroes met with each other" (Darian, 1978: 37). The power of the Ganga is assumed to be infinite: "The Ganges alone seemed to carry a meaning, and I could not understand what she said" (SR: 26). The answer could be received through the *Kashi Khanda* (28.84-85): "O Agastya, one should not be amazed at the notion that this Ganga is really Power, for is she not the Supreme Shakti (*liquid form*) of the Eternal Shiva, having taken the form of water ?" (cf. Eck, 1982: 219).

The Himalaya and the Ganga are both described as great sacred symbols of Indian culture; the first one represents the glory and the truth, and the latter the deeper sense of humanity. Raja Rao further expands these symbols to encompass the whole lifecycle: "Truth is the Himalaya, and Ganges humanity. That is why we throw the ashes of the dead to her. She delivers them to the sea, and the sun heats the waters so that, becoming clouds, they return to the Himalaya. The cycle of death and birth goes on eternally like the snows and the rivers" (SR: 35).

Quoting Shankara's *Gangastrotam*, Raja Rao expresses his feelings to the motherly Ganga (SR: 32):

> *Devi Sureshvari Bhagavathi Gange ...*
> Saviour of the three worlds of restless waves,
> Clear is Thy water circling upon the head of Shiva,
> May my mind ever repose at Thy lotus-feet.

Like a human being, mother Ganga "has sat by the ghats, her bundle beside her. What impurity, Lord, have we made her bear" (SR: 33). The question of 'pure and impure' is related only to the degree of faith. The Ganga is the cradle of Indian culture and civilisation. Most of the ancient and puranic literature of Hindu dharma refers to it in different forms. These are a few quotations: the *Rig Veda*'s *Nadi Sukta* (X. 75.5-6) mentions it as the river of the highest merit; similarly many of the *Puranas* mention the glory and merit of the Ganga, e.g. *Naradiya* (II.38-84, 51.1-48), *Padma* (V. 60.1-127), *Agni* (110), *Matsya* (180-185), *Skanda-Kashi Khanda* (29.17-168), etc. Even the *Mahabharata* (III.85.87-97, XIII.26.26-103, XIII.36.26, 30.31) gives many details of the Ganga. Remembering an old Sanskrit prayer to the Ganga in Kashi/ Banaras, Raja Rao cites (SR: 33):

> *Kashi Kshetram, Shariram tribhuvana jananim ...*
> And nigh the riverbank Thy water is strewn
> With *kusha* grass and flowers,
> There thrown by Sages at morn and even,
> May the waters of the Ganges protect us.

Like an archetypal metaphor, one can feel that "The Ganges knew our secret, held our patrimony..." (SR: 34). This idea has been fully elaborated in the *Padma Purana* (V. 60.39)

> What need of expensive sacrifices,
> or of difficult penances?
> Worship Ganga, asking for happiness
> and good fortune,
> And she will bring you heaven
> and salvation.

The Ganga symbolises the flow of divine energy connecting the three realms of the universe, therefore it is referred to as 'triple-path river' (*'tripathaga'*), and "is said to flow on earth, in heaven, and in the underworld. In heaven she is called Mandakini; on earth, the Bhagirathi; and below, Patala Ganga or the Bhogavati" (Darian, 1978: 69). Rising in the snowy mountains of the Himalaya, she sheds the light of wisdom on this earth; this is her blessing to the earthly people (cf. SR: 35). This corresponds to the *Matsya Purana* (121.29-30), which states that her home is in the Milky Way, where "through the darkness she sheds her silver light". Only with faith and full devotion can one understand the divine message of the Ganga — the constant flow calling for purity. The novelist is hopeful that to the pilgrims glancing at Banaras "the Ganga would give them back their purity" (SR: 121).

3. Cosmology and Uniqueness

The organisation of space varies from one culture to another. The associations and feelings to a spatial unit (say, a settlement) have their historico-cultural background. It is the personal experience that reflects the place (a spatial unit) in different moods and actions: "like time, place is also diffused, therefore one never quite knows where its centre is" (Hall, 1959: 169). This reflection is exposed within the varieties of ordering. With the growth of cultural institutions, the realisation of the connection between environmental form and human behaviour could be made more clear (Sommer, 1969: 9). A city considered to be an advanced growth of civilisation reflects its dwellers' personality, and ultimately it also develops its own personality. Therefore, city is compared with a mirror: "Seeing oneself is what we always seek; the world, as the great sage Shankara said, is like a city seen in a mirror" (SR: 14). According to ancient texts on city planning, the *Shilpashastras*, there is an explicit connection between gods, men, rites, and the city plans (Lynch, 1981: 74).

Banaras, known as the cultural capital of India, preserved the sense of cosmic beauty; it can nevertheless be visualised only with the eternal vision. Kashi is comparable to Brahman, the *Kashi Khanda* (99.6) says: it is *paramatman* (the 'Supreme Soul'); it is *chidanandamayi* ('made of consciousness and bliss'); it is *nishprapancha* ('unwordly'); and it is *anakhyeya* (the 'unspeakable') (cf. SR: 399). Sage Shankara (8th century CE) called Kashi the City of Light:

> In Kashi the light shines.
> That light illumines everything
> Whoever knows that light, truly reaches Kashi.
>
> (Eck, 1982: 302)

The quest for understanding that light has been raised in a sacred metre of the *Rig Veda* (III.62, 10), which Raja Rao quotes: "Om, O face of Truth with a disk of gold, remove the mist (of ignorance) that I may see you face to face" (SR: 246). He realised that "It was India I wanted to see, the India of my inner being. Just I could now see *antara Kashi*, the 'inner Benares'..." (*ibid*, also SR: 360). This cosmic beauty of Banaras has been described in various ancient *puranic* texts. According to the *Vamana Purana* (II.26.9) the two rivers, the Varana in the north and the Asi in the south, are said to originate from the body of the primordial person, *Purusha*, at the beginning of time. The *Jabala Upanishad* (2) described these rivers as the mystical veins of the subtle body: "It is called Varana because it obstructs (*Varayati*) all sins of the senses. It is called Nashi because it destroys (*nashayati*) all sins of the senses ... And, it is the place where the nose and the eyebrows meet. That is the meeting place of heaven and the world beyond". This esoteric interpretation indicates the novelist's quest to realise the 'inner Banaras'; he further noted, "The road to the infinite is luminous if you see it as a city lit in a mirror" (SR: 22).

It has been mentioned that "Kashi is the pious Hindu's name for Benares, the sacred city of Shiva, the Great Ascetic and Destroyer of the Universe. It is here, at the city's main cremation ground, that Shiva and Parvati created the universe at the beginning of time; and here that 'the corpse of the universe burns at the end of time. Only Kashi Survives'" (Parry, 1980: 88). The *Kashi Khanda* (26.80, 52.21) and the *Kashi Rahasya* (2.32-33) both declare: "whatever is known as a 'creature' — from Lord Brahma down to a blade of grass, in the four categories of beings — gets liberation in Kashi". It is through this cosmic understanding that Banaras is considered eternal; it is a place where "the dead do not die nor the living live. The dead come down to play on the banks of the Ganges, and the living who move about, and even offer rice-balls to the manes, live in the illusion of a vast night and a bright city" (SR: 22). Moreover, it is also considered as a city of predestination (SR: 17), as it is pre-determined that a soul will certainly get liberation in Kashi.

The night in Banaras symbolises a calm and peaceful place where one can meditate and mitigate worldly attachments. The great sages have experienced this vision: "Night, a rare and immediate night, was covering the Benares sky. Somewhere on these very banks the Upanishadic Sages, perhaps four, five or six thousand years ago, had discussed the roots of human understanding" (SR: 23-24). The idea of the religious merit of Kashi attracted people from all parts of India, especially as pilgrims (SR: 120, 121, 251). With the merit of the rituals performed, the pilgrims can look at the world as "holy and full of light and gentility" (SR: 252). According to the *Matsya Purana* (180.47) "Banaras is the most sacred *tirtha* among all the *tirthas* of India, this is the seat of liberation from transmigration as Lord Shiva looks after everybody". The intensity of religious merit becomes very high at auspicious moments of time. One such example is the Kumbha (SR: 402), which is held on special positions of planetary conjunctions, i.e. Jupiter x Aries or Taurus, Sun & Moon x Capricornus, each after three years at Haridvar, Ujjain and Nasik, and again when Jupiter x Scorpio or Sun x Capricornus, it is held every eleven years at Prayaga (Allahabad) (cf. Dubey, 1987, 2001). On this occasion pilgrims use to visit Banaras as a part of their sacred path and ritual performances.

Since the ancient past Banaras has also been famous as a seat of learning, along with being the holiest *tirtha*. The *Kashi Khanda* (96.121) calls it the seat of wisdom and knowledge. This multiple merit attracted scholars from different parts of the country to settle and test their own understanding. In this way "Buddha himself had walked and had washed his alms-bowl — he had gone up the steps and had set the Wheel of Law — a turning" (SR: 11); this happened during the 6th century BCE at Sarnath, a northern suburb of Banaras. Following the same path Kabir (CE 1398-1518) preached the doctrine of neo-Vaishnavism in the line of Ramananda (CE 1299-1410), his adopted guru, for whom Kabir said "Now, My Lord, be Thou my Guru and I thy disciple" (SR: 11). This enlightenment paved the path for a poor weaver, Kabir, to become so great a devotee, poet and reformer. Again, following the path of Ramananda, Tulasi (CE 1547-1623) settled down at Bhadaini Ghat near today's Revan Palace and completed his great epic the *Ramacharitamanasa* during the period 1574-1584, which retells the story of Rama in the language of the people. In his memory that *ghat* is known today as Tulasi Ghat. Many great sages and founders of various religious groups came to Kashi to pay their homage and to receive the message of supreme bliss, e.g., Shankara (8th century CE), Jnaneshvara (ca. CE 1294), Guru Nanak (CE 1469-1539), Vallabhacharya (CE 1478-1539), Chaitanya (1485-1533), etc.

4. Territory, Place and People

The dialectics of man's views of earth, i.e. earth as a hostile, alien place, and earth as man's true home, indicate the sense of placelessness and the degree of territoriality, further identified with fixed symbols and landmarks. Hall notes: "Beginning with the bacteria and the simple cell and ending with man, every organism has a detectable limit which marks where it begins and ends" (Hall, 1959: 162). Of course, any territory can be visualised with human settlements, but only through the values attached to them one can perceive the invisible messages given by those elements. In this context "literature is one of the agencies involved in attaching values to places" (Lutwack, 1984: 35). It is through one's vision that a place is identified as good or bad; in fact, places are neither good nor bad in themselves but in the values attached to them" (*ibid*).

The spiritual values and messages of place-learning have been fully described by Raja Rao in the context of the description of a territory and its natural features:

> Meanwhile Manduadih, Balapur, Hardatpur, Rajatalab, Nigatpur passed by: little hamlets with green all around and clusters of ancient trees by pond or on mound, that seemed to guard the tradition of the race. One remembered that it was here that the Aryans, when they first entered the country, camped under the ancestors of these trees, and the Ganges flowing by brought them the richness of green wheat-stalks, the yellow of sesame and the gold of sugar cane. It was somewhere here, too, that Gargi and Yagnyavalkya must have walked, and out of their discussions by wood-fire and by river-steps was our philosophy born, and that noble, imperial heritage of ours, Sanskrit, the pure, the complete, the unique. He who possesses Sanskrit can possess himself. (SR: 34-35)

Perhaps Raja Rao attempted to describe the Panchakroshi pilgrimage route through this description, but he has mistaken the real route with the GT road, which he actually described as the delimiting route starting from Manduadih and interconnecting Balapur (actually it is Balirampur), Hardatpur and Rajatalab. Moreover, he also wrongly refers to Nigatpur, while in fact there is no village of such name.

On the other side of the Ganga, an annual celebration of Rama Lila, a cycle of plays (called environmental theatre) which narrates the epic story of Lord Rama has been held in the small town of Ramanagar since the 18th century. (As every day's scene takes place in a different natural surrounding, it has been called 'environmental theatre'.) During the 31-days period of the play, the whole city becomes "creativity of sight" (Kapur, 1986: 59). The novelist refers to this city as the real city of Rama, where "every year people still come down to see the festival of Rama, and men and women and the royal family with horses, fife and elephants enacted the story of Rama" (SR: 21). Ramanagar lies at the southern end of the city of Banaras; at the northern end is Sarnath, where the Buddha turned the Wheel of Law (SR: 304).

Banaras is also famous for handicrafts, miniatures and brass-work, sweets with *bhang* (hemp: *Cannabis indica*) taken as an intoxicating drug, etc. Says Rao: "what I loved most were the shops, with their magnificent copperwork, inlaid with lacquer and ivory; the many bunches of false hair hanging from the roof; the multicoloured bangles; and the rich, fervid smell of *bhang*, as it was given mixed with butter-milk and spices. The Benares silk shops too were splendid, with saris of such intricate designs as to make one marvel that people still prepared such wonders and sold them for money" (SR: 25). This is an expression of the first glance of smellscape and colourscape. Banaras can also be visualised as an animalscape, especially around the major temples where animals like monkeys (SR: 10), bulls, goats, etc., roam freely.

Even since the third century BCE, there is evidence of prostitution in Banaras. A detailed description of this institution has been given by Damodar Gupta, a poet secretary of Jayapida, king of Kashmir (CE 779-813); his epic work, *Kuttanimatam*, presents a vivid picture of Banaras in this context, with emphasis on the minute details of the prostitutes' skill, garments, decoration, tricks and varieties. Moreover, temple priests were involved in protecting these activities. Says Raja Rao that one can see "the lovely smile of some concubine, just floating down her rounded bust and nimble limbs, for a prayer and a client. The concubines of Benares are the most beautiful of any in the world, they say; and some say, too, that they worship the wife of Shiva, Parvathi herself, that they may have the juice of youth in their limbs" (SR: 12). But at present the condition of concubines is a subject of pity, in fact it is a black spot on the culture of Banaras. Under their shelter, crime, deviant behaviour and black marketing are flourishing (Tripathi, 1986: 251-255). The religious connotation argued to maintain prostitution has its own history; the Buddhist monks during the 12th century, the Gahadavala period, were enjoying sex as a ritual practice, as mentioned in Krishnamishra's *Prabodha Chandrodaya* (3.9), a text of that period (cf. Motichandra, 1985: 144). Similarly, the city was also famous for necrophagous ascetics (*Aghoris*), whose offshoots are still found nowadays (cf. Parry, 1982).

5. The Major Deities

According to popular belief, every inch of space and every stone has divine essence in Banaras; says the *Padma Purana*, "Making a pilgrimage there in Banaras every day for a whole year, still she did not reach all the sacred places. For in Banaras there is a sacred place at every step" (Eck, 1982: XVI). Kashi in itself symbolises the whole world, therefore everything on earth considered powerful and auspicious is transposed here. Every stone is described as some form of Shiva, everywhere Shiva is present: "I am beyond imagination, form of the formless, form of consciousness and Bliss; Shiva I am, I am Shiva" (SR: 114). Moreover, "Benares looked after the saints, not the cruel people of the sacred city — each Sadhu sat, a Shiva" (SR: 12). Following the daily pilgrimage (*nitya yatra*), many Banaras dwellers pay their visit most commonly to Vishvanatha, and in the vicinity, to Annapurna, Dandapani and Dhundhiraja (Eck, 1982: 136).

Among the four major deities of daily pilgrimage, the novel only describes Annapurna (Fig. 30a) and Kala Bhairava (another form of Dandapani; Fig. 30b). Annapurna (literally: 'filled with plenteous food'), a form of the consort of Shiva, the patron deity, is also called the 'Mother of the Three Worlds'. It is believed that "by the promise of Annapurna, everyone will have lentils to eat and Ganges water to drink in Kashi" (Eck, 1982: 305). Describing the magnificent beauty of the icon and the power of Annapurna, Raja Rao mentions (SR: 26):

> How beautiful the Devi looked, in her saffron Sari and with dark forehead bejewelled, and what strength emanated from her, what depth of peace.
>
> O Thou who has clothed Thyself in cloth of gold,
> Decked in ornaments made of many and varied gems;
> Whose breasts rounded like a water-jar
> Are resplendent with their necklace of pearls;
> Whose beauty is enhanced by the fragrance of the Kashmir aloe;
> O Devi who presides over the city of Kashi,
> O vessel of mercy, grant me aid.
> *Annapurna sada purne.*

Shiva's ruling deputy who serves as *kotwal* (chief police officer) of the city of Banaras is Kala Bhairava (the Lord of Time and Death). According to the *Kashi Khanda* (31.43) "He is the Black One, who has also assumed the duties of the God of Death in Kashi". Even Death, it

Fig. 30. (a) Annapurna, a sketch based on an old painting (after W.J. Wilkins, 1882), and (b) Bhairava.

is said, is afraid of Kala Bhairava! While chanting the prayer to Kala Bhairava, the novelist quotes (SR: 21-22):

> I worship Kalabhairava, Lord of the city of Kashi,
> Blazing like a million suns;
> Our great saviour in our voyage across the world,
> The blue-throated, the three-eyed, grantor of all desires;
> The lotus-eyed who is the death of death,
> The imperishable one,
> Holding the rosary of the human bone and the trident,
> *Kashikapuradinatha Kalabhairavam bhaje.*

It is therefore said, "Banaras is eternal".

6. Death, Manes and Meaning

According to the *Kashi Rahasya* (13.25b-27a, 39), among the seven sacred cities bestowing salvation, Kashi is the greatest, as the other six cities and all the *tirthas* take refuge in Kashi and dwell there in order to increase their own power. This merit has made this city the city of the dead and the manes, comparable to Gaya. Says the novelist (SR: 10):

> ...in Benares there may be many dead, and all the dead of all the ages, the successive generations of manes after manes, have accumulated in the sky. And you could almost see them layer on layer on the night of a moon-eclipse, fair and pale and tall and decrepit, fathers, grandfathers, great grandfathers, mothers, sisters, brothers, nephews; friends, kings, Yogis, maternal uncles — all, all they accumulate in the Benares air and you can see them. They have a distanced, dull-eyed look — and they ask — they beg for this and that, and your round white rice-balls and sesame seed give the peace they ask for. The sacred Brahmin too is pleased. He has his fifty rupees.

Following the ancient tradition, for many Indians the polis consists not only of the living members of the family and the community, but also of the ancestral spirits who populate the Indian cosmos (Kakar, 1982: 4). These spirits can be invoked to seek support. There is a variety of functionaries specialised in this profession. There live several varieties of *karmakandis* (ritual performers) in Banaras; among them *ghatias* (priests at ghats), *pandas* (pilgrimage priests), and *Mahapatras* (funeral-rites priests) are notable (cf. Vidyarthi, et. al. 1979: 91- 125). In various funeral rites rice-porridge or balls are offered to the ancestors, as this is considered to have the capacity of ensuring immortality and providing them a place in Yama's world with the gods and divinities (cf. *Atharva Veda* IV.34.3). The *Mahapatras* are famous for their rigid rules and their greed for gifts.

The belief in the high spiritual merit of dying in Banaras has its origins in the historical past, where it has been fully described in religious texts and treatises. People of religious faith, especially Brahmins, wish to die in Banaras; it is a quest for realisation — "Oh, I am growing old; I want to go to Benares... I must now go to Benares" (SR: 24-9). This feeling has been fully elaborated in the *Kashi Khanda* (40. 162).

> Here why should a man dwell in a solitary place?
> And what is the use of turning from the pleasures of the senses?
> And what is the use of practising Yoga
> or sacrificing to the gods?
> For, without these one gets *mukti* easily in Kashi.

With a wish to die in Banaras people come to the city at the eleventh hour and get shelter in hospices such as Kashi Labh Mukti Bhavan, near Godaulia crossing. They have faith that "they may die in peace, for dying a good death is as important as living a good life" (Eck, 1982: 329).

Banaras being described as the city of death and *mukti*, it is quite natural that the funeral pyres could be perceived as "natural illumination" (SR: 21). Among the two cremation *ghats*, Harishchandra Ghat gives the message of peace and realisation of the self (SR: 25).

Among the main rituals and performances realised by pilgrims, offering the ashes of the cremated dead to the Ganga (*asthi-visarjana*) and lighting lamps to ancestors are the most common. People from different parts of India come here to perform *asthi-visarjana* (cf. *Vishnu Dharmasutra* 19.11-12) — the act which helps the soul to get a better place in Yama's realm (SR: 234). People who perform pilgrimage to Banaras for the above-mentioned ritual, as also for offering light to the manes, will be benefited with the highest religious merit. Raja Rao cites such an instance when a man is going to Banaras for this purpose, and his wife says, "Well, he goes, my Lord, to Benares; to bring light on the manes" (SR: 250). According to the *Harivamsha Purana* (I. 21.1) the post-funeral rites are of the highest religious merit; similarly the *Vayu Purana* (III. 14.1-4) also describes its merit in many ways.

In the funeral rites and ancestral worship, the offering of rice-balls has a high religious merit; it has been mentioned even in the *Taittiriya Samhita* (I.8.5.1). The ancient mythology as interpreted in the *Bauddhdyana Dharmasutra* (11.8.14) mentions that during the ancestors' rites manes come in the form of birds (mostly crows) to eat the rice-balls. Making use of satire, Raja Rao asks "...whether the Brahmins of Benares are like the crows asking for funeral rice-balls, saying 'Caw-caw'..." (SR: 12). The priests performing ancestors' rites maintain a register, well classified according to the area, lineage and genealogical tree of their customers; with their sharp memory and quick response they attract new visitors and ultimately convince them to offer more gifts in cash and kind (SR: 9-10):

> They knew my grandfather and his grandfather and his great-grandfather again, and thus for seven generations —...and for each of them they knew the sons and grandsons (the daughters, of course, they did not quite know), and so, they stood on their rights ... 'Pray, Mother, how could the manes be pleased?' So Little Mother yielded and just fifty silver rupees made everything holy.

7. Banaras is Banaras

Kashi has been famous for its distinct way of lifeworld and its styles, and also as a universal city. Therefore it has many names, five of them being the most important: Kashi, 'City of Light' (*Kashi Khanda* 26. 67); Varanasi, 'the City lying between the rivers Varana in the north and Asi in the south' (*Padma Purana* 33.49; *Matsya* 183.62; *Kashi Khanda* 30.69-70; *Vamana* 38, etc.); Avimukta, 'Never forsaken by Shiva' (*Matsya* 180.54); Anandakanana or Anandavana, 'Forest of Bliss' (*Kashi Rahasya* 14.39); and Mahashmashana, 'Great Cremation Ground' (*Padma Purana* I.33.14). The unique sacred topography of the city makes it unparalleled among all the cities in the world. The *Matsya Purana* (180.47) says that Banaras is a unique city and the highest in bestowing salvation to those who live here — any living organism: men, animals or reptiles. Following this idea the novelist too expresses, "Benares is Benares, Kashi the Holy, and whatever sins you commit in Kashi — well, there even a dog, or a bull, or a four-shoulder Brahmin attains liberation" (SR: 191).

Concerning Westerns visitors to Kashi, Eck writes (1982: 18), "virtually everyone who visited the city, from Ralph Fitch in the 1500s through those who went there in subsequent centuries, expressed astonishment and even repugnance at the panoply of images". But even some of the Westerners saw this city in the vision of Indian culture, like Keyserling who visited Banaras during the early 20th century, he notes: "Benares is holy. Europe, grown superficial, hardly understands such truth any more... Here I feel every day as if soon, perhaps even today, I would receive the grace of supreme revelation... Every would-be Christian priest would do well to sacrifice a year of his theological studies in order to spend this time on the Ganges: here he would discover what piety means" (Keyserling, 1969: 118-22). Considering both cultural milieus, Raja Rao compared Paris and Banaras: "Paris is a sort of Benares turned outward, and where but in Benares would Baudelaire be more real, more understandable, more perfect, and in every dimension?" (SR: 52). The novelist overlooked here to narrate the capacity of Hindu mythology to create living images, which at once integrates the universe and the microcosm, and also an existent lived-world (cf. Eck, 1986: 41). Moreover, it is in Kashi/ Banaras/ Varanasi, among all the *tirthas* of India, where one can see the best integration of myth, cosmos and lifeworld.

Comparing the 'valley of art' as from the artistic point of view, Banaras can also be placed at a distinct level; one can easily compare it with the Grand Canal of Venice, the murmuring flow of the river Isar in Munich, the colourful sky in Paris on an after rain afternoon, with the reflection of light on the old and new houses — whatever fantastic scenic beauties there are in the world, they cannot reach to the level which Banaras has preserved.

8. Epilogue and Destination

The novelist feels that, "Life is a pilgrimage, I know, but a pilgrimage to where — and of what?" (SR: 26). He has certainly reached quite near to his destination — to understand the 'inherent and invisible spirit' of Banaras. But he has not completely missed seeing the black spots on its glory; no doubt this is a different vision: "Benares seemed hateful to her: the whole of the North, but for the Ganges, was one desolation of dirt" (SR: 27). As a pilgrim, the novelist missed visualising the most sacred sites and areas of the city like the temples of Vishvanatha, Sankatamochana, Durga, and those ancient temples demolished by the Muslims, as well as the divine scenic beauty of the *ghats* for which the city is well known. On the other hand, one can easily agree to the statement that the novelist has fully merged in the cosmic sensitivity of Hindu mythology, especially in respect to the concept of *tirtha*. With this view in mind, at most of the places references of the ancient religious scriptures are cited. This angle would provide a new line of understanding the novel, i.e. integration of image, historicity and cultural pattern.

9. Basic Reference

Rao, Raja 1960. ***The Serpent and the Rope***. Orient Paperbacks, Delhi. Reprinted 1968.

~10~

Metaphysics and Life-philosophy: Raja Rao's *On the Ganga Ghat*

1. Introduction

For Raja Rao, the Ganga is the symbol of the life-philosophy which flows like the cycle of life. In Banaras the Ganga flows from south to north and forms a half-circle, bending like the crescent-shaped moon on the forehead of Shiva. This conveys the message that the north-bound river wants to save her devotees from death; indeed, the south is the realm of death, Yama, and the north stands for well-being, Shiva. Millions and millions of devout Hindus have come to the city since time immemorial to sprinkle the sacred water of their faith on the *Linga* form of Shiva, with the pious motive of reaching their ultimate destination. This is the background theme taken by Raja Rao for his novel ***On the Ganga Ghat*** (1993; hereafter referred as **GG**:). The book is based on his visit and experiences in the city in 1963 (cf. GG: 44).

In this novel Raja Rao attempts to explore the drama of life as it unfolds in Banaras, a city that has preserved the vividity and peculiarities of life from every nook and cranny of India. And to this unique city, from all parts of India came kings, lords, poor, beggars, merchants, courtesans, crooks, students, mystics, seekers and givers of knowledge, businessmen dealing both with spirituality and the material world, simpletons and charlatans — all in search of meanings to life, or to get settled in the holy land, or to get refuge as all their other ways were blocked, or to pass their final days in preparation for the retreat to heaven. This diversity turns into complexity and forms a mosaic of the whole Indian culture. No less varied are the creatures of Banaras presented in the book: the gentle, brahmachari (*celibate*) Madhoba and his Mohini — a feminine presence, "something more than a goddess, a woman"; Bhim, the sage parrot; the Brahmini cow Jhaveri Bai; bounteous concubines like Nanna; and hard-swearing, mantra-chanting *sadhus* laughing at the foibles of others. *On the Ganga Ghat* is a collection of eleven stories, and marks Raja Rao's return to the short story after a gap of over a decade. The prose is exquisite: chiselled, sparse yet evocative and mesmerising.

2. The Ganga: Aesthetics and Motherly River

The Ganga has been a symbol of India's age-long continuity; its culture and civilisation flow in the form of the liquid energy of Shiva — the Ganga (Fig. 31). The history of the Ganga is the cradle of Indian culture. She is also portrayed as a symbol of natural beauty, over-flowing with deeper meanings and messages inherent in Hindu thought. Shiva's anger is cooled here by his liquid energy, the Ganga, who in its bowed form looks like the crescent moon resting in his matted hair. In the whole 2525 km of its course, it is only in Banaras that the Ganga takes a sudden turn, flowing from the south ('darkness') to the north ('light'). The Advaita philosophy of 'non-dualism' says that in the deep intensity of darkness germinates the seed of light that radiates wisdom. In Kashi the fire in the cremation grounds never stops; one after the other pyres flame, continuing the lifecycle. After all only the body burns, not the soul. Says Raja Rao:

> Look at that still string of electric lights, a string through the awake night which seems to deepen the river's truth. Once in a while a lean tongue of flame flares up some dead whose body was being slowly turned to ash, which would finally be dissolved into the Ganga. Pyre, and pyre again, became prominent as we neared the river. The flames seemed so alive, the only nightly action in this visible universe. The string of lights seemed but reflections seen from the other side. Who were they, the one, two, or three, which had died, banker, virgin, retired police constable or Maharaja? And the yogis must watch these pyres as they open their eyes after their midnight meditations. The pyre makes death alive. He who has seen a body burn, knows he will never die. (GG: 13)

Compare with the *Kashi Khanda* (53.43), which glorifies the integrity of Shiva, the holy city, and the Ganga:

> I am Vishvanatha, the Lord of the Universe.
> Kashi is the light of liberation.
> The waves of the River of Heaven
> are the wines of immortality.
> What can these three not provide.

Fig. 31. An image of the mother Ganga River, riding on a makara, based on a painting of the early 20th century.

Coming from the Himalaya, the highest mountain, symbol of the highest wisdom and cosmic integrity, the Ganga purifies all, making fertile the plains of north India, and finally merges into the Indian Ocean. The *Kashi Khanda* (28.86) mentions: "The Ganga, filled with the sweet wine of compassion, was sent out for the salvation of the world by Shiva, the Lord of Lords". Says the novelist:

> Mathematics is therefore like the Himalayas. The higher you go the holier it becomes. And near Kailas, on the snowy heights, and from Gangotri does the Mother Ganga emerge. 'Zero is Ganga, Ganga is zero,' he shouted as if he'd discovered a Vedic mantra. I tell you, you could grind castor pods at the hell-mill, the Ganga beside you. The Ganga purifies all. She gives song to the songstress, limbs to the brave, paddle-push to the boat, and child to the wife. 'O giver of gifts Ganga Mata,' says Shankar to himself, and in prayer, closes firm his eyes. (GG: 71)

The present condition of the river is alarming; as another novelist described it: "Ganga is no better than a ditch, undrinkable and filthy.

Nor has this holy river helped me find Ramesh, though I beg and pray with every step" (Payne, 2001: 230). However, for the devout Hindus "the dark water gives no roughness, of course one avoids drinking it" (GG: 79); however, so many people do drink it. This is the dilemma of life, where sacred beliefs and secular concepts oppose each other and also reciprocate too, thus making life more interesting.

The *Katha Upanishad* (IV.6) speculates, "He who was born of old was born of water. Right from the Waters, the soul drew forth and shaped a person". In Hindu culture, water in general and the Ganga water in particular is accorded high sanctity, and thus is used in many ceremonies including rites of passage. The Ganga represents the 'cosmic whole', thus the idea of 'home', and the *ghat* along the Ganga is the turning, the edge, the transitional and active space of human being. Certainly a Hindu house without Ganga water is no home: "Never a home be a home where Mother Ganga floweth by not" (GG: 81). The importance of the Ganga grew as different cultures and kingdoms prospered along its bank.

The Earth is symbolised as the mother in the form of a cow ('*Go* or *Gaia*'), who provides milk to her calves as the Earth gives life-substance to her creatures. The cow milk as the energy of the life-substance ultimately generates the divine energy possessed in the human body (cf. Singh, 1996: 196-97). The Ganga's source is called Gomukha ('the cow's mouth'). The cow and the Ganga are both a symbol of the nutrient energy, and, together with the physical mother and the Earth, are perceived in Hindu beliefs as the 'four mothers'. Jhaveri Bai, a sacred cow, meets the Ganga and watches her reflection in the Ganga water — its waving mirage slowly disappearing and getting re-created constantly: "The Ganges flows fierce and fresh on Jhaveri Bai's back. Head inturned and her horns unshaking, Jhaveri Bai contemplates her own face in the moving waters. There's magic in this picture that appears and disappears" (GG: 57).

3. The Distinct Banaras

Banaras presents a unique example of a place where the ballet of life has preserved all the contrasts. About that epitome of sophistry, the author said:

> In Benares everything — bullock carts, rags, human excreta (in cones or flat), fallen wayside hay, tree tops, burnt charcoals, abandoned bus horns, beggars, ugly names on worn walls (may be of politicians) — everything, everything benefits from all

> acts — for no act here has any consequence. An action must have cause and effect. In Benares there seems no reason for a cause, thus the result is, no effect. No act breeds an act. And so eternity, the bent meaning of the river. (GG: 7-8)

The *pandas,* specialised priests at the pilgrimage places, are the people who control the religious arena of the city. They, like parrots (e.g. Bhima, a character in the book), make their holes in the settlement and after the passage of time claim themselves as the owners. They have made their nests near to all the important *ghats,* and maintain close ties with their associated functionaries such as boatmen, flower sellers, barbers, and vendors selling ritual items. Raja Rao narrates:

> Bhim, the parrot, is among the eldest of the kingdom. Lean at the neck (much hair having fallen during these many decades), and with a wisp of white hood, he moves with natural serenity. He seems to have such privileged freedom of movement across the sky of Benares that even the vultures give way to him. (GG: 17).

The novelist has implicitly explained two circuits in Banaras. One is the inner circuit, delimited according to Puranic tradition and based on the pilgrimage route of Avimukta; the area amidst it is 'never forsaken' (*avimukta*) by Shiva. The holy territory of Banaras consists of the three sacred segments, viz. Omkara in the north, Vishvanatha in the middle, and Kedara in the south. The outer circuit is beyond the Avimukta route, almost spread over the western part. Of course, although Raja Rao has attempted to describe this route, he has only partially succeeded (GG: 22). In fact, he took the divisions of inner and outer as a metaphor of the two opposite sides of life for which Kashi is well known: the City of Light and also of Delight. High and low divided by a route! Right is a symbol of auspiciousness, and left of impurity. The left always cries, and the right cheats. The right is the age-old traditions of *dharma* (moral ethics) as ordained by the religious mythologies (e.g. Brahmins, rituals, *ghats,* priests, etc.). The left stands for the counterpart *karma,* worldly action with fruit (e.g. low castes, farming, fields, workers, etc). Always a tussle and interaction between *dharma* and *karma* goes on, superseding each other. Both sides never cross their limit, instead they help each other in their mutual survival and interdependency. The on-going drama is narrated here:

> … those to the right belong to one caste, to the left the other. To the left you have the weavers, the untouchables, the hide-sellers,

> the prostitute houses (of the poor and the accidental), and to the right you have the rajas, the concubines, the pilgrims, and the temples — and the river. The vultures of the right do not eat with the vultures of the left — there are strict rules not only about eating but about mating. You have on the right the vultures born life after life feeding on the fishes, the thrown-off meats of pilgrims, and even a good carcass or two. It depends on whose it is. But on the left you must eat all sorts of things, and even share a buffalo with crows or a host of curs. The vulture's cry to the left is like a policeman's whistle, sharp and one-noted, but the vultures of the right have long drawn notes, as if they were gentlemen accustomed to wait on Zamindars. And the two provinces are so clearly drawn that the two types of vultures — the vultures of the left and the vultures of the right — never invade each other's domains. That's the law. And the vultures, you may know, are great obeyers of the law. (GG: 22)

There also exists a group of intermediaries between right and left, *dharma* and *karma,* like the common people explained with the metaphor of 'sparrows' by Raja Rao:

> This is not always so true of the sparrows. These tiny commonplace populace of Benares are so mixed up in their mediocrities that they eat anywhere, and they mate anywhere, and in fact they peck at any grain, funeral grain, or pilgrim-leavings. They however marry only from the sparrows of the ghat sides, exception being made to those of Ramnagar, on the other bank. For reasons of bird-laws the Ramnagar side is counted as holy. The sparrows too follow the pilgrims sometimes when they make their sixty-league circumbulation of Benares. They go in groups and return by evening to their nests on the Dasi Ghat or the Hanuman Ghat side. The peculiarity however of the Benares sparrows is this: they are fearless. Commonplace they may be but proud they are. The story goes that once when Sri Rama was crossing the Ganges a sparrow stood on a side, and swore allegiance of all the sparrows to the Lord. (GG: 22-23)

According to popular belief in Kashi every piece of sand possesses the essence of Shiva; Shiva, the supreme, the Lord of this City has blessed the dwellers to be beyond the range of hierarchy — higherarchy or lowerarchy. For those who understand there is no master, no slave too:

Fig. 32. The Teacher and the Disciple: Symbolic view of *Yoga* (spiritual pleasure, left) and *Bhoga* (worldly enjoyment, right: preparing *bhang*), a 13th century image at Kardameshvara (with courtesy from Lannoy, 2002: 189).

"In Benares all dust is musk, in Benares all tears are nectar, in Benares there are no slaves and no animals! For all creatures are free. The mighty Shiva in his greatness takes his leap, and he dances" (GG: 55).

In Banaras, "*masti* is genial and tolerant in its commitment to a carefree way of life. Unawed by the sacred power of his city, the Banarasi lives in the present, untroubled by the past and believes in enjoying life to the full" (Lannoy, 2002: 189). However a scene appears on the surface, it would be different inside. Banaras is the city where *yoga* (spiritual bliss) and *bhoga* (worldly pleasure) mix in the various facets of life (Fig. 32); as it is said "But all Benares is one gup (*gossip*) — so one less or one more, who's there to care" (GG: 62).

The circle is a common symbol of infinity and the universe, and the spiral of the human consciousness and the lifecycle. God is a potter; using the rhythm of the wheel of time and the technique of his divine wish to play, He creates the world: " 'God himself is a potter. He made the wheel from which came this pot,' and he laughs, beating his chest with dire conviction" (GG: 83).

The circle emerges into infinity if its radius is infinite. By throwing a piece of stone into calm water, one can see the emergence of overlapping circles and spirals. From the centre outwards it further extends beyond sight. The role of man as an actor in this drama is the most basic. However, purity and piousness of his intellect (in the form of the Ganga of wisdom) are pre-requisites. A commoner, Bhola, when relaxed murmurs to himself and feels that his life also has some value. " 'Brother, all ends in a circle,' he repeats, and throws a stone to drive away a crow, and hop-hop it disappears. Then dipping the twig into the Ganga, he makes the triangle and the circle again. 'Till the triangle become the circle, you see, God will not be pleased' " (GG: 83).

The impact of the medieval devotionalism (*bhakti*) is strong in the life of the common man. Bahkti is popular as a friendly and interdependent relation between the divine being and his devotees:

> If the Ganga does not say
> Who then will go on naming Ram,
> If I do not say (!)
> You, alone will remain, O Ram. (GG: 83)

A common aphorism of Banaras says: "Death in Kashi is Liberation" — *Kashyam maranam muktih*. For death in Kashi is death transformed. There are many 'hospices' (homes for dying people) where people, mostly aged widows (from Bengal), pass their last stages waiting for death. Of course, this is a cruel Brahmanical tradition, people passing their last breathe in hospices feel neither guilt nor hatred for the tradition: "She felt no evil against anyone. She felt no love either. She waited for death as a baby bird awaits its mother's beak, a gnat or caterpillar for food" (GG: 92). It is a matter of speculation if people come to such hospices for passing their time or getting religious merit, or really with the intention to achieve liberation (cf. Justice, 1997: 46). However, the dead are brought to the burning *ghats* at all hours of the day and the night, and the biers are immersed in the Ganga and then left to dry off before putting them on the funeral pyre. In one of his last interviews before his own death, Raja Rao said, "People think that Banaras is about death. There's death everywhere. The burning bodies on the *ghats*, the half-burnt corpses floating down the river ... But Banaras is not about death. It's about eternity..." (Evam, 2002: v)

The city of Banaras is described metaphorically as the city beyond the gauge of space and time. It is said that the real Kashi, the eternal Kashi is suspended in the Void on Shiva's trident (Fig. 33). This immunity from time can only ever be real by an act of vision. The patron deity Shiva in his form of Kala Bhairava (Lord of Time and Death) controls this city. Raja Rao writes:

Fig. 33. Kashi on Shiva's trident, a 19th century painting.

> "The city of Kala Bhairav is no place, for everything is destroyed there as it arises. So I go where there is instant destruction; therefore all is. Where Shivji danced on the crematorium is where the world is real. Time and space are burnt to ashes. To live, you must dance," said the Sadhu and gyrated in the corridor of the wagon and in such a manner that the passengers (and Shivlal too) thought he would just jump out, and fly away. (GG: 102-103)

Narrow lanes, dirt, filth, charcoal smoke, obnoxious smells, leakage of sewers, open drains, scattered solid wastes, dispersed human excreta and animal dung, overflowing water, polluting habits of the dwellers — these altogether make the lifeworld of Banaras.

> In the gullies of Benares the smells are exuberant, the ladies' shy — shyness curves their saris to bent innocuity, but man's passion is in the starved shine of his eyes. The gutters go their way making time, carrying little broken claypots (that milk and tea and curd have used for man's satiations, and that ritual purity

> has destined for their formal destruction) — the gutters have broken baskets, little threaded sweetmeat trays, an ant-eaten umbilical cord, torn sackcloth on which bees sit for a better taste of funeral honey. The gutters leap through the side streets, open up by comers, and gay they go half full with dark moving fluids to any Ganga Ghat, and leap down under *pipal* [*Ficus religiosa*] trees. For all of here must be holy, and even the sewage has to rush in cascades, and be hallowed by the pipal's knotted roots. (GG: 123)

For all its filth, the Ganga is indeed the 'river of heaven' for devout Hindus. And some of this sanctity reaches out to the visitors and everybody else. But why, really, are we in Varanasi? Is it not perhaps to experience the closeness of death and its frightening everyday character? Raja Rao was sure that "Banaras has the best and the worst of India, but it is here that you see the human wanting to leave all that behind, the human wanting to be divine" (see Evam, 2002: v).

4. Shiva's City

The city dwellers are well known for worshipping several gods together, *bahudevapujakas*. The city is pluralistic and polytheistic at once, what Max Müller calls *kathenotheism* — the worship of many gods, one at a time or one after one. It is believed that the Supreme Reality can be approached and apprehended in many ways (Eck, 1982: 40).

> There's more mystery in the world than you know. In Kala Bhairav's temple, sometimes you can see monkeys, devotees of Hanuman come. Between the dog and monkey there's marriage in Benares. Madho has a great following among the dogs and the monkeys because he worships Hanuman. (GG: 37)

Further,

> For everything on earth, the good and the bad, come to the one single end — touching the holy feet of Sri Rama. (GG: 78)

One of the adages of Banaras says that no one sleeps hungry in the city as the Mother Goddess in her form of Annapurna ('plenitude of food') takes care of the devotees; also, in the form of Gauri ('radiant mother'), she gives the blessing to take away all sort of sins. " 'Mother Annapurna, take away my sins, my million, million sins. O mother!' Then he rose and fell prostrate before his own mother" (GG: 71).

According to the *Kashi Khanda* (98.49b-51a), "One who sees Vishvanatha makes all pilgrimages. One should always have the glimpse of Vishvanatha and always bathe at Manikarnika (in the Ganga river). True, true, over and over. True, true, over and over". The most common 'daily pilgrimage' (*nitya yatra*), very popular among the pilgrims and the city dwellers alike, focuses on the temple of Vishvanatha and the associated deities in its vicinity.

> Worship Vishwanath, the Lord of Benares,
> Whose locks seem delightful with wavelets of the Ganga,
> He who is ever adorned on his left with Mother Gauri,
> (He again) beloved of Narayana,
> And the conqueror of the Bodiless God (Kama). (GG: 76)

5. A Holy Dip in the Ganga: Towards Pilgrimage

The Ganga water is holy, but also provides secular merits. The milkmen of Banaras are known for deliberately increasing the quantity of milk with good Ganga water, earlier sold at one rupee and a quarter per *seer* (i.e. Rs 1.25 a litre; presently it is Rs 17 a litre). "For pilgrims Ganga is holy, and so is Benares milk" (GG: 53). Also, " 'There's always Mother Ganga for the orphan,' he said, and came to the holy city of Benares. He found no difficulty in finding a job: he looked so strong, he could lift a mountain. And in Benares there aren't such hefty people anymore" (GG: 33).

The devout Hindu man, following the tradition, soon after marriage worships the Ganga and wishes for a good successor (cf. Fig. 34).

> "And I went to the Ganga and said: Mother Ganga you will have to give me a son. He must be better than me. He must be much much better than me. He must neither smoke nor drink nor womanise. He must be pure (*aparna*) and great. And I threw some flowers at Mother Ganga. And you know how the Mother does, when she answers. She hissed her two-lipped hiss, as if she said the same thing twice over. When Mother Ganga is there what lack of greatness," he remarked and wept between his knees. (GG: 67)

Unfortunately, Raja Rao failed to describe the chain of 84 *ghats*, among which the most popular are the five called *Panchatirthis*; from south to north, these are: Asi, Dashashvamedha, Manikarnika, Panchaganga and Adi Keshava (Figs. 35, 36 & 37). He has mentioned

Fig. 34. Kashi: Worshipping the Ganga after marriage by groom and bride, and the family.

only the two cremation *ghats,* Harishachandra and Manikarnika, as well as Dashashvamedha (cf. GG: 119). Additionally, the beauty of the sun rise, which symbolises the meeting of the masculine divine fire (Sun) and the feminine divine water (the Ganga), has also been overlooked by the novelist. One can easily remark that Raja Rao has plunged so deep in the waters of the Ganga that he forgot to narrate the story of the riverfront *ghats* and their surrounding areas.

Mind is the centre of all human activities. Our whole life is a pilgrimage from one end to the other. We all are pilgrims, each carrying on his back a pot with his own traditions. Each tradition having its own specialities, distinctions, marks, and ways as ordained by the code of rules. Hinduism is an amalgam of many such varied pots, but the Ganga has its special dwelling-place in all the pots. Traditions paved the ways for spatial transposition of the Ganga all over India, or else its water is carried from the sacred site of Kashi.

> Man's illumination, however, is of the mind, yet he shapes his utensils for proof of his material disposition. I am a pilgrim, so I have a pot. One pot. Big pot. Small pot. Brass pots with tusk-beaks or silver ones with swan-heads, pots with cow-mouths or pots with just arches carrying handles, pots are pots and the Ganges has no choice. You dip and you bring it to your pilgrim

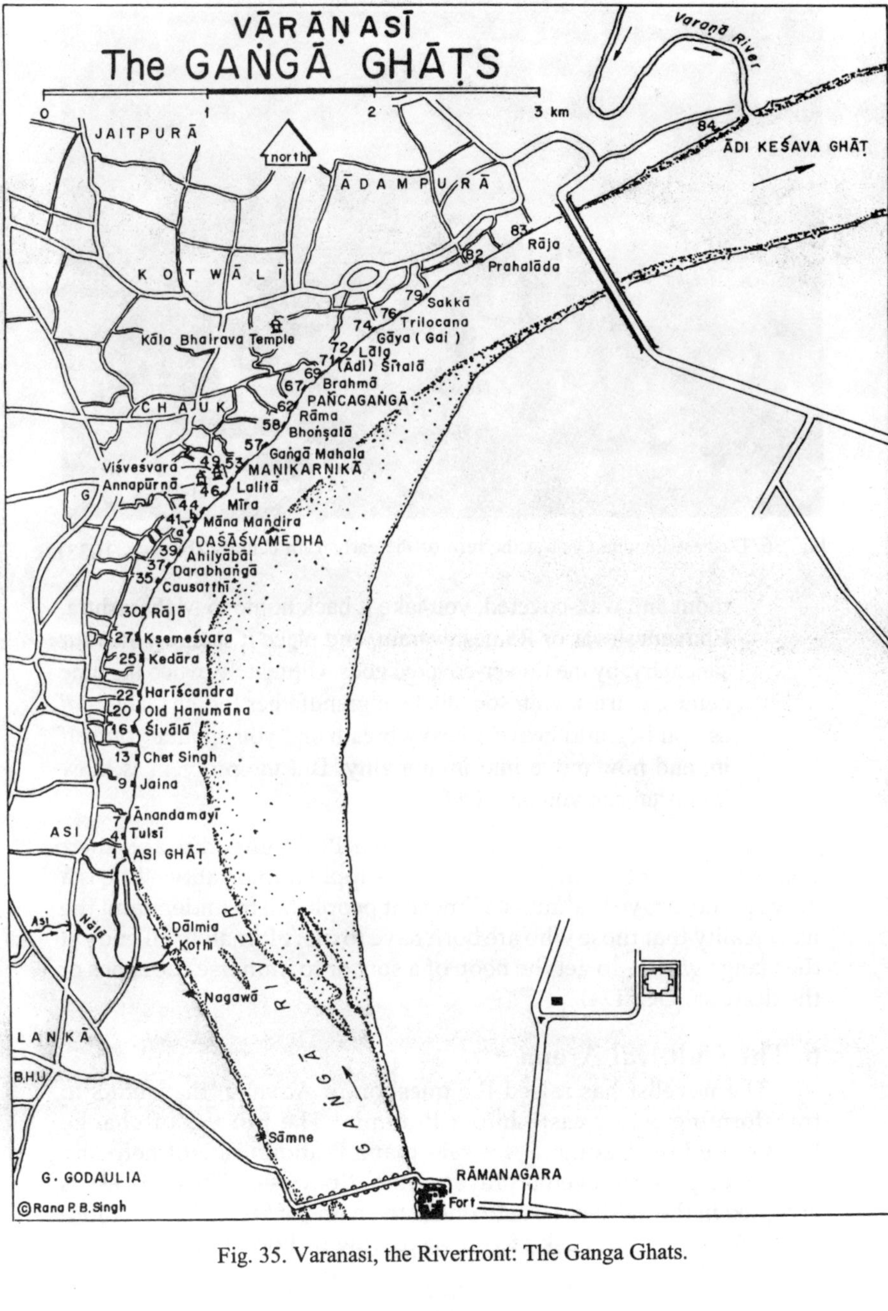

Fig. 35. Varanasi, the Riverfront: The Ganga Ghats.

Fig. 36. Dashasvamedha Ghat at the turn of the early 19th century (Prinsep, 1833).

> room and wax-covered, you take it back home to Maharashtra, Bhuvaneshwar or Rameshwaram, and place it securely in your sanctuary, by the flower-covered gods. Ultimately, when the time comes, you ask your son, uncle or grandfather for the Ganga-*jal* as you begin to heave a heavy breath and you sputter yourself in, and now move into immortality. But the problem is, how immortal can you be? (GG: 123)

The overseers of Hindu rituals, the Brahmins, through their dogmatic rules perform the business to supply immortality: "Life is a grave game, oh, ye brahmins". Innocent people fail to understand the hard reality that those who are born have to die; ultimately all ends at the Ganga *ghat* — to get the boon of a son, or to immerse the ashes of the dead (cf. GG: 124).

6. The Cultural Arena

The novelist has raised the question of Advaita, that refers to transforming a low caste into a Brahmin! The process of change transformed the tradition. It is said that a Brahmin cannot help any person, or perform even a prayer without payment. This process is accepted in the modern society under the name of *bakshish*, 'donation-gift': "And why not I ask of you, a sparrow be born a brahmin? The

Fig. 37. Ahilyabai and Shitala Ghats, Varanasi: a riverfront view.

wise Bhim the parrot says: Are you still there, O race of Bhagirathi? The brahmin is dead with his lucre as the English with their greed. In Benares, we know no caste but virtue" (GG: 24).

The dogs refer to the working class, who would not be taken care of after death: they cannot afford to pay the donations for the Brahminic rituals. "The dogs in Benares do not bark when you carry firewood — they know it's for the dead. They too would be dead one day, but there would, alas, be no firewood for them. Thus the common area of silence" (GG: 29-30).

Banaras is known for its funny stories, such as: the quantity of wood required for cremation varies according to the status of the dead in terms of wealth. "All the dead are not good. This much you learn too from the trade. For if he's an evil man you know he will need more firewood than any others, and the brahmins knowing all this will not wait for him till he's all burnt to pure ash (unless he is sort of a lakhpathi [who owns hundreds of thousands od rupees])" (GG: 31-32). Moreover, "sometimes one wonders whether the curs of Benares do not understand their talk" (GG: 32).

Raja Rao is regarded as one of the greatest theme-makers of women and their lives and predicaments; in fact he is regarded as the thematist of the feminine principle with rational sensitivity. His vision of the feminine is derived from Brahminical culture, Indian Vedanta, Upanishads, Puranas and finally culminates in Tantra. "And women,

I tell you, are the bane of Benares. There are too many of them and most of them seem to have but one job. Even the rich widows who come, they are not without casting eyes on a young male pushing his firewood cart to the ghats. Virtue does not grow easily in Benares. And vice has no better place. For all comes here to burn" (GG: 33).

One of the southern *ghats* is dedicated to Anandamayi Ma (1896-1982), a pre-eminent widow-saint of the 20th century. She was unassuming, simple, modestly attired in plain white cotton robes, and usually very accessible. Many of her followers were regularly going to her ashram and those gifted ones received flowers and beads from her, as in the book queen Rasomani, who would go in a palanquin with whisk-bearers, and she would sit and participate in the group chanting (GG: 91).

Since the ancient times Kashi has also been famous for courtesans. The rich aristocrats played a major role in promoting their culture, besides different kinds of arts. In fact, these coutesans were not vulgar prostitutes, but practiced many kinds of refined arts as music and dance, etc. In the early Buddhist literature the story of Addhakashi, a prostitute, is described in detail (cf. *Vinayapitaka* 2.359-60; Motichandra 1985: 40). Damodar Gupt's *Kuttanimatam*, a 9th-century text, is full of stories of beautiful women and courtesans (cf. Vishvakarma, 1987: 188-189). Many such women were servants in the Shiva temples. The tradition continued, and remnants are still visible today in different forms.

> The Benares concubines are famous through history. How come to Kashi Vishwanath and not taste of the honey of consecrated womanhood? "Lord, may she be handsome, and may she know love-making of such a wise, the earth knows no greater truth. Lord, the woman is the most beautiful thing you have created. The breasts and the waist, and the music that rises, curls, and falls, — and her dance is the dance that the Lord Shiva himself initiated mankind into." (GG: 104-105)

The lust for the never-ending desire to have pleasure leads ultimately to a suffering which has no end. If the self is awakened, then no need of worldly happiness. A sense of non-attachment helps in crossing worldly affairs.

> Man goes where he has to go but one day he will arrive where there's no going or returning. A car can always take you to the railway station. But you don't need (or do you?) a car to go to yourself? No. (GG: 44)

If one realises that this world is an illusion, then all its happenings are accepted as a game of pleasure.

> I tell you, you cannot live in Benares if you have no imagination which explains why Bhedia is so happy here. For him the world is imaginationings. To live in one's imagination is truly to live in heaven, has said some village vulgar singer, has he not? But that's the truth of the matter. (GG: 49)

The place is also known for "barbarian Banaras Brahmins", who are masters of ticklish rules imposed upon the innocent devotees, who succeed by hook or crook to cheat them. Virtually virtue falls at the feet of vice! (GG: 62). "And when Padma fell at the feet of 'this barbarian Benares brahmin' or the 3Bs as he called himself, he instinctively felt like falling at his wife's feet in return. How can virtue fall at the feet of vice? So he'd rise and stand and sometimes suddenly he entered into that august silence. There he saw no one, no, none" (GG: 63). No one can challenge, no one can change anything; it's better to be silent.

"Asleep after what you have revealed to me. A butcher may go to sleep after a slaughter, a tax collector after fleecing his client. But a brahmin boy dances with joy when a son is conceived by his spouse" (GG: 66). Why should they not be happy? There will be a celebration on the occasion of the rite of passage, and Brahmins will be fed with good meals. The Brahmins maintain the tradition of patron-client relationship and also maintain the recorded history of their clients' ancestors and their visits too. "You can ask any brahmin in Benares, where anyone else is, and somehow they will tell you, or take you to another who will tell you, all you want to know, where your daughter is, or your uncle. And he will even tell you, not only of all your ancestors, father, grandfather, and great grandfather, their names all written down in their family documents" (GG: 117).

Knowing all the pitfalls and filthy ways as well as many superstitious rituals, the dwellers enjoy their lives knowing the ultimate end for all of us.

> All, all we know. Such, indeed the brahmins of Benares. For, remember, what you find not bad and good in Benares, you know you will see no such truths any elsewhere on earth. Here, in this most sacred city, I can tell you, whoever wants to hear that in final wisdom, there is neither virtue nor vice, for both burn like those pyres on the ghats, equally — to ash. Don't you understand this? Even the curs here know it. (GG: 117)

7. Message: Flowing Ganga vs. Lifeflow

Every happening depends on context, situational demand and ultimate objective. In every sphere of life, surrounded by chance and changes, man attempts to make his destiny, however many times he fails. Awakening the symbolic meaning of a wooden cot, *charpai*, the novelist narrated the story of Banaras:

> Every event of life has a double meaning. There is no accident in existence. Yet there is the miracle of chance. To know you lie on a shaky *charpai* in this damp building, in what is perhaps the Rajghat College Guest House but, as it were, a nowhere of anywhere is to ask the question: Who made this rope that wove the *charpai*? And the tree, the timbers from which the *charpai* was made? Whence came they? What destiny brought the rope and the string together? ... Event is always single, simple. Event is action without object. (GG: 16)

Similar to the philosophy of 'action', as narrated in the *Bhagavad Gita*, Raja Rao also perceives life as a never-ending trail of actions, sometimes failed and sometime achieved: "Remember life is only a caravan, as the saying goes: Does one know what a fresh dawn would bring, once the desert night is over?" (GG: 39). It is said, it's not certain that darkness will continue forever; certainly after night comes the light of day.

The wheel of time turns its rhythm constantly. The cycle of action always rolls.

> The quiet Ganga flows. The dippers are dipping, the crows are cawing. The vultures vociferate from high pipal tops. On terraces the wet clothes of pilgrims hang with assiduity. The more the sun, the more holy would they be. The bazaars seem of a sudden silent — it's noontime and people like to eat and rest. Shalwar Khan now pushes the Naga's head down with the oboe and fixes back the lid of the serpent-box. And then drags out a bamboo-basket from his large cloth-sack. Putli will still come out from some terrace, boys, having disappeared before you, into the earth. Life is so like an oboe song. (GG: 50-51)

The Ganga originates from Gomukha, 'cow's mouth', in the Himalaya, that's how the cow and the Ganga are inseparable. The Earth is also symbolised as a cow. Jhaveri, a cow character of the book, always nourishes, like the mother earth who gave birth to Sita, the wife of Lord Rama. Jhaveri represents the flow of the Ganga. "Sita Devi, mother of us, I worship you, that my sins, my friends' sins, and all evils be taken away. Birth is so mean, Death is so low. Mother give us no birth or death" (GG: 56). And, ultimately, in the channel of time life flows.

Without purification and cleanliness, rituals are not fruitful. The cow, symbol of the Ganga and the Earth, cries. Bathing is a call to revive the intimate relationship of humanity with the divinity.

> The cow's tears are purer than your brahmin prayers. Come and see it there, if you will, by the Benares ghat. "God you made the elephant and the peacock, the bear and the porcupine — even the dog did you make and the hyena, creatures of the earth. But the cow, Lord, you made as your first child. Lord, I sink in your waters, I sink into my origins, Lord give me the gift of truth." (GG: 57)

Through mind, speech and action (*manasa, vacha, karmana*), awareness and unconscious attention prevail in everyone's daily life — this system of *dharma-karma* ('moral duty and justified action') represents the Indian 'lifeworld', symbolised as a 'water-flow'. The concept of 'life-flow' and 'water-flow' are the two sides of man-nature interaction. Like the two banks of the Ganga, *dharma* and *karma* are the two sides of *truth*, the river. But only by awakening (*chetana*) and wisdom (*jnana*) can one understand this.

> Life flows as you see, like the Ganga herself, simple and abundant, carrying princes and dancing girls, fishes and carcasses, the pyres burning on her side, reminding you that the Truth is but one indivisible flow. What is dream and which reality, then? (GG: 120)

If the human lust corrupts nature, then the life-flow would certainly turn to chaos. Presently the world is suffering by the combined pollution of non-awakening, individualistic ideas, and consumerism — all around self-centredness! It may be a turning towards dissolution, which will be followed by a new beginning. If the energy (water-flow) will stop, civilisation will be finished.

> What if the river should stop, Lord? (Like once she did, you remember, when you held her thunderous flow in your topknot, the moon smiling above her) What might the Vedas do then, and the fishes and the seeds and the sounds and the elephants?

> O, let water flow, Lord, that the earth turn not away from its fulcrum, whirl, earth, that the Ganga flow, round and around on herself, from earth to sky and from the heavens back to the Himalaya. The circle is the end of all beginnings as the Ganga is of water. (GG: 122)

The novelist gives a warning; nevertheless, in the Hindu mythological thought, the hope of a re-awakening, of a new creation, is always present.

> If the Ganga cannot grow dry one will never know deatḥ. Hence is she, the Mother of compassion. (GG: 125)

The distinct trilogy of Truth-Wealth-Trick begins as 'Truth Triumphs', and passes through 'Wealth Triumphs' to finally reach 'Trick Triumphs'; this trend has resulted in common frustration and unworthiness.

> Man is mortal is the grandest fib man ever invented. Foolish is man in trying to believe in such a lie. When knowledge, as Ganga, as *jnana-ganga*, flows, death is dissolved into truth. She is, as Sri Shankara said: She is *nija bodha rupa*, she, the form of Consciousness pure. (GG: 125)

> The object is not in seeing but in perceivingness. There is no here, Lord, there is no space, no movement, therefore I am the Ganga that flowing flows not. For where ends the flow? Nowhere. Where there is no end there is no beginning. Anything that is non existent at the beginning and also at the end, does not exist in the middle either, says the Great Gaudapada Acharya. He was, as you know, the Guru of the Guru of Sri Shankara himself. Thus, you fool, realise; the Ganga never flows. (GG: 125)

> For, where the flowing ends — *ap*, the is-isness of water begins. So, now Ganga, flow. (GG: 123)

8. An Epilogue: Towards the End

By self-awakening one can get that revelation 'similar' to the cosmic form of Shiva's body (Krittivasheshvara, cf. Fig. 38) which consists of all the eighteen forms of knowledge,

> The cessation of all mental activities is the supreme peace — that is the holiest of all holy places of pilgrimage, the Manikarnika

Fig. 38. Krittivasheshvara Lingam as Shiva's body in Kashi: 1 Omkareshvara, 2 Shrutishvara, 3 Mahadeva, 4 Trilochaneshvara, 5 Bharbhuteshvara, 6 Gokarneshvara, 7 Vireshvara, 8 Chandreshvara, 9 Avimukteshvara, 10 Dharmeshvara, 11 Madhyameshvara, 12 Jyeshtheshvara, 13 Vishveshvara, 14 Manikarnikeshvara, 15 Kapardishvara, 16 Kaleshvara, 17 Kedareshvara, and 18 Shukreshvara.

> (in me); the ever flowing stream of knowledge is the pure primeval Ganges (in me); (thus) I am the Kashika, of the form of pure Consciousness of Self. (GG: 121)

Archetypically, the KKh (33.167-172) mentions Kashi as Shiva's body, whose different parts are represented by eighteen lingams; at another level all these converge into one lingam, called Krittivasheshvara (Fig. 38). The number 18 symbolises the 18 branches of knowledge, including the 4 Vedas, 6 parts of the Vedic divisions, and the other branches (cf. Singh, 1994b: 213-213).

Mythology also refers to the Shiva lingam as the father-mother of the universe (SP-*Vidyeshvara Samhita*, 16.95), and thus the whole world is considered as a *Lingam* (KP II.97). This highest state of sacrality has been transposed upon the earthy territory as the abode of divine beings which has its manifestation in some transcendental sphere, often identified with Shiva's realm (cf. Singh, Rana, 2002b: 56).

Raja Rao has quoted here Shankara, a great thinker of the 8th century, who further said in his hymn to Kashi:

> If all this dwells within my body,
> What other place of pilgrimage can there be. (cf. Eck, 1982: 302).

"As the Ganges dissolves all acts of man so does silence dissolve all of speech. Man is never more a pilgrim than when silence carries him from darkness into light" (GG: 13). Raja Rao's vision of silence and the experiences of life may be compared to the nature of the Buddha's silence. It is known that his thought leads to a kind of pessimistic nihilism. Said Lannoy (2002: 234), "Not the nihilism of the modern West — negation of being, from which we instinctively recoil in horror — but that most un-Western nihilism which speaks, ...to reach the deep unease at the heart of modern Western civilisation, reaching out beyond the confines of the place in northern India where the Buddha first articulated his thought, to embrace the timeless dilemmas of all humanity." Close to Raja Rao's vision are Nobel Laureate Octavio Paz's (1971: 96) words:

> The Buddha said everything one can say with words: the errors and achievements of reason, the truth and falsehood of the senses, the fullness and the void of the instant, the freedom and the slavery of nihilism... But his silence says something different... What the Buddha's silence says is neither negation nor affirmation. It says *shunyata*, absolute emptiness: everything is empty because everything is full, the word is not a statement because the only statement is silence... Vibrations, waves, signals and responses: silence. Not the knowledge of the void: an empty knowledge. Buddha's silence is not a knowledge but something after knowledge: wisdom. An un-knowing.

To continue the discourse a little further, one can note that the Buddhist experience of Nothingness is not construed as threatening, but rather as a benediction. Its pessimism is so radical that it includes the negation of the negation: it denies death with the same logic with which it denies life. Eliade says that the Buddha offers the practical means "of being reborn to freedom, bliss, and the unconditioned state of nirvana...if one knows death already here below, if one is continually dying countless deaths in order to be reborn to something else — to something that does not belong to the Earth but participates in the sacred — then one is living, we may say, a beginning of immortality. It would follow that immortality should not be conceived as a survival after death, but rather as a situation one is constantly creating for oneself, for which one is preparing, in which one is even participating from now onward and from this present world" (Eliade, 1960: 227-228).

A simple life is a good solace and the best healing after repentance. Banaras is not a city where one can easily fulfil his ambitions, as the whole culture is full of obstacles (GG: 53). "Who can do anything in Benares that all do not want to see? If no one sees, the monkeys are there to see, always. The monkeys too got intrigued. This young man is playing some trick (for you may not have heard the Benares monkeys know as much as you do of the smell of money)" (GG: 109). A folk proverb says: If the simplest food of fried chick peas and Ganga water are available in Banaras by the blessing of Shiva, never leave Kashi as nowhere else can one find the whole family of Vishvanatha.

> How simple is the truth if only we listen to ourselves. But we prefer to listen to the crows on the Ganga Ghat, to the chatter of brahmins at the funerals (and in our temples) and to the ekka [horse cab] drivers (who frighten you with talks of death and taxation) and to those dead to death, the sadhus. The fact of the fact is simple. One cannot go to the Ganges. (GG: 125)

Ignorance distorts the moral sense of human beings; it can be removed by wisdom and self-realisation. The lust for power corrupts man. "The more the man threatened the more he wanted to go *there*" (GG: 104). Lord Krishna, preaching to his friend Arjuna, taught us (*Bhagavad Gita*, 4.42):

> Kill therefore with the sword of wisdom
> the doubt born of ignorance
> that lies in thy heart.
> Be one in self-harmony, in Yoga
> and arise, great warrior, arise!

This leads to the emergence of the dynamic force of play, i.e. thought-action: "It is the force of creation that brings being into existence" (*Bhagavad Gita*, 3.3). The novel ends with this message, symbolising the beginning of awakening: "One cannot go to the 'I'. For if you dare have a deep look on the Ganges evenings, and see the Ganga unflowing, then you know there is no Ganga. Water is just water. So, O, Mother Ganga, please be gracious, and, — flow" (GG: 125).

9. Basic Reference

Rao, Raja 1993. ***On the Ganga Ghat***. Orient Paperbacks (vision Books), New Delhi and Bombay.

~11~

THE MUSLIM WORLD: BISMILLAH'S *The Threadbare Woven Shawl*

1. Introduction: the Novelist's March

In the history of Hindi literature, Premchand's writings awakened society between 1920-1930 by presenting lively portraits of poor artisans, peasants and people of similar social groups. In spite of his close physical proximity (his residence was at only six kilometres from Varanasi City), he did not describe the *Jullahas* (Muslim weavers) of Banaras, a class of people struggling for existence. Of course, the novelist Phanishwar Nath Renu continued his line of approach during the 1950s, but he also did not write about the poor masses of an urban society. This gap has been filled up by a young but established novelist, Abdul Bismillah (b. 5 July 1949; Fig. 39), who has a deep sense of belongingness to this community through his stay in the weavers' world for more than a decade and his vision as a participant observer. It is because of his mind set-up and social interaction, as he is also a Muslim, that the lifeworld of the weavers is narrated vividly in his novel, ***Jhini Jhini Bini Chadaria*** (*The Threadbare Woven Shawl*; hereafter referred as **AB:**). Various aspects of the weavers' life are illuminated through various angles and mirrors of vision — their depression and suppression while merchants perceive them happy and better off, their inter-personal relations and their struggle for maintenance — all these critical issues and contrasts are presented through their words.

Ultimately the novel does not end only with frustration or a chaotic chiaroscuro, but rather it gives insight for the realisation of hard facts and inspiration for revolution. In this way, it presents an in-depth vision of literary art and provides a path of social awareness. Various issues related to landscape, identity and social condition, the life, social world and belief systems, the reactions, exploitative world, and finally weavers' sense of realisation have been highlighted in the way the novel narrates, and further compared with contemporary

Fig. 39. Abdul Bismillah.

scenes. Bismillah's close study of the weavers detects different sub-cultures with their distinct worlds within the composite weavers' culture. Such dialectic approach in historico-materialistic purview leads the novel to project historical and social realities.

In contextual perspective, the novelist himself has expressed that "in the novel I attempted to make a living portrait of the total life of the weavers". Moreover, he wants to show the degraded condition of the average weavers, the downtrodden — how do Seths and loom owners exploit them? The novelist depicted several such aspects magnificently in their natural setting. How a sari produced by an average weaver's craftsmanship reaches the world market, but alas! he himself leads a suffocating life ... one can find such scenes everywhere (cf. AB: 164).

The novel is divided into two parts named warp (*tana*) and weft (*bana*), which respectively refer to the longitudinal network of threads and the crossing and intersecting warp. These two parts are separated by the novelist's explicit expression of writing referred to as a 'contextual part' (*Chhepak*, AB: 161-165). Metaphorically, the two parts symbolise the social-religious-economic world (*tana*), and the world of awareness and the experiences (*bana*). Thus, by weaving together these two parts, *'The Threadbare Woven Shawl'*, written by Abdul Bismillah, presents the whole life of the weavers of Banaras with vividity, distinctiveness and contrasts, all in the purview of their experiences and the places associated with them (cf. Fig. 40).

To illustrate the weaver's habitual style of conversation, the novelist has not hesitated to use frequently even vulgar abuses; the most common are 'coitus' (*burchodi*, used 24 times), and 'product of the vagina' (*bhousaria-wallah*, 13 times). In total fifty-two times such abusive words appear in the novel, but in no way are they used out of context. The above-cited peculiar words of abuse are very commonly used among the weavers or even the folk-Banarasis.

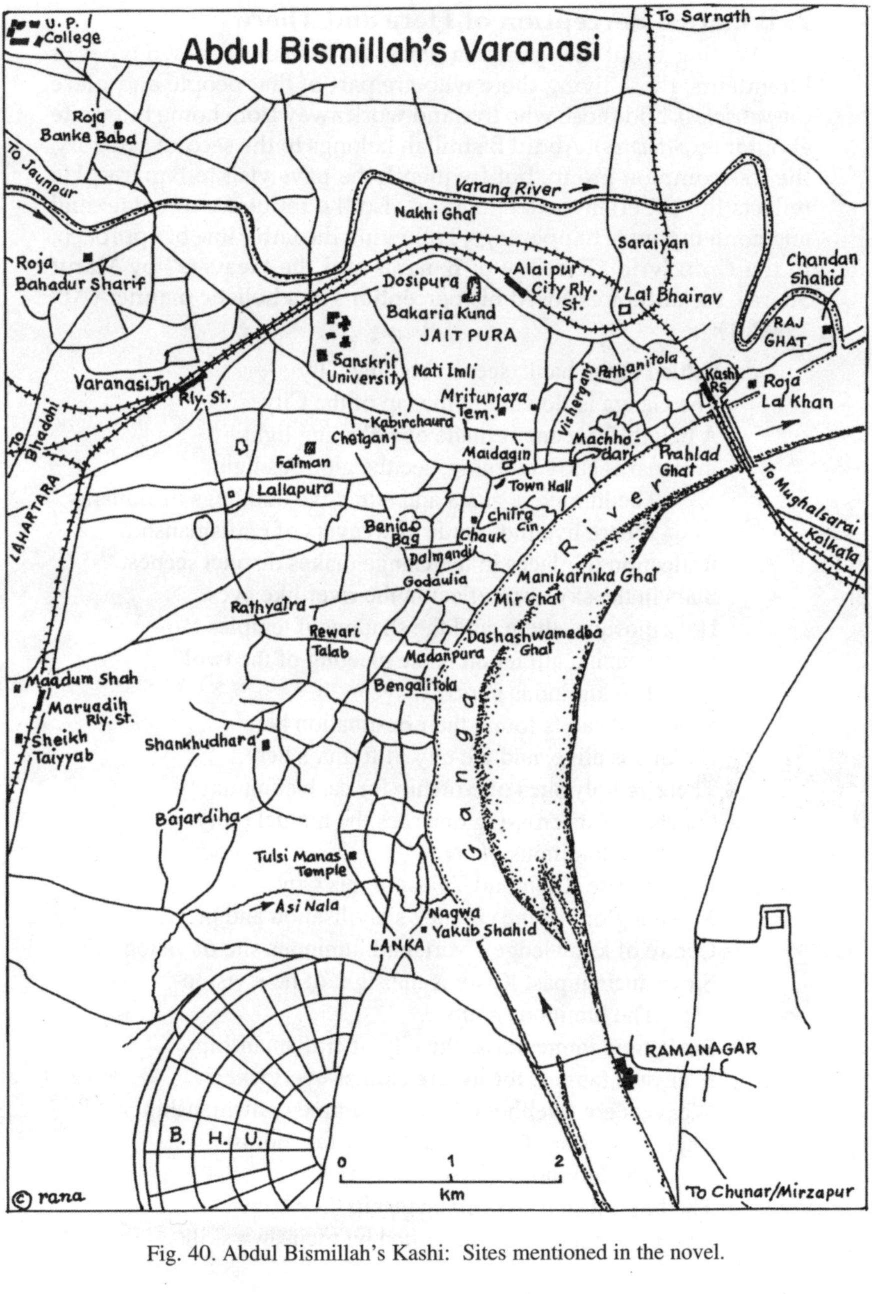

Fig. 40. Abdul Bismillah's Kashi: Sites mentioned in the novel.

2. Banaras: Perception of Here and There

Writing about the spirit of a place, we can consider two types of litterateurs: those living there who are part of that people and place (*in-patriotes*), and those who live and work away from home but write about it (*expatriates*). Abdul Bismillah belongs to the second category, the less common group, but frequently he pays visit to Banaras. He reflects the experienced feelings, as also the influence of contextual and contemporary happenings. Following the latter line of approach, in the Urdu lyric "The City of Banaras and the Weavers" by Maruf Sharifi, the author exposed his perceptions in a holistic manner (AB: 199-201):

Settled at the bank, see the shining City
The Ganga is flowing in the lap of the City.
A delightful scene is made of reflecting light
In Banaras early morning, see the glorious light.
  The luminous *ghats* and attractive buildings of Banaras,
  Where live thousands of weavers of craftsmanship.
Reflection of places in the Ganga makes distinct scenes,
Stars in the sky also reflect in the river like eyes.
Holy mosques there, and the shadow of temples too
How amazing attraction is the meeting of the two!
  The luminous *ghats*...
Sages and saints found their destination here
Buddha is alive, and the city of Rama's here.
There're holy sites of worship for each community
On each of its crossing one sees the mutual unity.
  The luminous *ghats*...
In past were Kabir and Tulasi in this City
Making glory of the country's civilisation and piety.
Centre of knowledge — art, and luminous site of vision
Since ancient past Kashi is the sight of new vision.
  The luminous *ghats*...
Since time immemorial the city of craftsmanship
Is always famous for its silk clothes everywhere.
Weavers got livelihood by their unique craftsmanship
Their houses are fully inhabited by the looms.
  The luminous *ghats*...
The highest state of craftsmanship they know,
Deserted, but became inhabited by their own skills.

The line of patriotship as shown by Gandhi
With that zeal weavers operate the thread in looms.
    The luminous *ghats*...
Ultimate product of the devotion they show
Grandness of art of craftsmanship they show.
With hope to get the reward of their labour
This idea in mind, during dawn they go to the bazaar.
    The luminous *ghats*...
Decorators of our motherland's border
Promoters of the purity of Habb's daughter.
Even the first man learnt culture from them
These weavers do put your face under cover.
The luminous *ghats* and attractive buildings
    of Banaras,
Where live thousands of weavers of craftsmanship.

The textile and silk industry in Banaras has a historical base, as recorded in the Vedic and Buddhist literature. During the 12th-14th centuries its glories reached a zenith, and by the turn of the 20th century Banaras became famous for its saris (Srivastava, 1986: 205, 206). Presently Muslims make up for one-third of the population of the city; and there are about 1400 Muslim shrines in the city (Fig. 41).

The morning scene at the Banaras riverfront has been often extolled for its fantastic beauty; in fact, "for picturesqueness and grandeur, no site in all the world can well surpass that of Benares as seen from the river Ganges" (Sherring, 1868: 9). This natural scenic beauty is referred as *Subahe Banaras* ('morning-view Banaras'). But this scene today has also a much more material dimension, which reflects the poor condition of the society (AB: 185):

> Not too much rush along the *ghats*. A few devout-typed ladies are taking their bath, and a few scoundrels are watching them. A few men are also bathing and performing oblation rites ...At the *ghats* beggars carrying begging-cups in their hands are asking alms while shouting 'Hail to the mother Ganga'. In one of the nearby *dharmashala* [pilgrims' rest-house], a few persons are still sleeping, including two poor teen-aged girls... One can see easily their perturbed saris and a glimpse of their breasts... From the other side of the Ganga, from the back of acacia trees the sun is coming up.
> In this new age, this is the 'morning-view' scene of Banaras.

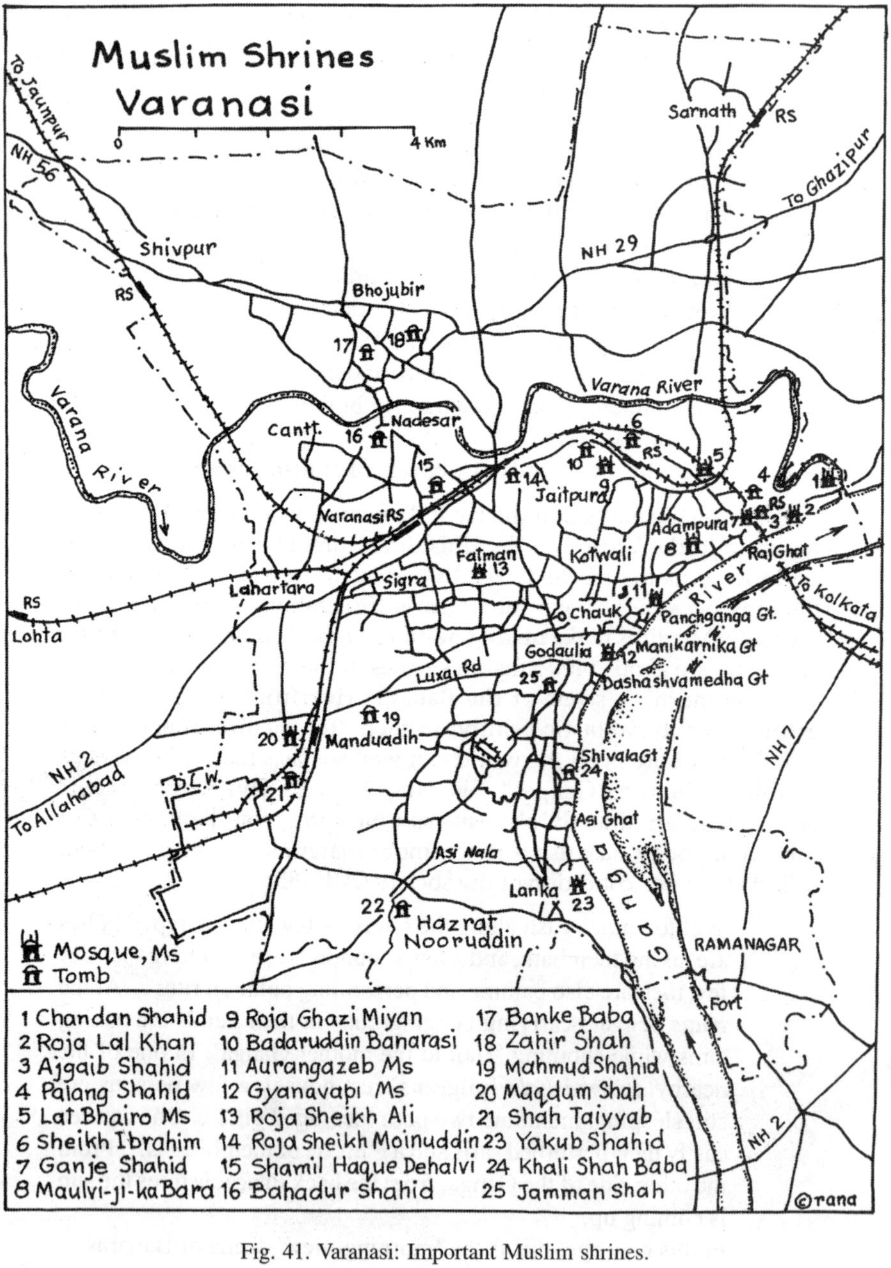

Fig. 41. Varanasi: Important Muslim shrines.

Banaras has been a great seat of learning, therefore a large number of educational institutions (*madarasas*), related to various sects and cults and named after them, are still flourishing,: "Everywhere one sees there are countless madarasas. This is a city of *masjids* [mosques], temples, *ghats* and *madarasas*. One is called Matal-ul-Ulum, and some other Mazhr-ul-Ulum. One *madarasa* is Farooqia, another Hamidia. A small university of Arabic medium has been recently opened here too" (AB: 38). The management of the *madarasas* is a subject of conflict, as many committees claim to have control over the same *madarasa*; in this way two such committees are trying to overcome the management or the same *madarasa* in Madanpura (AB: 39).

During the auspicious month of *Shravana* (July-August), a large number of Hindu fairs and festivals are held in Banaras; among such fairs, Mrityunjaya Mahadeva and Manas Mandir are famous for attracting large crowds (AB: 70). Some fairs are associated with special rituals, like Tij Mela at Ishvargangi and Shankhudhara, which are particularly related to womens' festivals. But now the glorious days of ceremonial grandeur have passed. The question arises: "Where is that scenic Kashi? Where has its glory gone?" (*ibid*). Of course, still all those fairs and festivals are held, but show and decoration have replaced to a great extent the sense of devotion and sanctity. In spite of this tendency, some unique religious celebrations are still performed in the traditional way. During *Ashvina* (September-October), Dashahara is still celebrated in its full form. In most of the *mohallas* (neighbourhoods), Ramalila is celebrated (AB: 189). In Ramanagar it is performed over a period of 31-days, where the actors, pilgrims, kings, and gods together make a world of cosmic creativity; it "is sustained every year with undiminished passion" (Kapur, 1986: 59).

Ashvina is specified for the worship of images of the goddess, especially by the Bengali citizens. In their own neighbourhood, "in Bengali Tola the creation of images of Durga is on at full speed and glamour. Beautiful images of the divine feminine. The four-handed goddess is trying to kill demons. But these clay-made goodesses don't know that many among her devotees are now trained in a 'demonic sect' " (AB: 189). By the use of satire in the last sentence the novelist expresses the defiled condition of the celebrants.

A central site for public gathering in Banaras is Benia Bag; this park serves many purposes, from public lectures of leaders to spacing the goat bazaar. Says Bismillah, "Any leader visiting the city addresses the people in Benia Park — Smt. Indira Gandhi [late Prime Minister] had organised several rallies here; if a circus comes to the city its tents are also installed here, and during Bakr-Id a great bazaar of goats is held in this park too. The whole environment smells with the bad odour of he- and she-goats. Roads are covered with layers of goat dung" (AB: 104). The multiplicity of uses of the same space and its changing mood according to the changing environmental conditions are well expressed here. This extreme character is common in Banaras. Some areas are well known for their polluted environment, like the vegetable market in Vishesarganj: "during the rainy days everything is covered by mud and dirt — all roads become dirty, muddy and polluted with a black filthy silt, and an obnoxious smell pervades all" (AB: 98-99).

Banaras has its distinct culture of courtesans, even since ancient times, but at present their condition is very degraded. They are famous for promoting the institution of open love and sex, including prostitution (Motichandra, 1973: 8). There are two main areas where most of the brothels (numbering 70) are located, i.e., Dalmandi and Shivdaspur. According to a survey, about 266 persons are engaged in this profession. In spite of the "Suppression of Immoral Traffic in Women and Girls Act 1956" (cf. Husain, 1978: 1), the profession is still well alive in the above mentioned two places as also at some new places where some women practice it on an individual level. This situation has been narrated in the book:

> At Nakkhi Ghat near Alaipur railway station (Varanasi City) a professional prostitute lives. Now prostitutes have vanished in Dalmandi. If somebody wants to enjoy sex, this is the right place to visit, otherwise one can go to Manduadih (Shivdaspur). Hanifwa visits Nakkhi Ghat; it is cheaper and nearer too. (AB: 29-30)

The above narration indicates how proximity and cheap rate are the basic considerations of the weavers who visit brothels. In fact, the poor weavers waste their savings to enjoy sex and pass their life in a bad economic condition. Tegh Ali, a poet of Banaras folk culture during the late 19th century, has depicted this issue through his mastery of satire. He is cited by the novelist in this context (AB: 71):

> I break my breakfast by chewing gram,
> While *khajja*-sweet with cream is reserved for you,
> O my darling!

The typical Banarasi breakfast is a combination of *puri/ kachauri, jelabi* (ring-shaped saffron-coloured sweet cooky), curd and mixed vegetable consisting of germinated gram, pumpkin and potato (AB: 185).

The city possesses the mystical power of imparting peace, which can be received only through a state of faith. Such spiritual glories are vividly described in ancient scriptures. This distinct quality attracts people in search for peace. Many who are sick of Western materialism come here in search of peace. Among these people Hippies are notable; one can see them roaming everywhere in the narrow lanes. "They are dressed in torn clothes, or sometimes naked faces, or wrapping their face in cotton shawls, while walking they stop and enjoy smoking cannabis, and kiss their female partners. They are scattered all-over the city" (AB: 71). Their inflow is increasing day-by-day. But at the other end the question arises: "Are they trying to make our country a slave?" (AB: 185). With their flow drug-addiction has been introduced, and the frustrated young generation are becoming addicts.

In spite of the increasing numbers of modern vehicles such as motorcycles and auto-rikshaws, the traditional man-driven rikshaws are still prevalent. And, the rikshaws-pullers have their typical way of doing their job — this is also a unique feature of Banaras: "The rikshaws-pullers of Banaras are quite notorious. If any college girl would ask they will carry them to Lanka, but to others they reply that they're engaged!" (AB 20).

Several minor aspects of this city reflect its distinctiveness. The city faces a very bad condition with the drastic rise of prices, like the whole of India: "Prices are rising by leaps and bounds. Oh! O! Allah! Is it your wish" (AB: 12). People of the city are so much tolerant that they are habituated to electric cut-offs, a most common feature in the city even today (AB: 61, 69); in spite of so many complaints, no one is eager to comply. Side-by-side, "rich persons are swallowing the poor like bigger fishes swallow the little ones" (AB: 58).

The electoral system has its own ways and network of process and functioning. The students election (in universities and colleges) presents a glimpse of such a scene, where caste-politics and charismatic leadership always pay: "Preparation for the students' union election started. But the examination of the previous session has not yet been held. Anyway the election has to be held. Sharifuddin is also contesting for a post. And now he is involved in conducting a survey of Muslim voters" (AB: 67). Caste-politics is deeply rooted in elections, and contestants always keep record of the students of their own caste. Show and public marches against the Vice-Chancellor are common features, whatever issues there may be, like admission policy, etc. Such situations always make the campus environment tense (AB: 96).

The election period has its own distinct seasonal mood. Using comparisons, the novelist exposes this condition: "Poor men get disturbed when their special festival comes closer, or their daughter's marriage comes closer, similarly rich people and lords are disturbed when elections near. ... And, many seasonal leaders are also born in this period to work in politics" (AB: 203). The presence of an M.L.A. (member of the Legislative Assembly) is an important and auspicious occasion for his supporters. He is known as the right agent to get the work done from the government offices: "Whenever Mr. M.L.A. is at home [at Banaras], each morning different persons like showmen, *gundas*, loafers, flatterers, fake-admirers, outspoken persons, and even culprits — all pay a visit there to convey their messages with the object of getting support to get their works done" (AB: 207). To make their request more convincing and strong, bribes and the offering of gifts are very common (cf. AB: 31). Similarly, several other issues of the culture of this city could be highlighted, but the novel studied here gives a major emphasis on the Julahas' lifeworld and their belief systems.

3. Julahas: Folk history, Identity and Poverty

Banaras has been famous throughout history as a river port exporting cotton and silk products. Even in 600 BCE many neighbourhoods in the city were inhabited by weavers (Kosambi, 1970: 124, 125). Patanjali (2nd century BCE) described the fine silk products from Banaras, and similar references are also found in Pali literature (Sukul, 1974: 43-44). But no Julaha is aware of his ancient past and historical lineages. In fact, *Julaha* ('the ignorant class') refers to Muslim weavers, and it "was the common name until the 19th century, afterwards they insisted that they should be called *Ansaris* after a claimed Arabic ancestor who practised the art of weaving" (Pandey, 1983: 116). The word 'Julaha' is today never used by weavers to refer to themselves, though it is often used by others. Presently "all the weavers call themselves *bunkar*, whether independent craftsman, dependent manual labour, master weaver or partly-owner of a firm. Almost all of these are Muslims and call themselves *Ansari*, also a synonym for weaver' (see Kumar, 1988: 49-52).

According to oral history, weavers claim their settlement since the Muslim period, when they migrated from Lucknow (AB: 10). But some knowledgeable weavers claim that "during the reign of Ashoka (BCE 272-232) we came from Arabia and introduced our craft, and slowly after the passage of time we made our distinct place" (AB: 228).

There are many social groups among the weavers, which may be easily identified according to spatial affinity. Some are called Alaipuria (resident of Alaipura, a neighbourhood), others Madanpuria (resident of Madanpura), Mauwallah (migrants from Mau, a town in a nearby district), and Banarasia (the old settlers of Banaras). But all are similar in profession and identity, in spite of several occurrences of group conflict (AB: 10-11).

Altogether, there are over 50,600 looms in Banaras. They are concentrated mainly in three areas: Alaipura (18,200), Madanpura (6,000) and Lallapura (3,300), where about 60,000 weavers work, according to the statistics of 1985-86 (Dube, 1986: 201). One of the characters of the novel, Iqbal trying to awaken the weavers, says "There are two hundred thousands of weavers and forty thousand looms which produce saris worth 250-300 million rupees. But in return we receive only a *lungi*, buffalo-meat, naked-poor children, and wives. Nothing more!" (AB: 228). They live in the worst state of poverty (AB: 11), but today they are seriously thinking that "should we tolerate the exploitation and torturing environment, or raise our voice against these evils" (AB: 235). In fact, whatsoever the area may be "there is no difference between Mau and Banaras. Any place is always the same for the poor" (AB: 170).

Buffalo meat is cheap (5 rupees a kilogram at the time of the novel; presently it is Rs 30 per kg; AB: 46), and the low-economic status weavers can afford it. The buffalo meat-shops at Alaipura and Machhodari are well known (AB: 87). This meat is a symbol of poverty (AB: 9, 143). Even in religious fairs like Bahadur Shahid Mela, Bakr-Id, Ghazi Miyan Mela, Muharram at Lat Bhairav, etc., varieties of dishes made of this meat are popular (AB: 62, 74, 87, 104, 124). The *kima* and meat-*pakora* of Dalmandi are well known among weavers (AB: 21, 88), which they enjoy on off-days or on special occasions.

Poverty is the greatest disease and a divine curse; sometimes weavers have not even a few rupees to pay the fee of a doctor (AB: 66). But like most poor people in India, weavers too think, "in life there are several necessities which a man never fulfils, but after death these needs automatically get reduced to a very limited quantity — a piece of cloth, water, soil, incense and camphor. Altogether these are the items needed by a corpse for its funeral rites" (AB: 172).

Their poor economic condition does not allow the Ansaris to enjoy good and costly wine. Only on particular occasions do they enjoy such wine (AB: 47). Lat Bhairav is the most important place where Julahas drink *tari* (toddy), mostly in the evening time (AB: 182). The novelist has explicitly described a drinking scene:

> Good *tari* is available in the morning — the neat and pure, but it is reserved only for those *jawans* [young people] for whom committing crimes is considered an act of pride. But those who don't want to do what society calls crime, visit such places at dawn taking benefit of the shackle of shadow. Wearing a *lungi* and carrying a toddy-ladle (*tonga*) in one hand, a cap on their head, talking about Allah, praising Pakistan and abusing India, they gather in this area like herons at the time of dawn. (AB: 15)

Economically well-off Ansaris also perform the pilgrimage to Mecca, i.e. *Hajj*; after their return they entitle themselves 'Haji' and receive more respect from their community. Sometimes one can find very funny names of Hajis, like Haji Bandar (monkey), Haji America (USA), Haji Kabaristan (graveyard), Haji Jhuthe (false) in Madanpura, and Barahim Mircha (chilli), Bau Dabba (box), etc. in Alaipura (AB: 97). Many of the Hajis practice 'going outside for pleasure and relaxation' (*bahri alang*). *Bahri alang* "is a concept related to geography, and equally a matter of mood, time and a ritualised pattern of activities" (Kumar, 1986: 42). Some Hajis, like Haji Amirulla, daily go to *bahri alang* in the morning after Fazir's prayer. (AB: 26)

4. The Banaras Weavers: Their Lifeworld

Poverty and religious rigidity go together (cf. AB 26). With the belief that poverty is the result of Allah's curse, weavers don't expect any change in their condition. They say, "What to get and what to give? What happened in the ancient past, will continue today. One can't change and challenge any rule of Allah! Oh! Who was poor, will continue to be poor in spite of several attempts. To whom Allah made rich will always be rich. Getting loans can't remove poverty. Beggary and being lord of a kingdom, both are blessings of Khuda [God]" (AB: 44). Weavers feel that if life passes by Allah's wish, certainly in future too it will go on similarly, and they feel themselves damned (AB: 125). Searching for an alternative place to get rid of exploitation would never show the way as everywhere exists the exploitative environment (AB: 127).

The hope that some divine power can help to improve their poor condition encourages superstitions. The weavers feel that Chandan Shahid would certainly give his help to form a co-operative society (AB: 46). Moreover, "everybody in the Julaha community believes that a ghost has possessed Rehanwa, therefore it is a hard task to get a groom for her. Father Bashir is unable to think what to do and what not to do. Age and time both are passing slowly, slowly" (AB: 99). The reliance on shamans provides a means by which unexpressed and inexpressible psychic states can be immediately expressed (cf. Levi-Strauss, 1963; 167-205). The auspicious Melas (fairs) related to shamans record many such activities. Of these Melas, Bahadur Shahid, near Kachahari on each Jummerat [the eve of Thursday in the month of Radjan] and Makhdum Shah at Akbarpur in Faizabad are notable (AB: 74, 82-83).

To have a hysterical personality is also a common feature among Julahas. They feel that "hysterical attacks are the result of the possession of some malignant ghost, and can only be cured with the help of shamans and faith-healers" (AB: 60). In fact, "to be the helpless victim of one's society, the stars, one's unconscious, or mental disease are now our culturally sponsored myths of passivity and this forms the basis of current hysterical alternatives" (Krohn, 1978: 188). The therapy system based on shamans is related to "a much larger system of knowledge which the Muslims call *ilm-i-ruhani,* or soul knowledge", and the mystic power received through it is called *ruhani-takat*, soul force (Kakar, 1982: 32, 35). Poverty, illiteracy, and a strong sense of superstitions in taboos and rituals altogether make the Julahas' lifeworld.

With the passage of time "a lot of changes took place in the city of Banaras, and in the country or even on the international scene. Thus, many modern means and ways have been introduced, but in no way the mentality of the middle class Julahas has changed" (AB: 142). Their name 'Julaha' itself reflects their identity as 'the ignorant class'; furthermore, they are believed to never be loyal even to their parents (AB: 143).

The worst part of religious rigidity can be seen during the conflicts between two groups of Muslims, i.e. Shia (believing Ali as the Prophet's successor), and Sunni (orthodox). The mosque and graveyard in Dosipur muhalla is always a subject of conflict between these two groups (AB: 214). Such conflicts are considered to be a good occasion to superimpose superiority of one's group for political and economic gains. Jealousy is another common evil among Julahas; in fact, "no neighbour or kin would be happy to see a peaceful family" (AB: 232).

The competition in giving donations for constructing mosques, provides on the other hand an opportunity to show their economic status. The pityful Julahas offer their valuables and ornaments as donation; one should not be left far behind! The house of Allah is under construction, let us donate unendingly, and by this merit a seat will be reserved in heaven (cf. AB: 15). But ultimately a poor Julaha, in spite of his will, is unable to give a substantial amount (cf. AB: 17). The hierarchical approach to interpersonal relationships, as in organisational activities, is clearly visible. Competition in this context helps in the formation of various groups and associations. In Banaras, "there are many religious associations (*anjumans*): Anjuman Shams-e-Ilahi, Anjumane-Irfania, Anjumane-Ilahia, Anjumane-Bachkania, Anjumane-Islamia Kadimi, Anjumane-Gulamane Rasul, etc. Attended by young boys of age 10-12 years old to the middle-aged of 40 years, these anjumans invoke the preaching of the holy *Quran* as revealed by Hajrat Muhammed and his four disciples...These associations also organise lyric-competitions based on the original composition and music and are awarded accordingly" (AB: 205).

The economic scarcity and tough life make the home-atmosphere disturbed; and "if the home-atmosphere is so bad, whatever form of healing one will use, no effect can be expected" (AB: 110). Such conditions put obstacles in the education of the girls; girls are not acquainted with the changes taking place in the rest of the world, neither are they familiar with their glorious history and culture (AB: 234). Very few Julahas are familiar with their own great saint Kabir (CE 1398-1518) who worked as a weaver and tried to awaken his pupils (*ibid*). Presently, "What to say about our mothers, ourselves, our fathers, our wive's native families and their in-laws families — wherever or whosoever, no one has peace and ease; all the (Julahas) are leading a suffocating and filthy life." (AB: 145).

The owners of the sari-firms and the middlemen always exploit and cheat the dependent Julahas, while they claim to be honest and humane. This reminds one of the Orwellian utopia: "Oh! This is strange! Those are really dishonest, claim them as honest; those really thieves, are accepted worthy! Could you please let me know if any Seth is presenting his duplicate products as duplicate? No, never! ... These owners have a great mastery in turning duplicate products into real ones, and with this art they are doing good business" (AB: 229). Additionally, "so many illegal concessions are also taken from us. Those who work as labour at the owners' house they are the worst victim" (AB: 230). Even their own kinsmen who are in the medical profession cheat the pitiful Julahas, while they hope they will get more sympathy and support from their kinsmen: "He hopes that, being a Muslim, the doctor will take more care of a fellow Muslim patient" (AB: 211). But this illusion was washed away when that doctor cheated the poor Matin (AB: 212). His fellow Muslim doctor, Ansari, refused to see Matin's wife in spite of several requests and appeals to his humanity (AB: 75). But Doctor Gupta, a Hindu, readily went to see Matin's sick wife without even charging the fee (AB: 76). In fact, here the question of caste and religious affiliation does not arise, but rather the sense of human service.

Most of the Julahas suffer due to a political-religious stigma. Lack of national feeling is a most common feature. "When Pakistan defeated India [in cricket] every Muslim boy in the area began to dream of being Imran Khan [a great cricketer from Pakistan]. In opposition, there is not one but several Gavaskars [India's prime cricketer]" (AB: 37). The novelist presents a scene of Muslims being sympathetic to Pakistan after India's defeat in cricket (AB: 184):

> The betel-leaf (*pan*) shop was overcrowded. Kikki, the shop-keeper was speedily busy in preparing *pan* as he was murmuring something. Everybody was cheerful and smiling. Latif was sure that Pakistan had won the cricket match. Whenever Pakistan wins, Kikki offers *pan* to everybody free of cost; but the moment he hears about the defeat of Pakistan he will close down his shop.

During peak floods, the Muslims get a malignant pleasure: "When Muslims see a house-roof or a cow or buffalo floating in the Ganga, they feel so happy as if they had seen the moon on the occasion of the Id" (AB: 241), because of their religious animity with Hindus.

But, after all the worldly activities will not stop at all:

> Whatever drastic changes may occur in the national political structure, whatever important person may die, whatever accidents may happen, whether the most honest be defeated or the dishonest rewarded, in spite of all, the societal functioning would never be stopped in any way, like growth of grass every year, and like silk-worms eat mulberry leaves and precacious silk threads taken from their bodies. (AB: 124)

Similarly, the Julahas' lifeworld is also passing away in the river of change.

5. Marriage, Divorce, and Education

The Julahas who belong to the middle-class always attempt to create a balance between their state of economic suppression and the social liabilities they have to fulfil. As Bismillah says, "liabilities and helplessness had made him [father] so weak that he was unable to raise his voice against social evils, and ultimately the marriage was fixed [his teen-aged daughter's marriage was settled with an aged groom already having five children]" (AB: 99).

The popularity of marriage between cousins among the Muslims helps to reduce its cost to a certain degree. It has been observed: "Among Muslims all over India cousin marriage is performed. It is complementary to that of planned hypergamy, and demand of reciprocity of mates between two families regardless of their material and social standing. Cousin marriage reduces costs to both parties" (Miller, 1981: 155-156). But there are also examples of some rich men among the group of master weavers or owners of sari-firms who have a kept-woman (cf. AB: 26).

The daughter is mostly considered as an economic burden, as on the occasion of her marriage dowry is an essential need among the low class Muslims, as with Hindus. Similarly, like Hindus, they have no right to get a share in the parental property. Presenting to the reader a marriage farewell song, the novelist using similes narrates the feelings of a bride; the bride says (AB: 102):

> O my friend! Why my father is
> sending me to some other's village.
> To my brother he gave the parental house,
> and to me, eviction from home.
> From one forest to another I'm passing away
> and became thirsty at the end.
> From the palanquin, out of veil I've seen
> there is no more father, nor his village.

The system of frequent divorce and the complete predominance of husbands upon their wives is the saddest spot on the Islamic tradition. Divorce is a very common feature among Julahas: "What right a women has in our society? Whenever you think, push her back with your foot and get a divorce! What more use one wants of a woman? Cleaning the threads, cooking and washing dishes, giving sexual enjoyment in bed, producing children, and services in all the respects. In all these acts, if she makes some offense, then one can follow the rules of Islam and say loudly that he has divorced her — Divorced! Divorced!! Divorced [*talak*]!!!" (AB: 57, also 83). And ultimately, Islamic rules and society will sanction it. In another way divorce produces a psychic state of having committed a criminal act, as the husband always feels disturbed after getting divorce (cf. AB: 183). This social evil is like leprosy on the body of society (AB: 174). The mental state of the husband after giving divorce is comparable to the one of a sick monkey watching the ground in isolation (AB: 188). On the other side, the woman too becomes completely discarded and alone, deeply feeling the lack of her husband and children; weeping is the only means of consolation that she has (AB: 155).

According to Islamic tradition, a woman once divorced can't be accepted again by the same husband, until she is re-married to somebody else and passes at least one night with him, followed by divorce from him (AB: 65). But the question remains unanswered. How can one suddenly break the sentimental relation! How love and affection can be thrown into the dust within a second while saying *'divorced'* three times? Is it possible to break love like an unripe thread with this pronouncement? No, never. But the fear of social traditions, religious taboos and the compulsion to follow the ways of one's predecessors altogether prevent the challenge to this stigma. Those who challenge it face the danger of not being accepted by the community (AB: 231). And ultimately they abandon themselves to their destiny.

Illiteracy and lack of consciousness towards education are other negative features prevailing among Julahas. A psychic fear about the lack of opportunities even after education restricts their desire to get proper education. Julahas feel that "modern education is unable to open new ways for our children, as it cannot help in the art of weaving; moreover, our children are not going to be employed as judges or district collectors" (AB: 158). The Islamic education, of course, is considered to be worth paying for, with a view to being aware about the teachings of Islam, but it never helps to improve their economic condition even a little over the condition of bare survival. Therefore, "teachers in the *madarasas* work as weavers in the day hours, and teach in the school after dusk" (AB: 40).

The community has established some Ansari schools, where teaching is performed from grade 1st up to intermediate class (12th). In spite of all the facilities and encouragement found there, the Julaha children are not benefited by it, neither are they serious to get education (AB: 91). Cheating, manipulations and competition for administrative supremacy are common in these *madarasas* (cf. AB: 27). But at least these institutions familiarise the Julahas with the great Julaha poet of the 15th century, Kabir, and the present Urdu lyric writer, Nazir Banarasi (AB: 13).

6. The Julahas' Belief System

The Holy *Quran* prescribes five duties for every Muslim: to believe only in one God, i.e. Allah, and that Mohammed is his prophet, to pray (*namaz*) five times daily, to give alms, to fast during the month of Ramajan, and to make a pilgrimage to Mecca (Hajj) at least once in a lifetime if at all possible (Makky, 1978: 39). Of course, every Muslim certainly tries to follow these duties, but people also vacillate in their obedience to the rules. During the month of Ramajan (the month of fasting) Julahas use to take tea behind a curtain at a reliable shop, confident that no other fellow is watching (AB: 80). The pilgrimage to Mecca, Hajj, provides religious merit and also the opportunity to bring foreign goods: "The world is going fast! One has to take care of his children. [While starting for Hajj pilgrimage] My wife has asked for two lady-watches, my daughter has asked for a tape recorder, my son has warned and requested for a Seiko-brand wrist watch and also for a camera — all to be brought during the return. How can I deny it to them? After all, no sin is there; I will bring all these things for my own home, not for smuggling or for sale, then why should Allah be angry?" (AB: 176). But the custom officers will probably charge a duty, therefore Haji Habibulla was mentally disturbed.

The belief system is fully dependent upon the concept of faith. If the Mufti (*moulvi*) announces that he has seen the Moon on the first day of the waxing moon, everybody will believe him (AB: 87). In a similar way they fix the dates for other festivals and religious happenings, including Urs of Sheikh Tayyab Shah Banarasi in Manduadih, which is held between Id and Little Id (AB: 91).

Their faith is so strong that even in the construction of a house and the selection of an architectural design religious code is given prominence: "Now this house of 'English-cum-Ansari Style' has been finally constructed, and with the advice of Seth Gajadhar Prasad the 'entrance-ceremony' has also been performed, purely in the Islamic way" (AB: 239). A recitation from the *Quran* is followed by a grand feast attended even by reputed persons of the city (*ibid*). Such feasts are a good occasion to show one's prosperity and to get popularity. Also, "the Haji after performing the Hajj pilgrimage distributes sweets, earth from Arabia, sacred water and even chocolate — an additional modern item" (AB: 178), and guests and receivers pay their obligation to the Haji; why should they not be obliged, after having so easily got offerings from the holy land of Arabia!

Animal sacrifice "commemorates Abraham's willingness to sacrifice his son", and "also symbolises the believer's preparedness to give what is dearest to him. It marks the Muslim renunciation of idolatrous sacrifice" (Makky, 1978: 41). The festival of Bakr-Id is considered to be the festival of sacrifice. On this occasion a large mass of Muslims gather to purchase animals for the sacrifice. Some areas are famous for this specific animal fair: Kachhi Bagh, Bari Bazaar, Chhitanpura and Pathanitola are famous for buffaloes (AB: 103), while the biggest bazaar for goats is held at Benia Bagh (AB: 104). Of course, immigrant Pathans have always encouraged goat-sacrifice albeit Ansaris / Julahas are fond of buffalo meat. Moreover, the sacrifice of a camel is also ritually essential, therefore every year a camel is sacrificed in a particular Muslim neighbourhood (AB: 105). With the belief that this sacrifice has a connection with Hajrat Ibrahim [Abraham] (AB: 106), they usually think that "the meat of a sacrificed buffalo can never be indigestive however much one will eat" (AB: 108). The Islamic rule that "even seven persons can share the purchase of an animal for sacrifice" (AB: 106) relieves the poor Julahas from this economic burden.

The environment that follows Bakr-Id reminds one of hell (AB: 107):

> Smell! Obnoxious Smell!
> Bakr-Id has passed, but its smell still remains in the air. Everywhere, there are garbage pits where tons and tons of remains and leftovers of sacrificed buffaloes are laying rotting. Somewhere their veins are decaying, somewhere filthy excreta from discarded stomachs came out. Somewhere the remaining hoofs of baby-buffaloes, and at other places the decomposed eyes of a buffalo. The whole environment is a scene of filth.

Muharram is a month dedicated to mourning in memory of the death of Ḥassan and Husain for the Shia branch of Muslims. During the period of the waxing moon, every evening wrestling-shows and competitions are organised, mainly in such places as Shahid Baba in Koila Bazaar and Chhitanpura near Iman Chauk; other places are Kachhi Bagh, Bari Bazaar and Bakrabad mohallas (AB: 110). During the 10th to the 13th day of the waxing moon, the *Tajia* (a decorated replica of the tomb of these two martyrs, Hassan and Husain) is carried out in procession. The Tajia of Langre Umar Hafij is made out of pieces of diamonds and precious stones. The Tajia is kept under a tent on the 9th day and the procession continues till the 13th day of Muharram (AB: 112; cf. Fig. 42).

Muharram is the festival of grief and compassion, therefore many youngsters show their feelings by physically torturing themselves. In

Fig. 42. Muharram procession (after Prinsep, 1833).

fact, "these youngsters want to show the depth of their piety and grief for the murder of Husain. Shia youngsters even cut their faces with blades, which results in clearly visible blood marks on their faces. Many of them badly hurt their back with iron-chains" (AB: 115).

Among other celebrations, the ones that the Julahas most commonly attend are the *mela* (fair) of Ghazi Miyan, which is held for a week during the Hindu month of *Jyeshtha* (May-June) in the *mohalla* of the same name. The *mela* starts on Sunday at the graveyard of Ghazi Miyan (in Bari Bazaar) and is shifted to a new location every evening — "On Monday at Nakkhi Ghat, on Tuesday at Kachhi Bagh, on Wednesday at Chhitanpura, on Thursday at Benia Bagh and on Friday at the Purana Pul. In this way the whole week becomes a scenic period" (AB: 61; cf. Fig. 43).

The *mela* of Chandan Shahid is also popular among the Julahas: "This *mela* is held every year on Thursday in the Hindu month of *Chaitra* (March-April). There is a graveyard near the confluence of the Ganga and the Varana, known as Chandan Shahid (Fig. 44). Credit needs to be given to the Muslims of India for searching so many *shahids* (martyrs of Islam) in the soil of this country, who project their mystic power to the common men on each Thursday. Chandan Shahid is one of them" (AB: 46). It is believed that this site has the mystic power to get relief from endogenous madness, which occurs because of excessive worry, anxiety, or by some physical illness, as well as disorders caused by demonic spirits (Kakar, 1982: 97). With this faith Matin visited the tomb of Chandan Shahid and offered him flowers and sweets, probably his blessings will help in getting the co-operative society formed (AB: 46).

The Julahas of Banaras also pay a visit to the *dargah* (tomb) of Shah Qasim Sulaimani (1549-1606), an Afghan saint and take an active part in the Urs (ceremonial commemoration); this dargah is in Chunar, about 40 km south of their city. He was born at Peshawar and at the age of 27 took to an ascetic life and performed the pilgrimage to Mecca and Medina. During Akbar's reign (1556-1605) he was not molested further than having his place of residence fixed at Lahore; but on the accession of Jahangir his enemies represented to the king the danger of allowing Shah Qasim to attract so large a number of followers. The saint did not please Emperor Jahangir who put him in prison at Chunar in 1606, where he finally died the following year. The annual offerings and fairs take place in the period of 17th-21st days of the Islamic month of *Jamadi-ul-awwal*, and also on every Thursday during March-April. All classes and sections of society irrespective of religion and caste attend these fairs and prayers (cf. Singh and Rana, 2002: 246). This

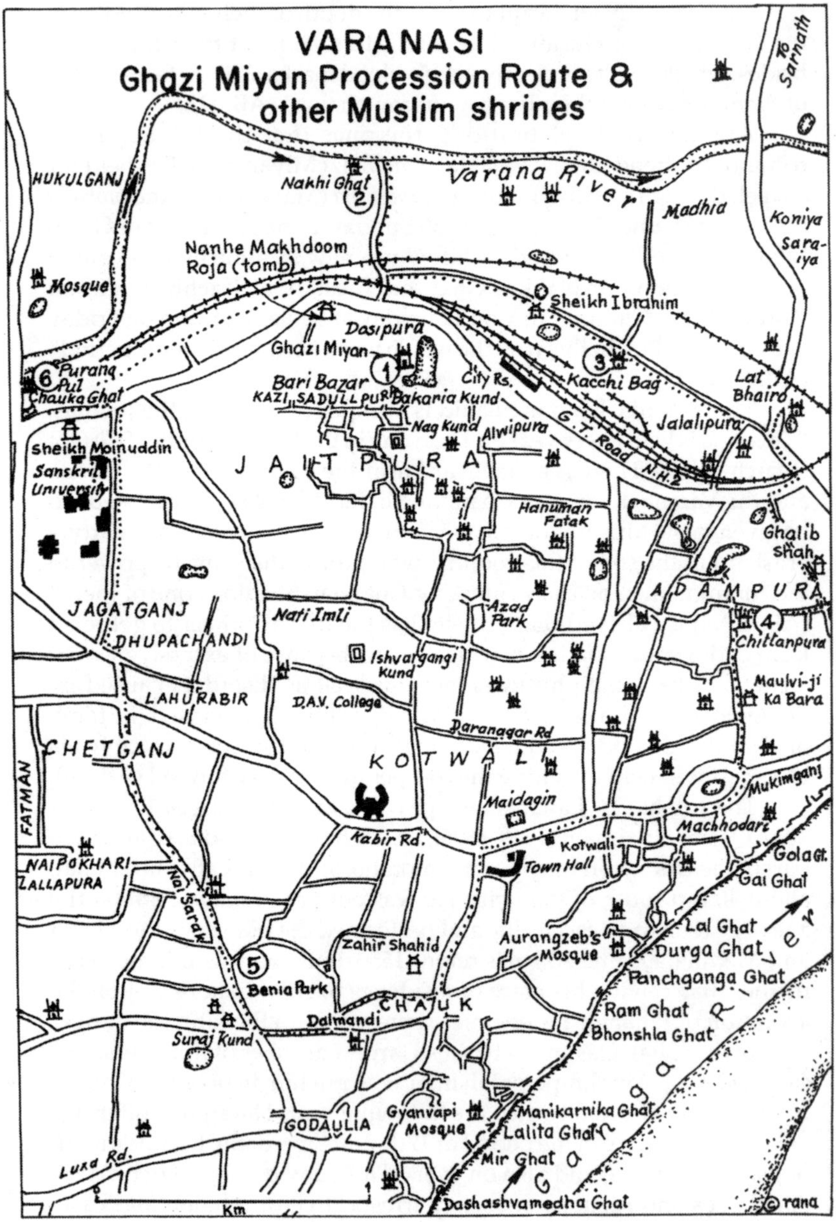

Fig. 43. Ghazi Miyan procession route, & other Muslim shrines.

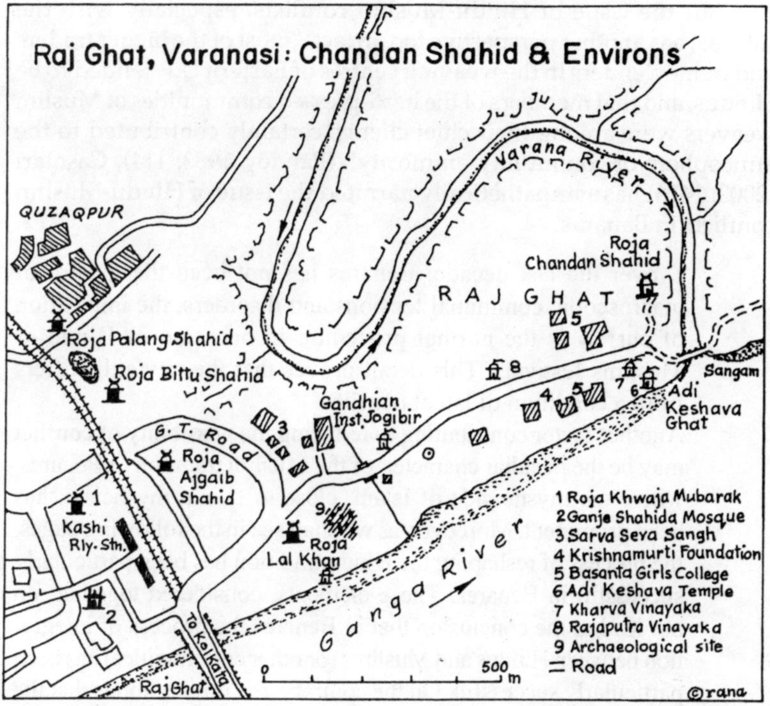

Fig. 44. Raj Ghat, Varanasi: Chandan Shahid & other Muslim Shrines.

annual fair provides an opportunity to go outside for relaxation and picnic, obtaining also a religious benefit (AB: 147).

7. Hindu-Muslim Conflicts

The religious contrast between Hinduism and Islam, of course, encourages group conflict. This takes its worst shape with the involvement of people who have vested interests. Group conflicts between Hindus and Muslims, and also between Shias and Sunnis, can be seen side-by-side. Even the issue of supremacy of power promotes group conflicts, and this reaches a climax when the prayer ground is being converted into a war-field (AB: 33):

> A very moment before, this was a holy site for prayer, and now it is converted into a battlefield. But whatever it may be, prayer or war, a person having false conceptions in his mind will always be in his own world of obsession.

But the issue of Hindu-Muslim conflicts, especially with the Julahas, has another perspective too. In fact, "most of the bigger traders and moneylenders in the weaving centres of Eastern U.P. tended to be Hindus, and that members of the hard-pressed communities of Muslim weavers were among their chief clients, certainly contributed to the atmosphere of community animosity" (Pandey, 1983: 114). Casolari (2002: 1416) has sympathetically narrated the issue of Hindu-Muslim conflicts in Banaras:

> ...over the last decade, Benares has not been the theatre of macroscopic communal tensions and disorders, the imposition of curfew is the normal procedure in occasion of Hindu or Muslims festivals. This detail proves that the city still suffers from a condition of latent conflict.
>
> Another factor contributing to reducing the possibility of conflict may be the peculiar character of the Muslim tradition in Benares, where the mystic side of Islam, close to Hindu mysticism, has been prominent. Moreover, as we shall see in the following pages, the process of reshaping the Hindu tradition has been particularly successful in Benares. These elements, considered together, do not lead to the conclusion that in Benares the process of integration between Hindus and Muslims (or other communities) has been particularly successful. On the contrary, the impression is that the hegemony of the Hindu community has been overwhelming.

The religious celebrations with procession are the main occasions for Hindu-Muslim riots. Among them the Hindu's Dashahara and the Muslim's Muharram are notable; "on both occasions religions come on to the road. So openly religion stands keeping its head downwards. In spite of this, people say it is the road to truth, the ultimate truth. And for this truth people give their life!"...Such riots are now common, therefore, "it is sufficient to say that a conflict between Hindus and Muslims started. In this country now the direct meaning of conflict between Hindus and Muslims is riot" (AB: 191). Holi, the colour festival of the Hindus, is also an occasion of conflict. If a Hindu throws colour on a Muslim, even by mistake, this often results in conflict and tension; but there are also tolerant Muslims (AB: 45-46).

There are two streets in Madanpura mohalla, one of which is dominated by Hindus and the other by Muslims. Hindus want to pass their procession with the icon of Durga by the Muslim dominated street. And "Muslims don't want it, otherwise their faith may be in danger. In the Hindu dominated street Muslims built an Imam Chauk and they put their Tajia there, but Hindus don't want it, otherwise their faith may be challenged" (AB: 190).

In order to control the riots, the administration usually declares curfew in those areas more prone to troubles: "On the occasion of [Hindu's] Dashahara and [Muslim's] Muharram there [Kheri Bag] happened a great riot, which resulted in casualties to hundreds of people. In the language of the administration, there was curfew for ten continuous days in the 'sensitive mohallas'— twenty-four hours a day. Many died due to lack of water. Corpses started decomposing, but there was no relaxation even for performing their funeral rites" (AB: 167). Such riots cause immense damage on the business of weaving communities wheresoever they may be — Mau, Azamgarh, Ghazipur and Banaras.

The ancient sites of Hindu temples, which were demolished by Muslim rulers, are also centres of Hindu-Muslim conflicts. In 1669, by order of the Mughal emperor Aurangzeb, three most important temples of Banaras were completely demolished, and on their sites mosques were built: Vishvanatha, Lat Bhairava and Beni Madhava temples. On the occasion of the Muslim festival Bakr-Id a large crowd of Muslims meets at Jnanavapi mosque (beside Vishvanatha Temple); this creates a tense atmosphere (AB: 89). According to a folk tradition, a Brahmin scholar of Persian wrote a poem in which he satirises Islam (AB: 90):

> O king! Look at the mystery of our shrine,
> If it's demolished it becomes the house of Allah.

The prayer of Id is performed in the Fatman Idgah at Lat Bhairava: "In fact, the importance of Lat Bhairava becomes more auspicious because there exists a temple in this mosque-compound. And the existence of a temple in the compound of a mosque is possible only in this city of Banaras. It is said about this place that an English Collector had ordered that *puja* [Hindu worship] and *namaz* [Muslim prayer] both should be performed here, but it never happened so" (AB: 89). The calm acceptance of Muslims for prayer by Hindus shows their sense of tolerance.

The occasions of Hindu-Muslim conflicts and riots are considered to be a good time for political leaders to gain popularity, especially during the period immediately before legislative elections (AB: 193). As "counter-answer to Hindu's shouting 'Hail to Lord Shiva, Hail to Lord Shiva' (*Hara Hara Mahadev*), Muslims raise their slogan, 'Allah is the only universal Lord, Allah is great' (*Nar-e-Takbir, Allah-ho-akbar*)" (AB: 194). To get cheap popularity political leaders organise assemblies of Urdu lyrics, to be attended both by Muslims and Hindus (AB: 197).

Dumont in his book cites the discerning observation of Beni Prasad to the effect that "the difficult transition to a democratic ideology was left entirely in the hands of the middle classes, where rivalry developed between members of the two communities 'for the few available posts' " (Dumont, 1980: 319, citing Prasad 1945). This can be easily discernible in the weaving business where hierarchical control is a common feature.

8. Exploitative World

Hierarchical inequality is common among the weavers; moreover the "growing gap between requirements and availability of skilled personnel" (Lipton, 1977: 177) further promotes inequality, leading to more exploitation of the bottom class.

The persons involved in weaving can be classified into five hierarchical groups from lower to higher: *dependent weavers* working under another's roof, *dependent weavers* working in their own home, *independent weavers, master weavers,* and *owners* of sari-firms (see Kumar, 1988). These persons are further connected with a chain of middlemen brokers (*dalal*), commission agents (*Kothidar* or *Adhatiya/ Kothiwal*), wholesalers (*thokdar*), and retailers (*khudra vyapari*). The upgrading of a person from one group to another depends upon the skill and strategy he has, but in this march of competition many have also failed: "Some persons started their career as labourers and became workers, then shared weavers, sellers and sometimes owners. But Matin was a person who from shared weaver fell down to labourer" (AB 77).

Most of the times, the owners behave in a harsh way with the workers: "Loom owners never give rest to the weavers, rather they always scold them for their slow work" (AB: 98). As many weavers are in debt with the owners (*Girasthas*), they feel relaxed in their dealings with them: "*Girasthas* always wait for such moment in which some client-weaver will visit them for asking a loan! Getting back the debt gives a particular feeling of enjoyment which one can't get from other acts!" (AB: 48).

The owners also give mental torture to the weavers by delaying payments: "For paying the cost of saris, Seths [owners] generally give cheques which can be cashed only after a month or so, but the poor Julahas need immediate money to purchase goods for their daily subsistence" (AB: 139).

The business of making duplicate products and their sale at the price of original ones maintain the counterbalance between agents and brokers: 'Duplicate pieces of Banarasi saris reach the middlemen and agents through brokers, and they get more benefit. Many Muslim brokers perform this duty only on a very low commission as they can't do any other job' (AB: 92).

In spite of raising voices against exploitation, nothing seems to improve. For reducing the price paid for the saris, Seths always find numerous defects in their manufacture (AB: 19). The owners cut the sum of donations done for political support from the cheque they pay to the Julahas (AB: 209). Most of the Julahas have to suffer this exploitative cycle, which always starts soon after every legislative election (AB: 213).

Julahas felt the need to form a co-operative society through which they would obtain an optimal benefit for their work, but to create such a society needed so many complicated channels that the Julahas ultimately failed (AB: 20-21). They fully realise that the whole network of brokers, merchants, loom owners, shop keepers and Seths all exploit them at different levels in different ways (AB: 223). For their benefit the government passed several laws and rules, but there are many loop-holes through which they continue to be exploited (AB: 220). By being more aware of legality, by their monetary supremacy and by taking help or bribery, the owners and Seths make their own co-operative society, which results in finally stopping even the idea of opening a Julahas' co-operative society (AB: 117-120).

Julahas are aware of the situation, but there does not exist any way to escape from it: "What to do! No alternative at all! Everything that we have is part of our debt — loom or silk. We have to rely only on our physical strength and skill. Even the governmental loom agencies are the ancestral property of loom owners?" (AB: 158). With the passage of time the burden of indebtedness increases, and it reached a stage when all the other doors for getting out are closed (AB: 176). Having these feelings, they arrived at the conclusion that "life is meant to eat and be merry! Somehow let us pass it" (AB: 221). But this is not the end of the story. If there is a seed of awakening, there lies a ray of hope too. Only crying will not resolve anything, rather mass awakening is essential.

9. Realisation and Raising Voices

Julahas live in the hope of future prospects. "When will that day finally come when a common weaver labourer will have the right to live a good life? He should be treated not like a labourer, but as a great artist or craftsman..!" (*Never*!) (AB: 78). The monotheist teaching of Islam is so much affirmed and strong (cf. Dumont, 1980: 32) that a Julaha feels that no one can rise in this profession because of the fact that their destiny is the subject of Allah's wish. Even if his prosperity increases, he would only be an 'Ansari' — what more? "But becoming an Ansari of Banaras is not a greater thing than being a Julaha. Therefore, he wishes that [his son] Ekbal should get a proper education and will become not a clerk, but an officer!" (AB: 64). However, the regularity and requirements of the daily life can't be stopped; one has to continue his work to maintain his subsistence:

> From Chittanpura to Kachhi Bag and from Madanpura to Bajardiha, all the work is going on as in the past. Everything is going on its usual way also in Semra, Bahadurpur, Lohta, Lahartara, Pandeypur, Harahua, Chaubepur and the nearby villages. Weavers from the countryside, both Hindus and Muslims, come daily in the morning to Banaras to work on looms owned by some one or the other, and for few coins they sell their craftsmanship and hard labour. (AB: 123)

Domestic affairs and the bad economic position together suppress the Julaha's life, which results in disappointment and distress:

> My wife is a patient of tuberculosis; she needs nutritious food. The Seth usually finds defects in my saris. The government continuously increases the price of goods. How can one operate this vehicle of life? (AB: 19)

Education is considered as a strong tool for change. "But what can one gain after getting education in an English school? Will he have to do his own professional job? Let him be a little older, he would go to Golghar carrying sari-boxes" (AB: 35). But some other father feels: "What will be the result of getting education in an Islamic school [*madarasa*]? Will he have to become a Maulvi? Or will he move from one mosque to another throughout his life with a long beard and a mat? No! Not at all!" (AB: 35).

There exists a third line of thought too: "Getting education in a *madarasa* has several benefits. During the day hours he will have free time to help in weaving. We do not have to die like Matin. We have our own loom" (AB: 35). In course of time "the rich are becoming richer, and the poor poorer". This has been perceived by Julahas:

"Those devoted to their craftsmanship and hard labour are mostly poor, and the middlemen are becoming richer" (AB: 216). The basic root-causes are the structure and taboos of the society as ordained by the Islamic laws, therefore "change in the system is the first essential task before doing anything. Let us remove social evils first" (AB: 217).

Under the skilfully managed network of the bourgeois, Julahas are unable to get a new way of relief or even the required leadership. Julahas have lost faith in the leaders: "He is now one of the leaders of the Communist Party. He was unable to do anything else, but now he is a leader!" (AB: 175). With false assurances, community leaders manage to get the votes of the Julahas, but after winning the election they don't care about them anymore: "Community leaders attract the Julahas with the false assurance that they will fight against the Seths and the middle-agents, and [with this propaganda] ultimately they win their game" (AB: 176).

For benefit, assistance and help "there are about two hundred co-operative units in Banaras helping to purchase goods and to sell products. ...But most of these are false units" (AB: 227). Of course, "the government has given a loan of Rs 640 millions to 29 societies. And 61 societies received a grant of Rs. 2,578,000 from the Reserve Bank of India, but nobody knows where the money has been spent at all. We know that you have not received a single rupee. The whole sum was distributed among the middlemen" (AB: 229). Strike "is considered to be the only way to to give strength to their demands, but it always deteriorates the condition of the poor. During a strike in Banaras, Mau and Mubarakpur in 1981, all the weavers faced a terrible situation" (AB: 135). Such issues were also raised in the newspapers, but no positive results occurred (AB: 136).

Revolution can only be started by the young generation that can't abide by the old rigid rules (AB: 236). Even the Islamic rules need to be challenged: "All are superstitions. ...All the rites are made by their organisers to continue their profession of cheating and getting economic gains. We have to do what is right..." (AB: 225).

10. An Epilogue: Towards a Conclusion

In its vividity, clarity and lived experiences, Abdul Bismillah's novel is a worthy portrait of the weavers' world, written with fearlessness and sympathy for their craftsmanship. With this perspective, he has been successful in describing the inside realities. Their present condition has not changed much since the late 19th century, according to a report presented in 1907: "In the majority of cases the weaver at present lives a hand-to-mouth existence; his method of working, the appliances he uses, and the amount he has to pay to the moneylender to obtain money to purchase his materials, cut down his earnings to such a narrow limit that these are barely sufficient to supply his daily wants" (Pandey, 1983: 108). Each and every aspect of this report has been fully described in the novel with experiences, expressions and clarity. In fact, a balance has always been maintained between insiders' feelings and outsiders' reflections.

Through his intimate sensing the novelist has yielded understanding as well as a first hand knowledge of the weavers' world. A realist and sympathetic treatment of their sufferings go together in Bismillah's novel. The novelist expects that in the end every weaver will realise his capacity and capability — this would be the real achievement of the novel. The novel ends in this spirit with Kabir's provoking verse (AB: 246):

> O Saints! The storm of knowledge's blowing now,
> All the walls of illusion are falling down
> and deception is unable to protect them.

11. Basic References

Bismillah, Abdul 1986. ***Jhini Jhini Bini Chadaria***. (*The Threadbare Woven Shawl*). A novel in Hindi. Rajkamal Prakashan, New Delhi.

Bismillah, Abdul 1996. *The Son of the Loom*. Translation of *Jhini Jhini Bini Chadariya* from the Hindi original by Rashmi Givind. Modern Indian Novels in Translation Series. Macmillan India Ltd, Madras.

~12~

THE MODERN LIFEWORLD: SHIVPRASAD SINGH'S *The Street Turns Yonder*

1. Introduction

With the help of Shivprasad Singh's novel ***The Street Turns Yonder*** (*Gali Age Murati Hai*, in Hindi, 1st ed. 1974; 2nd ed. 1991, hereafter referred as **ST:**), it is attempted to provide different perspectives on the lifeworld of modern Varanasi. The novel contains vivid accounts of the cultural personality and lifeworld of Banaras. The city is perceived as the holiest city of Hindus and as a microcosm of India. On one side, it is well known for its sanctimony, sacred glories and heritage, and on the other for theft, roguery, *masti* ('joie de vivre'), *mauj* (delight), *phakarapan* (carefreeness), and *akhkharpan* (headstrongness). Due to the high-intensity of its spiritual magnetism, people from different parts of India have settled in the city and have formed a mosaic of life styles and lifeworlds, called *Banarasi*, yet maintaining their age-old traditions and regional linkages (Singh, 1980: 43). In attempting to critically expose this point, Shivprasad Singh has been successful in projecting the multiple aspects of the cultural personality and lifeworld of Varanasi.

The cartographic view of the cultural landscape and the identification of places mentioned have been presented through maps, both existent and perceived. Additionally, the novelist's cognitive maps of the city are drawn at two levels — memory-based, and knowledge-based. The novelist's utopian man has been sketched out and compared with Mandeville (Singh, 1985: 296-297, 310-311). To widen the horizon of observations and descriptions, the milieu and meanings are compared at some places with contemporary works.

2. The Novelist's Urban Experience and Criticism of the Book

In this chapter, *The Street Turns Yonder* is considered as a base onto which to project place and modern society. Here his main intention is to capture the temporal theme of student unrest in Banaras.

Fig. 45. Shivprasad Singh

He worked on modern society in the 1970s using the students' reactions of the late 1960s against the present system of education and the use of English for teaching as his core themes. That is why there appears to be a discontinuity in describing the landscape and culture of the city. The novelist feels that since the city has been the strongest seat of learning and education, this theme should occupy the central position and that social degradation and students' reactions are the result of that time. He further stresses the need and demand of the society to know the modern culture of Varanasi. These are the main forces behind writing *The Street Turns Yonder*.

The selection of Varanasi and the disturbed social scene for his background reflect the novelist's experiences from his early education to his employment in Banaras. Shivprasad Singh (Fig. 45) was born on August 19, 1928, in a village about 50 km north-east of Banaras. He first visited the city in 1947 as a young student when he was admitted to the 11th grade in the U.P. College. He received his M.A. in Hindi literature in 1953 and his Ph.D. in 1957, both from the Banaras Hindu University. Soon afterwards he joined the department of Hindi there as a lecturer, and was promoted to professor in 1983. He finally retired in 1988, and he left this mortal world on 28 September 1998.

Before starting the novel, the novelist had devoted his energy to walking around Varanasi, meeting the people, watching the activities and rituals and also critically examining the basic writings on the city, ranging from mythologies and religious treatises to contemporary historical sources. With this involvement, the novelist cites such sources and experiences frequently, and so his narration becomes more relevant in understanding the culture.

It is commonly believed that *The Street Turns Yonder* is mainly about the student movement. This, of course, is the setting; nevertheless, it is about something wider than that — the search for humanity in the holiest city of India, the uniqueness and distinct personalities of its dwellers, the horrors of terrorism which developed as a subculture and the philosophical and archetypal aspects of the sacred territory and the northerly flowing of the most sacred river, the Ganga (*Ganges*). The Ganga is taken as a simile for the lifeworld of Varanasi.

It is clear from the author's conversation that "the spiritual magnetism and contemporary culture" were the forces that inspired him. His ideology is expressed in the very first page of the novel: "If my friend is rich, I never mind accepting his richness. But I never beg courtesy from anybody irrespective of the closeness that he may have" (ST: 13). Predominantly, at first he felt that the feelings of the Hindus toward Banaras as a beautiful, cosmic and sacred city are close to reality, and at different places in the novel this is fully described. The novelist feels that writing a novel about such a city needs a certain state of realization and experience, especially a struggle for survival among the accidents and sufferings in life. His own struggle to get a job in the Banaras Hindu University and the tragic death of his two children, including the death of his daughter in 1984 due to severe illness, were part of his repository experiences.

He feels that in the dense darkness of his life, he had created a light through writing the novel to satisfy his own soul. Above all, 'death' is the real truth of life; those who realise this fact can tell the truth explicitly. The novelist says that he had experienced personally the sorrow of the dying glories of this city but learnt to have peace in the darkness. Of course, the tale and narration are based on imagination, but the underlying realities are always preserved in *The Street Turns Yonder*. In the field, both with the novelist and alone, the present author found most of the characters of the novel in and around the sites and spots described in the novel. Though they speak for themselves, the identity of the location at some places is, admittedly, inaccurate. Reising (1986: 166) has rightly warned: "the text's actual meaning is not a position or idea articulated by an author through a text, but a struggle within the writer that the Lawrentian critic can discern by trusting the tale".

Replying to his critics, the novelist says in the preface to *The Blue Moon* (1988: ii) :

> Only those can understand the novel in full who have lived in Varanasi like the dwellers of the city. One can't perceive the eternity of this city by showering a few drops of the Ganga water on his body, or only watching the scene while sitting on the ghats. It is essential to have experience of the holy dip in the

Ganga, lived experiences of the street culture and participation in the festivities and sacred journeys as a *pilgrim* not as a *tourist.*

Above all, every person has the right to say whatever he experienced, as an outsider or insider. The novelist is successful in narrating his experiences through his descriptive power and sheer virtuosity. In his own words the novelist says metaphorically:

> I attempted to project the varieties of images of this distinct city which are sometimes dark, muddy, swampy; however, there is a light and life too. Also, there is "the light of spirituality" shining at various places in the novel. "The turning of the street" is the "turning of life". Who can narrate it without deeper experiences of sufferings?
>
> (*Interview* on October 7,1992)

In the novel itself the novelist has captured almost all the possible characteristics of the most common places and has also given more emphasis to the places in the central part and those along the Ganga river. Even imaginary plots, characters and associated sites are (indirectly) closely related to reality. This shows the novelist's deeply rooted experiences and feelings.

The novel is at most places strong on descriptive details and frequently refers to history, illustrated with mythologies linked with imagination. However, the novel has been criticised on this ground. Reviewing this novel, Krishnanath (1975) has rationally highlighted its weak and strong points. He has indicated that "how others have seen the novel, I don't know. That is their job, they do it. I would need that much of liberty as the novelist has taken himself" (cf. *Ibid*.: 3). Following this analogy, I have also taken liberty in my approach and vision to analyse *The Street Turns Yonder.* Krishnanath's review deals only with the storyline of the book, and fully neglects the social-cultural perspectives for which personal surveys and understanding of the city are necessary. Here the latter aspects are given due consideration. But the reviewer accepts that the novelist has tried to visibly be in every place and in every activity in the city of Banaras (*ibid:* 4). This statement has been exemplified with the help of the novelist's cognitive maps. He further remarked that "this is an attempt to view Puranic myth from the vision of modernity, and modernity from the vision of Puranic myth" (*ibid:* 3). One can say that in another sense this is the merit of the novel, since it projects the continuity and contradiction of tradition.

Krishnanath is doubtful about the meaning of the 'title'; he feels that only the novelist knows it, or perhaps not even him! To throw light on this issue he suggests reading the novel from the end:

> Which is this street?
> Not the street, it is Gol-ghar
> Golghar... ! Keep patience. Move on the road, and
> at the turning go out. Wherever you want —
> Maidagin or Chauk, you can go.
>
> (*op. cit.* 6, ST: 491)

Mishra (1974: 58) feels that publishing the novel in a series of parts in the Hindi fortnightly *Dharmayuga* (from Delhi) has resulted in a lack of continuity and of narrating climax of events. Moreover, in spite of covering so many spots and plots the novel has not managed to paint the unique colour of the city, known as *Banarasi* (*ibid:* 57). He further comments that the depiction of this colour was not possible only through literary sources or imagination, a convincing picture can only come from deep experiences of the lifeworld of the city. It seems that emotions have overcome the creativity of the novelist. He again says metaphorically that "since the novelist missed the way, he rarely attempted to search, and whenever he attempted, he exposes only his emotional bonds" (*ibid*: 58).

Agyeya (1974: 62) is of the opinion that the novel is full of mysteries of non-contextual provokings, and one can only admire the attempt which ends without any goal. The novel is disappointing as it lacks a constant flow of thought and also any objective. His comments are further extended by Srivastava (1974: 74), who says that his presentation of the realities is misleading, and most of the characters never follow the contextual environment prevailing there, but rather fulfil the wish of the novelist (*ibid* 76). He adds that the author, in fact, ultimately realises that his Vishvanatha (the patron deity) is now blind, and Annapurna (the chief goddess) carries the burden of old-age (*ibid*: 78). It has also been observed that the novelist is biased and never overcome to the stereotype bond of a professional novelist; this indicates that he is interested in making a story suited to some action-movie for the middle class Indian audience (cf. Krishnanath, 1975: 78). One of the renowned critics, Namwar Singh (1980: 4) remarked that "the overuse of similes by Shivprasad Singh poses a serious threat to the very existence of the story itself"; however, this is not true in most of his writings.

The novelist's own student, K.P. Singh (1985: 4) remarked that "the main features of his personality are his self-centred, self-praising and unsociable nature. Of course, he is keen to appreciate the feelings of human sense, but always fails to escape from overcoming his own personality" (*ibid*: 11). Moreover, his usual style of painting life is by "using the flash-back system", which indicates his own emotional feelings rather than an overall picture of the lifeworld of Banaras, while he never accepted.

These literary criticisms are not taken into consideration for writing this chapter, instead emphasis is laid on field experiences while describing the spirit of place, people and culture.

Of course, at some places the novelist's identity supersedes the character (e.g. ST: 13-15; 30-39), and at other places non-contextual lengthy descriptions are given, like a picnic at Sarnath (ST: 279-286). Such instances make the reading quite dull. However, with its masterly vividity, symbolism and real scenes the experiential feelings are presented with superb descriptive power, and the sheer virtuosity with which Shivprasad Singh handled the Hindi language. Through field study one can find most of the notable characters roaming in the areas mentioned, where they speak for themselves; however at many places the locational identity is misconceived.

The cognitive maps of Shivprasad Singh (cf. Singh, 1985: 296; Fig. 46) are developed from his own mental topography of the city. He was asked to draw the maps in reference to the places mentioned in the novel (Fig. 47). His perception of the edges in the four directions — the Ganga river in the east, the Asi stream in the south, the Varana in the north, and the Panchakroshi route in the west — is clear and strong. In a physical sense, there is a contrast between reality and perception to a certain extent. However, directions, relative locations and relative scales are close to their actual counterparts. The novelist's cognitive map can be compared with a 'real' map showing the important places mentioned in novel (Fig. 46 and 47). It is obvious that all the characters are closely associated to the areas nearby the Ganga. This experiential presentation clearly indicates that the novelist has a high level of awareness towards the Ganga, but not towards the cityscape.

3. The Canvas

While starting to write a novel on Varanasi, Shivprasad Singh decided to prepare a set of three volumes dealing with the modern, medieval, and ancient cultural personality of the city, comparable to

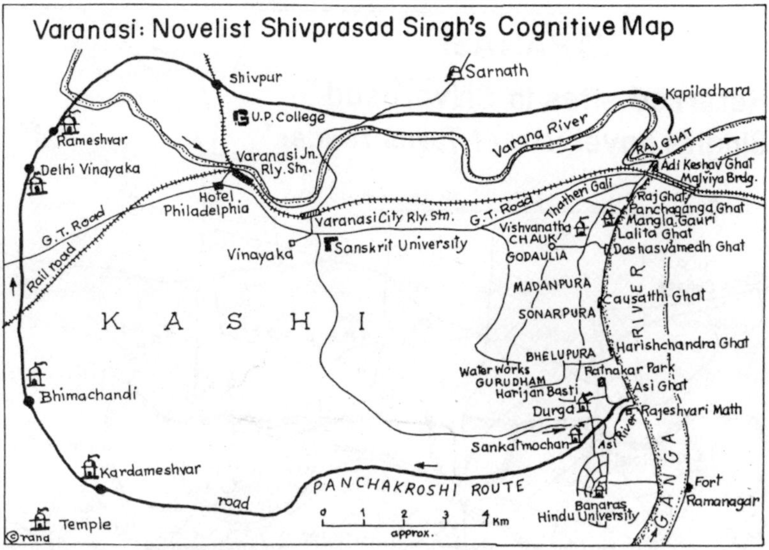

Fig. 46. Shivprasad Singh's Cognitive Map of Banaras.

Lawrence Durrell's *Alexandria Quartet* (Faber & Faber, London, 3 vols., 1957). The city of Varanasi provided a backdrop and shaped the view of the Indian social world that he sought to convey in his three novels. He worked on modern society in the 1970s using the students' reactions of the late 1960s against the present system of education and the use of English for teaching as his core themes. That is why there appears to be a discontinuity in describing the landscape and culture of the city. The novelist feels that since the city has been the strongest seat of learning and education, this theme should occupy the central position and that social degradation and students' reactions are the result of that time. He further stresses the need and demand of the society to know the modern culture of Varanasi. These are the main forces behind writing *The Street Turns Yonder*. Of course, taking benefit of the contextual differentiation, Singh narrated the lifeworld of Varanasi.

While writing the novel studied here, under the contextual background Singh also presented some glimpses of the ancient historical accounts. Four such accounts refer to the ancient view. The first is the mythology of Harishachandra at the cremation ghat (ST: 33), taken from the *Markandeya Purana* (VIII). The others are the story of Devodas (ST: 192-194) from the *Mahabharata* (XIII.31. 26-28), the origin and loss of rivers at Panchaganga (ST: 347-348) from the *Kashi*

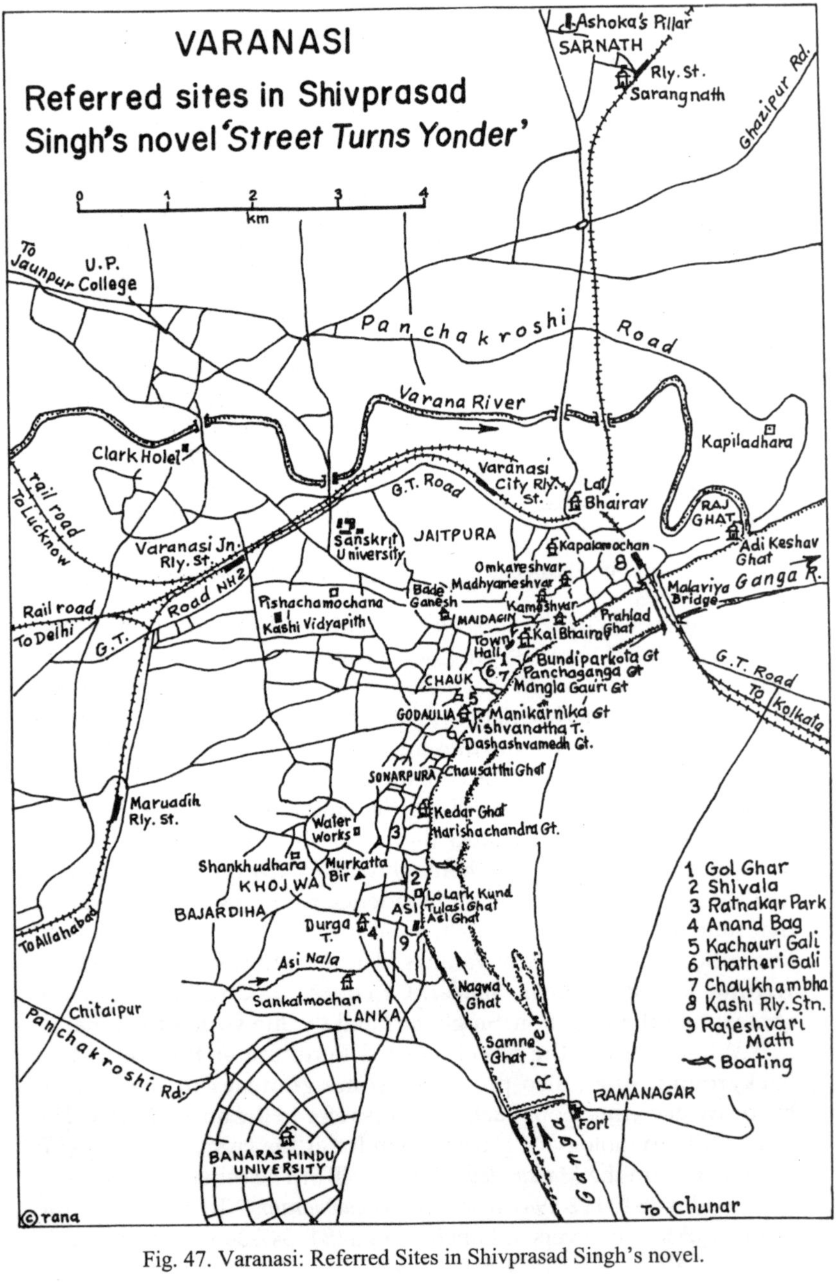

Fig. 47. Varanasi: Referred Sites in Shivprasad Singh's novel.

Khanda (59), and the story of king Brahmadutta's manipulative strategy for purchasing horses (ST: 273), from the *Tandukanali Jataka* (Pt. I. no. 5). These mythologies may be metaphorically analysed with a view to understanding how worthiness vanished, how a diplomatic strategy was implemented to remove superstitions and terrors, how sex destroyed the merit of chastity that resulted in a curse, and the manipulative strategy to get something, respectively.

The period of the 1960s and early 1970s was famous for student agitations throughout the world. How could a city like Varanasi, a well-known seat of learning, be left behind in this march! The 'youth and their reactions' is the main issue around which the rest of the subject matter takes turn. Nevertheless, the vivid form and pattern of the city's cultural glory and heritage were also described. Singh thought that the latter provided a background for the former. He further believed that "in spite of all reactions, struggle within the fast growing crowd, the youth has not reached the right turning. ..Why?" This novel attempts to answer this basic question, but could not successfully arrive at a conclusion. Varanasi is one of the most ancient continuously living cities in the world, where crowds of hippies are found at most of the old but neglected temples — this does indicate conflict between the old and the newly developed wealthy culture. Stafford Beer (1975: 44) has rightly lamented:

> With so many of youth growing up,
> In the hippies, let's not work, professional-protesting pattern,
> There seems little hope for change
> In the foreseeable future.

The basic issue, related to the medium of teaching, instruction and government activities, was to replace English with Hindi, then only in a real sense independence would be achieved. The students' movement started against English, but stopped at the question of removing the police force (PAC) called to suppress them. "*Adjustment* is the real slogan of Indian society, *competition* is a false show" (ST: 318). The other important issues taken into account are the unique personality of city, the immoral educational scene, the Ganga's multidimensional and living character, lifeworld and turnings, etc. along with several other themes. The coverage of so many themes was not an easy task. The more closed and traditionally preserved a society is, the harder it is for its members to isolate themselves from each other and from society as a whole; and the greater the desire to do so in the interest of nurturing a self or self-integrity.

The concept of *mandala* compared with turnings, reflecting upon the circle of life, has been well preserved in the novel. The narrowness of the streets show how situations change a man in a particular way, and the turnings indicate moments of change; both go side-by-side in accordance to the contexts. It is this reciprocity that the lifeworld and lifecycle are represented in different contexts. The spontaneity of the *mandala* has been expressed in Western psychology by Carl G. Jung, whose conclusion is worth comparable to the above analogy developed by Shivprasad Singh:

> … the unconscious trend to regard spirit and matter not merely as equivalent but as actually identical, and this is flagrant contrast to the intellectual one-sidedness, which would sometimes like to spiritualise matter and other times materialise spirit.
>
> (Jung, 1972 : 29)

4. Physical Aspects of the City Personality

The high sense of sacredness of the number 'three' is vividly symbolised in Varanasi. In a physical context, Varanasi is famous for three unique sacred entities: the northerly flow of the Ganga as base, the two cremation ghats as places of the last rites of life, and overall the golden temple of the patron deity, Lord Vishvanatha (ST: 32-33). This natural and fantastic beauty can't be established only by its physical attributes. Singh notes that the beauty of Varanasi can't be perceived easily without some obstacles: "Everybody wants to see the beauty, but glancing is not possible without any obstacle; Varanasi is beautiful but without impediments how can one see that!" (ST: 13).

The number *three* again corresponds with several trio-notions: the three forms of Shiva having their independent territory (Omkareshvara in the north, Vishveshvara in the middle, and Kedareshvara in the south). Three rivers delimit the edges of the city, i.e. the Varana in the north, the Asi in the south, and the Ganga in the east (ST: 38). The number three refers to the integrity of three realms, the three qualities and three original gods in the form of Shiva who has three eyes. In fact, Shiva is a universal god, having control over the three realms (with three eyes), the four directions (with four arms), and the five elements (with five forms); altogether this points to 'wholeness'. Moreover, since the patron deity of the city is Shiva, necessarily the city possesses a universal identity (see Singh, 1986).

The Ganga provides an arc (ST: 246), and the circle drawn taking the distance from Panchaganga Ghat to Dehli Vinayaka as radius limits the most sacred territory (ST: 113). This description is vaguely presented; it should be from Madhyameshvara to Dehli Vinayaka, which corresponds to the Panchakroshi route (see Singh, 2002: 26). It is mentioned, "this is the only city demarcated by a route of five *krosha* (11.6 miles) like thread in the garland and Shiva lingams as flowers" (ST: 343). On this route Dehli Vinayaka serves as a watch god of the western gate of Varanasi.

With the use of symbols and metaphors the milieu of the Panchakroshi route has been presented. The pilgrims perform the circumambulation in *purushottam masa* (intercalary Hindu month in the leap year; ST: 341). The architectural beauty is symbolised with the religious and divine understanding. About the grand Shiva lingam at Parma village, Singh expressed: "Here is a human-size Shiva lingam; a great snake takes round and tightens up the lingam. ...This indicates that energy is always curious to get Shiva in her arms, but Shiva accepts that appeal as a divine ornament. The heat of infinity bounds him, but Shiva, after becoming cool, puts it on his forehead" (ST: 344). This clearly indicates the mystic and divine power of Shiva. It is unique that all the gods/ demigods from the various holy sites of India came to Varanasi and were spatially transposed as lingam in the form of *Ishvara*.

In the Panchakroshi route, after every two lingams (total number 108) lies a weight-tower (*bojhatek*) to get the pilgrims relaxed from their weight (ST: 344). This physical fact has full theological explanations; Singh expressed:

> I thought earlier so, but now know that these weight-towers are for those who were exiled from the city by the curse of Kapaleshvara, and who therefore can't get relief from the sin of murdering Brahmins, and thus ultimately are not allowed to enter the city. It shows that the city is reserved for Brahmin sacrifices. (ST: 344)

The high sense of sanctity and spiritual magnetism of Varanasi attracted people from all over India (cf. Singh, 1980: 43), among them migrants from Bengal, Gujarat and Bihar have a distinct identity (ST: 68). The former two are famous for Mother Goddess worship, and their deep faith is visualised in the grandness of their celebrations, decorations and varieties of rituals (ST: 61; 83).

The filthy environmental conditions are concentrated in the areas where Harijans are settled. Poverty and adaptive mode of living are mixed together, resulting in a neglected social world cut off from the rest of society. The hero, Ramanand, says:

> As soon as I entered along with Nandkishor in the *harijan* neighbourhood, I was blown by obnoxious smell... In front of each house lies sewerage, at all the gates there are garbage-pits. Both sides of the streets are filled with urine and excreta. In the name of domestic animals, most of them have goats... (ST: 183; also 188)

Harijans always feel the negligence of society:

> We are poor, *harijans*. That's why our prestige has no value at all. Even chastity is measured on the scale of caste and purity-pollution. (ST: 245; also 186)

Though the city does not have a strong industrial base, still there are slums-like settlements everywhere as in more developed cities. Harijan *bastis* are typical examples. Comparing Banaras' sanctified glory at one end, and its filthy environment at the other, the invisible and the dark side can be felt together. With the use of simile the city is described thus: "In the silence of night and the environment of darkness, the houses of Banaras look distinct. Everything is stopped, as if a photographer would try to catch the picture of the city in a very dim light..." (ST: 246). Here the photographer is the divine spirit, darkness the dark-side and the dim light the evil part of the society — poverty and filthiness. This makes clear that in spite of divine presence man is solely responsible for creating dark spots in this holy city.

5. Metaphor and Milieu: The Spots

One of the most popular couplets in Varanasi says, "Widows, bulls, stairs and ascetics; only by avoiding these can one enjoy Kashi" (cf. ST: 114). Indeed, the narrow lanes filled with crowds and wandering cows, bulls and ascetics are unique features of this city (ST: 361; see Singh, 1988: 23, Fig. 48). In spite of the natural beauty of the city along the Ganga (famous for purity), the city presents a dirty and filthy environment:

> ... Every river dreams to carry the load of an excellent city like Varanasi. Similarly, each country is hopeful for its youth to continue and make the old traditions more relevant and useful (as preserved by the ancestors) out of the ruins and garbage. The hope of this great city can't be lost in nothingness. (ST: 276)

But the situation is not very promising. This statement reminds Muktibodh's (1975/1964: 51) poem "Self-expression of an ex-reactionary":

Fig. 48. Four Faces of Kashi: the cartoonist's view.

You do have sorrows,
I too have sorrows.
We're suppressed under a ruined house.
It is difficult even to cry,
impossible...
Even to move.

This is comparable to Singh's exclamation (ST: 80, based on a Bengali song):

Brothers!
Let's hear the story of the life-less city.
On brick and remains here,
its pains and sufferings engraved.

A content analysis of newspapers gives the impression that the city is reserved for sinners: "It is a lifeless and unknown city, and famous for corrupt deeds and murders as reported in daily newspapers. This has given me impression that Banaras is the city of *gundas*" (ST: 337).

The city abounds in mythological stories where the gods and sages manipulate things to their advantage; in later days similar examples of stories of black marketeers and smugglers follow this tradition (ST: 102). One of the explanations for this state of things is inferred from the story of Harishchandra, who had to tolerate all kinds of torturing tests for being a follower of the path of truth. Later on he went to heaven with all his subordinates, leaving only liars and wantons in the city (ST: 33). Hemachandra's *Kumaracharita* (3.59; written in CE 1184) referred to this city as *thaganam sthanam* ('the abode of thieves'). Another text of the 12th century, Pandit Damodar Sharma's *Ukti-Vyakti Prakarana* (38.28-30) also gives similar descriptions (see Dubey, 1985: 38).

Even as late as in 1856, Svami Dayanand, the founder of the *Arya Samaj*, was defeated by failing to explain a false sacred metre from the *Upanishads*. He stood confused, and ultimately he was declared defeated: "The art to make right from anything wrong has flourished well in this city. The city is famous for the art of making anything wrong look like real through manipulations" (ST: 45).

The only city having dead-body homes where its carriers come, wait, relax and proceed to the ghats, is Varanasi. These houses have also a special sense of *joie de vivre* and delight:

> ...Formerly I never understood the function of corpse carriers, but when the city became an abode of *joie de vivre* for me, and I too became one among the many street wanderers, I slowly realised I realised the naturality of this. ...Death is also a celebration. If you cannot believe it, watch the duties of the corpse-carriers. After burning the corpse, followed by a holy dip in the Ganga, they eat *puri-kachauri* at the street-shops in Kachauri Gali. Frequently they talk to each other about the various stages and happenings of the cremation of the corpse. While talking, they never express any emotion or attachment to the dead — as if the talk was serving the function of *chatni* [a spicy sauce dish] to put one more mouthful of food in the belly so easily. (ST: 280)

In many places the novelist has commented on the notorious activities of the *pandas/ ghatias* (priests at the ghats). The movie *Sangharsha* ('struggle'), released in 1963 and based on a novel in Bengali, highlights various such deeds performed by the *pandas*. These include murder, cheating, forgery, illicit sex, crime, etc. In Singh's novel too, such instances are mentioned at various places. Self-praise is the most common feature of almost all the *pandas* (ST: 255). In course of time they fall into degradation by drinking wine in the company of low-status people and taking part in corrupt deeds; therefore they are sometimes called *gundas* (ST: 256). The *pandas* project themselves as contractors to help the souls in crossing the Vaitarini (mythological obnoxious river lying between heaven and hell), which souls have to cross after death. People having high faith in the realm of the dead (*yama loka*), and wishing to get a place in heaven, naturally contact the *pandas* to perform sacred rituals. The novelist reacts to this attitude, and says that *pandas*, in fact, never guarantee the crossing, but rather degrade the person and victimise him under the shadow of sacred rituals (ST: 174). They are even involved in encouraging pick-pocketing and other criminal acts happening at the ghats (ST: 200).

In the city daily instances of terrorism can be noted: "Terrorism is a great disaster. It is like a black cloud moving all around every time" (ST: 275). In fact, "it is a hatred item, it never originates outside; it is like the germination of bacteria in the human body. ...It is an infectious disease which spreads over a large mass" (ST: 275). Everybody is fearful and suspicious about others, like in the Orwellian negative utopia: "Big Brother is watching" (Orwell, 1949: 17, and 175). A culture of 'gangster oppression' is now a common scene.

Under the banner of so many names, and under the shadow of hypocrites like the Orwellian *dualact*, there are many persons degrading humanity and justice. The novel mentions:

> You think that you are following your path rightly, that there exists no relation with other happenings! But this is a false notion of yours. You may not quarrel with anybody, but somebody may certainly quarrel with you. He may put your life in serious trouble.
>
> That's why I said, to be alive there is a need of training. And you give all training of those kinds, I said. (ST: 214)

The personality of Bakkad Guru / V.N.P. Singh reflects a complete view of the mentality of terrorists, who under various shadows do all kinds of inhuman acts on behalf of others, for which they receive money in return (ST: 214; 225). Such people are the overall controllers of the network of the system. But Banaras has been famous for even the high morality of *gundas* (see several stories by 'Rudra' 1967, chapter 8 of this book). In the present novel the personality of Rajulli shows a similar character. The hero expresses: "In my short life I have seen so many *gundas*, but Rajulli is distinct among all, he worshipped humanity. I think that except those who became *gundas* by profession (the loafers), the rest are open-minded and kind hearted ... I am happy that still such kind of *gundas* are living in Varanasi, of course like an abridged edition of a book" (ST: 351).

In spite of several such strange situations, the lively culture of *joie de vivre* and being carefree is maintained in the city. Remarking on the continuity of this tradition, the novelist cites the story of Tulasi, a great Bhakta-poet of 16th-17th century: "Tulasi, the great poet of the people ... You know! Tulasi consumed poison throughout his life for the good of the society and gave nectar to the mass of the community" (p. 77). Tulasi was a symbol of the carefree; the novelist says (ST: 57):

> Call me wanderer, ascetic, washerman,
> Or Sari-weaver, whatever you like,
> I take food from alms, that's why there's no need
> To implore or beg anybody, whoever he may be.

With such strong emotional bonds, the city creates an environment of carefreeness and delight. Watching side-shows is everywhere very popular:

> This is a unique city. No room to move, no straight passage to go ahead here and there, but if a showman comes, citizens stop all the activities and watch the show. ...In this crowd, the show-watchers will try to make room somehow to watch the show very closely. For this attempt, a strong competition starts. (ST: 106)

As in Calcutta (Kolkata), the kaleidoscopic scene of the celebration of Durga Puja appears in Varanasi. The city has the unique glory of combining these three ingredients: devoted faith, decorated lighting, and dancing programmes. In the same period three regional representations of festivities happen — Durga Puja of Bengalis, Garaba of Gujaratis, and Ramalila of Bhojpuri-Hindus. Such scenes, reflecting a microcosm of India, are found only in Banaras (ST: 80). A glimpse of the deteriorating Bengali culture can be seen with young people' watch for sex in Durga Puja. One of such youths expresses: "Let us move to the Ghat, there exists another face of beauty. There one can see beautiful girls (*achha mala*)" (ST: 81).

The dualistic nature of culture is seen even with the style of taking food. How urbanites feel superior to ruralities can be seen in this context. "This specific style is reserved for only rich men, i.e. to eat slowly, so that they may not think that somebody is an over-eater. Just imagine this! Even the style of taking food is affected with the culture of richness..." (ST: 95).

Hindu culture is dominated by the ordinances of Brahminism, therefore a Brahmin is perceived as equivalent to a god (ST: 187). On the other end instances of reactions are notable everywhere, especially among untouchables (*harijans*). The hero Ramanand asks a *harijan* girl, who in turn reacts against Brahminism while exemplifying her experiences:

> ... I am awakening my Brahmin soul to bless you for well being, and you are weeping!
>
> Your blessing will never be fruitful. Your *mantras* are now dead. Milk for medical aid is now scarce, and you are talking about a milk-bath. If I have no home or even companion, how would my children be happy? Before coming out from the womb my children had to be sacrificed! Do you understand...?
>
> Ramanand was pleased, and commented: This is the real spirit of the female energy. (ST: 172)

Begging is another impartial part of the scene. An intelligent beggar says, "you can get alms only if you pose in a pitiful way. If you would behave morally, you would be abused. At least you have to learn a lesson" (ST: 243). He clearly says that the whole world is a beggar: "The Giver is only One (God), and the whole world is a beggar. I have seen how big persons do anything for money — request, defile, immoral deeds, tolerance and what not!, even beggars cannot behave like this" (ST: 231). It can be compared with the saying that "money is everything, so everything is justified for money".

Some of the important temples now provide shelter for sex and crime. One wandering ascetic warns the hero Ramanand:

> You will be punished for your honesty, and be suppressed and pressurised for your modesty and worthiness. You are too tender. Have you not seen couples mating in the Sankata temple? What have you thought about these holy temples? There are snake-retreats underneath these temples where boa-snakes wander, rats jump and go into the mouth of death. All kinds of corrupted deeds are performed there. Are these acts right? You are living in the university. Tell me, whatever happens in the temple there, is that right? Tell me the truth! (ST: 198)

The condition of the charity houses, *maths* (monasteries) and widow-homes is deteriorating day-by-day. *Maths* are now becoming rats' shelters, and also the victim of unauthorised capturing (ST: 23). The present condition of the government offices is comparable to the widow-homes. Discarded widows come to reside in these homes, where they pass their time collecting food, gossiping, abusing each other and talking about their memories of younger days related to love, sex and prosperity (ST: 97).

One of the most distinct occupations in Varanasi is sari weaving. But the condition of the weavers is very pitiable. They are victims of exploitation, bindings and demoralisation (see chapter 10, pp. 246-247). Thatheri bazaar is the main centre of the sari trade. One Muslim sari-weaver (*Julaha*) repents: "If my product is so poor in quality, please leave it so... If this is your way of dealing with business, our wives may well sit at the houses of prostitutes. ... Even the cost of silk will not be reimbursed..." The merchant bargains: "My dear! Take ten rupees more; why are you so angry? We are not purchasing without paying the price..." (ST: 262). The city is famous for bargaining in most of the economic exchanges.

The novelist believes that good and bad run side-by-side since the origin of humankind; indeed they are opposites that cannot stand independently.

6. The Ganga: Metaphor and Meanings

As the Ganga symbolises Shiva's energy, she has also three forms — heavenly river, earthly river, and underworld river (Singh, 1987a: 316). This river is considered as the most sacred. The whole Hindu lifecycle is related with ritual purification by water, especially of the Ganga; in fact, the same concept of 'lifeflow' may be symbolically represented with 'waterflow'. We can bring to attention here the concept of *Gangaisation*, a process of transposition and perception in which many rivers or water bodies are conceived as being the Ganga during sacred baths and on other auspicious events. The Ganga river has received special importance in Hinduism as 'purifier'; in fact, she may be said to be the cradle of Indian culture and civilisation (cf. Singh, 1987a: 316-17). This idea has been reflected metaphorically by depicting the Ganga in twenty-one colours (compare: 7 circuits, *chakras*, multiplied by 3 mythical realms, *lokas*, equals to 21) in Kashi, which can be categorised into seven groups. It is to be noted with sadness that due to serious threat by human encroachment causing physical and cultural pollutions many of the good colours are progressively

Fig. 49. The Cognitive Map of Banaras: Kashi's Real Map.

turning into blackness. A sensitive walker has expressed that "a walk along the ghats presents another image too, one of poverty and crowding. And, another is of filthy and polluted scenes created by the garbage piles, sewerage, breeding diseases, drains carrying human waste directly to the stream, occasionally floating corpses and also pouring toxins from India's burgeoning industrial sector" (cf. Singh and Rana, 2002: 103; Fig. 49).

6.1. Distinct Beauty

The northerly route of the Ganga in Kashi is like a bow-bend. This unique setting naturally encourages everyone to think over its historical past. All rivers are conceived as feminine in India. The Ganga looks like a chaste virgin girl who has placed the pot of Indian culture on her bent waist; how grand this ever-lasting and immortal light in arc-form is! (ST: 19). It has been compared to the description given in the *Brahmavaivarta Purana* (*Kashi Rahasya* 2.13.38):

> What is that divine light
>   reflecting over water in arc,
> Which even during the cosmic flood
>   remains as it always was.

Just after the annual flood the ghats are covered by silt and clay, therefore many people go into the current by boat for taking bath on the other side. The morning scene at that time makes one think of a young female-snake trying to bind the city (ST: 126). Ganga delimits the eastern boundary of the sacred territory of Kashi (ST: 341). One of the five most sacred ghats, Panchaganga is considered as the site of the meeting of five rivers, while one can see only the Ganga (ST: 347). The novelist omitted to mention that the Yamuna and the invisible Sarasvati joined the Ganga at Prayaga/ Allahabad (127 km upstream from Banaras), and together they arrived to Kashi when Bhagiratha led the Ganga across north India (*Kashi Khanda* 59).

6.2. Medium of Transport and Shelter

The constantly flowing stream serves as a channel for transport, especially for carrying patients from the congested parts of the city. Even at the more crowded peak times, one can easily travel by boat between Asi and Panchaganga ghats (ST: 308). Moreover, for boatmen the Ganga is a shelter where they pass most of their daily routine; and during the hot season, the Ganga helps to give relief from heat. During the time of hot-winds (*loo*), the children of poor boatmen happily bathe and swim the day long. Like a mother, the Ganga serves these children by relieving them from the *loo*. Thus, she serves as a means of transport, subsistence, shelter and relief (ST: 353).

6.3. Cursor of Flood

The water level of the Ganga starts to rise after *Ganga Dashahra* (10th waxing fortnight of *Jyeshtha*, (May/June), but soon after the rains start the increase gains momentum, and slowly the steps at the ghats get submerged; the width of the river also slowly increases (ST: 37, 57). The situation becomes worst at the times when water reaches into the lanes; everybody takes all precautions for safety. The people compare this with the cosmic flood (ST: 70). It appears as if the Ganga was trying to replace the city, and having failed now enters into the lanes (ST: 71-72):

> The flood water left all its moral orders, and, failing to push back the arc-sited city, started flowing wherever it found way. The Asi Bridge merged into the belly of the drain. On the Durgakund-University road and the bridge there, the water flowed with a murmuring sound. Looking into the current of the Ganga one can imagine a grand charisma. The basement of Ramanagar fort, and the trees lying around, all gone into the water …The sun was rising. The floodwater was flowing with a unique gurgle sound…

We can compare this with Khushwant Singh's description of the monsoon rains:

> And the sound or water spouting down from the roof, the gurgle of the gutters and of the rain falling in torrents was like a lullaby… (1959: 105).

Describing the peak flood of 10th September 1967, Singh says:

> Someone was bounded somewhere, and some other man was entangled somewhere else. In spite of not willing to, Sichanna was in the grip of Jhulani. Bhagtin doesn't want, but was living in the tight hold of the Pujari. There developed a flood-time relationship. But up to what extent the flood of new blood can tolerate such bonded-illegal relationships? No longer at all! (ST: 78)

This metaphorical statement indicates the challenge to physical (land) and psychological (mind) states of extremities and consequential boundlessness.

During the flood, the Ganga becomes more voluminous and speedy. Under the shadow of clouds, the muddy water of the Ganga appears to be completely black (ST: 246). During this period, the two cremation ghats become more polluted, but, endowed with strong faith, people continue to perform their ritual performances there without any hesitation.

6.4. Multiplicity in Seasonal Beauty

In different seasons the Ganga reflects rays of vivid colours of beauty, providing different inspirations and moods. During the rainy season the meeting of clouds with the river looks as if the clouds wished to kiss the river, one can especially contemplate this scene looking from Asi Ghat towards Malaviya Bridge in the north (ST: 18). In November, near the open fields bordering the Ganga around the Asi area, one can enjoy the sunrise and its reflection on the quiet and calm Ganga. The wavy movement of the reflected light upon the river calls for thinking on the divine (ST: 125). In this season the beauty of the all-covering greenery spotted by the yellow flowers of mustard on both the sides of the river is overwhelming (ST: 267).

In the mornings of April the Ganga shines showing her whitest face. Dressed with a light-blue sari, the white face of the Ganga indicates that, in spite of darkness, there lies the most pious and clean body (ST: 232). In *Jyeshtha* (May/June), the blowing winds carrying sand sometimes form a mirage. These natural beauties are unparalleled in any part of the world.

6.5. Place of Daily Rituals and Routines

Since the ancient past the Ganga has been serving as an altar of rituals and sacrifices. It is the place where, according to mythology, king Harishchandra sold his son as a sacrifice to follow the path of truth (ST: 15). Pulled by the river's high mystic power of sanctity, people from all parts of India came and got settled along her borders (ST: 23). A holy dip in the Ganga keeping full faith in her purifying power is the normal ritual practice among the settlers (ST: 295).

6.6. Flow and Theology

The pilgrims and devotees come close to the Ganga and pay regards to her as a motherly river, shouting: "Hail to the mother Ganga..." (*Ganga maiya ki jai*) (ST: 13). More than others, boatmen strongly perceive her as mother (ST: 353). The holy river is thought to be constant, ever-lasting and ever-flowing even during the cosmic food;

it preserves the divine light described in the *Kashi Rahasya* (ST: 19; compare the *Kashi Khanda* 26.67).

The Ganga conveys a message of peace and silence that is comparable to the pigeons living in the nearby houses. Indeed, doves themselves are considered as a symbol of peace (ST: 134). One can realise the meaning of silence at the banks of Ganga; this silence itself is self-realisation (ST: 146). For those not having that state of mind, the Ganga will slowly indicate the notion of non-attachment (ST: 161; also 319). This metaphor shows that like water, life has a cycle of flow, movement and interaction.

Life reaches its climax in death, the return of the soul to its origin. This message is metaphorically expressed by the northerly flow of the Ganga: "A river coming from the north has to flow towards the south, but it is only in Kashi where it turns back towards the north, conveying the message: return to the origin..." (ST: 357). The Ganga calls for travelling back to the earliest beginning of the world. This message manifests the transcendental value of place and life. It clearly attempts to answer the Vedic quest — "Who am I ? From where did I come ?" (*ko aham, kuta ayatah*). Ultimately, the body made of the five basic organic elements (i.e. earth, water, fire, air and ether) will be again decomposed into these five elements after death; this is the cycle of life.

6.7. A Site for Sinners and Thugs

The ghats are well known as a place for cheating and sins (ST: 200). On the steps beggars sleep in the open space after becoming tired with their daily routine; it is their shelter (ST: 57). Like a mirage, the Ganga is also a great site of forgery (ST: 347); deviant youngsters even have sex in the boats at dusk (ST: 160).

Scholars have described the Ganga in historical, philosophical, geographical and geological perspectives, but the lived experiences and feelings of the Banaras-dwellers have been presented in this novel with vividness and symbolic reflections.

7. The Polytheistic Character of Hindu Society

Most of the narration and plot of stories of the novel are gleaned from the regional context, but they really project a pan-Indian scene, especially the Hindu social world, which is well known for its 'multiple arrangements' (see Eichinger Ferro-Luzzi, 1983: 4). In all spheres of society, Hinduism records paradoxical expressions and adjustments, but it can't be described as *hassliebe* ('hate-love' as the Germans say).

Hindus are proud of their ancient glory, but distressed for the ongoing cultural deterioration. Since man is the most sublime creature on the earth, "to know the man perfectly is essential. Only then one would intermix with others. But who knows the other perfectly?" (ST: 313).

The quest and search for the complementary half-part (male and female energy, i.e., *Yin* and *Yang*, as so many other sets of pairs) has continued since the ancient past, and hopefully will continue in future. Hindu mythology notes that Shiva with his trident (the three forks symbolising thesis, antithesis, and synthesis) divided all life-organisms into male and female. Search from both sides is always going on with a view to forming unity. The specific form of Shiva representing unity is known as 'Ardhanarishvara' (god half-male and half-female). This divine form creates the mysteries in the ever-expanding universe (ST: 196). But due to illusion, the unreal looks real, and the real looks dark and unreal.

Simplicity is one of the ways for being human, which is the need of the time: "Don't be a big man, this does not matter, rather be a real human being" (ST: 355). Of course, one has to pay a heavy price for becoming so simple, with the result that life becomes fearful: "You are so simple that you are even unable to say a word against injustice. That's why anybody can easily stress and destroy you without any hesitation" (ST: 46). This statement reminds the need for mixture in all the pure materials. Bimal Mitra says, "Absolute truth is a false notion. A little bit mixture of falsehood makes the truth a real appearance, like a golden ornament cannot be made without mixing some other metal" (Mitra, 1985: 260; also 254-264).

Life is considered like a place where everybody is a guest: "Here everybody is a guest. Someone for a few days, others for a longer period, but everybody is a guest. There, the question of hostship does not arise" (ST: 93). We can juxtapose this with Shakespeare's expression in *As You Like It* (II. viii, 139):

> All the world's stage.
> And all the men and women merely players.

The modern world is too complex. Its root-causes are uncountable; also, "it is worthless trying to know the root-causes" (ST: 318). But optimism gives a new path to life: "If society wants to destroy you, struggle and teach them a lesson. Don't be disappointed" (ST: 61-62). Of course the novelist's own life was full of sorrows and sufferings; he encouraged the youth to struggle for rationality. Nowadays Orwellian negative thoughts are encouraged with appreciation in the society: "Worthiness is a curse. Ignorance is strength" (Orwell, 1949: 17). Similar expressions are also found in Singh's novel studied here.

The social norms and rules as ordained by the *Dharmashastras* ('Books of Religious Order') are biased towards males and make such adjustments to get escape for males without excuses. The Nobel laureate novelist Naipal (1977: 53) mentions:

> Hinduism has not been good enough for the millions. It has exposed us to a thousand years of defeat and stagnation. ... Its philosophy of withdrawal has diminished men intellectually and not equipped them to respond to challenge...

The present novel also mentions such reactions but such cries result in negligence in the society:

> "Let these *shastras* be burnt", she expressed with anger, "all these *shastras* are to torture women... How amazing are the regulations of the social world! How amazing these *shastras* are!" (ST: 149)
>
> ~~~~~~~
>
> Harimangal exclaimed, 'we are against the *shastras* since childhood; therefore, they are neglected at home and not accepted in the society. (ST: 150)

Youth is not really reacting to the traditional norms and rules of the society, but rather struggling for individualism:

> Rajjo laughed: Whatever the *-ism* may be, either socialism, equalitarianism or Gandhism, all are somehow or other a garment. Man is the same man as was in the past. ... The struggle of the youth unrest is the competition for capturing position, somehow to avail opportunities even without deserving, and nothing more than that. Within the tight underwear we all are animals. (ST: 291)

This reminds us of Jonathan Swift's saying "Principally I hate and detest that animal called man" (*Letter to Pope*, Sept. 29, 1725).

Hindu society is deteriorating not only in terms of family affairs (ST: 337), or by breaking such social ties like inter-caste marriage (ST: 299), rather the whole basic nature of democracy in India has changed its mottoes, at least in practice. Politics has become just a means to get the chair of power (ST: 274-75), and now the motto followed is that "the Government is *off* the people, *bye* the people, and *far* from the people", as paraphrased after the famous address given by Abraham Lincoln (*Speech*, Nov. 19, 1863; cf. Singh, Rana 1999: 57). An honest character shuns taking any part in politics (p. 275).

Adjusting to injustice and misdeeds and flattering to please powerful persons with a view to maintaining one's position and getting undue benefits are common in Indian society; of course, their roots go to India's ancient past (pp. 90, 318). Through the back doors there exist many job opportunities that do not exist through proper channels (p. 245). Under various colour of dress, there exists man in animal form; specific dress clearly denotes a particular group of the society or idealism (ST: 144).

The deeds and actions of police are beyond imagination. With terror and torture they can do whatever they like. Torture and brutality are very common acts of the Indian police (Naipaul, 1977: 115). The machinery of administration is made in such a manner that an attempt for transformation turns into ruins so quickly. Says the novelist, "Many enthusiastic persons tried to make this machinery more humane through a radical change, but in response the machinery itself took their lives. In fact, it never provides another chance to have them survive and to be human" (ST: 178). Adjustment is the great slogan we learnt from our ancestors (ST: 176, 318).

All three possible ways to respond to the circumstances of life are described with several examples, viz. neutrality (as cited above), depression, and reaction. The climax of depression may lead to suicide. At some stage, when all the ways to lead life are closed, a man tries to get relief through the act of suicide. Jamana, presently a wandering ascetic, remembered his bad days in the past and expresses how he thinks afterwards:

> If life is felt to be useless, the realization between 'to be' and 'not to be' is lost; then the only way to eternal peace is by committing suicide! ... With a great destiny we are born as human beings; however, if life becomes depressing and terrorised like that of beasts, then suicide is not a bad retreat. (ST: 235)

The city of Varanasi is perceived to be a refuge for sinners ? an extraordinary cultural notion in this city where "a thousand persons perform religious singing in groups (*kirtana*) honoring the murky lamp; there are few people who can tolerate the light of truth" (ST: 243). Compare Chaudhuri (1979: 172), who cites a Sanskrit couplet based on Wilson's translation from the *Vishnu Purana*:

> For those who are ignorant of the revealed scriptures and the sacred traditions, who have abandoned purity and proper conduct, and for those who have nowhere else to go, for them Banaras (Varanasi) is the refuge.

Despite these problems, a great country like India and its culture survive. When the hero Ramananda raises his voice, his experienced friend replies:

> Oh! Stupid! How could you be alive without combatting these smugglers, politicians, liars and rowdy persons living under white garments? Obviously you can survive, but life would be even worse than death. (ST: 120)

The distress and disappointment make the novelist react with a sarcastic 'utopian' vision. He opines that the mythological sage Vishvamitra will create a new form of man to annihilate human attributes that get in the way of man's social ambitions:

> I am Vishvamitra. I would make a man whose arms will be in the legs so that without bending down he may touch the feet of elders (so-called). One of the eyes will be in the back to watch the critics at the back. I will remove both the ears of man. No need to hear any person's prayer. No need even to do this as man never hears even with ears. I will put only a hole at the place of the nose ? there is no need for facial beauty. (ST: 303)

The line sketch of this utopian man (see Fig. 50) is comparable to Sir John Mandeville's illustrations inspired from 14th-century travel accounts (cf. James, 1972: 121-22). Expecially the three sketches of Mandeville's utopian man portrait the animality, hunger and loss of intellect, as well as the brutality of man. Vishvamitra's divine man is imagined with some of the basic 'drawbacks' resolved through the replacement of different parts of the human body; now man is freely adapted to his own degradation.

Of course, most of the utopian thoughts are related to a good place out of no place, but here the novelist attempts to create an extra-ordinary man out of defiled man. This proposition at least encourages thinking over the issue of making man a real humane species.

8. Place Speaks: Awakened and Dead

The space, which by human transformation converges into place, has also possesses a sense of expression in two ways — positive and

Fig. 50. All Possible Worlds: Utopian Man. (A) Animal Man, (B) Hungry Man without Head, (C) Brutal Man (cf. Sir Mandeville's 15th century World; after James, 1972: 122); and (D) Vishvamitra's Divine Man.

negative. With a self-awakening, one can realise the aliveness of a place:

> Place is also alive, Tiwari! One's own place is as much acquainted as one's own wife, and you can not behave in whatever manner you want without any hesitation and suspicion… (ST: 145).

The environment of a place and a person's emotional bondage in its connection characterises the multiple sense of perception:

> For the first time I realised that place has also a sense of aliveness. Like humans, even places are sometimes alive and sometimes dead, I heard so. Place can't be only this; it can suck the blood, like rainy clouds it can also stimulate the regulation of blood in a dying person. I realised this only within ten minutes that I was going in a state of transcendence… (ST: 361)

There are some sacred places which are famous for silence, peace and relaxation, generating a new insight of life (e.g. Durga Temple; ST: 41), and at some places one realises the non-attachment to this world as everything is mortal — subject to death. Among the latter places the cremation ghats is notable. It has its own unique personality:

> It swallows everything in his mouth. Sometimes visitors find it fearful, because terrorrific scenes and obnoxious smell are there. For workers, boatmen, washermen, funeral priests, those who work there day-and-night, this place is like their garment — it is neutral for them. (ST: 317)

The specific character of a unique place is the understanding of silence, which conveys its message through mute language. Time talks, space speaks, only when one learns the language of silence:

> Silence is also invaluable stuff. If you don't disturb it, it will be reflected with the light of an unbelievable self-confidence (and self-realisation), and if disturbed it will change its mood and warn you like an excited snake's hood… (ST: 146)

A metaphorical explanation for the increasing sins among Banaras-dwellers may be found with the help of the logical story of the Dhutpapapa river, once existent at Panchaganga Ghat but now relegated to a shallow-hole. It is a matter of controversy "whether Dhutpapapa removes the sins committed by Kashi's citizens, or it swallows them, or puts sins into depth, and flowing innocently underneath…" (ST: 347).

There are two unique mystic forms of supernatural demigods for which Varanasi is famous, i.e. Bhairava and Bir. Bhairava is considered as a terrifying form of Shiva who, by replacing the lord of death (Yama), looks after the misdeeds and accounts the worldly activities of any person living in Kashi. As divine guardian of the eight directions, Bhairava controls all the sacred territory of Kashi through his eight notable forms: Ruru (at Hanumanghat), Chanda (at Durgakund), Asitanga (near Briddhakal Kupa), Kapali (known as Lat Bhairaṿa in Alaipura), Krodhan (in Kamachha), Unmatta (in Deora village along the Panchakroshi route), Samhara (in Gaighat), and Bhishana (in Lohatia, known as Bhuta).

Out of the eight Bhairavas, two are represented in the novel. Unmatta, literally defined as 'excited', who symboles the reaction against evil, calls for being more practical in place of idealism. He inspires the hero, "Live on the surface bravely, and search for your bread" (ST: 356). The city of Varanasi is famous for manipulating to defeat the worthy and truthful, therefore Unmatta warns us to become alert about that (ST: 45); and even, from a sexual point of view, he inspires us to unite with one's lover (ST: 139). He further warns to be well aware about one's own capacity for doing any job (ST: 186); and also to do something to make the nation stronger: "Wait and see the happenings! This great country is not made just only for destruction" (ST: 276). Chanda Bhairava, the killer of evil doers, is now under the grip of cheaters (ST: 41-42); therefore one has to be aware and escape from such practices.

Kashi has been famous for Yaksha worship that goes into historical past, even before Shiva worship. Yakshas are considered as the assistants of Bhairava, and guardian demigods. According to folk tradition their number is believed to be fifty two, but in fact their number might have been fifty six, in parallel with the fifty six Vinayakas whose shrines are lying at the intersection of the eight directional radials and the seven atmospheric circumferences (Singh, 1986: 308-309). Among the Birs, Lahura, Bhoju, Murchali, Daitrya, Dyoriha, Dhyondiya, Brahma, Karman, Manika, Deora, Bulla and Murkatta are still active and worshipped on different auspicious occasions in different neighbourhoods. The Murkatta, literally 'whose head has been cut down', symbolises the defeat and loss of intellect: "All the intellectuals in your department (of the university) are attacking each other with swords of abuse. Tricking was common, but now direct attacks started. This has provoked the loss of their *heads*. All are now Murkatta (beheaded) Birs" (ST: 165).

9. Immoral Educational Scene

Since the present period, the *Kali Yuga*, is known as the era of falsehood and conflicts, one can realise this most prominently among the higher educational institutions, like universities. As early as in 1958, in the convocation address of Gorakhpur University S. Radhakrishnan remarked: "We are passing through an era where evil can't be punished and intellect can't be rewarded." Juvenal also noted: "*Prohitas landatur et alget*" (Honesty is praised and starves; from *Satires* i. 74). The Nobel laureate Albert Szent-Gyorgyi warned alarmingly: "We are helpless in the face of this terrible strain of idiots who govern the world". This trend has gained momentum slowly with the passage of time. Universities have lost their boundaries:

> University has its boundary from the remote past; but deviant youths' reactions destroyed it. Outside youths are constantly entering into the campus to enjoy the inside life. Nobody knows who those youths are. ... There is a unique thing with them, that even if they would want, they would be unable to have a feeling of reverence for the university. How could this be? They are not in touch with books, the teaching community, or they have no fear at all for failing in the examination (as they are not enrolled)... (ST: 271-272)

Moreover, the increasing corruption in examinations encourages this tendency (ST: 39). Yearly strikes and late examination are common routine (ST: 340).

The university hospital (B.H.U.!), especially the student ward, is now a retreat for relaxation and good health. There "some students are really ill, and some come to get rest and improve their health. In every corner of life leaders are available. For example, there are leaders among thiefs and robbers in jail, similarly there are leaders among the patients (in the student ward)" (ST: 340).

Of course, the devoted teachers never relate politics with teaching, but they have to pay a price for that. In fact, "in India the path of truth and worthiness is made of thorny bushes, and always unstable, therefore people avoid following that path" (ST: 30). Under a good teacher to get a scholarship is also a problem (ST: 93). To adjust with the situation many teachers try to prove themselves as ultra-modern while "taking tea-coffee, breakfast, and dinner with students". This is the identification of the so-called modern intellectuals (ST: 165). Such tendencies are rapidly increasing.

The main root of students' unrest is assumed to be the generation gap (ST: 270). There is a strong competition to occupy every position: "whatever it may be, chair or position, wealth/property, opportunities, or even women for sex, with everything there is a tussle between the old and new generations to control it" (ST: 103).

In coping with the western culture, the whole energy of students is getting swept away from self-realisation, rationality, and proceeding towards a real aim. They are becoming deviants (ST: 349). To enjoy the lust of power they manipulate everything, but always cry for saving democracy (ST: 273). Moreover, sex-involvement is also becoming their part:

> All students' unrest is moving around sex! Why? Even in Bengali society, in the name of struggle only sex and drinks are accepted as their motto. Children do not like their parents because parents do not procure them enjoyments... Everybody is trying to live his own life. (ST: 164)

This trend of becoming more individualistic and self-centred encourages the loss of integrity in society, especially extended and joint family.

The issue of language is not a basic one, but it is one of the tools for charismatic leadership. Concerning this question we are still slaves: "What will happen to the country which is trying to seek solution through magic, superstitions and charisma! ..The question of language is also the same!" (ST: 117). India has no national language and English is still accepted as a second language, even after fifty years of independence. However, we proudly mention our rich cultural history of around three thousand years.

Similarly, many such issues are raised in the novel, which encourage thought about the city's educational environment, which was at some time most respected throughout the world. In spite of having at present five universities and several colleges, along with other indigenous institutions and Sanskrit schools, an educational vacuum is visible everywhere. The real aim of education should be to make the man more humane and divine.

10. Concluding Remarks

Mankind is at the turning point, but with a careful decision only the right turnings should be chosen. Metaphorically, the novelist suggests, life is not only a circle or straight line but rather a series of turnings. From one turning one goes out and reaches other turnings. Varanasi is famous for such a distinct network of street-turnings ? symbolising human life. The narrow lanes symbolise the human problems, including unrest and frustrations. The novel ends with this sense of perceiving the spatial structure of Varanasi, associated with symbolism: "Be patient. Follow on the road, and at the turning go out: wherever you want to go, you can go ? Maidagin or Chauk" (ST: 361). Maidagin and Chauk are, respectively, the symbols of the 'open plain' and the 'road-crossing' and refer to two life situations. Man is free to select one of the conditions for passing life. Human wills and wishes are the processes that enable us to control a path of passing life.

He felt that a hundred cultural dissertations need to be written to project the cultural heritage and glories of the multiplicity of Varanasi. Considering the Ganga as the symbol of 'lifecycle' and 'lifeflow', the lifeworld of Varanasi has been painted with the use of metaphors and symbols related to the river. The cyclic march of life and the flow of the novel both become counterparts to one another.

The changing personality of Varanasi and its distinctiveness are the result of a symbiosis between materialism and spiritualism. The angle of vision is important to understand the eternal feelings and external expressions as narrated by Shivprasad Singh through his in-depth tour of the city and seer capacity of describing vividity and distinctions. Whether his *Street* is narrow/wide or closed/open, depends upon the differences in individual perception.

Relph has rightly warned, "One cannot continue endlessly to use more science to solve the problem of science, just as more alcohol does not cure alcoholism" (1984: 223). Let me close the above narration with a quotation from the *Katha Upanishad* (ii), where the Lord of Death, Yama, says:

> The good is one thing, the pleasant another; these two, having different objects, chain a man. It is well with him who clings to the good; he who chooses the pleasant misses his end.

11. Basic Reference

Singh, Shivprasad 1991. ***Gali Age Murati Hai*** (*The Street Turns Yonder*), in Hindi. 2nd ed. Vani Prakashan, New Delhi; First published in 1974 by National Publishing House, New Delhi.

~13~

THE CONTEXT OF STUDENTS' MARCH: KASHINATH SINGH'S *Our Front*

1. Introduction

The decades of the 1950s-1960s were a period of students' struggle throughout the world. Students became conscious of their rights and position; in fact, a new wave of awareness arose among them. A city like Banaras, which records a continuous history of educational status since ancient times, certainly had to play an important role in such movements. In this spirit the city of Varanasi too sparked with several lights of students' struggle during the 1960s. Even during the 9th century BCE the city was famous for high scholastic learning. Since the ancient past the city records many folk-tales of educational and philosophic discourses. In 1968 there were incidences of student unrest throughout West Europe and North America; this clearly indicates that the issue became a universal problem during that period. American universities, including ones like Columbia and California-Berkeley, also experienced such happenings. The French Students' movement influenced many students even in Varanasi (Shivprasad Singh, 1974: 361), especially in the Banaras Hindu University. The Ministry of Education, Government of India, early on listed the causes as "loss of leadership by teachers, growth of economic difficulties, general loss of idealism, absence of social life, a sense of fear and insecurity, and unhappy living conditions" (ME, GOI, 1954: 3). Segal (1968: 243) further adds, "On several occasions, most markedly during the disturbances at Banaras, students used violence, stoning police and destroying properties". It is also to be noted that, "Banaras Hindu University served as a base for those interested in agitation in the city, hence the prominence accorded to student activists, and a recognition of the collective authority assigned to Hindu scholars in the city" (Freitag, 1989: 226).

During India's freedom movement, Banaras Hindu University had played a leading role, and during the late 1960s masses of students again became conscious of their rights and raised the question pertaining to the language of instruction. Around this issue two novels have been written by scholars associated with the department of Hindi, Banaras Hindu University. In 1972 Kashinath Singh released his novel, ***Our Front*** (*Apna Morcha,* referred hereafter as **SF:**), a small novel oriented towards the philosophic activities and real feelings and experiences that the students had during that movement. Another novel by Shivprasad Singh entitled *The Street Turns Yonder* (*Gali Age Murti Hai*) was published in 1974 (see chapter 12).

The novel by Kashinath Singh is the first novel of its kind to deal with the students' movement. Its fourth edition was released in 1985. The novelist feels that the young generation, which was born after India's independence (1947), has been frustrated with the present-day situation of disappointment, isolation and anger, and disliking the age-old traditions, ultimately they fight against the administrative system. In 1967 the movement against the question related to language and communication had been felt crucially. It is therefore quite fitting to the situation that the novelist selected this theme. The novelist feels that it was the first incidence in history, at least in the history of the city, that those students agreed to struggle collectively for a particular purpose (Kashinath Singh, 1985: 6). In the present chapter, the novel *Our Front* has been taken as source material for the interpretation of the students' culture in Varanasi during the late 1960s.

2. The Background

The novelist informed us that the present novel was meant to be the first part of a planned voluminous novel, but by the pressure of time he was compelled to make the present version (102 pp.). Unfortunately his aspired voluminous work was never published! The author's own rural background of the Bhojpuri culture of the middle Ganga valley is implicitly expressed in the novel. But on the other hand, he never attempted to follow the contemporary thoughts and writing style, but rather reacted against such dogmatic rules and succeeded in establishing his own mark with a view to highlighting the negative utopias of society. Therefore at some places a vulgar tone could be noticed. This novel documents the story of the new revolution in the history of educational institutions — how issues like the medium of expression and teaching can influence the total socio-cultural set-up of the common mass of people! Other important issues, such as the relevance of education, the role of the big universities, the status of language as script or expression of life, and the differences of vital necessities according to different class of people, etc. are also raised in this small novel.

In spite of being an active leftist involved in teaching since 1965, Kashinath Singh always maintains his rural personality with pride and pleasures. Never caring for what others say, the novelist feels that his writing is not a show, it is an essential part of his experienced personality; therefore idealism has been superseded by real and harsh experiences.

Of course, the novelist rarely tried to directly reflect upon the Banaras Hindu University, yet from the happenings in the novel one can very easily recognise many recent occurrences that happened in the University. For comparison of the two situations, many factual statistics of the Banaras Hindu University are given in this chapter.

This small novel has some unique features, which clearly depict the social environment of Indian students. First, it is a typical example of the popular local culture and its transitional phase. A simple student comes from a rural area and tries to establish his identity in the crowded environment. Students come with definite expectations backed by the economic support of their families, but the system does not provide them a proper way to fulfil their expectations. Secondly, and closely related to the above theme, is the class-consciousness and regional feeling; of course, this has not been fully illustrated in the novel, except at a few places. Additionally, the ideological struggle has been well described. Thirdly, the feelings of the elite groups, which try to impose their supremacy and strategy for their personal gain, are fully treated. That is why many times vulgar words are used to portray the lived experiences in a realistic way. Fourthly, the local cultural colour of the students' unrest has been projected in a very wide spectrum with a view to understanding the students culture of that period, which is still very much the same or became more complicated in the present circumstances.

3. Education: the Basic Question

Primarily education is the way of getting knowledge, but at present it is essentially meant to get a good job. This situation was there even before independence. The late national poet Maithilisaran Gupt (1912/1986: 153) expressed:

> That education is useless,
> which has no use for nation's progress.

The constant search is to understand the basic causes of crises human beings face; this can't be realised either through lectures or through the books. "We want to know some of the basic and small issues, like — a person works hard throughout his life, even then why is he still poor? When so many items to eat are available, why are people dying of hunger? When the whole city is full of colourful, decorative clothes, why are so many persons naked? When so much knowledge and so many books are available, why are people still foolish and illiterate? The thing called happiness, what is that rare thing? Who has made these rules, regulations and laws?" (SF: 21)

The educational institutions, especially the university, do not provide an answer to such basic questions, and do not even inspire the students to think over such issues of vital importance. In a sense the students are becoming deviant, lacking in conscience towards the real meaning of education, for which the whole system is responsible. The system is regulated by its rules and laws; accordingly, "whatever you want, you can choose to eat; whatever you think, you are free to speak; whatever you like, you are free to live with! Sure, there is no need to seek permission to do anything! ... We are free to say anything, but in our presence my home is being destroyed, and we were silent! ..Why is it so? (SF: 21). If such questions are asked to our elders or teachers, they consider us dissolute and depraved persons."

The students do not know why they get education. Whenever this question is asked, they will keep completely silent and quiet. Moreover, nobody can help them to get the answer to this question. Neither can they adjust in the rural environment of the middle-income family, nor can they devote themselves to some other job to earn some money to support the family, except education. The University, (e.g. Banaras Hindu University) is considered as an industrial estate, the whole structure of which is now out of order (*Dinman* 1983: 13).

One free-lance senior journalist, Sushil Tripathi, had been writing under a column "Disturbances in Banaras Hindu University" in a popular Hindi daily from Varanasi, *Aj*. In one of his articles, "The danger of learning in the capital of all knowledge" (1986), he detailed out the negative spots of B.H.U. Referring to the historical importance of this seat of knowledge, he pointed out that once the city was a great centre attracting scholars. But at present the brain is leaving this site for some other place which can provide better opportunities to test their intellect and for integrated research. In fact, it is claimed very openly that the university environment is afflicted with regionalism, casteism, kin-kithism and loss of national consciousness. The university life has crossed its limits what ideally ought to be (Tripathi, 1986: 238-239). On February 3, 1987, Basant Panchami, anniversary of the foundation of the Banaras Hindu University, the police fired on a students procession marching to the foundation site to worship Sarasvati ('the Goddess of Knowledge'). Many students were badly beaten and the *puja*-scene was transformed into a battlefield. Such happenings reflect the increasing rifts between students and teachers, and also the defiling of the cultural tradition. In fact, "the university is now the seat of administrative bureaucracy and students' suppression — in no way a seat of learning" (cf. *Dinman* 1987: 20-22).

According to the western perception, the role of Banaras Hindu University (BHU) was to propagate the essence of Hinduism and invisibly to promote fundamentalism. Casolari (2002: 1417) narrates her viewpoints that, "The foundation of the BHU was the accomplishment of Malaviya's efforts to strengthen the Hindu sense of identity and cohesiveness. ... Malviya's project of founding a Hindu University was part of a wider project for the promotion of Hindu education, and it also attracted many other organisations and supporters in other parts of northern India. ... The BHU was thus finally absorbed in the milieu of the militant Hinduism. ...From the point of view of a secular observer of the 1930s, the BHU therefore presented itself as workshop of communal ideas and policies." This view is challenged by an insider sociologist, Ashok Kaul (2002: 4), who says that the earlier remark is an example of vested interpretation. The founder of the university, Pt. Madan Mohan Malviya, was in fact an open and liberal Hindu leader and reformer, mentor of Mahatma Gandhi, who gave his first revolutionary address in the campus of the Banaras Hindu University in Hindi. Every institution is a subject of transformation on the line of the societal demand and cultural change.

The general perception of a university has been to consider it as a seat of learning. But now it has become only an agglomeration of buildings and teachers. The newcomer gets the first impression that "the university has high buildings, tall trees, green grasses, reddish-yellowish flowers — all around a green map, .. but there is no teaching environment, no learning either!" (SF: 9).

Life in the university is deteriorating. The novelist noted:

> To this university students come from every corner of the country and are willing to learn how to lead life. Somebody help them to make life easy. Whatever life they have experienced in their

> neighbourhood, they don't want to continue. Anyhow people are living and passing that life, but it is not meant for us. Such a life is beyond tolerance. Such life was tolerable during the British rule as we were slaves. But that life even today! Ah impossible!! According to what the elder people say, we are now even worse than in those days; this cannot be tolerated! There should be at least some difference between slavery and independence. (SF: 19-20)

The novelist further exclaimed, "Where has the glory of this University gone? Is this our real India? A poor, hungry and naked India? Are there many Indias? And above all our own university — a place full of plants where at the name changing seasons one can enjoy only the spring. In which India does this scene exist?" (SF: 25). This expression clearly indicates that the people attached to the university are not aware of India's countryside — its critical problems and socio-economic and cultural conditions.

4. The Language Issue

Most of the educational institutions in the Bhojpur cultural region (eastern U.P. and western Bihar) are facing the problem of the medium of instruction. Hindi, as the predominant spoken and written language, received priority. But the issue of language is not only related to the medium of instruction, but also to the will to understand the local culture and to be in close touch with it. Since language is the best symbol of cultural affinity, it needs consideration accordingly. The novelist is conscious of this:

> Based on my previous experiences, I can tell that the meaning of language is not 'Hindi' or 'English'. In fact, language refers to the style of life, the manner of life. Language means the language of democracy, the language of democratic right, the language for the right of independence and right to lead a good life. We are fighting for such manners and customs. (SF: 79)
>
> ... Our language must be strong enough for constant counter-actions against such threats. Request is the habit of slaves; we have to desist from this habit. (SF: 79)

These kinds of feelings have historical precedents; in June 1877 Bhartendu Harishchandra had raised his voice in his famous poetic speech at Allahabad:

Language is symbol of growth,
the root of all development.
Without knowledge of one's own language,
one can't satisfy eternal feelings.
Brothers! don't delay now,
arise and destroy ignorance.
Enhance thy language,
it's the base of all wisdom.
(Sahai, 1905: 50)

It has been said that language is not an implicit issue as such, because "everyone is speaking and expressing himself, but does everybody get daily bread? The foreign rule has suppressed our mental thoughts, which resulted into our bad habits and behaviours. People have lost the conscience that poverty and desperateness should also be the issues of agitation. What independence is there? we even lost the sense to understand! People have lost the sense even to smile and laugh openly" (cf. SF: 42).

The spots and incidents described by the novelist express the cultural connotations of language, and since man has power to think, he has to express his feelings, therefore our thought is our language. If the expression is confined to an external gate, the whole cultural sense will be "in prison" like Apollinaire's end of the poem:

All is quite.
There are only two of us in the cell:
I and my mind.
(Olsson, 1980: 18e).

In the university environment at present, both 'self' and 'mind' are in prison because of the lack of thought-process and teaching-learning bearings for which these institutions were originally made. The younger generation, those born after India's independence in 1947, while getting education faces the problems of dissatisfaction, scolding, loneliness, depression and disappointment againt the system. The novel *Our Front* highlights these theme in varying contexts (see SF: 6). These problems still exist at varying degress and in different ways.

5. The University: Casteism as Base

Casteism and politics are the two faces of the same coin. With the passage of time students and teachers both became somehow entangled with different groups formed on the basis of caste. This compartmentalisation process has resulted in the growth of several competitive groups fighting for power-control. It has been felt that only those people with the powerful caste receive due attention. The novelist painted a scene in which the head of the department very quickly neglects even the genuine requests of a teacher, of a different caste:

> Brother; only their voice can be paid attention,
> they are Kayastha (Lala); while I am a Brahmin. (SF: 31)

The issue of lobbying and casteism has been widely given attention in many daily newspapers in Hindi and English. In Banaras Hindu University prevails an "advent of academic anarchy":

> Lobbying and casteism by the teachers and by the non-teaching staff, on the basis of provincial proximity, affect policy-making decisions and youth organisations. ... Since the Brahmins and the Kshatriyas are at loggerheads, the Kayasthas and the Bhumihars use this conflict by playing the balancing role. ... Casteism, rampant among the teachers and the officials, also casts its influence on the student leaders. ... The student leaders also influence the university authorities to a great extent and casteism and communalism are also prominent among them. (*NIP* 1981: 2)

The root of casteism goes back to the history of Banaras Hindu University. According to a report, the foundation of caste politics was laid when the University was founded in 1916. "Those who formed the faculty were called 'Brahmin department' and those who made up the administration were called 'Kayastha department' even in the days of Mahamana. The latter was expected to 'help' the former and not 'control' it" (Singh, B.M., 1983: 22).

The Gajendragadkar Committee Report on B.H.U. seems to accord indirect approval to communalism and casteism by quoting the singular statement of a non-Hindi area student — "favouritism is shown to 'Singhs' who belong to the Thakur/ Rajput community". However, this is considered to be a fallacy as shown in a Report by an M.P., (late) Rajdeo Singh, an old student of B.H.U. (1968: 6-7). The caste-wise structure of teachers shows the asymmetrical trend that certainly influence casteism and regionalism (see Table 1).

Table 1. **Caste structure of teachers, Banaras Hindu University**

Caste	1968-1969		1979-1980		1983-84 #		Aug. 2004 §	
	No.	%	No.	%	No.	%	No.	%
Brahmins	364*	48.7	597*	44.5	314	25.0	286	26.1
Rajputs	39	5.2	125	9.3	168	13.4	151	13.8
Bhumihars	—	—	—	—	131	10.4	124	11.3
Kayasthas	105	14.0	204	15.2	169	13.4	134	12.2
Bengalis	—	—	—	—	184	14.6	106	9.7
South Indians	—	—	—	—	176	14.0	126	11.5
Bania	180	14.4	179	13.3	116	9.2	112	10.2
SC & ST	—	—	—	—	—	—	19	1.8
Others	133	17.7	238	17.7	—	—	37	3.4
TOTAL	749	100.0	1343	100.0	1,258	100.0	1,095	100.0

Note: * it includes Bhumihars; in 1968-69 and 1979-80. Bhumihars, Bengalis & South Indians are not mentioned. Sources: Singh, 1968: 7; # unofficial estimated survey (382 posts were vacant in 1983-84), and *Dinman* March 1983: 16; § estimated as on 1 August 2004, note that about 457 posts were still vacant.

In an interview related to casteism and regionalism (especially among north Indian Hindi speaking people), a sociologist answered that "minorities come close together for preserving their rights, while those in majority are always in conflict" (*Dinman*, March 1983: 16).

6. The Department

Many departments of the university are now operated through the system of power control and bureaucracy. With the passing of time a bureaucratised environment is growing in the departments, where faculty members are counted in number but lose all sense of social harmony and personal academic pursuit. The basic question is: would the trend reach a stage where teachers will forget their ultimate professional duty — that is to say, can they forget that they are teachers? This syndrome is comparable to the Orwellian negative utopia — "can man forget that he is human?" Those who are fed up with this system fail to make any change in spite of their efforts. This reminds us again of the Orwellian note that "man is born as nothing but a blank sheet of paper on which any given society writes its text" (Fromm, 1983: 261). This may be paraphrased as "in the present circumstances a teacher is appointed as nothing but a blank sheet of paper on which the department writes its text".

The bureaucratic supremacy of the respective heads of departments can be understood by observing their relationship with their colleagues. The novelist openly discloses:

> The Head (of the department) gives weight only to the language of buttering, flattering, or threatening. My colleagues are experienced to use these according to the need of the time. People say it was not so in the formative days of the university. After the passage of time by the entrance of un-qualified teachers, those never deserving to be teachers in the university, this practice has flourished drastically. (SF: 29-30)

Those who are close to the Head naturally get individual benefits in terms of the allotment of classes of their choice and different kinds of remunerative jobs; moreover, they convince him to allot unfavourable subjects to the teachers who are not of their liking. With such acts flatterers get a negative pleasure, a sign of power and dignity received under the shadow of the head:

> I have recommended him [the Head] to allot you such subjects for teaching, with the aim to give you something to think about throughout the session ! (SF: 31)

The worst part of bureaucratic rule is noticed in the appointment of teachers. A lecturer exclaimed: "Do you think that I take part in politics? If I would have done this, by now I would certainly be a Reader (*associate professor*), do you understand?" (SF: 68). A professionally devoted teacher cries against the manoeuvred appointment, "I understand WHY: I do not understand HOW" (compare Orwell, 1983: 68).

Commenting on the bossism of the chairman of the department, a Finish scholar narrates a story from the West, which is however very similar to the situation here:

> Do not imagine in your naivety that you have been given the offer solely because you are a brilliant scholar. No, it is but the first step on the road to dependency, and the ulterior motive is to be given innumerable favours in return. In the course of time, if you are not constantly on the alert, there is a great risk that you will become the professor's personal secretary. You will be asked to see to all kinds of minor tasks that were not specifically agreed upon at your appointment. These tasks gradually increase in number and variety, and will eventually trap you in a web of duties, depriving you of the most precious thing that you have as a human being: time. (Gothoni, 1996: 47)

A report in a leading Indian Hindi weekly refers to the highest state of negligence, the wicked tactics and partiality used in appointments, in the article called "the destiny of an over-qualified", published under the series "The Burning Question" (*Dinman* 1982: 7). The same case with current evidences has further been flashed recently as one of the typical examples of several such happenings in the university. The research publications, both qualitative and in number, and an international recognition of a junior teacher encourage jealousy, boycott and ultimately obstacles in getting an academic promotion (cf. *Ravivar* 1987: 23).

Another report highlighted the manoeuvring, kin-clanism, biases, and bureaucracy in several projects running in many departments of the Banaras Hindu University (*Aj* 27 August 1986: 4). It has been found that these projects are treated as means of illegal earnings; moreover, manipulations in data are also a common feature (*ibid.*).

A recent happening shows the intensity of the situation. Deeply disturbed by the working culture, an associate professor (reader) of musicology and the only teacher in the department, Mr Anil Bihari of the Banaras Hindu University has resigned on 6 May 2004. This drastic step has raised a question mark against the working culture in the university. In an interview at the railway station while waiting for the train, he exposed: "by regularly following the never-ending formalities, I don't want to spoil the precious moments of the rest of my life. This university has lost the environment of work ethics and human values, and one will lose most of his/her time in following the bureaucratic complexities of the department. Neither one can work 'freely', nor 'creatively', but rather as a machine where any human sense does not exist. Most of the teachers are not devoted to teaching and lack any sense of human service and ethical values. Of course, there are talented students, but such teachers are rare who can shape their intellect. Attracted by the illusion of considering this university as a great place where creativity is always encouraged, I joined it; however after only one year I faced the hard realities of the complex bureaucracy, where in the name of the system torturing is offered as a reward" (*Hindustan*, a daily, Varanasi edition, 7 May 2004, p. 2).

7. Teachers and Students

What is teaching? Is it preaching or pontificating? Everywhere lies a dilemma. There is no environment that could provide an opportunity to learn 'the ways of living life'. "In the name of 'something/ somebody' there are 'we' and 'I'. Sometime back I too joined this university with the hope to learn that way but in spite of being humble, innocent and faultless, I got the punishment for teaching the way to students. And now I suggest that they read books" (SF: 20). Further, there is thought-conflict between *they* (students) and *I* (teacher):

> They say — We are reading books for the last 20 years.
> I say — Be disciplined.
> They say — We tolerated discipline too much.
> I say — Try to learn fighting against troubles.
> They say — Not us, but our forefathers struggled and died... and, in fact, this discipline needs to be challenged now.
> I say — Keep patience.
> They say — For what?
> I say — Don't cry uselessly, be quiet!
> They say — You too! Be quiet, O broker of administration!"
> I say — Go, be vanished from here!
> They say — Why shall we go? We pay rent for hostels, fees for education, the colleges are running for us; you are running to your ends, and why and where should we go?
> They say, and say again — Gentleman!
> You are a very good man but be quiet.
> You may be a scholar too, but useless. Is it not possible that you just don't teach, but limit yourself to regularly draw your salary? (SF: 20).

A horrible scene exposes the teachers and their personality; inside realities are also disclosed here:

> The situation of universities becomes very unusual since some teachers, those who are entitled to be suited in the Normal or JTC schools, got appointment there — they got that chair with the help of the language of buttering-flattering-threatening. You can talk about reading-writing-learning. But they tell us who their connections are — mafias or friends. Naturally both the groups will be unknown to each other. The third variety of teachers are those having less interest in teaching but very active in having control over the Head of the department, by knowing the rules and regulations of the university on their finger-tips. All the codes of conducts and rules and laws, they remembered fully. The position of the Head is quite critical. One can escape from these rules, but how to escape from those *gundas;* and if you want to escape from *gundas* you have to follow those bureaucratic rules. (SF: 30)

Sometimes to establish himself at a different site, a teacher gets entangled in student politics, but ultimately he has to be a part of that network; a teacher exclaimed:

> Bungling is a common feature in the university. In the beginning, to become popular, I too submitted myself to the will of the students, but I soon realised my mistake. It is essential, of course, to revolt against the bad deeds rather than to be a part of them, but it is still more important to be alert so that someone will not be able to throw you out of the scene. ... But without fundamental changes at the grassroots, no revolution is possible in the university, as the *institution* (of bungling) is a part of it. In this sytem every cunning student will forge his own father's signature, and teachers will attest its authenticity. (SF: 35)

The orientation towards money and materialistic gain is so important that professional worthiness has been outdated. A teacher says: "Once I went to Iran, then purchased a piece of land. If somehow I manage now to go to Canada or America, I would make a house" (SF: 10-11).

One of the factors responsible for the increasing number of such teachers is the lack of interest in their professional duty. With relatively less competition and struggle, only average intellects are coming to join this profession, and moreover, they have no devotion and loyalty to the profession: "If they were not teachers, where would have they gone ? Nowhere at all!" (SF: 11).

Concerning the quality of teachers, as a warning to students Gothoni says (1996: 46-47):

> The professors are not the omniscient geniuses that they sometimes pretend to be. Their capacity is limited in many ways. They are human and occasionally bothered, as indeed are all human beings, by feelings of inferiority. Make it a priority to learn to distinguish between the first- and the second-rate professors, the wise distinguished scholar and the mundane plodder Do not let the mere title impress you. Develop an inner sight and the ability to detect the real nature of the person. Separate the agreeable from the disagreeable. Remember the basic rule: beware of the unscrupulous, put your trust in the modest and humble!

A similar condition is also prevailing among the students. After the passage of time their status and glory has fallen down. The novelist suggests to the father of a student: "If your son is a rogue, loafer and lethargic, and the villagers dislike him; if he is a hell and you are completely disappointed with him, please send him to get admission in the University" (SF: 12). "Betrayal is increasing among them — slowly, slowly. They don't want to study from their heart and mind. In spite of this they feel they have no alternative except studying. They always create some disturbance in the classroom" (SF: 22). In fact, they don't know what to do and what not to do: "Ultimately, tell me what you want? You don't know even who's your real enemy? You yourself are thrusting a pole in your own anus!" (SF: 48).

With an aim to get solutions and to be aware of the root-causes of chaos, students invoke teachers for guiding them in the search for the right path:

> To know the real cause of problems students visit senior professors who inform that if you want to create disturbances (a means of revolution), then there are several issues — manipulations in the appointments, corruption in the examinations, bureaucracy in administration, clerks crossing their limits, peons disobeying after several requests, busy in making their unions. ... Students have no rest, they go from one door to another" (SF: 38). ... But try to be aware of the plain realities. Since students are lacking rational thought and are becoming deviants, the consequence is quite challenging. (cf. SF: 41-42)

The temporal relationship between teaching and learning has also some problems. The number of teaching days in a session needs to be cited as an example. Out of 365 days (one year), about four months are wasted as vacations and summer, winter, Dashahra and Divali holidays. From the remaining 240 days, 40 Sundays are to be taken out; and out of the 200 days left, 50 days are allotted for death and birth ceremonies of our leaders as well as for special occasions. Therefore only 150 days (5 months) remain for teaching. Moreover, the absence and non-seriousness of students and even of some teachers during this period of teaching are also well known (cf. Munshi, 1986: 11).

8. Concluding Remarks: the March ahead

Singh's novel *Our Front* is one of the best diagnostic surveys on the issues of student unrest, and far from the prescriptive notes. In support of the scene many negative issues and utopias are disclosed so openly. If the university is considered to be a 'sick-factory', as referred to by some analysts, the diagnosis is the first requisite before the treatment. In this context this novel needs to be taken as a first hand document. We should also think that the present condition is the result of time, but one must not always to criticise the institution, as it is our institution and "we must make of it what we can" (Relph, 1981 : 212).

It has been rightly realised that "the whole university is like a settlement amidst the jungle surrounded by the military. Everything is quiet stifling" (SF: 72). Every year constant threats of strikes and unrest lead to things being postponed— *sine die* — a consequence of deviant march. To what extent police control will help the way to the proper operation of law and order! Due to lack of education, certainly the policemen use to ask for identity cards from the teachers, and they can terrorise others with their rifles. The novel ends with this remark:

> That's right, you have rifles, but — I smiled and took a blank piece of paper from my pocket — this is my front! On this paper, I have never learnt to excuse people like you, even myself and my people too ! (SF: 102)

With his deep insight and conscience, the novelist has been successful in planting the seed of awareness in the educational environment of this city of learning, Varanasi, which is passing its life in a shadow of darkness. But, remember what Gothoni (1996: 83-84) said, "Academic circles and intrigues have not changed that much since the birth of the university as an institution, and frankly I do not think that they will change in the future either, despite the honest and well-meaning (bureaucratic) attempts to improve and reform university studies: the reason is, man does not change.

9. Reference

Singh, Kashinath 1985. ***Our Front*** (*Apna Morcha*). A novel in Hindi. Rajkamal Paperback Pub., New Delhi. 1st. pub. 1972.

~14~

THE PLACE-BALLET: KASHINATH SINGH'S *Assi of Kashi*

1. Introduction: Reflections

Places, as perceived, consist of a physical setting in which the complexity of natural aspects and the diversity of their qualities make the ground. Moreover, places are also constituted by their human setting where people live or have lived, perform their works in their ways, create images and evolve their emotions. Thus, the combination of physical and human settings results into a personality of place that is reflected in the life style and lifeworld of the people living there. Geography studies the earth as the home of man; and phenomenologically it seeks to understand how people live in relation to everyday places, spaces, and environments (cf. Seamon, 1979). The focus of study in such purview is an exploration of everyday movement in space, and the creation of place by human activities in time, i.e. the two functions in the 'totality of environment', viz. time-space routine, and body-ballet.

Time-space routine is a set of habitual bodily behaviours which extends through a considerable portion of time. The time-space routine has a certain holistic pattern which, like movement itself, is an essential component of daily living. On the other side, body-ballet refers to a set of integrated behaviours, which sustain a particular task or aim like manual skills or artistic sensibility (Seamon, 1980: 157). Finally, the place-ballet is a fusion of many time-space routines and body-ballets in terms of place (*ibid*.: 159). On this line, here the neighbourhood of Asi is narrated as a place-ballet where the market place and a specific tea shop create an atmosphere of vitality, camaraderie, excitement and even gaiety (cf. Seamon and Nordin, 1980). It is argued that people are inescapably bound to place because of their bodily beings, physical interaction and emotional bondage, reflected in the drama of place-ballet.

The cyclic march of life and the narration of the novel become both a counterpart to one another. When a place is envisioned as ballet, space-place becomes a live organism through emotional bonds and interpersonal contacts, and thus place-ballets become the heart of the neighbourhood (cf. Seamon, 1979: 56). By the continuity of the chorus of raillery and slang the neighbourhood of Assi has been a model of hard realities in practice. 'This practice, a peculiar form of vagabond language, always hangs over the outskirts of legitimate speeches' (Luitz Pound's remark, as in Sanyal, 2002: 52). The abusive words and slang used here are mostly unparalleled, contextually good and transparent, and above all they directly convey insightful messages. We can compare this to an arrow that speedily moves to its end after leaving the bow.

The city of Banaras is divided into over 350 mohallas/ localities (neighbourhoods, or wards), identified by separate revenue records, settlements and closed boundaries. Assi is one of the mohallas, bounded by a sense of place, and marks the southern oldest settlement in the city. The essence of the concept of neighbourhood is the common recognition of an area's identity by residents and visitors, on the basis of some number of distinguishing traits. However, there will be a constant suspicion between insiders and outsiders. The perception of neighbourhood identities, boundaries, and even designations, may vary among people and over time, but there always exist the processes of interconnectedness, continuity and distinctiveness. The neighbourhood of Assi possesses all of these qualities. Describing the regional personality of Assi, Katz writes (1993: 3):

> Banaras is considered to be a microcosmos of the vast Indian subcontinent with representative colonies for most of the geographical regions of India. There are, for example, Nepali Banarasis, Tamil Banarasis, Maharashtrian Banarasis, and Bengali Banarasis. Many diverse neighbourhoods can be linguistic and cultural worlds unto themselves, though interconnected through overlapping economic, social, and religious systems. Many of these neighbourhoods harbour a reservoir of age-old traditions that deserve further study. ... The cultural hub of the southernmost section of the city is known as Assi. This 'hub' is surrounded by a number of culturally related neighbourhoods, such as Bhelupura, Sonarpura, Shivala, Khojwa, Lanka, and Nagwa. Occupying approximately one third of the metropolitan area of Banaras, this southern sector of Assi with its adjacent neighbourhoods is also considered to be a microcosmos of the sub-continent.

Fig. 51. Kashinath Singh

There has been a very strong tradition in European literature to record the climax and fall, contradiction and identicality, high and low, the radiance and the darkness, as well as the sacred and the profane of the culture, life, traditions and distinctiveness of the old cities (cf. Scott and Simpson-Housley, 2001), but in Hindi literature there is a dominance of mimicry. This novel is a fresh addition on this line of mimicry. Living in this city for the last four decades and being a regular participant in the place-ballet of Assi, the author's claim for critical experiences is acceptable. The author himself has been one of the characters. The names of many of the characters are real names of real people, and the essence of the stories, plots and incidences are also real as claimed by the novelist Kashinath Singh (Fig. 51). However, under this shadow the author tries to narrate his own reactions against Brahminism and unsuccessfully pontificates on the sacred lessons of Marxism.

The recent most so-called 'autobiographical novel' on Banaras is Kashinath Singh's ***Assi of Kashi*** (2002; hereafter referred, **AK**:). There are five thematic stories, of course chained in continuity, that were published earlier independently. These are: 'Let Us See the Show of Wood'; 'O Saints! There's More Conflicts in the Home'; 'Assi of Saints, Non-saints and Stupids'; 'O Pandey! Which Immoral Idea's Behind You?'; and 'Which Thug Has Looted the City' (AK: 9). A critic opines that these five stories are in fact essays, which cannot be labelled as reminiscences, autobiography, reportage, or regional novel; better to call them 'five wonderful essays' linked together. It would be an injustice to set this literary work within a bounded field of writing (cf. Sanyal, 2002: 54). Here the emphasis is laid to describe the contents, messages and exposition of coexistent cultures as communicated in *Assi of Kashi*.

In the southern side at the bank of the Ganga exists the historic neighbourhood of Assi, named after the rivulet called Asi (Fig. 52). At

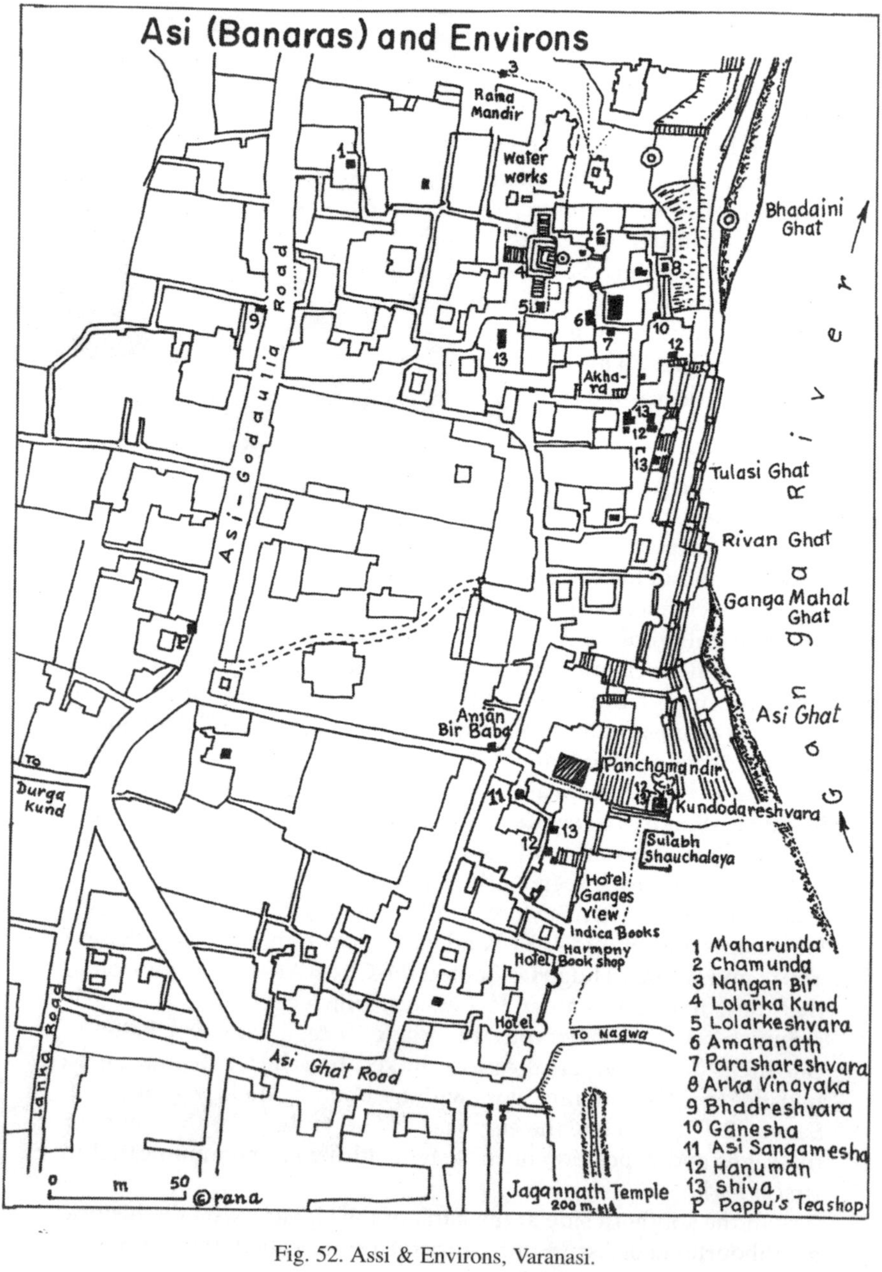

Fig. 52. Assi & Environs, Varanasi.

the Assi crossing is the crowded tea stall of Pappu. At this stall dialogues, discourses, and scenes of reciprocal abuse are constantly going on. Some of the distinct personalities of the city pay regular visit to enjoy this place-ballet and always imprint their mark. Never-ending discourses and brainstorming sessions, full of slang and railing, run from morning to late evenings. Those willing to join are welcomed, and those not are free to go. This novel is a 'life-show' presentation of the city and the neighbourhood, and their tales and the tales' tales. This area has a bad name among the so-called high-class conservative people, but not among the common men, as the author believes. Common men and common readers are the inherent parts in the plot/s of this novel (AK: 7).

The author is fond to such an extent of ridiculous ways of expression, which includes frequent abusive language, ostentatious reflections and boisterous remarks, that he lays himself open to ridicule. Among the Hindi scholars, the author is called blasphemous because of his challenges to the so-called soft-spoken, submissive and respectable language, in place of the folk and illiterates. At several places he tried to show his reactions to the society in a hyperbolic way, like his criticism of Brahminism and the political party BJP. By using the tricky way of praising and criticising himself, the author assumes that he has succeeded in portraying a negative image of Assi, which stands for a microcosm of Banaras. Taking help of contextual difference the author has cited names of medieval period saints who challenged the conservative traditions of Hinduism. To hit and be hit by someone, to humiliate and be humiliated by somebody, to abuse and be abused by others are common characteristics of the Aughar (Aghor) culture. These are the moral rights and duties too of the citizens of Assi. Kabir (CE 1398-1518) was the initiator of this tradition, which was completed to perfection by the Aghori saint Kinaram, CE 1627-1755 (AK: 38). The novelist is known for his satiric writing and rough speech, which has provoked his disrepute. He is so deeply involved in a deadly combat against the superstitious tradition and culture, that he ignored to narrate the puranic glory and the radiant past preserved in the bricks, stones and rituals still continuing in Assi and along the ghats.

The author has warned, "This edition is only for grown up and matured-minded people, not for teenagers and old people, and not even for those who are not acquainted with the rude language of Assi. ... And those find vulgarity, abusiveness, low profile and so many alike, are called '*chutiya*' ('product of a vagina', used as an idiotic address) by Assi-dwellers. Such people are requested not to read this novel and make themselves unhappy unnecessarily" (AK: 11). In the neighbourhood, when meeting somebody the Assi-dwellers say 'Hail to Lord Shiva' very loudly, followed in a low voice by *'bhonsari ke'* ('coming from a vagina', used as an abusive address), or *'harami kahin ke'* ('lousy bastard', used to call someone wicked) (*ibid.*). It is a folk saying, but anyone frequently using satire and rude language is said to be a dweller of Assi. "Here all are called 'Guru', not by their surnames like Singh, Pandey, Yadav, or Ram. Whosoever is born is called 'guru', and this title is imposed upon the dead ones too. This [Assi] is a well demarcated area across any strata in the social hierarchy" (AK: 12). Abusive expression is one of the rare resources of the indepth narration, cultural context and finally implicit expressive capacity of a language. Such expressions possess rare qualities of communication and the power of intense impacts. When all other means of expressive words failed, rude words are the only alternative.

The Assi area as a representative neighbourhood of Banaras is a cultural mosaic, and possesses all the attractions of the non-sensuous world too. The uniqueness of Assi area as described by Katz (1993: 331) is worth mentioning here:

> The neighbourhoods of Assi are also religious grounds. As an integral part of the ancient pilgrimage of Banaras, they constitute a part of the all-India tradition. These neighbourhoods have their own special sites of sacred power such as Ganga's confluence with the Assi River at Assi Ghat, Sankat Mochan Mandir, Tulsi Ghat Mandir, Kedarnath Mandir, Durga Kund Mandir, Lolark Kund, and Krim Kund. Many famous religious figures such as Vallabha Acharya, Baba Kinaram, Kumarasvami, Tulsidas, and even more recent figures such as Anandamayi Ma, Gopinath Kaviraj, and Svami Karpatri have lived in the neighbourhoods of Assi. These factors add to the special sense of Assi religiosity. But it is the residents of Assi who truly maintain the traditions and religious nature of their community. Without the support of the community, the religious personages and their institutions would be only hermits and enclaves unto themselves, island dwellers and islands in a temporal sea.

Samuel Johnson has rightly remarked that, "Every man has a right to say what he thinks truth, and every other man has a right to knock him down for it". A basic question is that if abusive language and slang have been a part of human culture since the ancient past, how can it be called 'rude' and 'useless'? If this is the plain reality, then it must also be accepted as a part of communication and literature. A critic has suggested that "the use of rudeness in stories should be like that of the apex on a pyramid, a precious stone in the ring, the poison in the snake, and like an oil lamp in the dark night. ... It should be like a thunderbolt for a short period but flashing the light in the sky of darkness. ... Life has also nudes, but nudity is not life. There should be nudity in art, but the sublime and supreme art is not only art. ... If nudity is unable to help the realisation of sufferings, inhuman deeds, compassion, piety and to awaken the feelings of the readers, and also encourages one not to understand the hard realities, in such a situation the nudity of language is an 'abuse' on the name of literature" (Sanyal, 2002: 52).

With a critical examination, the author satirically recorded the on-going ballet at Assi, and successfully exposed his own perception, experiences and portraits as a part of the various scenes. This reminds us Samuel Butler's remarks that " Every man's work, whether it is literature or music or pictures or architecture or anything else, is always a portrait of himself" (cf. *Ways of the All Flesh*, ch. 14). Kashinath Singh's novel *Assi of Kashi* is a first and unique literary book on the richness and intensity of the vagabond culture of a city. This novel is like a 'knot', Assi, synthesising the two contrasting cultures symbolised by the two rivers. The Varana in the north of Banaras represents the realm of Shiva and symbolises 'life', and was also a resort of great men of letters who followed the wide path of idealism. Assi, by its location in the southern part, represents the realm of Yama (Lord of Death) assisted by his subalterns — a group of people enjoying life as carefreeness, *joie de vivre* and headstrongness, and always keeping the toughness of life on the tips of their penises. Assi has been a refuge for reactionaries, revolutionaries and revivalists (cf. Sanyal, 2002: 55); at some plots the author tried to present himself as the true representative of the culture of Assi!

Another pertinent question is that to what extent the author has maintained his moral right to write this novel? Does he has such a deep experience as one of the characters, and also has he maintained a balance between the normative description of the hegemonic Brahminism as referred in the post-Vedic and puranic literature, and the real and in-side experiences of the contemporary downtrodden commoners? At many instances the author has succeeded, however at many other places he has been superficial. Some of the inter-contextual stories are copies of the well-known medieval storybooks that he included in his novel in the form of folk tales. Obviously he is master in the art of paraphrasing stories into another context of his liking. The story of "the jackal and the she-jackal who were running after an old bull with the impression that his testicles will someday fall like a ripen fruit which they will eat", taken from Vishnu Sharma's *Panchatantra*, an early-medieval book of stories (cf. Bhagwan Singh, 1995: 175-184), is compared by the author to the Indian political game. "The Indian government, a combination and alliance of several parties, is like an old bull's testicle — loose and swing as described in the *Panchatantra*. The parties in the opposition wait for its fall, but it will never fall in the near future" (AK: 92).

2. Banaras and Assi

If the Bhojpur region is the lunatic fringe of India, and Banaras is the lunatic fringe of Bhojpur, then Assi is the lunatic fringe of Banaras — the heart of the heart. And one says this with all the due bias of a Banarasian who loves his neighbourhood. "What a spectacular scene and a great pleasure is to be in Banaras, and nowhere else; not even in Paris, nor in Iran. Pleasure is an emblem of this city" (AK: 12).

Different cultures, taboos, traditions and totems have been brought together, and together they form the mosaic of Indian culture. Among them, we can find the following groups in Assi: (1) One is formed by the students of fine art, easily identifiable by their boards, sketch and colour pens while drawing sketches of cows, bulls, dogs and beggars. Obviously the city is famous for all these unavoidable features. (2) Another group consists of students of music and people interested in the annual musical concerts at Tulasi Ghat's Dhrupad Mela. Their dresses are distinct in colour, design, tone and looseness, and they carry musical instruments like sitar, tanpura, etc in their hands. They mostly walk in the company of their 'gurus'. (3) A third group is made up of journalists — crude and not reliable. They abuse and criticise the owners of the presses and newspapers, and publish only those items liked by them. They always claim themselves to be secular but publish news of fundamentalism and of the vested interests of politicians. News items like riots, murder, looting, robbery, rape, etc., are published with interesting stories and attractive and touchy titles. (4) A fourth group consists of the teenagers of the newly-rich upper middle class ('*gobardhanadhari*'). Most of the time they roam the streets with their new brand of motorcycles, such as Hero Honda etc. (5) There is also another group made up of political leaders, who believe in 'total revolution', that was born reluctantly from the nursing home of the political parties who disowned them. It is quite possible that these parties kicked them out because of their 'immaturity', ego, or rude behaviour, that didn't allow them to adjust to the party (AK: 24).

All these groups have chosen a common place for their discourses and activities. This place is Pappu's tea stall, where people also enjoy hemp-pellets (*'bhang ki goli'*), a mild narcotic paste made of *Cannabis indica*. In the evening different groups sit there and enjoy gossiping together with tea and hemp-pellets" (AK: 17-18). The art and style of gossip is a social practice since the beginning of civilisation. The gossip assemblies are the most known example of the continuity of such a tradition. Assi is a distinct place where gossip itself is conceived, perceived and practiced as an art of life, which should be called 'gossipology'.

Assi is not like the other neighbourhoods of Banaras. The author adds, "Assi is like the great book of grammar, *Asthadhyayi* (composed by Panini in ca. 500 BCE), and Banaras is its 'commentary'. For the last 30-35 years many Americans retired from 'capitalism' come here and wish that the whole world should be its 'commentary'. ... But nothing happens only by wish!" (AK: 12). For the author, Assi is a very special place. He says, "Assi for me is Bodh Gaya, and the holy fig (*Ficus religiosa*) at the ghat is the Bodhi tree for me, under which I received enlightenment" (AK: 12).

The Assi-dwellers perceive Asi Ghat as the king of all the ghats. "However, another ghat is named Raja Ghat ('king's ghat'). The city either starts here, or ends here. ... The holy fig (Bodhi tree) at its bank has the ghat for its natural setting. One can experience its fantastic adjustment with the rhythm of seasons, especially in the floods. ... This ghat, a superb combination of tunes of musical vibration (*soundscape*), colour of nature (*colourscape*), lines and edges of the ghat (*riverfrontscape*), and chirping of birds (*chirpscape*) is a spectacular combination of natural scene and cultural pattern. From morning to evening there will be artists sitting on the steps with their pencils, brushes, canvases and boards, as also photographers, practising singers, ladies singing in honour of the mother Ganga river, mystics yogis around the fire-pits. The rest are boatmen, wrestlers, sadhus, groups of chanters, and all sort of beggars" (AK: 98).

> Incense chips, incense sticks and smoke of marijuana [*smokescape*] are part of the cold and calm air around the ghat. And, this scene is combined with the sounds of ringing bells from the temple, the sounds coming from the moving boats and

> the shining rays reflected by the jumping fishes. But believe me, in the words of Jaggu the boatman 'since last few years this ghat has been changed by the Westerners into their permanent colonial houseboat. Everyday 250-300 Westerners, alone or in pairs, sit on the steps till late night!' (AK: 99)

> See the past. This whole Kashi was only the story of cremation! Nothing else! What was here! There was only a great cremation ground! Kashi means the great cremation ground. Whatever history or mythology might say, people say it this way! It is said that only corpses came here — in fact not coming, but carried by: on the soulders, in the bullock carts. From long distances! In the overall scene was the Ganga, and the banks covered with forests. No scarcity of wood! People carried corpses, cremated them and before the dawn retuned to their homes. ...In this way, this city has evolved from the fire, smoke and the remained ashes. (AK: 99)

Owing to different immigrants who came to this city for solace, peace and sacred merit, and as a consequence of various invasions, Banaras developed a diversified community structure while preserving its regional characteristics (cf. Singh, Rana 1980). In this manner Banaras has evolved a mosaic of social-cultural spaces which represents the whole of India. Brahmins from different parts of the country came and settled around the important Hindu temples. Payne (2001: 16) in her novel on Banaras describes this scene: "I came here imagining a water garden, people of a thousand different sects living in quiet harmony, with their doll-like god-figures blessing every act of life. It was a child's dream of Eden".

The Sarayuparina Brahmins are the priests of the Vishvanatha Temple, and also the major temples of the Omkareshvara Khanda (the northern part). The priesthood of the southern segment, Kedara Khanda, is controlled by the Gauda Brahmins from South India; however, in the Bhadaini and Assi areas, temples are mostly under the management of the Sarayuparinas. South Indians are mostly concentrated in the Kedara Khanda, but the Tamil people are also around the Vishalakshi temple. Maharastrians are settled around Durga Ghat and the Chowkhambha and Brahmanal areas, and Gujaratis are concentrated in Hatakeshvara (Haraha Sarai), Bhaironath and near Kath-ki-Haveli and Soot Tola.

Sikhs occupy many pockets of the city like Bari Ash Bhairo, Gurubag, Agastakunda and Chaitanyamath at Visheshvarganj. Sindhis have established Sadhubela Ashram at Bhadaini and pilgrims' rest houses at Agastyakunda, Kamachha and Assi. Recently Sindhis have settled in Gulab Bag, Maldahia, Orderly Bazar and Kamla Nagar. Bengalis are concentrated in the Jangambari, Ramapura, Bangali Tola, Sonarpura and Bhelupura areas. Several areas of Varanasi are dominated by different minority groups, like Kashmiris and Punjabis in Lahori Tola, Nepalis in Dudhvinayaka and Nepali Khapra.

Muslims are settled mostly in the suburban areas in the north, i.e. Alaipur, Jaitpura, Adampura, Kamalpura, Machhodari and Nakhighat. During the Muslim rule the military officers destroyed the noted Hindu temples and converted them into mosques, and the neighbouring areas were populated by them. The neighbourhoods of Lallapura, Nawabganj, Doshipura, Daranagar, Alaipura, Aurangabad and Madanpura are other areas where Muslims are concentrated.

Says the author, "In course of time, Kashi became a sacred place of pilgrimage and the place of *dharma* ['moral codes'] and liberation from transmigration [*moksha*]. This spiritual significance attracted kings, lords and rich people from all over the country. They started constructing palaces, mansions and rest houses along the ghats! The patron temple of the area was surrounded by people of the original place and prevailing social group. From south to north along the Ganga river are the Sindhis, Agrawals, Gujaratis, Maharastrians, Punjabis, Bengalis, Tamilians, Kannadis, Nepalese, and others who formed their closed neighbourhood in span of time. Later came Muslims, and they also settled down wherever they found space, and thus was their own neighbourhood formed. All the states and their representative castes settled along the ghats" (AK: 100). In fact, "the whole city was sitting up high along this curve of shore, and down at the far end in this bluish haze, she could see the fine lines and arches of the distant railroad bridge" (Payne, 2001: 57).

3. Ridiculous Ways & Symbolic Message

Banaras is open to all, in the same way as in ancient India several groups of invaders came, settled and finally became part of the soil of India. Of course Banaras is not so friendly a culture in the beginning, however it later accepts all the newcomers. "After the Emergency (late 1970s) and during the 1980s there happened a strange incidence! ... Certainly there had been attacks on India from time to time in history — by the Yavanas, the Hunas, the Kushanas, but one by one, and one upon other. However, in a similar way, young students came from the neighbouring states and districts like Arrah, Sasaram, Bhojpur, Chapra,

Ballia, Ghazipur, Azamgarh, Jaunpur, Gorakhpur, Deoria, and from other parts too to get education in the university, and they got shelter in the neighbourhood of Assi" (AK: 17).

The ghat area possesses a spiritual magnetic force, inspiring people to share people's sufferings and bring them solace. "After a long gap, attracted by a magnetic force, I unknowingly reached Assi Ghat and sat down under the Bodhi tree, where a 'Poets' Assembly' was held a few years back under the banner of 'Poets of the Masses, amidst the Masses' on the occasion of the 60th birthday celebration of Namawar-ji, the noted Hindi critic. This meeting was attended by Nagarjuna, Trilochan, Kedarnath Singh, Arun Kamal, Bhagat Rawat, Abdul Bismillah and others [*all well known leftist Hindi scholars*]. Today I found nobody here, except myself and a singer-yogi with his *khanjari* (a small tambourine). It was the first time that I saw such a scene. There was a smell of marijuana (*ganja, Cannabis sativa*) all around, and a pretty foreign girl was watching the singer's performance and listening the song:

> Listen O people of this world,
> The world is made of wood.
> Life is like wood, and death too,
> This is the mystery of the wood. (AK: 31)

"Assi is a slogan centre, not only the voice of Banaras, but also of western Bihar and eastern Uttar Pradesh (*Purvanchal*). A slogan initiated here, in span of time becomes a popular voice in the whole of Purvanchal" (AK: 36).

"Friends, Assi itself is 'an encyclopaedic Wishing-Tree of words and phrases' — the world knows it. Assi does not possess any thing, except framing [*formation*] of words. It exports this crop in the country and outside too. About fifty years ago this area had produced two words in its 'farmhouse' —'management' and 'programmes'. Programmes were not suited to its taste. Programme means 'liquor'; open the bottle, put the drink in the glass and enjoy! Convene the programme — making the country unstable, disordered and disturbed in all the possible ways. If someone thinks to get the country stable and organised, and save it from disturbances and loss, then enjoy *bhang* [intoxicant hemp]! *Bhang* is not like liquor, available in the ready form that one opens the bottle, pour in the glass and drink it. For this one has to 'manage'! It needs time to make it wet and soft, clean, and finally paste it on the stone. It takes hours of time. That is how 'management' means preparing *bhang*. For making *bhang*-paste ready 'time' and 'patience' are both essential. 'Programme' is not meant for those who can't spare time and are tightly busy! " (AK: 74).

> Listen O Sadhus! Where water is, life is there! Where the Ghat is, market is also there! Thus speaks history! History says that from the womb of the Ganga, the city was born! She is the mother. She's mother because three-fourth of the inhabitants of the city depend on her — ritual-priests (*pandas*), family priests (*purohits*), barbers, washermen, boatmen, fishermen, carpenters, flower-sellers, funeral-associates, sweepers, retail sellers, ascetics, sadhus, beggars, tour guides and masseurs — innumerable professions and uncountable castes are getting subsistence from the river since centuries. The rest fourth of the inhabitants include contractors and suppliers of sand, canal and bridge constructors, engineers, officers and also Indian and foreign-based governmental and non-governmental (NGOs) institutions involved in the issue of environment and pollution and in the 'campaign to clean the Ganga' (Swachchha Ganga Movement). They all are getting their sustenance here. One group passes life at the lowest level of subsistence, and others enjoy a lavish and extravagant life. This is the present scene, not a past one. (AK: 99)

Directly challenging the progress and workings related to the Ganga cleaning projects, poet Surendra Bajpayee recently provoked (as cited, Singh, Rana 2003) in this way:

> Society has two faces: dirty mind and dull people,
> Intention is not clear, but wish to clean the Ganga.
> On the contract of terror, taking dips in the depth,
> This always happened so, Why are you lamenting?

Pappu's tea shop in Assi (Fig. 53) is a centre of all types of activities and performances. This shop is always crowded by the regular visitors who are constantly involved in political discourse and debates, teasing and abusing each other, and are well-known for self-praise and specific identity. Their debates never stop, from morning to evening. Those who want to join in, or those that leave at any moment, both are welcomed here. This shop is a 'live show' of the culture of Banaras ? controvercial, contrast, disgraced, however attractive and politically awakened (AK: 7). "Assi-dwellers, especially those belonging to the community of Pappu's tea shop, think that abusing anybody and addressing him with rude titles is their moral duty" (AK: 36). "Pappu's

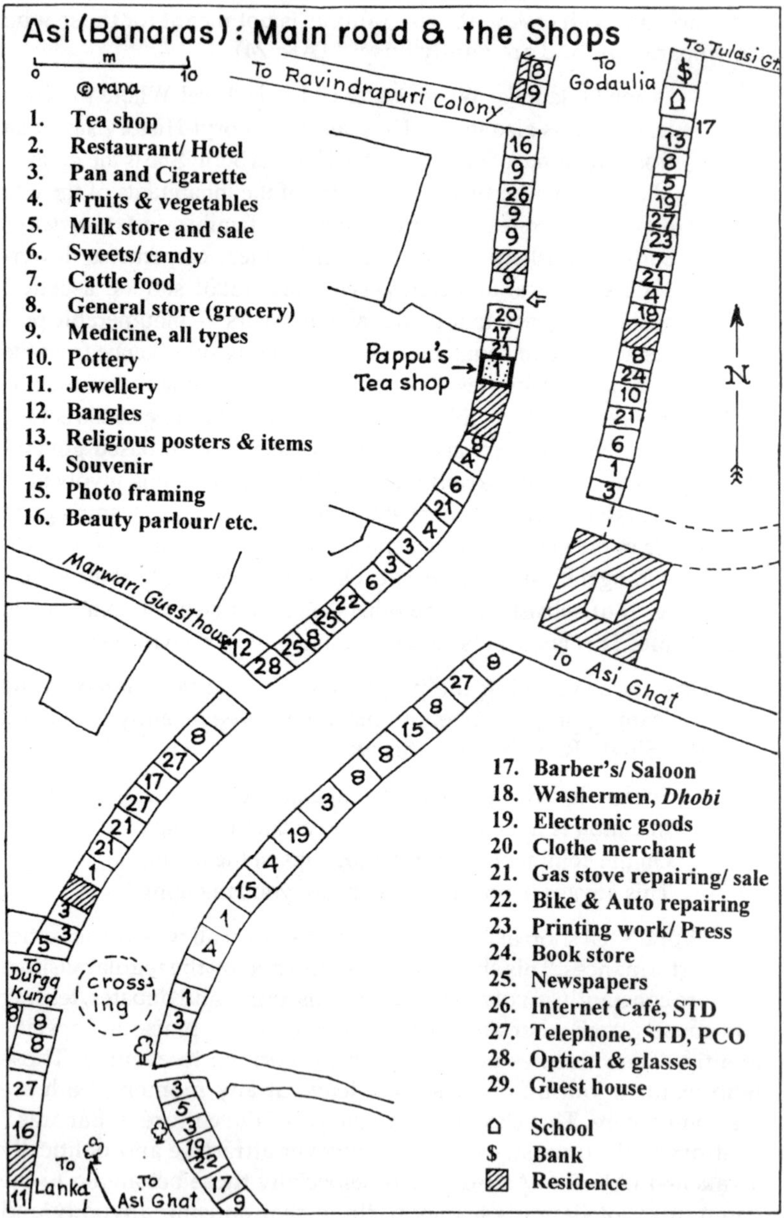

Fig. 53. Assi Bazaar, the main shopping area and Pappu's Tea shop.

tea shop is a companion's resort for artists, journalists, politicians and civilians, where they pass their daily life and share their feelings and experiences with each other" (AK: 20). One of the members of Pappu's tea shop said, "Is this not a great country, where for the cremation of a corpse a fee in the form of bribery is required! But we talk about idealism!" (AK: 25, also see AK: 34-35). Notes Segal (1968: 279), "Bribery— or what is delicately called 'grease money'— is ubiquitous, for import licences, building permissions, civil service appointments, agricultural aid, liquor permits, for almost everything that requires administrative sanction, even for school examination results".

4. The Place-Ballet: Socio-cultural Dilemma

As the name so thy fame. The word Banaras itself refers to the 'juice of life', which certainly includes a combination of up and down, good and bad, sweet and sour, simple and complex, and so many similar dualities. Assi's social diversification has been accompanied by a polarisation of the population into a hierarchy of classes and groups: upper and lower castes, pure and polluted, rich and poor, landowners and tenants, businessmen and commoners, modern professionals and traditional functionaries, old settlers and recent migrants, conservatives and westernised, Indians and foreigners, and so on. This combined pattern of diversity, distinction and dispersion created a variegated mosaic of urban culture regulated by the politics of pluralism and the unique social styles, despite constant internal tension and group conflicts.

"Assi has now turned into a museum, especially for Westerners. Whatever you want to see about the Banaras of the past, come here and watch" (AK: 155). The impact of consumerism and materialism is a part of the new culture. Says the author, "To survive in this city, money is the only necessity; to earn money one needs to know the tricky art of earning, and today everybody knows the art of that tricks" (AK: 159).

"Assi has until now preserved the spirit of laughter and pleasure — and what not" (AK: 162). The arena of Assi is a distinct example of the self-identifying behaviour of Banarasis that is locally known as *'Banarasipan'* — an integral mixture of *mauj* (delight), *masti* (joie de vivre), *phakkarpan* (carefreeness), and *akhkharpan* (headstrongness). Said Raja Rao (1989: 16), "The unreal and the real are so co-adjacent in Banaras you lose trace of the one, while you are wholly with the other".

> It is not disgraceful to say, 'The most stupid area in India is Purvanchal, covering western Bihar and eastern Uttar Pradesh'. ... A folk tale says that rhinoceros, while roaming for food, run

at 30/40 km per hour, but for excretion run back again to their habitat site; they will never stop on their way for excretion. This is similar to the conduct of the people of Purvanchal. In the past people were coming here for marketing, pilgrimage, domestic rituals and visiting courts for legal disputes, however they always returned back to their home for excretion! That is how the people of Purvanchal are known as the most stupid, absolutely useless, idiots, lethargic and indolent! When all the earlier settlers, kings, lords and merchants occupied Kashi, then the landlords and rich people of Gorakhpur, Deoria, Basti, Faizabad, Ballia, Buxar, Arrah, Chhapra, Sasaram, and so many other places thought over to settle here — this Kashi is ours, and we don't have any house here for shelter! Strange! (AK: 100-101)

5. Social Dilemma

The intensity of the satire is so deep that the author leaves himself open to ridicule: "Recently I heard that someone looking old, named Kashinath — a teacher in the university who writes stories — sits very frequently in the evenings in a shop, 'Rajesh Brothers', at the platform of Marvari Seva Sangh, along with some stupid friends. By his appearance how can one think that he is a writer or a poet!" (AK: 17).

Among the innovative cultural codes, beggary is an innovative cultural code. A new style of begging is to ask donations for cremating a corpse, taking benefit of the compassion of people — a new way of emotional blackmailing! (AK: 80).

So many people with high educational degrees are roaming around Assi without employment. They don't have money even for a cup of tea or a mouthful of betel (AK: 84). Such people sometimes adopt the means of beggary to earn money. Obviously, this is an example of the worst impact of individualism and consumerism. The Assi-dwellers perceive politics as means of survival and in several ways practice politics on the name of employment bureau for unemployed people (AK: 35).

Chauthiram Yadav, a professor of Hindi in the Banaras Hindu University, stresses the point that he never keeps company with Brahmins, but instead makes friends with Rajputs (AK: 43). This satire refers to the traditional perception that the company of Brahmins changes one's mindset to superstition and false belief systems. On the other side, Bhumihars are known for their alertness and cunning nature. "But, above all, a Bhumihar is a Bhumihar — incomparable!

An old proverb says 'be watchful and careful of **B**hai, **B**hatija, **B**hanja, **B**hand, **B**hut and **B**humihar — the six '*Bhas*' (viz. brothers, cousins, nephews, jesters, ghosts and men of the Bhumihar caste, respectively (AK: 46). A Bhumihar says, as the folktale referred, 'I am a Bhumihar! A hundred years thrust into one place, the next hundred years stood by there, next hundred years lay down, and next hundred years decomposed here" (AK: 89). This folk satire refers to spirit of existence a Bhumihar inherently possesses.

Addressing a Brahmin professor, the author says, "O Chaube, professor in the university. Do you know that Malaviya-ji had founded this university to teach the students how to commit sodomy with democracy! These youngsters learn how to cast forged votes during the elections" (AK: 70). The present educational crisis is result of that basic ideology; originally education is a cultural process to train man into a human being who will follow an ethical code in the service of humanity. The present education is only meant to train people to earn money, by hook or crook. The universities are now factories producing unemployed graduates.

The recent reservation policy for low castes has several negative consequences. In spite of being poor, the high caste youngsters have very few opportunities to get a job. "A Brahmin blesses the down-trodden and depressed class people with the words 'should you be born in your next birth in a family of Brahmins or Kshatriyas'. ...Soon afterwards, in a very low voice the Brahmin says 'You bastard, when you will knock one door after another unsuccessfully in search of a job, then only you will realise the pain of being a member of a high caste" (AK: 75).

Among the different localities of the city, Assi is disparate and distinct. "Assi is like an island in the Ganga of crowds and people struggling for survival. ...To live a life on the island requires a unique style, even since the time of Tulasi (CE 1547-1623). Whosoever came in this area carried some tradition, and keep them alive even today. Those traditions will always be here, in addition to the new cultures that are absorbed" (AK: 76). Satirically the author expresses, "Of course Tulasi wrote the *Ramacharitamanasa*, the great classic of the medieval period, but instead of giving supremacy to Lord Rama he preferred to eulogise Hanuman, 'the monkey military commander of Rama'. Who talks about Rama, except the 'Vishva Hindu Parishad' and its leader Ashok Singhal! How many temples of Rama and his wife Janaki are there? Except on the festive day of Rama-navami (the birthday of Rama) where does Rama exist in the eyes of devotees? See Hanuman

— wherever you go, on Tuesdays and Saturdays his shrines will always be full of devotees. The crowd of visitors starts since the early morning and continues till midnight — no room to move and no space to stand! In fact, the image god-form Hanuman is barely an imagination of the poet, and his establishment as a divine being was accomplished by Tulasi!" (AK: 97). Further, the author adds, " A human can be changed into a divine being by anybody, to transform a monkey into the human species took a trillion of years, but Tulasi in a short span changed a monkey into the shape of a god!" (AK: 97).

On the basis of a proverb, a representative personality of Assi, Dr. Gaya Singh exclaimed, "Don't trust the following, viz. Tiwaris among Brahmins, riding on a camel, a stepmother, cholera, a record-keeper among the Kayasthas, pumpkin among vegetables, ...and add to the list the most recent, i.e. American women!" (AK: 111).

Caste consciousness is increasing and becoming more complex too. Its most common use is to mobilise the electorate on the basis of their caste affiliation. "Elections are based on caste consciousness and the sense of unity is based on numerical dominance. ... Everybody pontificates about secularism, but in practice everybody in elections is involved in the power game of casteship" (AK: 51). The whole drama of political campaign is result of vested and personal interests based on individual gain or the well being of his own caste-group (AK: 56).

From the historical past Brahmins have been the Law Makers; they explained and interpreted the rules and traditions according to their choice and favour. "Brahmins are so cunning and tricksters that when some group is against them, first they enter into their company and, slowly like white-ants, destroy the whole group. They did this with Buddhists and they are now doing this with Kanshiram (the leader of the scheduled castes); Kanshiram always abuses Manu (the law maker of Hinduism) but use Manu's tricks and succeeds through his hypocrisy to gain hegemonic control" (AK: 65). The author adds further, "The Brahmins offered swords, bows and arrows to the Kshatriyas and encouraged them to always keep themselves busy in war, to fight and protect society. On the other hand they were busy in producing children with their wives. See these stupid Kshatriyas! Kshatriyas always were busy in outside, and Brahmins inside. With bow and arrow they were running after deers, and inside their houses life was moving delightfully " (AK: 65).

According to Mahatma Gandhi, "politics without principle is the cause of the global crisis. Whatever direction and ways concerning science, international relation or trade, war, education and ideological acceptance one proposes or selects are motivated by politics. And if it follows the track of immoral principles it destroys the social harmony." Gandhi has emphasised the need of spirituality as the first step of politics and governance (cf. Singh, Rana and Singh, Ravi, 2002: 72-73). But the reality is very hard.

To explain the difference between 'idealism' and 'realism', he uses symbols, satire and mythology. An experienced political worker explains that "Idealism is children's book for beginners, and good for competition and award. If Krishna would have followed 'idealism', Arjuna and Bhima [the heros of the epic *Mahabharata*], both would have been killed very early. ... If a faithful wife follows 'idealism', how could she have sexual relation with others? Do you know any ideal wife not having sexual relation with others? Keep 'idealism' very high for exposure, but live your life at the 'lowest' ? this is our so-called tradition? ... I've already said a thousand times that 'idealism' is a gold ornament, which is not to be worn everyday! Only on the occasion of marriage and such special occasion these ornaments are put on! Let us use the practice of 'idealism' once or twice in an year, but throught the year do the 'real politics'" (AK: 34). Corruption is the oxygen for democracy. Is there any nation where democracy exists without corruption? Try to keep eyes on all the nations of the world; where does such a huge number of local and regional parties exist, except in India! (AK: 34-35). Emotional blackmailing and hypocrisy are the essential part of political strategies in India; its history goes back to the early period of independence. And reached its climax in the period of (late) Indira Gandhi, who used the weapon of emotional feelings and got support of the Brahmins (AK: 60-61).

6. Unparalleled shows

The religious importance of Banaras has been the main force that drew Brahmins to settle down in the city since the past. In course of time their number increased. "In numerical dominance, Ahirs stand after Brahmins. Brahmins first exploited the area of Assi-Bhadaini; it was an isolated but great island under the control of priests. Later the landlords and rich people built rest houses, temples and resorts and handed them over to Brahmin overseers, who were thus benefited by their financial support, and on the other hand their children could get education in the city. Thus they have been fortunate to enjoy the cream. ... Under the shadow of Brahminism these priests keep the real owners involved in corruption, and torture the common public. But whatever inhuman deeds and sins Brahmins commit, there is no rule to punish them" (AK: 101).

The medieval South Indian saint-poet, Basavanna (§ 820; cf. Ramanujan, 1973: 20), laments while praying to Shiva:

> The rich will make temples for Shiva.
> What shall I, a poor man, do?
>
> My legs are pillars, the body the shrine,
> the head a cupola of gold.
>
> Listen, O lord of the meeting rivers,
> things standing shall fall,
> but the moving ever shall stay.

With the means of mythology, the author has narrated the hidden side of respectable institutions, something that the social norms never allow. "Rama asked Lakshmana, his younger brother, while indicating a wounded dog: 'Who has bitten this dog?' The dog replied, 'a Brahmin'. Rama wondered what to do because no legal rule of punishment existed to punish a Brahmin, even if he be a culprit. The dog was asked what he wanted. The dog said, please bless the Brahmin that he will be reborn as a Mahant [chief of a monastery] in his next life. ...The dog later said, you know I was a Mahant in my previous life, and in this life I am serving as a dog in the same monastery. This cycle will continue. ...Being a Mahant one can perform social service to all. In the monastery there will be many young and beautiful girls of 20-25 years old, who are nevertheless called 'Mata-ji' ['mother']. The bastard attendants in the monasteries are always addressing them as Mata-ji. The devout Collector [i.e. the District Magistrate] has come, and will stay overnight. He should be treated well! First we will serve him good food, and in the night he will enjoy lovely pleasure [*bhoga*, sex]..." (AK: 88).

This story presents two opposite views of life, called *yoga* (spiritual happiness) and *bhoga* (worldly enjoyment). Lannoy (2002: 189) describes this last as a symbol of the lifeworld in Banaras, what is referred as *masti;* he said "*Masti* is not cynical, it doesn't send up the serious side of sanctity, but in a way that is inimitably Hindu, it makes sure there is always room in religious matters for a sense of humour [*and physical pleasure*]. *Masti* is genial and tolerant in its commitment to a carefree way of life."

"I've heard that the USA has invented an 'anti-smile syrup'. After birth, one drop should be given to the child, and he will never laugh in his whole life. People say that it is under the process of test in Japan (AK: 151). ...What you call 'anti-smile syrup' is in fact the TV (television), Gaya Singh added thus" (AK: 162). In this TV there is always a channel of your choice, whatever you like (AK: 158).

> "You're crossing all the limits. What do you know about the Christians? They are lower even than *Chamars* ['leather workers, untouchables']. Lord Shiva can in no way tolerate that a Christian should live aside him" (AK: 130).

Bahari Alang ('outside entertainment') is a live tradition and an essential part of the culture of Banaras; it is enjoyed in closed groups and in places of solitude. This is a matter of mood, time, and a ritualised pattern of activity. These recreation places are outside the city territory. As the city expands, the *Bahari Alang* places shift. This tradition is culturally accepted as 'the flavour of life' (*'jivan ka ras'*). To enjoy that flavour special food is an essential part; a menu is fixed that consists of *litti* or *batti* (baked balls of flour), *dal* (lentil soup), *bhat* (boiled rice), *chokha* (smashed eggplant dish) and *churma* (a sweet made with flour, clarified butter and sugar). Except the last item, the rest are cooked on an open fire using cow-dung cakes as fuel. "A traditional juice *Thandhai* (a cool drink made of milk) mixed with *bhang* (intoxicant hemp, *Cannabis indica*) is a popular drink during summer in Banaras. But this shop has made a different experiment by serving *bhang* with tea, and this is a 'hit' like hot cakes since last thiry years" (AK: 42). This is one of the common practices to experience the pleasure of joie de vivre and carefreeness.

As the author explains, "*Bahari Alang* means a place without settlement. In the language of Assi it is a place of an undisguised silence. Everybody is free to walk naked and to speak any form of abusive or boisterous language. The *Bahari Alang* consists of even enjoying hemp (*'bhang ki goli'*), going to the other side of the river for open toilet, smoking drugs, putting marks on the forehead, chewing betel-leaves, using a scarf instead of pants. This is different to a picnic, because in *Bahari Alang* no member of the family is allowed to attend (with an intension to avoid them the vulgarity of the show). After independence the whole area across the river Ganga remained as *Bahari Alang*" (AK: 169). *Bahari Alang* is an impulsive trip, i.e. full of appropriateness for the lifestyle Banarasis live in. Says Kumar (1988: 89), "*Bahari Alang* is always described by a Banarasi as being the quintessential Banarasi activity; to be a Banarasi means to enjoy *bahari alang* and *bahari alang* is that which is most loved by Banarasis".

On the auspicious occasion of the colourful spring festival of Holi is celebrated the 'Holi Assembly', known for its rude performances of poetry — unique and unparalleled. "O People! See the spectacular charisma of Lord's (Shiva's) land, Kashi: 'the unparalleled show must be seen'. None of the human parts is without action! Any issue, that may be like LTTE, Khalistan, terrorism, the Babari mosque dispute, national or international matters and current affairs of national and international parties — all are within the range of coverage by the 'weapons of abuse'. Whatever be your interest, enjoying rude language, or political satire, or any other rough issue, it will be presented in front of you. If you may not conceive the direct meaning of the word, this assembly provides you music of vigorous, uprooted and rapturous" (AK: 19-20). This is an example to get experience and by participation practice the provokings of postmodernism!

> Enjoying hemp-pellets is a cultural symbol of Assi. If there is a culture, there certainly has been a tradition too to survive it. That tradition for which Assi is renown all over the world is the 'Fool Poets' Assembly' (*Murkh Kavi Sammelan*) held on the occasion of the festival of colours, Holi. This assembly, a great festival, is the only one of its kind in the whole world! Thousands of people from different parts of the country and also from abroad come to watch it and enjoy. ... The traffic was jammed and movement of crowds stopped. No room to move. ... The guardian and protector of this celebration is Dr. Gaya Singh. ... When the police authorities issued an order to stop the Fool Poets' Assembly, Gaya Singh warned them, shouting loudly, "You bastard Sharma! How can you dare to abolish the tradition of Kashi? What power do you have to attempt to destroy a tradition that is being followed for thousands of years! Police officers like you come and go; but Assi was existing in the past and will exist in the future too! (AK: 19)

On the occasion of 'Fool Poets' Assembly', celebrated on the 1st April every year since, the environment of Assi area is transformed into 'heavenly abode of fools'. The fool-poets' assembly has been an unparalleled show for the organisers, attendants and spectators ? all share the joy of being part of it; they enjoy the political slang of *'Feel Good'*!. In a more organised way this took its turn in late 1960s at Dashashvamedha ghat. This celebration is an Indian edition of the Fool's Day introduced by British in the colonial period. Thomas Carlyle (1795-1881), when asked the population of England said, "thirty millions, mostly fools". The people of Assi feel that making or being fool is a manifestive art like a form of *yoga*. Of course in the transformation and process of acculturation the Banaras dwellers lost so many age-old traditions, however they revived such assemblies in different ways and in different forms. They proudly feel that they are the kings of this great art. From individual foolness to national foolness we march ahead in blooming the glory and fragrance of the art of foolness.

The latest fools' assembly held at Assi Ghat and at Dashashvamedh Ghat on 1 April 2004 had been unique where the foolish citizens competed with foolish politicians and ultimately succeeded to make the public fully foolish. This assembly was organised by their association, presently chaired by a noted man of letters Pt Dharmasheel Chaturvedi. Banaras is the city of knowledge, and the art of being or making fool is one of the superb arts; Banaras cannot be lag behind by not florishing this art!. It reminds what Lord Byron (1788-1824) said:

> I'll publish, right or wrong:
> Fools are my theme, let satire be my song.

And also what Jonathan Swift (1667-1745) said:

> Hated by fools, and fools to hate
> Be that my moto and my fate.

"The shepherd-like Bhajapais (followers of Bhartiya Janta Party, a political party inclined to Hindu nationalism) conveyed to the protectors of the tradition of Assi that the Fool Poets' Assembly should be stopped. It is rude, nude, filthy, erotic and ridiculous. If someone wants to celebrate it, he should go out of the city! Go to the sandy tract on the other side of the Ganga river where nobody from this side will hear it. If you insist in holding the Assembly, the consequences will be police firing, serious confrontations and killings, etc." (AK: 19).

7. Insider vs. Outsider Perception

In many incidences an insider knows what others can never know; at the other end an outsider understands and constructs a rational interpretation for many other aspects, which an insider cannot do. There always exist a dilemma between the two viewpoints. But, in fact both are a counterpart to each other. "Have you heard the story of Diana, an Australian tourist, who was victimised by a bastard guide, a rough, dissolute and stupid fellow, she was ultimately murdered after a gang rape. ... There are incidences of murders of foreign girls whose dead bodies are found in a lodge, at the bank of the Ganga, etc." (AK: 125).

"Banaras is dying, but not from happenings such as the one of that foreign woman. She [Diana] represents the whole city situation, but I know the situation in Assi. It is obvious from the data how much imported heroin, brown-sugar, hashish and morfine are consumed near the ghats! Everywhere sex stimulant drugs are now on sale. The innocent older people are the victims. ...In all the inner lanes smuggling of US Dollars is growing rapidly (AK: 112). Drug addiction is becoming common among the youngsters because of the impact of Western tourists. These youngsters are unemployed loafers, who always run after beautiful girls for sexual enjoyment. They mostly sit at the tea stalls and try to cheat the visitors" (AK: 81).

The foreigners have purchased many houses under the names of local people, and they pass their lavish life here. They have spent a lot of money in repairing and extending these houses. They have even contracted fake marriages to arrange for their visa. They have started 'cyber cafés' in collaboration with local people — to be used by them for their personal contact and communication. We think of this as the process of 'globalisation'. "They are free to come here as many times as they want, and stay here up to the period they like. But think of us? Have we capacity to visit America even once in a lifetime? Our house is their house, but their house is theirs only, not of ours! ...Don't think of today, think of the future. In the near future they will tell, "Assi is decaying, dying, being demolished; give us a chance and we will renovate it — make it radiant, shining. Tomorrow they will make Banaras attractive, the day after tomorrow they will improve Delhi, and as the next step they will adopt the whole country like a baby! And, at the end while becoming too late we will know that we are in whose arms — motherly Yashoda, or demoness Putana?" (AK: 112-113). This narration explain the clash of two cultures, ideologies, life-styles, and ultimately in favour of naïve showing reaction against foreigners, however local people never try to stop their entries directly because they are the rich resource for the generation of wealth and improving economy. Foreign girls choose for boy friends and in some cases husbands, locals from the group of barbers, singers, book-sellers, those are easily managed. Such girls are involved in double tracks, double business — research and also drug business. By this trick they get student visa and easy entry into the universities. "How can one say that they are tired of Western materialism and fast life, and dissatisfied with machines and the money which gets them a lavish life?" (AK: 105).

A good number of foreigners are living in Assi as 'paying guests', mostly in the houses of low caste people. It suits to their pockets and they receive more respect and care than from high caste people (AK: 116). They make most of their companions and friends from persons of the lower castes (AK: 106). They are mostly backpackers and low income tourists or students, from all the corners of the world (AK: 118). Everywhere walking couples or groups of foreigners are part of the scene in Assi, and many of them would be in Indian garments — kurta and pyjama, or sari and chunari — worn though with a very doubtful elegance (cf. AK: 77). These foreigners walk here and there — on the road, in the lanes, they sit at the tea stalls, on the ghats; they are dressed in the Banaras style using undergarments, scarf, long gowns — any dress looking like dress to have the sense of joie de vivre. They sit at the cheap tea stalls and avoid the crowd. But nobody cares for their presence (AK: 104).

Most of the foreign researchers try to interpret or misinterpret Indian culture and its traditions and taboos according to their background, pre-conceived perceptions and ideologies. Catherine, a representative of this group, has written her own observations of hospices ('dying homes for the old'), where a majority of the women were found begging or getting shelter and food from other sources. She also noticed that a group of wandering mendicants (*sadhus*), who project themselves as great mystics and ascetics, are moving in ultra-modern cars with robust bodyguards carrying guns. They run chains of monasteries with the support of their sturdy and mafia devotees, and they themselves are entangled in several illegal cases (cf. AK: 109). However, there are many *sadhus* living a very simple life, who always help the visitors through soul healing and moral support; sometimes they live a beggars' life. Since Kashi is considered as the greatest holy place, all types of monasteries, both headquarters and branches, exist here.

Widowhood is a time of crisis in women's life. It has been remarked that "in their self-identification, the widows make a stereotype of beggary. Hunger and sickness reduced them to a sub-human level" (Saraswati, 1985: 111, 116). Catherine, a foreign scholar, reports her experiences of visiting hospices ('dying homes for old people'): "in each of such houses, according to the register 50-60 widows live there, and each one receives a paltry pension from the department of social welfare. ... However, I counted that hardly about ten widows were present there, the rest of the rooms were locked. Many of them do begging for their livelihood. Where have those widows gone? In what condition they would be? Some of the 'widows' introduced to me in no way look like 'widows" (AK: 109).

Said Catherine, " 'I've collected all sort of data pertaining to widows, bulls and ascetics. I noticed a great change during the last five years. If you don't mind let me add that Banaras is dying! The Banaras that was once read, heard and understood — is now at the edge of dying!' Listening to the hard realities is always painful. Gaya Singh, symbol of Assi par excellence, reacted against this statement, 'What do you want? Do you wish that the whole city be full of monasteries and widows? Do you wish that wandering bulls may defecate everywhere and make the lanes filthy? Do you wish that the bearded *sadhus* should make a fool of the common man even today? ... How can she dare to say that 'Banaras is dying'? In this Banaras we exist, and you are and myself and Assi too. These idiot foreigners come here after crossing several seas. These foreign visitors try to kill Banaras, and then propagate that 'Banaras is dying its own death'!" (AK: 110). In this purview Banaras may be considered as a desert, comparable to the Latin proverb used for Calcutta (Kolkata) — *Magna civitas, magna solitudes*, "a great city is a great desert" (Chaudhuri, 1970: 20). Chaudhuri further narrates the inside story of some Indian cities in north India that may be compared to Assi and Banaras, "They do not contain organised societies. They are formed only by the falling detritus of the stratified rocks in the villages, which are not only being quarried and dynamited but are also breaking up of themselves through an economic and social weathering to which the geological furnishes no parallel" (*ibid.*: 21-22).

8. Concluding Remarks: Awakening and Message

Understanding the maintenance of civic order in the life of Banaras, especially Assi, is a complex whole. On one side is the constant struggle to maintain a balance between tradition and modernity, and at another is the Hindu mindset that accepts the consequential tension as part of the lifeworld. This is the secret for enjoying life in this part of the world. It is like a slowly retreat towards death that Assi is moving under the drastic and constant threat of a team of people studying river pollution. The second group is made up of smugglers and the third of racketeers and *gundas*. The fourth is the government machinery and the bureaucrats. Amidst all such groups passes the life of common man! Where has the glorious tradition of our Assi gone? Alas! Everything on this earth has to go through the process of transformation — Assi too! (AK: 171).

The Assi-dwellers perceive the world and its turning like wood. "Wood is a symbol of the lifeworld and the lifecycle. In childhood we slept on a wooden cot. Being young we played games with a wooden stick, learnt writing letters on a wooden board, our early teachers trained us while beating us with a wooden stick, in marriage the rituals are performed sitting on a tiny wooden stool, the first night of our love passed on a wooden cot, in old age a wooden stick is a dependent means, and finally, on a wooden funeral pyre we will be cremated. This is the mystery of the function of wood" (AK: 31). Among the visitors, some use the culture as a sacrificial fire to purify themselves, some use it as an administrative tool, some use it as a boat to cross this world of illusion, while others use it only for fun and as a resource for business (cf. AK: 31). The chain of religiosity that maintains the continuty of tradition in Banaras is completely missing in Kashinath Singh's novel on Kashi. But one should remember what Katz (1993: 331) has finally concluded:

> The religiosity of Assi is supported by the special nature of the *tirtha* (a place of pilgrimage), but maintained by the common folk of the community. The entire community is drawn together in this task. Each section of the community, and every individual, share in maintaining the Assi tradition. This concept of total community engagement ... is what I regard as the factor behind the vitality of Banaras tradition and the unity of the society. Placing aesthetic values as well as the love of the dwellers and the love of the friend in the centre of community traditions are the secrets behind the success of Indian didactics. As long as the dwellers of Assi are actively engaged in tradition, the religiosity of the community will endure.

"Friends, I feel a sort of humiliation or repentance to say that the worst of all the organic species is the human being! When this specie gets higher education, then it becomes even worse! And, above all, if a person becomes a writer or poet, then she/he has lost all the values. Everywhere she/he searches 'meaning' — be it there or not" (AK: 31). This is comparable to George Orwell's satire, "Man is the only creature that consumes without producing. He does not give milk, he does not lay eggs, he is too week to pull the plough, he cannot run fast enough to catch rabbits. Yet is is lord of all the animals" (Orwell, 1945/1976: 9).

"It's too much. The world is too much! I'm tired of all this business. It may be air or water, whatever comes first do business out of it. First pollute and get benefit, then for cleaning do the business of cleaning. To what extent will this continue? Nobody knows!" (AK: 138). This reminds William Wordsworth's one of the *Miscellaneous Sonnets*:

The world is too much with us; late and soon,
Getting and spending, we lay waste our powers:
Little we see in Nature that is ours;
We have given our hearts away, a sordid boon!
The sea that bares her bosom to the moon;
The winds that will be howling at all hours,
And are up-gathered now like sleeping flowers;
For this, for everything, we are out of tune. (I: 33)

Together with drastic rise of prices, the tiresome suffering of common masses is provoked by the author (AK: 146), as:

For some people multinational companies,
For someone the temple,
For someone entertainment,
For the rest the drastic rise of prices.
All are enjoying their own business.
Hail to thy Vrindavana Bihari [Krishna],
Hail to our dharma,
Let non-dharma be lost,
Let's have the sense of helping others.
Hail to our Lord Shiva.

9. Basic Reference

Singh, Kashinath 2002. ***Kashi ka Assi***. (Assi of Kashi). A novel in Hindi on the Assi area (southern part of Banaras). Raj Kamal Publ., New Delhi.

~15~

Banaras is Wherever You Are?: Following Pankaj Mishra's *The Romantics*

1. Introduction: Canvas and Critique

The character of the place acquires recognition through the social individuals who, with their constitutive function of religious ethos and the functioning activities tried to use, allocate, understand and reflect the sense of spirit among the various places through the passage of time (cf. Silk, 1984: 170). One can allude to reality through vision, perception and feeling of the people or through text-interpretation as the texts speak for themselves. Moreover, the power of imagination to understand the invisible qualities is another aspect of the learning process (cf. Relph, 1985: 1), which will be essential to interpret while explaining a writer's vision.

Richard Lannoy, who during more than four decades of his life photographed and reflected deeply about the city, wrote, "Benares [i.e., *Banaras*], in its unimaginable antiquity, belongs not just to Hindus, but to Muslims, Sikhs, Buddhists, Jains and Christians. But it also belongs to everybody. I have come to the conclusion after many years that Benares is not just a physical locality, a cultural entity, a historical marvel of continuity and a city on the Ganges. It extends deep into the collective unconscious of mankind, an archetype which infiltrates into the dreams of millions — without its name even being known to them. Strangely, the closer and more detailed one's acquaintance with it all becomes, the more its unique particularity is revealed as based in the universal. A sacred city dreamed into existence over the ages, it is also a state of mind. As an old saying puts it: *Benares is wherever you are*" (Lannoy, 2002: 58). However, if someone is *'nowhere'*, or *'lost somewhere'*, then where will Banaras be?

In contrast to Lannoy, Pankaj Mishra (Fig. 54) paid only a short visit to the city of Banaras in 1989. Through one of the characters of his novel, Samar, he has tried to narrate his experiences (PM: 3). Mishra, who is basically a journalist, was born in 1969, and is a regular contri-

Fig. 54. Pankaj Mishra.

butor to the *New York Review of Books*, the *New Statesman*, and *Outlook* magazines. ***The Romantics*** (hereafter referred as **PM**:) is his first 'so-called *novel*', and has been taken into account as resource for this chapter. One of the e-zine ('electronic magazine') critics has remarked, "Samar in any case comes across as a 'detached' individual, probably because he is also the character through whom Mishra views the rest of the cast and in that sense seems to represent a part of Mishra's own personality. This 'detached' approach makes Samar an extremely wishy-washy character who just seems to blunder along life's by-lanes, going where his destiny takes him, with minimal dissent". Any idealist reader, those trying to get some insights of the uniqueness and complexity of Indian culture as revealed in Banaras, will be dissatisfied and also confused; however, one should sympathetically keep in mind the idea that Mishra is a trained and practising journalist and has already published his first travelogue, based on an industrial town of Punjab, ***Butter Chicken in Ludhiana*** (Mishra, 1995; hereafter referred as, **BC**:). This latter book will also be cited in contextual perspective, as this book also contained a small chapter on Banaras which was incorporated in detail in the later book (1999).

Following the shorter way to reach a destination, he tried to get himself crowned by an image of a top '*novelist*' (!) through propaganda in the media. However, one should also remember that such dual lifeworld of real existence and reflective exposure is also a characteristic of Banaras. Of course, the book is indigestible for those who love Banaras as a romantic landscape, lifeworld and a supreme coexistence of opposites where death and life form together the mandala of creation and continuity. By finding here and there some trash about Banaras, the residents of the city and many readers have developed a misconception that Banaras is the basic background of the book! The novel reminds us of Samuel Butler's remarks that "Every man's work, whether it be literature or music or pictures or architecture or anything else, is always a portrait of himself" (*Ways of All Flesh*, ch. 14, as in Singh, 1985: 314). It is also to be kept in mind that Mishra, perhaps, gave emphasis not so much to the common realities, but more to his own experiences of life, whether linked to Banaras or not. This situation has created mis-conception.

Mishra wrote whatever came to his mind, putting aside the spirit of place and deeper experience that results in their variety, distinction and changes in a longer period of time. This attitude has resulted in many factual mistakes. The title, *The Romantics*, has itself no relation at all with the subject matter. One western student, living in Banaras for many years, expressed that "there is no ground even to criticise the novel on the basis of Banaras as a background because there is no Banaras in it". He further said, "the tale in the novel is just a stereotyped and re-cycled material, leaving no fertile ground for 'self-reflection', or to know India" (based on an interview, December 2003). If you are unable to tolerate the obnoxious smell of the filth and sewerage, better to take a metaphysical dip in the two novels by Raja Rao, already described in previous chapters.

In most of the incidences and stories the narration is of an individualistic nature, thus making it as a table book or travelogue. And, one may agree upon the fact that the characters are initially engrossing, and the East-West amalgam held really tight for some time. While interacting with the students from the West living here for a long time, one obviously feels that Mishra has never tried to be inwardly part of this culture: to say Banarsi or Western-Banarsi, but has rather created a sketchy and topical scene completely non-reliable and false. In Indian thought it is said that even in intense darkness there lie some rays of lights! Let us search for that; this chapter is an attempt on that path.

"To fully appreciate the book," Wilson had written about *Sentimental Education*, "one must have had time to see something of life" (PM: 251). To what extent Mishra succeeded on this scale is a matter of debate. Eudora Welty has rightly expressed that "Location pertains to feeling; feeling profoundly pertains to place; place in history partakes of feeling, as feeling about history partakes of place" (qt. in Young, 1979: 52).

From the late 1980s, a mass of low-budget tourists, back-packers and hippie-type wanderers from the West started to encamp on the city scene. Mishra describes that period: "When I first came to Benares in the severe winter of 1989 I stayed in a crumbling riverside house. It is not the kind of place you can easily find any more. Cut-price 'guest houses' for Japanese tourists and German pastry shops now line the riverfront; touts at the railway station and airport are likely to lead you to the modern concrete-and-glass hotels in the newer parts of the city. The new middle-class prosperity of India has at last come to Benares. This holiest of pilgrimage sites that Hindus for millennia have visited in order to attain liberation from the cycle of rebirths has grown into a noisy little commercial town" (PM: 3).

In fact, "the people, objects, ideas, processes... interact with another to produce hybrid qualities, unique people" (Peet, 1985: 99). This is more true in the case of Banaras. However Mishra has not reached the experiential state of involvement; it has been said by an interviewer that he "understood very little and misunderstood much during those months there".

2. Insider (Banaras) Vs. Outsider (Benares)

It is not a surprise that Mishra, an expatriate and young author, has the ambition to cover a very wide canvas; perhaps he had the intention to please the West. His spelling names in the colonial manner, 'Benares' for Banaras and 'Ganges' for Ganga, is a testimony to this. Similarly, the name of the road-railway bridge at Raj Ghat, earlier called Dufferin Bridge, was changed to Malaviya Bridge in 1952, but in the novel the British name is used (cf. PM: 40). Additionally, he rarely tries to understand the cultural process in terms of continuity, maintenance and transformation, that resultantly making the place distinct and a symbol of Indian culture. Of course, he introduces the city in a romantic manner: "This is as it should be; one can't feel too sad about such changes. Benares — destroyed and rebuilt so many times during centuries of Muslim and British rule — is, the Hindus say, the abode of Shiva, the god of perpetual creation and destruction. The world constantly renews itself and when you look at it that way, regret and nostalgia seem equally futile" (PM: 3).

As remarked by an e-zine ('electronic magazine') critic, the novel has several topographical inaccuracies. No one can see the Ganga from the town of Mussourie, but through the mountains. And, neither does the river hurtle through Haridwar, but rather meanders and gurgles while on her merry way. Never in mythology does Haridwar appear as a miniature of Banaras (cf. PM: 142-43), nor Banaras is described as a sister city of Allahabad (cf. PM: 8). The city, which possesses strong and varied traditions of culture, attracts a huge mass of tourists, around 200,000 from abroad and a million pilgrims every year, and possesses the attraction of enjoying these traditions and the landscape by participation and involvement. How can one affirm so boldly, "The city, its antiquity, its special pleasures, held little attraction for me" (PM: 6), without having tasted it?

If one is not clear about his perspective and has no wish to be part of the local culture, e.g. Banaras, he will be lost in a jungle of complexity and will be a victim of confusion and aimlessness, like Debbie, a character of the novel, who was not sure why she is here and what she should do! (cf. PM: 160; cf. Fig. 55). However, many people oppressed by the Western 'bourgeois' way of life, and attracted to Eastern mysticism, music and easy life come here in search of solace (PM: 17). But the hard realities of cultural crises challenge the romantic image. Thanks to the sympathetic attitude of westerners and their wish to adjust; remember, the best way to relax in cultural crises is 'adjustment' (*samjhauta*). "My mind was full as always of something I had just read, and I quoted Flaubert, from some probably inaccurate translation, about how one should live like a bourgeois but think like a bohemian" (PM: 45).

'When one is in India, one has to behave in the same way as the people here do' as expressed by (PM: 47). The increasing flux of Westerners, with many of them staying in the city for long periods, has resulted in many changes in the local society. At every nook and corner cheap guesthouses are coming up like frogs at the start of the monsoon. For western tenants the rates are high (PM: 5), but for the westerners' pocket (favoured by the currency change), it is still very cheap. Making some adjustments with Indian friends, some westerners are buying houses and enjoy life: "a house in Benares, something for which people he knew saved and scrounged all their lives" (PM: 48). In his first novel Mishra describes Banaras as a city of laureates and great maestros: "According to her, Benares, city of light, of Shiva, Raja Harishchandra, Kabir, Tulsi Das, Ravi Shankar and Bismillah Khan, was now a molester's paradise" (BC: 219). But after four years, when he published his novel on Banaras, he completely missed that facet of the personality of the city. Perhaps he never read even Salman Rushdie's *Midnight's Children* (1981), two pages of which describe the riverfront in a wonderful manner:

> Yes, that was where it happened, in the palace of the widows on the shores of the Ganges in the oldest living city in the world, the city which was already old when the Buddha was young, Kasi Benares Varanasi, City of Divine Light, home of the

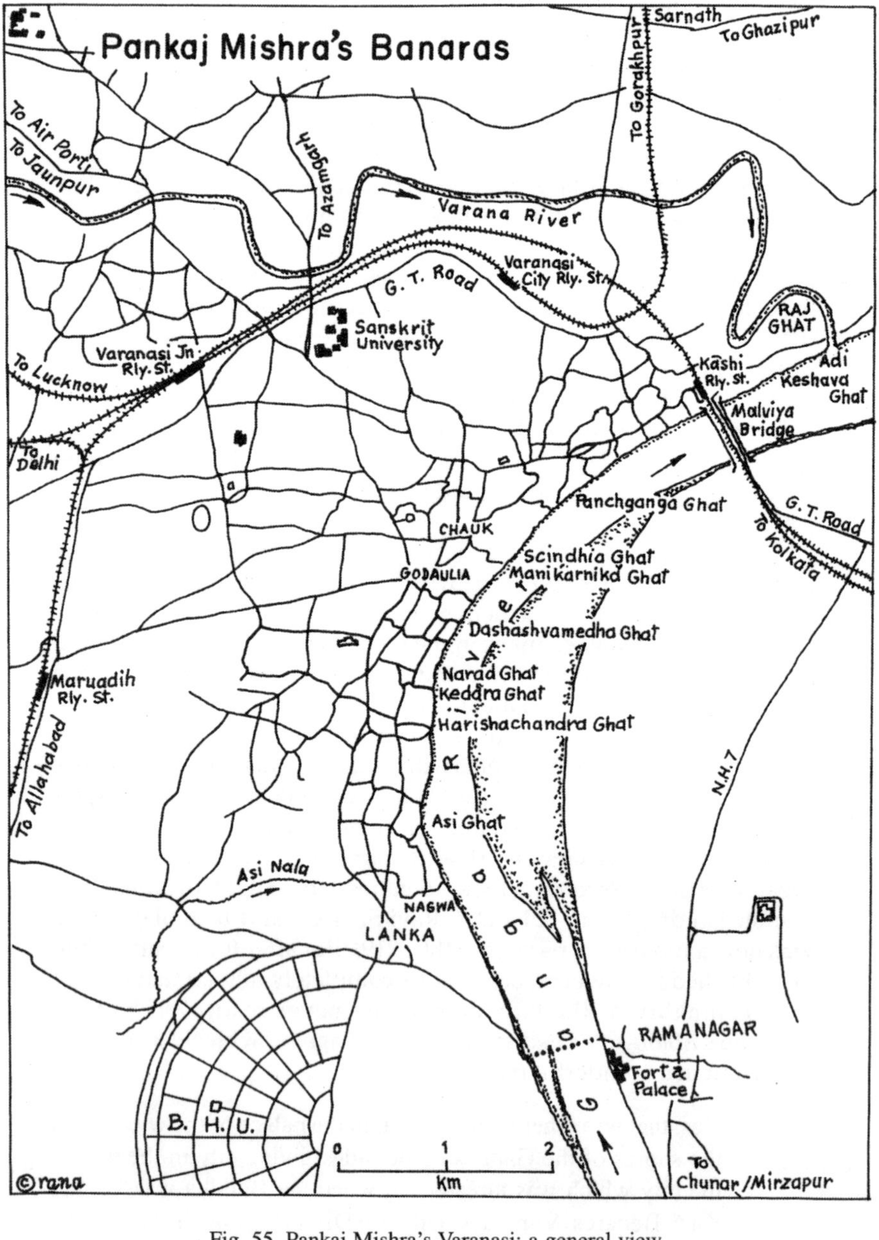

Fig. 55. Pankaj Mishra's Varanasi: a general view.

> Prophetic Book, the horoscope of horoscopes, in which every life, past present future, is already recorded. The goddess Ganga streamed down to earth through Shiva's hair ... Benares, the shrine to Shiva-the-god, was where I was brought by hero-Shiva to face my fate. (Rushdie, 1981: 432)

Rushdie adds (1981: 433):

> Follow the river, past Scindia-ghat on which young gymnasts in white loincloths perform one-armed push-ups, past Manikarnika-ghat, the place of funerals, at which holy fire can be purchased from the keepers of the flame, past floating carcasses of dogs and cows unfortunates for whom no fire was bought, past Brahmins under straw umbrellas at Dasashwamedh-ghat, dressed in saffron, dispensing blessings ... and now it becomes audible, a strange sound, like the baying of distant hounds ... follow follow follow the sound, and it takes shape, you understand that it is a mighty, ceaseless wailing, emanating from the blinded windows of a riverside palace: the Widows' Hostel! Once upon a time, it was a maharajah's residence; but India today is a modern country, and such places have been expropriated by the State.

The increasing pressure of cultural interaction challenges the old ways and rules of life. This is quite painful for people whose life is run by age-old tradition. How can one accept so easily the alien ways? "But she didn't remark on the potential awkwardness of Catherine's visit, or on how Anand had explained Catherine to his parents. Patroness, girlfriend, fiancée: they all would have been alien and difficult concepts for them" (PM: 50).

On the other side, many of the foreigners, leaving aside their traditions and careers, get mental healing here. "He had told her about his life, his various careers, how they brought him little satisfaction in the end. Catherine said, 'He has suffered a lot of pain.' It was Benares, she said, that had healed him" (PM: 56). But this is not so easy. Frequently, the foreigners feel insecure and suspicious with society, like Catherine who wanted to share her loneliness and insecurity with the local people (PM: 60). This is reciprocally true with the local dwellers, who always see the Westerners with a suspicious eye. The doubts, distress, a kind of invisible fear concerning impact of Westerners on the local tradition and the resulting challenges to be faced — all converge to the chaos in the society. There are also examples of foreigners who have settled here and adopted the Indian way of life, including marriage with an Indian girl, and who fascinated the local dwellers (PM: 57). One such character is Mark.

Cruelty and casteism go together, in fact they are now part of the social structure ? treating people as a commodity. Mishra thinks that its roots go back to the past: " 'The cruelty,' Rahul said, 'is unimaginable, and it goes right down to the bottom of the social structure. Everyone is cruel to everyone else. Rajputs to Bhumihars, Bhumihars to Yadavs, Yadavs to Harijans. The modern idea of regarding people as individuals with their inalienable rights is still centuries away here. For the man with wealth and power everything is in his domain, whether land or human beings, is his property. It is very difficult for an outsider to understand this way of perceiving people as property, but that is the dominant ethos of this region" (BC: 226-227).

3. Mishra's Own Saga, and Scenes of Banaras

Mishra narrates his experiences as recorded in his memory and tries to discover the world of Banaras through his own imagination, awe and wonder (cf. PM: 36). But to remember is not necessarily to understand. Indeed, that very gap between memory and insight is what haunts Samar, one of the main characters.

In spite of his wish he has not succeeded to "find a way of sharing my experience of Benares, and find some way of integrating it into daily life" (PM: 15). Through eastern heart and western mind Mishra tried to share the experiences, but perhaps succeeded only marginally: "We didn't kiss even once" (PM: 143). Mishra was highly impressed by "the great thing about the European novels and films that they have no inhibitions about sex and nudity..." (PM: 58). However, in Indian culture these are forbidden themes! Mishra has failed here to make a balance, or to be straightforward on any of these routes.

Pankaj's own emotional, autobiographical story, full of self-praise and pontificating while he himself sitting on an ivory tower, is symbolised by the personality of Samar (cf. PM: 64-74). An e-zine reviewer said that "Samar is a 'detached' individual who projects himself as 'wishy-washy character' who just seems to blunder along life's by-lanes, going where his destiny takes him, with minimal dissent".

Complaining about his father, Samar claimed that he "had built no house to pass on to me, and there wasn't much money. But he could set aside a small allowance that would see me through college" (PM: 72). Moreover, "Benares was a choice by default" (PM: 73). But this contrasts with the further narration: "I knew more people, and their presence in my life filled me with new emotions and alerted me to old inadequacies" (PM: 73).

However, a big question is: do the dreams turn into reality?: "'It's the story of my life,' he had said. I couldn't see it, then, but in Benares I had been among people who, like Frédéric and his friends, had either disowned or, in many cases, moved away from their provincial origins in order to realise their dreams of success in the bourgeois world" (PM: 250); but these people measurably failed either in adjustment, or in achievement at different levels and in varing degrees!

The Banaras dawn (*'subahe Banaras'*) is an image well known for the sunrise, its colourful reflection on the palatial buildings along the ghats, and the picturesque scene created by the meeting of the changing colours of light and the increasing ritual activities. Slowly slowly the darkness is replaced by light; here life starts from the sacred act of holy dip in the Ganga to daily work in the places of work. Those ignorant of this breathe of the cultural life create their own fussy image: "Morning brought Benares, huddled under a dark canopy of rain clouds; shuttered shops and broken roads and slime-covered drains and defecating men passed our weary eyes" (PM: 144).

4. The Ganga, the City, and the Pilgrims

The Ganga river is the vital and aesthetic force of Banaras. Out of the 84 ghats along the riverfront Mishra has only touched upon four ghats, and rarely any detailed plot was developed along the ghats. The main cremation ghat, Manikarnika Ghat, where 90% of the cremations take place (on average 150 corpses daily), has not been mentioned. Here are some paragraphs related to the ghats:

> On Harishchandra Ghat, among piles of wooden logs and mounds of swept-up ashes, there was a lone burning pyre, and the grieving friends and relatives of the deceased stood motionless around it. At Kedar Ghat, the piercing oboe-like sounds of shehnai from a wedding procession travelled over the water in brief gusts. Up ahead in the far distance, a train rattled across the Dufferin Bridge, its windows flashing the last of the day's sunlight. (PM: 40)

> She barely noticed the city sliding past us, the ghats with their isolated groups of people and solitaries, the tattered beach umbrellas, the melancholy widows in white saris, the stray coils of smoke from funeral pyres at Harishchandra Ghat. (PM: 269)

> We were halfway to Dashashvamedh Ghat, its throng of bathing devotees partly visible behind the plume of black diesel smoke that one of the empty anchored boats breathed into the air. The boat slid forward in smoother bursts now. A small breeze blew in from the other side, ruffling the water and making Miss West, as she spoke, draw her shawl around her even more tightly. (PM: 272)

"She often spoke of her tramps through Benares in a way that attached significance to the smallest things. Coming into the house from somewhere, she would remark on the quality of the light over the river" (PM: 76). What 'quality' of light, nobody knows for lack of any description!

The oil-lamp ritual, *arati*, in the morning and evening along the main ghats is certainly an attracting scene, which can provoke a comparison with Haridwar; however the only passing sentence about it does not give any sense of understanding (cf. PM: 142-143).

With the increasing impact of tourists' demand, the wish to earn more money from the foreign visitors, and the drastic encroachment by the migratory population, the riverfront of Banaras has been transformed into an ugly scene. Those lovers of the tradition and architectural beauty are distressed by such transformation. However, in the novel none of the character's eyes catches this decadence nor feels sad; strange to know that the riverfront has not changed. "The riverfront was unchanged, but the view on the other side of the house had altered. A new shed of corrugated iron stood in the temple courtyard. The roof of the facing house had higher balustrades, stubs of iron girders sticking out of the uncemented brick wall" (PM: 264).

On the 13th day of the dark fortnight of *Phalguna* (February-March) falls the marriage day of Lord Shiva, called Maha Shivaratri. Varanasi is the abode of Shiva, that is why this charming festival is especially celebrated here. In all the Shiva temples, grand decorations (*shringara*) and celebrations are held, but the Vishvanatha Temple (Golden Temple), Vishvanatha Temple in B.H.U., Adi Vishveshvara (in Bansphatak), Mritunjaya (in Dara Nagar), Trilochana and Kedareshvara temples are the most popular. The Vishvanatha and Mritunjaya temples are visited by around one million devout Hindus to have a glimpse of the special *shringara*. During the festival a procession is taken out from the Mritunjaya to the Vishvanatha temple. "In Benares's calendar, teeming with festivals, Shivratri occupies a special place. Millions of pilgrims visit the city that day to bathe in the river; and it was to witness their slow exuberant late-afternoon progress through the streets and alleys of the old city that I arranged to meet up with Catherine and Miss West on Dashashvamedh Ghat" (PM: 160).

The other equally important bathing festival is the full moon day of *Karttika* (October-November), which attracts more pilgrims from all over India than any other festive occasion. On such occasions the city scene completely changed into a spectacular and picturesque environment, as narrated by the author:

"All around me, and in the far distance, swarmed a crowd of pilgrims, with not a patch of uncovered ground to be seen anywhere, pilgrims surging into the main road from all directions, through narrow lanes and maze-like alleys' from between houses leaning into each other; pilgrims holding marigolds and red hibiscuses, brass and steel, platters filled with lit diyas and sweets and vermilion powder, pilgrims wearing pink and purple saris, crimson and white turbans, glossy silk and threadbare cotton, pilgrims ochre-robed and naked — ash-smeared, matted-haired Naga sadhus with gleaming tridents, their long penises slackly swinging as they walked towards the ghat — pilgrims everywhere, chanting slogans in praise of Shiva as they went down the steps, past the coconut and flower sellers, the anxious-eyed cows and the fat priests under their tattered straw umbrellas, to the river, throwing rose petals over their heads, up towards where the monkeys balanced on electric poles, quiet and watchful" (PM: 160-161). Many of the stairways' walls to the riverfront are decorated with murals depicting Rama and Sita on the throne of Ayodhya, where sometimes ochre-robed sadhus with matted locks sit and relax (cf. PM: 44).

5. The Place-Ballet: Special Scene

As described earlier (see p. 299), the place-ballet is a fusion of many time-space routines and body-ballets in terms of place (Seamon, 1980: 159). The dwellers of Banaras (Banarasis) possess a distinct culture and environment that make its own place-ballet. Some of the scenes are touched by Pankaj Mishra.

On festive occasions, to eat and drink special sweet dishes and drinks is a common practice. The curd-shake with ingredients of sugar, spices and a paste of intoxicant hemp (*Cannabis sativa*), called *lassi,* is among the popular ones; similar to it is *thandhai,* a soft drink made of fresh milk. "It didn't take long for the cannabis to take effect. The voices and laughter grew louder; people grew careless in their postures: Mark slumped against a bolster, his back to the river and its fickle late evening traffic of tourist-laden boats, and Sarah was half-recumbent on the white sheet, her thandhai cup precariously perched upon her stomach. Several conversations grew around me" (PM: 13). It is wrong to say that "a real Brahmin never drinks lassi" (PM: 13); this is an example of superficial remarks and denotes lack of familiarity.

On the occasion of musical performances and concerts, the musicians wear "long embroidered kurtas and shawls that had been drenched in attar" (PM: 11). The musicians' dresses also create an attractive scene.

In the early morning, the ritual activities start at sunrise, characterised by bathing in the river Ganga, ringing of bells, offering oil lamps to the Sun god, devotional music, the roaring sound of the conch shells, and also other profane activities: "I got up early, awakened, more often than not, by the sounds from nearby houses: radios blaring devotional music, crying babies, wet laundry being slapped against the bathroom floor, the voices of people queuing up before the municipal tap in the alley below, water cannonading into plastic buckets" (PM: 20). Frequently and regularly in the morning and evening one could hear the sound of the bells in the shrines all over the city, especially along the riverfront. This transforms the whole environment into a 'soundscape', as described:

> The *tan..tan, tin..tin, i..ing..ng...*
> The sound from temple-tower,
> Giving message in the morning hour,
> Divine Beings are ready to bless,
> This is a call for glimpse and wish. (Singh, Rana 2002: 173)

With the help of analogy, the author portrays the light and dark sides of culture by citing a popular Urdu poem; however this poem should have been translated in a more authentic manner (PM: 26-27). Social and physical pollutions are symbolised by 'whitish leprous spots', and the poet is in search of light:

> This whitish leprous spots, this night's fangs like city —
> This is not: that long —looked and awaited city,
> Not that that city in quest of which I wondered
> Set out, believing that somewhere the friend will meet
> Somewhere must be the stars' last halting-place
> Somewhere the verge of night's slow-washing tide,
> Somewhere an anchorage for the ship of heartache.
> (PM: 26-27)

The southern part of the city was in earlier days covered by a green lush vegetation and less number of inhabitants settled in a natural environment. By 1916, when the Banaras Hindu University was built, the whole of the south was transformed slowly into a more built-up and institutional landscape. Lanka, the area near to the entrance of the university, was changed by drastic expansion, however it fulfils the needs of the people. Here co-exist two settings with a marked contrast: Lanka — the unplanned modern sprawl — and the university campus — planned, but still maintaining a natural setting. "After the construction of Lanka — box-shaped brick houses, shuttered shops, exposed drains, pavement vegetable vendors and tea shops spilling out over the road — there would be the ever-renewed surprise of the university's green open spaces; the broad tree-lined avenues stretching from one end of the campus to the other; the sprawling cricket and hockey grounds; the quiet cool groves of bamboo, banyan and mango trees" (PM: 21).

It is incorrect and strange to mention the two universities of Allahabad and Banaras, where in the past, "the Civil Service — originally set up by the British — recruited large numbers of students, from the universities of Allahabad and Benares. The number had diminished drastically in the last decade. But the old reputation had endured; these universities were still seen as portals to the Civil Service" (PM: 29). Who can trust such statements? These words show Mishra's vested interest to romanticise the colonial supremacy! Additionally, the description of students keeping pistols in their rooms, or throwing grenades at policemen are other such hyperbolic expressions.

Encroachment and seizing property of houses by force and illegal means are common in the older part of the city. The complex juridical system of ownership and possession of a house supports this tendency of illegal capturing. Many monasteries and their associated buildings were in course of time occupied by people; this provoked conflicts, court cases and social fights. Those fail or kicked away from this struggle certainly solace themselves philosophically: "Greed is the biggest evil. It eats away man, destroys families, sunders husband from wife, son from parents ..." (PM: 37, and 154).

The layout plan of the Banaras Hindu University is based on the symbolic cosmology showing the crescent moon on the forehead of Shiva. This design is not the representation of the cosmos as found in the Vedas, the author thinks (cf. PM: 76). The layout plan is further divided by roads following diameters and radials where "the various departments lay on the diameter of the semicircular plan; behind them were the hostels and playgrounds. Set in the middle of large lawns and gardens, the buildings looked like products of an extravagant imagination, the predominant style being Indo-Saracenic, a mishmash of neo-Victorian and Hindu-Islamic styles: cupolas, arcades, colonnaded balconies, castellated towers, porticoes, domes, minarets, all jumbled up together in stone" (PM: 76).

The layout plan of Banaras Hindu University was originally planned in 1915 by a famous philosopher-architect, Patrick Geddes, who wished to integrate together scientific tradition and cultural heritage in landscape and built space; but he was kicked from the planning on the recommendation of some anti-Indian British officers. At important places in the university campus stand statues of the founder of the university, Madan Mohan Malaviya (1861-1946), as if keeping eyes on his creation and blessing people. His statue is nowhere installed at any important intersection in the city, therefore the question of "forlorn, negligence, discolouring" does not arise (cf. PM: 77).

Among the inspirational figures behind the foundation of Banaras Hindu University was Annie Besant (1847-1933), the English theosophist and Fabian socialist and friend of George Bernard Shaw (1856-1950) (cf. PM: 77). Annie Besant had already started a Hindu School in 1892 in Banaras, and later on an appeal by Malaviya gave her school to him to start the **B**anaras **H**indu **U**niversity. In course of time, it became known by a punning acronym, BHU, similar to the creation *mantra* (sacred word) of Brahma, the Creator in the Hindu pantheon. Time passes by diversions and frustrations. The university also changed by the cultural transformation, however the essence of the seed (*bija*) has always been there (cf. Lannoy, 2002: 343-344).

Everybody is free to say what she/he thinks good, however as a social being it is rationally ethical to represent the common perception of the masses. Mishra is fond of describing ambiguous and filthy landscapes, but always in the abstract and without any aesthetic sense of respect. "The train swayed and clattered ahead through tangles of gleaming tracks. Benares appeared at last after a series of small deserted stations, and the view contracted: it was now naked brick houses, and messy electric wires and algae-covered ponds, around which sat early-morning defecators, gazing up meekly at the passing train" (PM: 254). He adds, "The train picked up speed; dust blew in through the windows. Benares — this part of it newly developed and ugly — soon petered out in ponds of stagnant water and rows of corrugated-iron sheds and yards filled with rusty junked cars and trucks" (PM: 105). It seems that Pankaj's narrow mindset, education and perception resulted to ugly description of the city. John Lane (2003: 161) has rightly remarked that,

> It could be said that our education lies in thrall to the market economy and to managerial and functional dictates. Our art is benighted by a clinical cynicism. Our Earth is being desecrated; our culture debased. Perhaps the full catastrophe has been camouflaged by the power of money over every thing and the spectacular achievements of technology, but the inhuman environments and fouled-up landscapes remain as a legacy to be redeemed.

Ignorant Westerners or in that sense even westernised Indians (e.g., Mishra himself) see this culture as 'filthy' and perceive the whole country as malicious image in a hegemonic dark colour. "Most of them couldn't think of India as anything other than an exotic hotbed of illiteracy, poverty and religion: they would come back from their travels around Benares, speaking excitedly of sadhus who had been standing on one leg for ten years, of beggar children without limbs and of the huge rats scurrying about in the alleys" (PM: 91).

The Nobel Laureate poet Rudyard Kipling (1865-1936) said in his imperialistic jingoism:

> Oh, East is East, West is West, and never the twain shall meet,
> Till Earth and Sky stand presently at God's great Judgement Seat;
> But there is neither East nor West, Border, nor Breed, nor Birth,
> When two strong men stand face to face,
> though they come from the ends of the earth!
>
> (from *The Ballad of East and West*)

This may be true in the context of technology, but not in terms of culture! Mishra may not be correct while saying that "the light has failed" (cf. p. 143, 144, and 277); in fact, it is faded, not failed!

Remember what the novelist Shashi Tharoor says (1997: 6): " The reason India has survived all the stresses and strains that have beset it for fifty years (after independence), and that led so many to predict its imminent disintegration, is that it maintained consensus on how to manage without consensus". This is very difficult to understand, but not impossible. We face a clash of cultures; as Hari Dam expresses (as quoted in Raine, 1997:10):

You live in time; we live in space.
You're always on the move; we're always at rest.
Religion is our first love; we revel in metaphysics.
Science is your passion; you delight in physics.
You believe in freedom of speech; you strive for articulation.
We believe in freedom of silence; we lapse into meditation.
Self-assertiveness is the key to your success;
Self-abnegation is the secret of our survival.
You're urged every day to want more and more;
We're taught from the cradle to want less and less.
Joie de vivre is your ideal; conquest of desires is our goal.
In the sunset years of life, you retire to enjoy the fruits of your labour
We renounce the world and prepare ourselves for the hereafter.

Banaras is also known for a culture of *'joie de vivre'* (*masti*), but in no way is it cynical. In fact, it is "genial and tolerant in its commitments to a carefree way of life" (Lannoy, 2002: 189). "The sadhu with matted hair did not look up as I passed him. Behind him, a boy attempting to ride a bicycle much bigger than he was tipped over and fell; a veiled woman watching him from the roof suddenly broke into laughter. The vegetable vendor kept on monotonously reciting the prices of tomatoes and cabbage" (PM: 147).

The increasing flux of low-budget tourists from the West and the growing pace of desire for money among the dwellers result in social evils like robbery, cheating, looting, etc.; this is a clear tendency towards cultural decadence. "Catherine was now working part-time at the French Tourist Information Centre. A steady traffic of French tourists passed through Benares, and they often ended up losing their passports or becoming seriously ill or getting robbed, or worse. It was her job to help them out" (PM: 43). As thy name, so thy fame; the name 'Banaras' itself refers to the mixture of the two opposite characteristics, the spirituality of *'yoga'* and the materiality of *'bhoga'*. For the western visitors it is shocking and unbelievable — "Catherine's unsettled and unsettling presence, her many alien, inscrutable emotions and preoccupations — I felt them beginning to work on me. Thoughts combined, interlocked, ramified. I felt tense, oddly exposed" (PM: 119).

To abandon oneself in the lifeflow of the zig-zag narrow lanes, where all the turnings and crossings lead one to somewhere and somehow, is considered a unique experience. This gives one a feeling of quest in search of 'self-realisation'. However, this is not an easy task. "I would make my own way back to Assi. I went through the ghats; I avoided the alleys, whose bright liveliness in the evening — the men playing cards or chess, the groups of loudly bantering men at tea shops, the snatches of sitar or sarod music floating out of open windows — depressed me. In my mind, I would keep thinking of things Catherine had said to me, turning them over, searching for signs of affection, and feeling more disappointed and saddened than before" (PM: 152)

6. Society and Defiled Culture

The predominance of Brahmins in the religious arena and their overruling authority on the ritual complexities is still noticeable in other facets of life, e.g. politics. If Brahmins feel unable to directly have the power of control, they use the power of emotion, religious texts and casteism. "He [a Brahmin] lobbied hard with the administration on their behalf to postpone exams, or to reinstate an expelled student; he worked overtime on the labyrinthine university bureaucracy to get more Brahmin students admitted into university hostels. He asked for nothing in return from those he favoured other than their votes for Brahmin candidates in elections to the student union. That was how he came to know me: he volunteered to help me gain a health certificate from the university infirmary, and I turned into one of the young Brahmin students under his protective umbrella" (PM: 22). The purity-pollution/ high-low caste hierarchy still prevails among the students, and even among the teachers. In the novel the downtrodden low-caste people are called 'lumpens' and even 'anti-social elements'; on the other end, Brahmins are described as studious and civilised people (PM: 23).

There was in the past a marked resistance to female education — a cultural stigma in Indian society. But in the recent past the situation has noticeably changed. There is some evidence to suggest that in the late 19th century Banaras, women did not receive any kind of formal education at all (Kumar, 2000: 152). The novel in no way tries to keep the readers informed about the contemporary scene. "Prejudices against female education were a feature of poor societies; I didn't associate them with England. Could it be that her father couldn't afford to send her to university? I wasn't sure, and didn't think it was the sort of question I could ask" (PM: 9).

Many incidences of Allahabad have been superimposed upon Banaras and its institutions, like Banaras Hindu University. During the last decade the situation of course improved in educational institutions. However, "the university had suffered a steep decline in the years since independence. Anarchy reigned behind the still impressive facade of its domes and towers. Academic sessions were in total disarray: examinations due in April were more likely to be held in December, if at all" (PM: 8). Many times the bad spots of the past are placed in the present context, as it was the ongoing scene. "The university's recent troubled past only further increased my fear. For some months, the campus had been the setting for pitched battles between the police and students (PM: 23).

Mishra's description engenders despair and depression, where any hope for goodness is lost: "It was Rahul, an old acquaintance, who made me look for an explanation in the changing character of Benaras Hindu University (BHU). Most of the women I spoke to had singled out BHU as the most difficult place for them in Benares. One wasn't much surprised by that. Of late, BHU's only associations were with rowdyism, inter-group violence, strikes, gheraos, and delayed academic sessions. Like the other great North Indian university of the past — Allahabad — it had gone into steep decline over a period of ten-fifteen years, and it didn't seem it would ever recover" (BC: 224).

There are cases when Western ladies fall in love with Tantric sadhus. At least a passing sentence in the book refers to one such case (cf. PM: 159). Mishra is only concerned with economic paucity in the poverty that he tries to portray, but focussing in only this aspect in no way explains the life-philosophy and ethical values of a society. Similarly, his passing remarks about cruelties in rural India give the impression that the whole world of rural India is full of cruelties (cf. PM: 170). Such flimsy remarks are irresponsible, sketchy and far from reality.

Mishra was too harsh in narrating the sexual harassment of western girls. He tells the story of Sarah, a student of the Wisconsin Programme in Banaras: "I haven't met a single young white woman in Benares who has not been molested, but still people quote American statistics at you. Here you may not be raped, but you still have no dignity in the eyes of most men on the streets. The degradation through verbal and physical molesting is much more than what rape does to you, because it is such a common casual everyday affair. And what's worse is that after some time it makes you feel unclean and corrupt. You begin to feel you are to blame for all this" (BC: 220).

A good number of tourists come here in search of solace. They are frustrated with the Western culture of materialism and consumerism! But many times they fail to receive anything of worth from

India. Mishra is right, to a certain extent, when he says that the culture of *bhoga* ('worldly pleasure') has replaced the culture of *yoga* ('spiritual merit') so much that the simple tourists have to pay the price of the cultural downfall. He narrates, "They come here basically to hang around the ghats, smoke dope, have some fun, and they go around in the most outrageous outfits. They wear these see-through tank-tops and halter-tops without bras, they go around in short shorts. And these young men who see them naturally get ideas. These sort of provocative clothes makes them think all western women are whores, just dying to have sex. And once they get that idea in their heads, it doesn't matter what you wear. I have never worn anything other than a salwar-kurta in Benares. I cover my head when I go out; you can't see a single inch of my skin, but I am still not left in peace" (BC: 220). The description continues, "The stories didn't really have to be coaxed out of anyone; the humiliations were too fresh in everyone's memory. And the stories were truly appalling" (BC: 221).

Comparing the present Banaras life with that of more than a decade ago, one can explicitly experience the downfall and cultural pollution. Sarah explained it with shock and suffering, " 'The verbal harassment,' she said, 'was there even then, but in a very minor sort of way. It was never as explicit as it is now. At the most people would say, 'Hello dear' or something like that. Now, you are lucky if someone does nothing more than expose himself in a deserted alley and ask you to suck his dick. Men come up to me while I am sitting by myself on the ghats, start up a conversation, and then before I know it, they tell me they are sexually frustrated and could I please help them relieve their frustration. It really is incredible!" (BC: 221). Who can rely on such general and extreme happenings, except Mishra himself? Such narrations are hyperbolic and indicate vested interests, most probably to defame a culture with a view to pleasing the western readers.

Banaras culture has declined so much that it is on the verge of loosing its civic and ethical sensitivity of culture: "Benares has changed so much in the last five-six years, all the crass vulgar middle-class culture that you see in a place like Delhi is here now, and all you can do is feel sad. You can't really do anything about it except leave. It breaks my heart to even think that, but that's how unbearable it has become" (BC: 222).

Trying to seek answers to the problem of cultural confrontation, Mishra thinks that we are basically in the presence of a clash of two civilisations:

> It is one of the most conservative cities in India, but it also has one of the largest foreign populations in India. So the confrontation between two sets of incompatible cultural values is rather direct here.
>
> The Indian response to this clash is as usual incorporate. It incorporates some aspects of the other culture, but those are really the worst aspects. So on top of a pre-existing distorted, valueless feudal structure you get distorted, valueless modernity. The two combine rather well, and on days when you get depressed about all this you wonder if their synthesis is not really the greatest achievement of contemporary Indian culture. (BC: 227)

7. An Epilogue: No Destination

The author finally arrives to the hotel, a symbol of a westernised ivory tower, and feels happy to play with his own gauge of "an unknown maze of potholed dark back alleys". Finally, "Water ran down my back; my socks were wet; my feet cold. But I was feeling quite calm" (PM: 270). One of the problems of criticism is whether to accept the reliability of incidences, narration of stories, and description of the landscape. Only a few incidences deal with the cultural landscape, which is the product of long evolutionary processes and human manifestations. The story and characters are merely stereotypes with no unique or even memorable characteristics. With many sweeping generalisations and confusions, Pankaj Mishra has tried to bash Banaras and to sell filth, poverty, and his own viewpoints about them. Misha believes more in 'illusion' instead of 'change'. " 'That,' he was saying, bringing out each Sanskrit and Hindi syllable precisely, 'is *sunyata*, the void. And this' — he pointed at the teeming conglomeration of temples and houses towards the north of the city — 'is *maya*, illusion. Do you know what our task is?' " (PM: 180). But if the sight is weak and the intensity of awakening is low, the perception will always be misty. From the other end, William Blake (1757-1827) explains this in his poem as:

> If the doors of perception were cleansed,
> Everything would appear to man as it is, infinite.
>
> (from *A Memorable Fancy*)

One of the e-zine (electronic magazine) reviewers has very passionately observed that, "The problem in the end is the sense of 'giving up' that seems to pervade every Indian character in the book.

Just as in 'Fasting, Feasting' and 'The Blue Bedspread', every character has a problem and is unhappy and troubled. When will someone write a book about normal middle and upper middle class life in India, about the fun you have in school, in college, in professional situations, and sometimes even at work? That there are people who are content and successful and not criminal and fat and paunchy with beaded eyes and greasy hands. And though you can never wipe away the backdrop of poverty and disaster, not everyone leads these lives. Do poverty, filth and decay have to be our only export?"

> So began my last days in Benares — days of gnawing restlessness and gloom! (PM: 149)

The gauge of civilisation is measured by the maintenance, continuity of good traditions and cultural codes in practice today. To talk only about the glorious past never gives a sense of respect and honour. Mishra finally laments: "What's funny is that while we were there, we really had been looking forward to Benares. From all that I'd read about it, it seemed like the cultural capital of North India. And I suppose, having seen it now, it is in a way. But culture isn't just about the past, about old temples and musical traditions and things like that. I think it also has something to do with the present moment, with how people treat each other in daily life, civic manners, a certain basic decency towards women, older people, and if you take that criteria, Benares comes right at the bottom of all Indian cities we visited" (BC: 223). Here Mishra is pessimistic and not right to say that 'Banaras is at the extreme bottom'! Most probably he just met the kind of people that crazy tourists usually meet: brokers, unemployed young lazy people, drug addicts and petty criminals, and that is how within his narrow thought he failed to narrate the rich, varied and beautiful scenes of Banaras. One has not to form an idea of all-pervasive unhappiness in the cultural chaos. Remember how Nirad Chaudhuri (1960: 280) has warned us: "The situation is tragic, not only pathetic, when seen in its eternal twilight. If any world had and has the right to put up this inscription:

> Through me you pass into the City of woe:
> Through you me pass into eternal pain;
> Through me among the people lost for aye.
> All hope … abandon, ye who enter here.
>
> ~~~~~~~
>
> The Hindu world has and had that right.

Nagananda Muktikanth wrote a poem to awaken the spirit of Hindu masses, named "To the name of Banaras" (as cited in Singh, Rana 2003), which says:

> Arise O dwellers of Kashi! Awaken now,
> Or in the camel-form march toward the West.
> Vacate the city, to leave it for invaders' wish
> Who can dilapidate it without any obstacle,
> And impose the curse of non-sensuality
> Upon your piety culture.

This noble call by the poet had inspired the people in Banaras during the movement to save Hindi and Hindu culture in the late 1960s. But presently we are at the edge of losing the capacity of self-realisation and awakening. The infection of mental pollution is more hazardous now. But the environment of crisis and chaos may be taken as diagnostic outlook, as narrated by British photographer and free-lance writer Lannoy (1998: 18):

> The riverfront has been corrupted by touts and by commerce directed towards the innumerable foreign vagabonds and somewhat aimless seekers of the exotic from every corner of the globe. Touting of the most obnoxious sort happens all the time, whether by children or adults. The irony or paradox of this corruption is that it is the negative side of that magnetism which Benares has exerted for centuries over people from all parts of the world. For today more than ever before, a great many ardent, serious, learned students, scholars, linguists, musicians, philosophers, archaeologists, sociologists, have flocked to the city, including eminent people in every branch of knowledge, and endeavour, whether at the university, the American Institute, the Centre of Buddhist Studies at Sarnath, and also students who gravitate round individual pandits and teachers.
>
> The cultural life of Benares is alive and well, even in a bedlam of disorder, decay, overcrowding, congestion and all the ills that we are accustomed to in modern India. It would be a sad day indeed if Benares would become just like any other over-crowded city, rather than the unique microcosm of everything fine in Indian spiritual culture.

8. Basic References

Mishra, Pankaj 1999. ***The Romantics***. Picador (an imprint of Macmillan), London, and Picador India, New Delhi. [Ref. as PM: pp]

Mishra, Pankaj 1995. ***Butter Chicken in Ludhiana: Travels in Small Town India***. Penguin Books India (P) Ltd., New Delhi. [Ref. as BC: pp]

~16~

Literary Images of Banaras: Towards Closure

The varied dimensions of experiences and human feelings, both of the individual and collectively, have been shaped in the purview of city and re-shaped by the transformation of culture and landscape. However, such studies have earlier been put at the margin in the academic arena where empirical models and Marxist perspectives were the leading paths. Both of these viewpoints failed to accommodate the varied aspects of human experiences that are rooted in space, time, happenings, and contexts. Cities are more than the built environment; in fact, they are also "an experience to be lived, suffered, undergone" (Preston and Simpson-Housley, 1994: 2). Literature is one of the media that provide sharing with these human conditions.

By the turn of late 20th century, the increasing impact of post-modernism, where 'meaning, metaphor and messages' are the core concern, has provided a fresh and more humane path of common sharing, understanding, and marching ahead. In the early 1960s Lewis Mumford's *The City in History* has successfully explained cities as places of human habitations. Similarly, Kevin Lynch's magnum opus, *The Image of the City* (1960) has opened opportunity to analyse and examine the images of the physical city. These writings influenced the cognitive approach, where aesthetics, values, images and faith systems are given consideration. Literature has been taken as a strong resource to portray the varied city images in different eras with common sharing. A reader meets to varied characters with whom he starts his journey, and at one stage find himself in a state of cultural rootedness. Meeting together is a start; Working together is a progress; Going together is a march; and Achieving together is a revelation.

Like any old and traditional city, Banaras too is an accumulation, not only in respect to demographic, economic or structural terms, but also in terms of the inherent possession of the spirit of place maintained in history and reflected in feelings and emotions. There is an enormous range of old and mythological literature glorifying or de-glorifying the city of Banaras. The unique physical setting of the city served as a special element of city image that symbolically narrated in literature. Of course, we see the city through the filter of the writer's imagination, which produces a very particular and idiosyncratic way of seeing: sometimes an ideal place like paradise, and at other time a victim of exploitation.

The essays in this book narrate the story of Banaras, in both moral and topographic terms, which record the upheaval, restating and degradation of human scale in different periods of time. That is to say that the city of Banaras, far from presenting a utopian ideal of glory, has also become symbol of disorder that offend a sacred cosmic order. In all the writings the worlds of nature and humankind seem to flow more seamlessly into one another, especially the serene beauty and power of the Ganga river is everywhere, nevertheless the contradiction of culture, i.e. high and low, also exist together. One should also remember, as exposed in the writings, that 'sacramental glory and manipulative culture go side by side'.

Possessing the spirit of divinity, the myths and traditions have maintained the vibration of life in this city since time immemorial. Of course, archaeologically it has been proved that since c. 1000 BCE the city has continuously recorded human habitation; that is how the city is known as one of the 'oldest living cities in the world'. Once Mark Twain (1898: 480) said: "Banaras is older than History, older than tradition, older even than legend and looks twice as old as all of them put together". Banaras is not the story of bricks and stones; it is in fact a living History in itself. During the 11th -12th century CE the city was destroyed at least four times by invaders. However, it survived and was repeatedly revived; the sites and holy spots were re-searched, the monuments were re-paired and re-built and the spirit was again re-awakened to re-unite with the primordial. In this way the eternity of life has survived in spite of several superimpositions or attempts to submerge it.

The multiple personalities of Kashi, portrayed in the literature, are projected as:

City of *light*, where every day the sunrise reflects on the crescent moon-shaped Ganga river, and finally illuminates the riverfront;
City of *delight*, where high degrees of pleasure and fun are experienced;
City of *plight*, where ups and downs always make life full of frequent and sudden changes;

City of *might*, which possesses the power of feeling and attraction;
City of *sight*, which allows clear vision to emerge where humanity and divinity meet;
City of *right*, where all the human deeds are righteously assessed by the patron deity Shiva, who then blesses and curses accordingly.

The *Kashi Khanda* (35.10) says, "The Ganga river, Lord Shiva, and the divine city of Kashi make the Trinity of grace and perfect bliss". This sentiment attracted people from all parts of India to settle down here and to make their own world, resulting in the creation of a vast cultural mosaic.

Marc Katz (*NGJI*, 1990: 134) has eloquently said, "One aspect of this great tirtha that has fascinated authors is its unique dualistic nature. Banaras is equally famous for its sanctimony as its inverse sanctimony: dirt, gundas, burning ghats and death, and the 'saucy' self-identifying behaviours of Banarasis which is locally known as *'Banarasipan'* — an integral unity of *mauj* (delight), *masti* (joie de vivre), *phakkarpan* (carefreeness), and *akhkharpan* (headstrongness). This local duality, which paradoxically unifies the realities of the ups and downs, and the purity and profanity of life, and also finds its way within the Banaras based literarture — to the delight of 'Banarasia' addicts who particularly enjoy this Banarasia *rasa* (taste)". The present book presents the literary images of Banaras, from the ancient to the contemporary.

There is a common saying in Banaras that as this is a resort of the Lord of the Universe, Vishvanatha, one does not have to leave it. This way the culture of Banaras is an example of 'self-identifiability'. It "is free from the ubiquitous 'other worldly' elements, and emphasises the cultivation of excellence in 'this worldly' life. It is because of its disregard for the diacritical marks of religion that it can accommodate a much wider variety of people who are otherwise separated from one another by religion, caste, language, or region. ... This 'reality culture' of Kashi also overlooks many of the traditional social values which are bred in the bones of narrow sectarianism, and it presents a certain style of life which is abhorrent to both orthodox Hindus and Muslims" (Saraswati, 1975: 52-53).

Taking literature as source material to reflect upon the perceptions of 'urban images' and experiential feelings, writers from various backgrounds have been selected, and hard realities of human social adaptation and the growing malaise in reference to belief systems have been analysed. Of course, as against deterministic thought, literature has been assumed as a mirror of social processes, but with addition of fieldwork and comparison with contemporary writings this line of thought works properly. The present book is an attempt to analyse the literary images of a single city, Banaras, based on the writing of several writers. Banaras, perceived as the cultural capital of India and the holiest city for Hindus, was taken here as a case study. Ten writers are considered independently and their writings are arranged serially time-wise (from the ancient to the contemporary) into fourteen chapters.

This book is a modest attempt to capture the spirit of 'Banaras through time' portrayed in literary images as evoked by the writings of ten authors from a variety of different backgrounds. This work presents images of the city of *rasa*: Varanasi, Avimukta, Thaganam Sthanam, Benares, and Banaras (all appellations of Banaras) based on the perceptions of various writers. Banaras is the oldest and holiest city of India. Hindus perceive Banaras as such a sacred place that if one leaves this world in Banaras then his or her soul will undoubtedly go to heaven. These and other images of Banaras have been supported by writings of the ten authors examined here. Obviously each writer has raised his voice according to the need of time, and almost all have attempted to prepare the portrait of Banaras in the manner it appeared, perceived, and in the manner it had spoken. Except Kabir (as the Kabir presented is taken from a contemporary author's writing), the original writings have been taken for analysing literary images, intimate sensing, belief systems and landscape.

One of the perspectives taken into the background is the appraisal of the richness of information that has been drawn from varied literary sources. The book begins with the ancient period, associated with the mythical king Divodasa and his son Pratardana, followed by the medieval period of the Gahadavala dynasty. The next essay begins with the fifteenth-century reformer poet Kabir. The successive chapters cover the culture of the 16th, 18th, 19th centuries and continues through the 20th century with writers such as Shivprasad Singh, Kashinath Singh, Abdul Bismillah, and Pankaj Mishra. All these writers stem from various philosophical, cultural, linguistic and religious backgrounds. This richness of resources has generated kaleidoscopic images of the city of Varanasi from temporal, spatial and, of course, experiential points of view. The selection includes an entire array of authors ranging from 'Banarasi' natives such as Kabir, Tulasi, and Bhartendu to visitors like Ghalib, and including the expatriate Indian writer Raja Rao. With this collection of writers we get 'insider' views along with the perceptions of 'outsiders'. The subject matter of the book is divided into fifteen chapters. The 1st chapter is a critical appraisal and synoptic review of the emerging field of literary geography and the search for identity in India. The following fourteen chapters chronologically evoke the images of Varanasi based respectively on the writings of each author. The last chapter (16) presents a summary and conclusion, and the synthesis of messages.

While planning to write on Banaras, Shivprasad Singh published a set of three novels dealing with the ancient, medieval, and modern city (see chapters 2, 3 and 12 of this book). The city of Banaras provided a backdrop and shaped the view of the Indian social world that he sought to convey in his three novels. He makes no claim to be a regional novelist, however, with contextual differentiation his novels contain details of landscape and concrete areas. He has published seven novels, all in the Hindi language. Three of these are on the culture and landscape of Banaras in three periods, *The Primordial Fire* ('Vaishvanar') on the ancient, *The Blue Moon* ('Nila Chanda') on the medieval, and *The Street Turns Yonder* ('Gali Age Murti Hai') on the modern city images and cultures.

The 2nd chapter portrays the culture and lifeworld of the Vedic Kashi as illustrated in the myth of Divodas, who is eulogised as the founder and the first sovereign king of the kingdom of Kashi. The story of Divodasa is first referred in ca. 1200 BCE, and continues in different versions in the Puranic literature till 10th century CE. The Vedic and Puranic descriptions narrate his story, which is taken as base for the novel, *Vaishvanara* (The Primordial Fire) by Shivprasad Singh. Issues like behavioural morals, the continuity of traditions, and the strategy for territorial control are here portrayed. This novel attempts to link myths, culture, landscape and historicity through the process of imaginary stitching by the novelist. The citation of the Vedic metres and other literary sources makes this novel more like a historical document.

The 3rd chapter portrays the Varanasi of the 11th-12th centuries (Gahadavala period), a glorious era in the history of this city, based on Shivprasad Singh's novel *The Blue Moon*. The Gahadvala period is known for cultural conflicts and a climax of glory, finally lost by the fall of this royal dynasty. The author has presented vivid scenes of anarchism and topophobia in the context of the people and landscape of Kashi. With the help of metaphors and symbols, both positive and negative aspects of the city are painted. Descriptions of the Ganga, mango groves, mahua trees, tulasi plants, suggest the importance of these objects in the lives of the people of that period. The canvas is so wide that the expression, meaning and message of the story told have sometimes not been fully expressive. Moreover, much emphasis has been laid on the dark spots in comparison to the shining ones. But after all, this work successfully attempts to tell the story of that period.

The 4th chapter explores the thought of the famous reformer poet Kabir, who was born in Kashi and lived most of his life in and around Varanasi. Thus, in his writings the social and ritualistic aspects of the Varanasi society are portrayed in the context of hypocrisy, inequality, and the stigma of the caste system. Kabir's role as a reformer attempting social integration through rational criticism has been narrated in two works, i.e. Bhisma Sahni's play *Kabir Standing in the Bazaar* (1981) and Rangeya Raghav's novel *The Warp of Loi* (1976). The latter work deals with the life of Kabir, and a marginal emphasis has been laid on Banaras and its culture, therefore it was not selected for analysis. Shahni's work highlights the landscape and lifeworld of Banaras and Kabir's role as critic and reformer, thus it helps to understand the real personality of Kabir and his vision of the Banarasi culture.

Tulasi's perception as a poet of Varanasi has been explored in the 5th chapter. Tulasi was a Rama *bhakta*; he wrote most of his works while living in Varanasi. In Tulasi's *Kavitavali*, and *Vinaya Patrika* one can get a vivid description of various religious and sacred sites of Varanasi. The city was thought of by him as a wish-granting cow, and also as a victim of the era of falsehood. Similar to Kabir's tradition, Tulasi also did not write any work directly on Banaras, but at several places he prayed to the divinities of the city and also described the downfall of the society, a real picture of late 16th-early 17th centuries CE. His alternative strategy for a middle path integrating Vaishnavite and Shaivite traditions encouraged a mass movement of Bhakti in the Hindu society. Among his writings where Banaras is mentioned, *Dohavali*, *Kavitavali* and *Vinaya-Patrika* are noteworthy.

Ghalib's Banaras is a splendourous city. In the 6th chapter Ghalib's perceptions and feelings about this city are discussed. Through Ghalib's verses one can truly understand an outsider's feelings regarding this city. According to Ghalib: "Banaras is a unique city, What more to say about it! Where is such a city born?" He even expressed his desire to settle in Banaras had he been young. Ghalib was a Persian poet who stayed for four months in Banaras and expressed his feeling in his lengthy poem, *The Light of the Lamp*. He was so much impressed with the religious landscape and the glorious beauty of the city that he only described this part and did not care for the negative side.

The rest of the seven writers have been synthesisers, looking into the good and bad points together in reference to context and milieu. But Raja Rao is much closer to Ghalib, and rarely attempted to see the dark sides. In fact, he symbolised many of the ancient-puranic descriptions through modern eyes, it is therefore with the citation of original sources that his symbols are expressed, trying to understand the invisible mystic power that the city possessed. A passing journalist purview of Banaras is portrayed by Pankaj Mishra in his first novel, *The Romantics*.

The late 19th century images of Banaras are depicted in Bhartendu Harishchandra's *Love-lorn Female Ascetic* (*Premajogini*). The 7th chapter surveys both negative and positive views of the landscape of Banaras. Bhartendu had a fond feeling for Banaras. In his play *Andher Nagari* he talks about the degradation of human values and the escalating importance of 'money' in every walk of life. The city has turned from the 'city of light' to the 'dark city' according to Bhartendu Harishchandra. The polytheistic character of Hindu society and religion has been fully described by Bhartendu. The worst impact of colonialism and the degradation of Hindu society have been given full emphasis, but he did not fail to highlight the sacred glories of the city as perceived in the ancient past, by referring to the *Markandeya Purana* (VIII). His famous poem "*Saw your Kashi, O people! I saw your Kashi* !" is so much valid today as when it was written in 1875. Of course, one can easily contend that it is a reflection of his saturated and frustrated mind, but on the other end one can easily justify it through keen observations and experiences. His description is so alive that it arouses social awareness even today.

The 8th chapter presents visions of the 18th and mid 20th century Kashi. Shivprasad Mishra's stories have been surveyed in order to fulfil this task. His statement that "Banaras has been famous for the dualistic qualities of man, the sages, and the loafers" is illustrated with pieces from his sixteen stories.

Banaras viewed by an expatriate writer, Raja Rao, is the content of the 9th chapter. Raja Rao's novel *The Serpent and the Rope* has been scrutinised with an aim to summon the inner personality of Kashi. In his novel Raja Rao calls Banaras a 'surrealist city'.

In his novel *On the Ganga Ghat*, Raja Rao explores the metaphysics of the drama of life as it unfolds in Banaras, the city which preserved the distinctiveness and contrasts of life that flows together with the current of the motherly river Ganga.

Chapter 11 studies the modern and socialist writer Abdul Bismillah's perception of the life of the Varanasi weavers and their lifeworld. Issues like place attachments, Hindu-Muslim relationships, the use of slang and their perceptual world are examined in this chapter.

For the outline of chapter 12, *The Street Turns Yonder* by Shivprasad Singh is the main resource, used for the purpose of evoking many 20th century images of Varanasi. For example, the word 'Banarasi' conjures up an image of typical Varanasi culture, which is characterised by *'mauj'* (delight), *'masti'* (joie de vivre), *'phakkarpan'* (carefreeness), and *'akhkharpan'* (headstrongness).

Chapter 13 depicts a very specific aspect of 20th-century Banaras: the theme of the student's struggle with all its dimensions, as narrated in Kashinath Singh's novel *Our Front*. The 14th chapter is a regional travelogue of a small but unique neighbourhood of the southern part, Assi, based on a recent novel, *Assi of Kashi* by the same author. This area is known for the wonderful mixture of *yoga* (spiritual life) and *bhoga* (worldly pleasure). To narrate his explicit experiences, the author has taken the shelter of vulgarity at different levels, however it may be acceptable. Kashinath Singh's recent novel on the locality of Assi is an attempt to portray the ugly but lived scenes and the cultural spots of this part of Banaras. Many of the narrations are similar to Bhardentu's, full of satire and with a robust exposition. Both of these narrations enable us to understand the 'maintenance and continuity of tradition' and 'acceptance of modernity and cultural transformation', which always exists in between conflict and adjustments at various stages, in different times and at various levels.

Chapter 15 is another example of an attempt to see the two faces of Banaras through the lenses of the West and the East. Pankaj Mishra's *The Romantics* is taken here as a base. This travelogue-novel gives an impression that the culture of Banaras is like mixed vegetables — potpouri, where it is difficult to describe the taste of anyone of them, however all together result in a unique taste. Here all the vegetables are blended in the colour of western viewpoint as the author perceived and believed it.

The details of the writers, their works and years of publication are given in Table 1.

Table 1. Varanasi (Banaras): Writers, Writings and Themes

Chapter, Writer (life span)	Title of work; language	Publ. Year	Main theme of Literary images
1. Introduction	A Critique	—	Review and Appraisal
2. Shivprasad Singh (1928 – 1998)	*The Primordial Fire* (novel), Hindi	1998	Landscape and culture in the 8th-9th cent. BCE
3. Shivprasad Singh (1928 – 1998)	*The Blue Moon* (novel); Hindi	1988	Cultural conflicts in the 11th century
4. Kabir (1398-1518)	*Kabir Standing in the Bazaar* (play); Hindi (by Bhishma Shahni, 1915-2003)	1981	Place and social evil in the 15th century
5. Tulasi (1547 – 1623)	*Dohavali; Kavitavali; Vinaya-Patrika* (poems); Avadhi	16th cent.	Hindu sacrality and the the lifeworld in the 16th-17th centuries
6. Ghalib (1797 – 1869)	*The Lamp of the Temple* (poetry); Persian	1827	Glory and feelings
7. Bhartendu Harishchandra (1850 – 1885)	*The Love-lorn Female Ascetic* (play); Hindi	1875	Topophobia in the 19th century
8. Rudra Kashikeya (1911 – 1970)	*The Flowing Ganga* (stories); Hindi	1967	Images in British period, folktales and history
9. Raja Rao (1909 – 2002)	*The Serpent and the Rope* (novel); English	1960	Reminiscences and city myths
10. Raja Rao (1909 – 2002)	*On the Ganga Ghat* (novel); English	1993	The life-philosophy and meaning
11. Abdul Bismillah (b. 1949 –)	*The Threadbare Woven Shawl* (novel); hindi	1986	Contemporary weavers' lifeworld
12. Shivprasad Singh (1928 – 1998)	*The Street Turns Yonder* (novel); Hindi	1974	Insider-Outsider view, dualistic culture
13. Kashinath Singh (b. 1937 –)	*Our Front* (novel); Hindi	1972	Students' struggle in the 1960s
14. Kashinath Singh (b. 1937 –)	*Assi of Kashi* (novel); Hindi	2002	Reminiscences of a part of the city and its culture
15. Pankaj Mishra (b. 1969 –)	*The Romantics* (novel); English	1999	Perception of East and West
16. Summary and closure	A synthesis	—	Meeting grounds and common scene

All the three basic imagery qualities of a city, i.e. generic, representing an encompassing ideal/ archetype (as cosmos); expressive, through the processes and artefact/ design (as organic entity); and cultural identity, reflected with the customs and colophons (see Reiner and Hindery, 1984: 133-4), are represented at different levels and in different degrees in the literary sources taken into consideration. Of course, metaphysically Varanasi is mythologised as a cosmic and universal city, it is also an amalgam of living-awakened sites, the holiest city and also the city of pitfalls of culture. Raja Rao expressed it wonderfully, "Banaras has the best and the worst of India, but it is here that you see the human wanting to leave all that behind, the human wanting to be divine" (see Evam, 2002: v).

A similar approach to highlight the polytheistic character has been made by Shivprasad Singh, who exposed at many places the dualistic personality of Banarasi culture. The main aim to awake mass awareness about the students' struggle, for which the novel was written, has ultimately not been achieved. This theme of students' struggle has been fully exposed with good and bad points in Kashinath Singh's novel *Our Front* (1972); in fact, this is a lively document on the theme and still fully valid — rather more valid today! In describing the hard truth, Singh could not stop expressing himself in a vulgar way. The same tradition has been followed by Abdul Bismillah in his novel on weavers. Both of these writers are inclined to be leftist in thought, therefore they rarely appraised the age-old traditions into their writings. Both have presented their long experienced feelings of the city in reference to their belongingness and hard perceptions without caring whatever criticism they would have to face.

With closer examination of the characters, acts, places, and plots of *Street Turns Yonder* one can get an in-depth tour of the city: I personally feel that no regional urban geography has yet grasped the lived scenes of Varanasi so completely. Most of the writings on Varanasi are religious and emphasise its glories, ignoring the "city-life" as experienced by its dwellers. In this way the novel becomes a source of data where attitudes, values, perceptions, feelings and a sense of faith together present the overall picture of such a complex and historic city. Imaginations and realities meet so closely that they become two sides of the same coin. This novel narrates "the twilight zone of rowdies, black marketeers and even corruption among the ritual priests at the *ghats*, it is with a sense of acceptance or, at least, an understanding that the scale of urban existence makes the presence of such people inevitable. Even if Varanasi is the home of sinners, this judgment does not depend upon some dialectical vision of a future city transformed into either a Babylon or a New Jerusalem" (Preston and Simpson-Housley, 1994: 338).

How to connect folk history with the incidences of history through literary works, this is what Rudra tried; without attempting to fit his work in the frame of either novel or story, he provided a substantial base to understand the lifeworld and landscape of Banaras during the 18th-mid 20th centuries. The river Ganga symbolises the continuity of tradition, existence and downfall, purity and sin — and so many spots of dualism. The aesthetic sense of environmental perception, the changing mood of tone of music according to seasons, and people's adaptability are expressed with an aim to understand the inside view of Banarasi culture. Additionally, the life symbols and metaphysics of the Ganga river as they appear in Hinduism are narrated in Raj Rao's *On the Ganga Ghat*.

In each of the chapters the major emphasis is on the individual's writing, but side-by-side sources from other references are cited for comparison and contrasts. Since the city of Banaras records a long experience in history as a centre of pilgrimage and mystics, everywhere the puranic literature is cited to indicate connections and historical perspectives of metaphor, symbolism and milieu. This book is an approach to integrate 'objective' and 'subjective' perspectives, however more emphasis is laid on the post-modernist viewpoint with an aim to project the inherent meaning, metaphors, metaphysics, messages — all playing their role in making the milieu of the city called 'Banarasipan'. Of course, no one can claim that this will be the end-product of literary images, but one can easily realise that the work will be helpful to understand the complex and multiplicit network of belief systems. For this purpose a rational balance is maintained between imaginative literature and lived experiences of the city through intimate sensing.

Paraphrasing Samuel Johnson's (1709-1784) remarks for London is well suited to the city of Banaras: "By seeing Banaras, one can see as much of life as the whole India can show." Moreover, "it is a city as rich as all India. But it is not an easy city to comprehend for those of us who stand outside the Hindu tradition" (Eck, 1982:6). A dweller who loves this city with heart and mind expressed the city metaphorically in terms of capturing space, time and tradition: "Banaras either of the past, or of the present, and would be of the future, was an historically important city of the past, and is of the present, and would be of the future. Banaras is not only a city, but a culture in itself... Looking at this city is easy, recognition difficult. Touching it is easy, capturing difficult. Making a portrait is easy, transformation onto the mental canvas difficult. In this way, in spite of easiness in outlook, in appearance it is a city of infinity" (cf. Gupt, 1984: 21).

The spatial and temporal changes of culture and landscape as reflected in the 'City images' have been vividly narrated in the works of the eleven writers mentioned above. Of course, in many of the cases the 'hard truth' of the surface often develop a theme of 'the City of Hell', yet there also appears an exposition of intrinsic realities which develop the sense of 'the resort of divinities'. There is a popular saying that "each and every particle of dust and stone in Banaras has the spirit of Lord Shiva" — the god of polytheistic personality; Shiva in the form of Ishvara represents the divine power of creation, protection, and destruction. This sense can be metaphorically seen through the literary works mentioned above. Such powers and actions go together and follow one another, developing a system of 'life-cycle'. Let me close the book with an appeal to join the road of literary pilgrimage, and to exchange our experiences:

> Path running towards crossing the boundary,
> Out of space, out of time and the image.
> Let's go beyond sky-arc of blue territory,
> In search of what lies across the image,
> Ultimately reaching the wholeness of cosmic limit,
> Where God and Human frame a unit.
>
> Singh, Rana (1995: 191)

REFERENCES

Agyeya, S.H. Vatsyayana 1974. Reactions of a novelist — *Street Turns Yonder. Naya Pratika* (a Hindi monthly magazine of literary criticism from Delhi) 1 (7), July: 55.64.

Aurobindo, 1979. *The Supreme Discovery*. Aurobindo Ashram, Pondicherry.

AV *Atharva-Veda Samhita*, trans. W.D. Whitney. Harvard Oriental Series, vols. 7-8, 1905. 2nd Indian reprint. Delhi: Motilal Banarasidass, 1971.

BP, *Brahma Purana*,1954. Gurumandala Granthmalaya No.XI, 2 Vols., Calcutta.

Bayly, C.A. 1983. *Rulers, Townsman and Bazaars*. Cambridge University Press, Cambridge.

Beer, Stafford 1975. *Platform for Change*. John Wiley & Sons, London.

BgP, *Bhagavata Mahapurana*, 1971. Sanskrit & English transl. Ed. G.L. Gosvami, 2 vols., Gita Press, Gorakhpur. Dt.: ca. CE 14th century, Ref.: X.66.

Bharati, M. 1986. When started Hanuman's worship in Vishvanatha's territory (in Hindi). *SANMARG*, '*Kashi Visheshank*' ed. K.K. Mishra. Sanmarg, Varanasi: 171-181.

BhP, *Brahmanda Purana*, 1976. Ed. J.L.Shastri. Motilal Banarasidass, Delhi. Dt. ca. 4th century. Ref. Varanasi: 2.3.67, 207.

Bismillah, Abdul 1996. *The Son of the Loom*. Translation of *Jhini Jhini Bini Chadariya* from Hindi original by Rashmi Givind. Modern Indian Novels in Translation Series. Macmillan India Ltd, Madras.

Buttimer, Anne 1976. Grasping the dynamism of lifeworld. *Annals, Association of American Geographers*, 66 (2): 277-292.

— 1985. Nature, water symbols, and the human quest for wholeness. In, D. Seamon and R. Mugerauer eds. *Dwelling, Place and Environment*. Martinus Nijhoff Pubs., Dordrecht: 259-280.

Casolari, Marzia 2002. Role of Benares in constructing political Hindu identity. *Economic and Political Weekly* (a weekly from Sameeksha Trust Publication, Mumbai), vol. XXXVII, No. 15, April 13-19: pp. 1413-1420.

Cassirer 1955. *The Philosophy of Symbolic Forms*. Vol. 2, Yale University Press, New Haven. Reprinted 1972.

Chaturvedi, Dharmasheel 1984. Gundas of Kashi. In K.K. Rai, ed. *Uttar Pradesh: Kashi Anka* (in Hindi). Dept. of Information and Public Relations, Govt. of U.P., Lucknow : 56-59.

Chaube, J. and K.L. Srivastava 1979. *Medieval Indian Society and Culture* (in Hindi). U.P. Hindi Sansthan, Lucknow.

Chaudhuri, Nirad C. 1966. *The Continent of Circe*. Jaico Publ. House, bomay. First publ. by Chatto & Windus, London in 1965.

— 1970. *To Live or Note to Live*. Hind Pocket Books, New Delhi.

— 1979. *Hinduism, A Religion to Live By*. Oxford University Press, Oxford.

Cohn, Bernard S. 1971. *India: Social Anthropology of a Civilization*. Prentice-Hall, Inc. Englewood Cliff, NJ.

Cosgrove, Denis E. 1979. John Ruskin and the geographical imagination. *The Geographical Review* (New York), 69 (1) : 43.63.

Dalmia, Vasudha 1997. *The Nationalization of Hindu Traditions. Bhartendu Harischandra and Nineteenth-century Banaras*. Oxford University Press, Delhi. Paperback 1999.

Darian, Steven G. 1978. *The Ganges in Myth and History*. University of Hawaii Press, Honolulu. Reprinted: Motilal Banarsidass, Delhi, 2003.

Das, Shyam Sundar, ed. 1970. *Kabir Granthavali* (in Hindi). Nagari Pracharini Sabha, Varanasi. Orig. ed. 1951.

Devereux, Paul 1990. *Places of Power*. Blandford, London.

Dinman (a Hindi weekly from the Times of India, New Delhi) 1982. The Burning Question: destiny of an overqualified, Vol. 18, no. 15 (18-24 April): 7.

Dinman 1983. Our Universities: Banaras Hindu University. A report by Chanchal, et al. Vol. 19, no. 11 (13-19 March): 13-16.

Dinman 1987. Police in the University (B.H.U.). A special report on students' unrest in Uttar Pradesh by Basant Srivastava. Vol. 23, no. 7 (22-28 Feb.): 20-22.

Dillitone, F. W. 1986. *The Power of Symbols in Religion and Culture*. Crossroad Pub. Co., New York.

Dube Rajendra Kumar 1986. Banarasi Sari industry: issue of its dignity (in Hindi). In, K.K. Mishra ed. *SANMARG, Varanasi Visheshank*. Sanmarg office, Varanasi: 197-202.

Dubey, D.P. 1985. Varanasi,. A Name Study. *Archiv Orientalni* 53 (4): 35-40.

— 1987. Kumbha Mela: Origin and historicity of India's greatest pilgrimage fair. *National Geogr. Jl. of India* 33 (4): 469.192.

— 2000. *Prayaga: the Site of the Kumbha Mela*. Aryan International Publs., New Delhi, illustrated.

— eds., 2001. *Kumbha Mela*. Society of Pilgrimage Studies, Allahabad; 5 essays.

Dumont, Louis 1980. *Homo Hierarchicus. The Caste System and its Implications*. Rev. English ed. University of Chicago Press, Chicago. Indian reprint by Oxford Univ. Press, New Delhi.

Durrell, Lawrence 1957. *Alexandria Quartet*. 4-vols. novel. Faber & Faber, London.

Dwivedi, Hajari Prasad 1971. *Kabir* (in Hindi). Raj Kamal Publ., Delhi.

Eck, Diana L. 1983, *Banaras. The City of Light*. Penguin India, New Delhi (Indian Reprint). 446pp., illustrated. Originally published in 1982 by Alfred Knopf, New York.

— 1986. Banaras: *cosmos* and paradise in the Hindu imagination. In, Veena Das, ed. *The Word and the World.* Sage Publ., New Delhi: 41.55.

Eichinger Ferro-Luzzi, Gabrilla 1983. *Cool Fire: Culture-Specific: Themes in Tamil Short Stories.* Edition Herodot, Goettingen.

Eidt, Robert C. 1977. Detection and examination of anthroposols by phosphate analysis. *Science*, 197 (30 September): pp. 1327-1333.

Eliade, Mircea 1979. *Patterns in Comparative Religion*. Sheed and Ward Pub., London.

— 1960. *Myths, Dreams and Mysteries*. Philip Mairet (tr.). Harvill Press, London; orginal in French, pub. Editions Gallimard, Paris, 1957. pp. 227-8. Mythes, rêves et mystères (1957). Editions Gallimard, Paris.

Evam 2002. Foreword, I, Banaras (by Raja Rao). *Evam* (Samvad India Foundation, New Delhi), vol. 1 (1 & 2): v-viii.

Freitag, Sandria B. (ed.) 1989. *Culture and Power in Banaras. Community, Performance, and Environment, 1800-1980*. University of California Press, Berkeley.

Fromm, Erich 1983. Afterward. In George Orwell's *Ninteen Eighty-Four:* 257-267.

Gold, John R. 1984. The death of the urban vision. *Futures* 16 (4) : 372-391.

Golding, Paul R. 1997. *Tales of Banaras. The Flowing Ganges*. (with Virendra Singh). Book Faith India, Delhi [Pilgrims Book House, Varanasi]. (Introduction, commentary and English translation of Rudra's *The Flowing Ganga*).

Golledge, Reginald G. 1985. Teaching Behavioural Geography. *Journal of Geography in Higher Education* 9 (2):111-127.

Gothoni, Rene 1996. *How to Survive in Academia*. Helsinki University Press, Helsinki- Finland.

Grierson, Sir George 1903. *Tulasidas : Poet and Religious Reformer.* Royal Asiatic Society of Bengal, Calcutta.

Gupt, Kamal 1984. Magnificent city of pre-history and modernity. In, Kaushal Kumar Rai, ed. *Uttar Pradesh: Kashi Anka* (in Hindi). Dept. of Information and Public Relations, Govt. of U.P., Lucknow : 21-23.

Gupt, Maithilisaran 1912. *Bharata Bharati.* Poems in Hindi 2nd. ed. in 1986. Saket Publication, Chirgaon (Jhansi).

Gupta, Mata Prasad, ed. 1968. *Kabir Granthavali* (in Hindi), Agra.

Hall, Edward T. 1959. *The Silent Language.* Doubleday and Co., Inc., New York.

Hawley, John S. and Juergenameyer, Mark 2004. *Songs of the Saints of India.* Oxford University Press, Oxford and New York.

Heidegger, Martin 1927. *Being and Time.* Transl. J. Macquarrie and E. Robinson. Harper and Row Publs., Inc., New York. Reprinted 1962.

Husain, Mozhar 1978. *Suppression of Immoral Traffic in Women and Girls Act* 1956. 3rd ed. Eastern Book Co., Lucknow.

Hussain, Yusuf 1959. *Glimpses of Mediaeval Indian Culture.* Asia Publ. House, Bombay.

Jackson, J. B. 1970. *Landscapes.* Selected writings; ed. by E.H. Zube. Univ. of Massachusetts Press, Amherst.

James, Preston E. 1972. *All Possible World.* The Odessy Press, Indianapolis, NY.

Jung, Carl G. 1972. *Mandala Symbolism.* Princeton University Press, Princeton.

Justice, Chistopher 1997. *Dying the Good Death. The Pilgrimage to Die in India's Holy City.* SUNY Press, Albany, NY.

Kaviraj, Gopinath 1965. *Kashi ki Sarasvata Sadhna* (in Hindi). Bihar Rastrabhasha Parishad, Patna.

Kakar, Sudhir 1982. *Shamans, Mystics and Doctors.* Alfred A. Knopf Pub., New York.

Kapur, Anuradha 1986. Actors, pilgrims, kings, and gods: The Ramalila at Ramanagar. In, Veena Das ed. *The Word and the World.* Sage Pub., New Delhi: 57-74.

Katz, Marc J. 1993. *The Children of Assi: The Transference of Religious Traditions and Communal Inclusion in Banaras.* Department of Religious Studies, Publ. Series. Vol. 12, University of Göteborg, Göteborg (Sweden); published PhD thesis.

Kaul, Ashok 2002. The other side of Banaras: An untold story of EPW. *Hindustan* (a Hindi daily newspaper), Special "*Subah-e-Banaras*", 30 May, Thursday: p. 4.

Keul, István 2002. *Hanuman, der Gott in Affengestalt. Entwicklung und Erscheinungsformen seiner Verehrung.* de Gruyter Verlog, Berlin and New York. (Series: Religionsgeschichtliche Versuche und Vorarbeiten, 47). In German with English summary.

Keyserling, Count Hermann 1969. *Indian Travel Diary of a Philosopher.* Translated from the German by J. Haolroyd-Reece. Bhartiya Vidya Bhavan, Bombay. Reprinted.

KKh, *Kashi Khanda* (of *Skanda Purana*), 1991-1998. Editor: Karunapati Tripathi. Sampurnananda Sanskrit Vishvavidyalaya, Varanasi. 4 vols. Sanskrit and

Hindi translation and commentary. Dt. ca. 12th-14th century. Contains 100 chapters and 11,624 verses.

KKT, *Krityakalpataru*, by Lakshmidhara, 1942. Ed. K.V. Rangaswamy Aiyangar. Gaekwad's Oriental Series Vol. XCVIII. Oriental Institute, Baroda.

Kosambi, D.D. 1970. *The Culture and Civilisation of Ancient India in Historical Outline*. Vikas Pub., New Delhi.

Krishnanath 1975. Gali Age Murati Hai. *Kalpana* (a Hindi Monthly magazine of literary criticism from Hyderabad) , 26 (11), Nov.: 3-8.

Krohn, Alam 1978. *Hysteria: The Elusive Neurosis*. International University Press, New York.

Kumar, Nita 1984. *Music and Popular Culture in Banaras*. Unpub. Paper in South Asian Conference, University of Wisconsin-Madison, Nov. 23 pp.

— 1986a. Patronage, identity and cultural change: five melas of Banaras. In T.P. Verma, et al. eds. *Varanasi Through the Ages*. B.I.S.S. Varanasi Pub. 4 : 159-170.

— 1986b. Open Space and free Home: pleasure for the people of Banaras. *Contributions to Indian Sociology* (n.s.) 20 (1): 41-60.

— 1988. *The Artisans of Banaras. Popular Culture and Identity*. Princeton University Press, Princeton. Published in India: Orient Longman, Hyderabad and New Delhi, 1995.

Lane, John 2003. *Timeless Beauty in the Arts and Everyday Life*. Geen Books, Devon (UK), & Viveka Fd., New Delhi.

Lannoy, Richard 1998. Is Benares burning. *The Sunday Times of India* (a daily from New Delhi), March 29: p. 18.

— 2002. *Benares, a World within a World*. Indica Books, Varanasi.

Lawrence, D. H. 1969. *Spirit of Place: Letters and Essays on Travel*. Ed. Alan C. Thomas. Dutton Pub., New York.

Levi-Strauss, Claude 1963. 'The effectiveness of symbols' and 'The Sorcerer and his magic'. In his *Structural Anthropology*. Basic Books, New York: 167-185, and 186-205.

Lipton, Michael 1977. *Why Poor People Stay Poor*. Temple Smith Ltd., London.

LP, *Linga Purana*, 1973 Ed. J.L. Shastri. English Tran. 2 vol. Motilal Banarasidass, Delhi. Dt.; earlier part – ca. CE 8th century, later part – ca. 12th century. Ref. canto 92: 190 verses.

Lutwack, Leonard 1984. *The Role of Place in Literature*. Syracuse University Press, Syracuse.

Lynch, Kevin 1960. *The Image of the City*. MIT. Press, Cambridge, Mass.

— 1981. *A Theory of Good City Form*. MIT. Press, Cambridge, Mass.

Makky, Ghazy A.W. 1978. *Mecca, the Pilgrimage City*. Croom Helm, London, for Hajj Research Centre.

Mallory, W.E. and P. Simpson-Housley, eds. 1987. *Geography and Literature*. Syracuse University Press, Syracuse.

MbH, *Mahabharata*, 1933-1959. Ed. V.S. Sukthankar (and others), 19 vols. Bhandarkar Oriental Research Institute, Baroda. Dt.: ca. BCE 4th century. Ref. VI.10.30; VI.14.6; XIII.154.23 and 168.25.

ME, GOI 1954. *Education in Universities in India, 1951-52*. The Ministry of Education, Government of India. Govt. of India Press, New Delhi.

Miller, Barbara D. 1981. *The Endangered Sex. Neglect of Female Children in Rural North India*. Cornell University Press, Ithaka.

Mishra, Ajay 2004. *Pakka Mahal* (in Hindi). Vani Prakashan, New Delhi. A novel dealing with the central and old part of Banaras.

Mishra, Pankaj 1995. *Butter Chicken in Ludhiana: Travels in Small Town India*. Penguin Books India (P) Ltd., New Delhi.

— 2000. *The Romantics*. Picador India, New Delhi. A novel on the perception and reflections of the Western visitors in Varanasi.

Mishra, Vidya Nivas 1974. Three New Novels — Criticism. *Naya Pratika* (7), July: 57-58.

Mitra, Vimal 1985. *Literary Reminiscences* (in Hindi). Vishvavidyalaya Prakashan, Varanasi.

Motichandra 1973. *The World of Courtesans*. Delhi.

— 1985. *History of Kashi* (in Hindi). Vishvavidyalaya Prakashan, Varanasi. 2nd ed., Reprinted 2003.

MtP, *Matsya Purana*, 1907. Anandashrama Sanskrit Series No. 54, Poona. Dt. ca. 8th-10th century. Ref. 180-185-411.

Mugerauer, Robert 1984. Mapping the movement of geographic inquiry: a commentary. In, T.F. Saarinen, et al. eds. *Environmental Perception and Behavior*. University of Chicago, Dept. of Geography, Res. Paper 209: 235-243.

Mukherjee, Vishwanath, ed. 1978. *This is Banaras*. in Hindi. Thalua Club, Varanasi.

Muktibodh, Gajanan Madhav 1975. *Chand ka Munh Terha Hai* (in Hindi). Lokodaya Granthmala No. 201, Bhartiya Gyanpith, New Delhi, Orig. Pub. 1964.

Mumford, Lewis 1961. *The City in History*. Secker & Warburg, London.

Munshi Mukundalal 1986. Personal appeal of a teacher. *Aj* (a Hindi daily from Varanasi), 20 July: 11.

Naipaul, V.S. 1977. *India: A Wounded Civilisation*. Penguin Books, Harmondsworth.

Nemeth, David J. 1987. *The Architecture of Ideology*. UC Pub. Geog. 26. University of California Press, Berkeley.

N.G.S.I. 1990. Book reviews: Singh, Rana P.B. (1989), *Where Cultural Symbols Meet. National Geographical Journal of India* (B.H.U., Varanasi), 36 (1-2), March-June: 129-146. [Nine reviewers]

NIP, Northern India Patrika (an English daily from Allahabad) 1981. A report "Advent of academic anarchy: BHU campus", Nov. 6: 2.

Niyogi, Roma 1959. *History of the Gahadavala Dynasty*. Oriental Book Agency, Calcutta.

O' Flaherty, Wendy D. 1973. *Asceticism and Eroticism in the Mythology of Shiva.* Oxford Univ. Press, Oxford, Delhi.

Olsson, Gunnar 1980. *Birds in Egg/ Eggs in Bird.* Pion Pub., London.

Olwig, Kenneth 1984. *Nature's Ideological Landscape*. George Allen & Unwin Pvt. Ltd., London.

Orwell, George 1949. *Nineteen Eighty-Four.* Commemorative ed. 1983. New American Lib., Inc., New York.

— 1945/ 1976. *Animal Farm*. Penguin Books, Harmonsworth UK.

Pandey, Gyan 1983. Economic dislocation in Nineteenth century Eastern Uttar Pradesh. In, Peter Robb ed. *Rural South Asia*. Curzon Press, London: 89 129.

Parry, Jonathan P. 1980. Ghosts, greed and sin: the occupational identity of the Benares funeral priests. *Man* (*N.S.*) 15 (1): 88-111.

— 1994. *Death in Banaras.* Cambridge University Press, Cambridge. Indian Reprint available.

Patel, Narsi 1977. *Carnival in Banaras.* The Author (12 pp. poems originally in Gujarati, published in 1957; translated in English by the author).

Payne, Peggy 2001. *Sister India*. Penguin India, New Delhi. A novel set amidst the turmoil of religious violence in modern day Varanasi.

Paz, Octavio 1971. *Claude Levi-Strauss: An Introduction*. Jonathan Cape, London, and Cornell University Press, Ithaca NY.

Peet, Richard 1985. The geography of human liberation. *Antipode* 17 (2-3) : 98-104.

Porteous, Douglas J. 1985. Smellscape. *Progress in Human Geography* 9(3): 356-378.

— 1986. Intimate Sensing. *Area* 18 (3): 250-251.

PP, *Padma Purana*, 1894. Anandashrama Sanskrit Series No. 131, 4 vols. , Poona. Dt. ca. 12th-13th century. Ref. I.33-37; IV.235-236; V.14; VI.278.

Prasad, Beni 1945. *India's Hindu-Muslim Questions*. London.

Preston, James J. 1985. Creation of the Sacred Image: Apotheosis and Destruction in Hinduism. In J.P. Waghorne and N. Cutler eds. *Gods of Flesh/ Gods of Stone.* Anima Publ., Chambersburg, PA : 9-30.

Preston, Peter and Simpson-Housley, Paul, eds. 1994. *Writing the City. Eden, Babylon and the New Jerusalem*. Rouledge, London & New York.

Prinsep, James 1833. *Benares Illustrated in a Series of Drawings*. I to III Series. Baptist Mission Press, Calcutta and Smith, Elder & Co., London 1834.

Radhakrishnan, S. 1971. *The Bhagavad Gita.* (Sanskrit and English). George Allen and Unwin, London.

Rai, Kaushal Kumar, ed. 1984. *Uttar Pradesh, Kashi Number.* in Hindi. Public Relation and Communication Dept., U.P. Govt., Lucknow.

Raine, Kathleen, 1997. All roads lead to India. *Resurgence* (Devon, UK), 183 (July/August): 7-11.

Ramanujan, A.K. 1973. *Speaking of Siva.* (Translated with an Introduction). Penguin Books, New Delhi.

Rapoport, Amos 1983. *The Meaning of the Built Environment.* Sage Pubic., Beverly Hills.

Ravivar (a Hindi weekly from the Amrit Bazar Patrika, Calcutta) 1987. Worms have eaten the Banaras Hindu University: A special report by Haribansh, et. al. Vol. 10, no. 26 (1-7 March) : 20-25.

Reiner, T.S. and M.A. Hindery 1984. City planning, images of ideal and existing city. In, L. Rodwin and R. M. Hollister, eds. *Cities of the Mind.* Plenum Press, New York: 133-147.

Reising, Russell J. 1987. *The Unstable Past. Theory and the Study of American Literature.* Methuen, London.

Relph, Edward 1981. *Rational Landscapes and Humanistic Geography.* Croom Helm Pub., London.

— 1984. Seeing, Thinking, and Describing Landscapes. In, T. F. Saarinen, et al, eds. *Environmental Perception and Behavior.* Univ. of Chicago, Dept. of Geography, Res. Paper No. 209: 209-223.

— 1986.Geographical experiences and being-in-the-world: the phenomenological origins of geography. In, R. Mugerauer and D. Seamon eds. *Dwelling, Place and Environment.* Martinus Nijhoff Publ., The Hague: 15-31.

RgV *The Hymns of the Rig Veda*, ed. J.L. Shastri, trans. R.T.H. Griffith, Rev. ed., 2 vols. Delhi : Motilal Banarasidass, 1973. Dt.: ca. BCE 1500, Ref.: 1.130.7; 10.179.2.

RvS, *Rig Veda Samhita*, 1940. Ed. Shripada Sharma. Svadhyayamandala, Anudha. Dt.: ca. BCE 1500, Ref.: 1.130.7; 10.179.2.

Russell, Ralph 2000. *The Famous Ghalib.* (Selected, translated and introduced by Russell). Roli Books, New Delhi.

Russell, Ralph and Islam, Khurshidul 1994. *Ghalib, 1797-1869: Life and Letters.* (Translated and edited). Oxford University Press, Delhi.

SaB, *Satapatha Brahmana*, 1882. Transl. J. Eggeling. Sacred Books of the East, vols. 12, 26, 41, 43, 44. The Claredon Press, Oxford. Reprinted, Motilal Banaridass, Delhi, 1989. Dt.: ca. BCE 1500. Ref.: Vol. 5: 4.7.1; 13.5.4.21; 14.3.1.22; 14.14.

Sachau, Edward C. trans. 1910. *Alberuni's India*. 2 vols. Truebner, London. (Book originally written during CE 1007-1033).

Schilder, Robert and Callewaert, Winand M. 2000. *Banaras, Vision of a Living Ancient Tradition*. Hemkunt Publs., New Delhi.

Sahai, Shivnandan 1905. *Harishchandra* (in Hindi). Hindi Samit, U.P. Govt., Lucknow, Rept. 1975.

Sanyal, Gautam 2002. Who will go, leaving aside the abuses of Kashi? *Hams* (a monthly magazine of public awakening in Hindi, from Delhi), 191 year, number 17, 1 August: pp. 52-55.

Saraswati, B.N. 1975. *Kashi: Myth and Reality of a Classical Cultural Tradition*. I.I.A.S., Simla.

— 1985. The Kashivasi widows. *Man in India*, 65 (2): 107-120.

Seamon, David 1979. *A Geography of the Lifeworlds*. Croom Helm Ltd., London.

— 1980. Body-subject, time-space routines and place-ballets. In, *The Human Experience of Space and Place*, eds. Anne Buttimer and David Simon. Croom Helm, London: 148-165.

Seamon, David and Nordin, Christine 1980. Market place as place-ballet: the example of Varberg, Sweden. *Landscape* (Berkeley, CA), 24.

Segal, Ronald 1968. *The Crisis of India*. Jaico Publ. House, Bombay. First publ. by Penguin Books, Harmondsworth, in 1965.

Sharma, Ramvilas 1966. *Bhartendu Harishachandra* (in Hindi). Rajkamal Prakashan, Delhi. 2nd ed.

— 1975. *Bhartendu Era and the Tradition of Evolution of Hindi Language*. (in Hindi). Rajkamal Publication, Delhi.

Shastri, Ganga Sharan 1976. *The Life of Kabir* (*Kabir Jivana Charitra*), (in Hindi). Kabir Bani Publ., Varanasi.

Sherring, M.A. 1868. *Benares, The Sacred City of the Hindus*. B.R. Pub Corp., Delhi. Reprinted in 1975.

Silk, C.P. and J.A. Silk 1985. Racism, nationalism and the creation of a regional myth. In J. Burgess and J.R. Gold, eds. *Geography, the Media and Popular Culture*. Croom Helm Ltd., Beckenham, Kent: 165-191.

Silk, John A. 1984. Beyond geography and literature. *Environment and Planning*, D. *Society and Space* 2: 151-178.

Singh, B.M. 1983. BHU: Pockets of excellence amid general sloth. *The Hindustan Times* (an English daily from New Delhi), January 28: 17 and 22.

Singh, Bhagwan (ed. & trans.) 1995. *Stories of the Pancatantra*. National Book Trust, New Delhi; in Hindi.

Singh, Kameshwar Prasad 1985. *Story-writer Shivprasad Singh* (in Hindi). Sanjay Book Centre, Varanasi.

Singh, Khushwant 1959. *I Shall Not Hear the Nightingale.* Grove Press, Inc., New York.

Singh, Namwar 1980. *Story: New Story* (in Hindi). Lok Bharati Prakashan, Allahabad. 3rd ed.

Singh, Pratibha 2004. *Shiva Kashi. Pauranik Paripekshya aur Vartman Sandarbha* (in Hindi). Vishwavidyalaya Prakashan, Varanasi.

Singh, Rajdeo 1968. *Gajendragadkar Committee Report on BHU, A Review.* Chauhan Art Press, New Delhi.

Singh, Rana P.B. 1980. The Socio-cultural space of Varanasi. *Art and Arch. Research Papers* (London) 17: 41.46.

— 1985. The personality and lifeworld of Varanasi as revealed in Shivprasad Singh's novel: a study in Literary Geography. *National Geogr. Jl. of India* 31 (4) 291-318.

— 1986. Shiva's Universe in Varanasi. In, T.P. Verma, et al., eds. *Varanasi Through the Ages.* Bhartiya Itihas Samkalan Samiti, Varanasi: 303-311.

— 1987. Toward myth, cosmos, space and mandala in India: a search in the geography of belief systems. *National Geogr. Jl. of India* 33 (3): 305-326.

— 1988. The image of Varanasi: Sacrality and perceptual world. *Nationol Geogr. Jl. of India* 34 (1) : 1-32.

— 1989. *Where Cultural Symbols Meet: Literary Images of Varanasi.* Tara Book Agency, Varanasi.

— 1995. Heritage ecology and caring for the earth: a search for preserving harmony and ethical values. *National Geogr. Jl. of India*, Vol. 41 (2), June : pp. 191-216.

— 1994. The sacred geometry of India's holy city, Varanasi: Kashi as Cosmogram. *National Geogr. Jl. of India*, vol. 40: pp. 189-216. Reprinted with revision in : *Ancient Cities, Ancient Skies*, eds. J. M. Malville and L. Gujral, 1999. Aryan Publ. For IGNCA, New Delhi : pp. 59-80.

— 1997. Sacredscape, cosmic territory, and faithscape: Goddess territory of Vindhyacala, India. *National Geographical Journal of India*, vol. 43 (3), Sept. : 237-263.

— 1999. Rethinking development in India: Perspective, crisis and prospect. In, David Simon and Anders Närman, eds. *Development as Theory and Practice.* DARG Ser.1.Longman, Harlow, UK: pp. 55-75.

— 2002. *Towards the Pilgrimage Archetype. The Pancakroshi Yatra of Banaras.* Indica Books, Banaras.

— 2003. *Battle of Gods, Battles of Men in Banaras.* A paper presented in the International Interdisciplinary Conference "Symbology, Myths, History: Weapons and Wars, from Rudra to Mahatma Gandhi": 19 - 20 May, State University of Milan, Napoleonic Hall, Milan, Italy.

— and Rana, P.S. 2002. *Banaras Region. A Spiritual and Cultural Guide.* Indica Books, Varanasi.

Singh, Rana P.B. and Singh, Ravi. S. 2002. Development in India: Scenario and Ideology. (with Ravi S. Singh). *Towards a New Regional and Local Development Research Agenda*, eds. Anders Närman and K. Karunanayake. Dept. of Geography, Goteborg University (Sweden), series B, No. 100 and Centre for Development Studies, University of Kelaniya (Sri Lanka), No. 1: pp. 65-78.

Singh, Rana P.B., Singh, Ravi. S. and Rana, P.S. 2002. Sacred Geography of Goddesses in Kashi (Varanasi). *Journal of Geography*, vol 3 (Theme: Social Geography, eds. H.N. Sharma and A.K. Bhagabati; Dept. of Geography, Gauhati University, Guwahati), October: pp. 11-35.

Singh, Shukdeo and Linda Hess, eds. 1977. *Selected Poems of the Bijak of Kabir*. Kabir Bani Publ., Varanasi.

Skanda Purana 1960-1965. No. XX, 5 vols. Gurumandala Granthamalaya, Calcutta ; in Sanskrit.

Sommer, Robert 1969. *Personal Space*. Prentice-Hall, Inc., Englewood Cliffs, NJ.

Srivastava, S.K. 1986. Tradition of textile industry in Kashi (in Hindi). In, T.P. Verma et al., eds., *Varanasi Through the Ages*. B.I.S.S., Varanasi: 205-207.

Srivastava, Parmananda 1974. Obstacles of the so-called students' reactions: criticism of the novel. *Naya Pratika* 1 (11), Nov.: 74-79.

Sukul, Kuber Nath 1974. *Varanasi Down the Ages*. K.N. Sukul, Patna.

Sukul, Kuber Nath 1977. *Varanasi Vaibhava*. (The Glory of Varanasi); in Hindi. Rastrabhasha Parishad, Patna.

Tarachand 1963. *Influences of Islam on Indian Culture*. Allahabad.

TC, *Tirthacintamani* by Vacaspati Misra. Bibliotheca Indica, New Series No. 1256. 1912. Asiatic Society of Bengal, Calcutta.

Tharoor, Shashi, 1997. A culture of diversity. *Resurgence* (Devon, UK), 183 (July/August): 4-6.

Tiwari, J. N. 1985. *Goddess Cults in Ancient India*. Sundeep Prakashan, Delhi.

Tiwari, Rakesh 1986. Rock painting of Mirzapur. In, T.P. Verma et al., eds. *Varanasi Through the Ages*. B.I.S.S. Pub. 4, Varanasi: 105-112.

Trilling, Lionel 1965. *Beyond Culture*. Viking Press, New York.

Tripathi, Rajneesh 1986. Forms of prostitutions in Varanasi, then and now. In, Kaushal K. Mishra, ed. *Sanmarg, Varanasi Number* (in Hindi). Sanmarg Office, Varanasi: 251-255.

Tripathi, Sushil 1986. The danger of learning in the capital of all-knowledge. In, *Sanmarg*, Special Publication: *Varanasi Issue,* ed. K.K. Mishra. Sanmarg Pub., Varanasi: 237.239.

TS, *Tristhalisetu* by Narayan Bhatta. 1915. Anandashrama Sanskrit Series No. 78, Poona.

Tuan,Yi-Fu 1974. *Topophilia, A Study of Environmental Perception, Attitudes and Values*. Prentice-Hall, Inc., Englewood Cliffs, NJ.

— 1977. *Space and Place, The Perspective of Experience*. Edward Arnold Ltd., London.

Yugeshvar, (ed.) 1994. *Kabira Samagra*. (Kabir's writing in total). Hindi Pracharak Samsthan, Varanasi. in Hindi.

Upadhyay, Nagendra Nath 1986. Kashi of Kabir and Tulasi; in Hindi. In, T.P. Verma, et el, eds. *Varanasi Through the Ages*. B.I.S.S., Varanasi (Publ. no. 4): 288-294.

Van Ghent, Dorothy 1953. *The English Novel: Form and Function*. Harper and Row, Inc, New York. Reprinted 1961.

Vaudeville, Charlotte 1986. *Barahamasa in Indian Literature*. Motilal Banarasidass, Delhi.

Vidyarthi, L.P.; Saraswati, B.N. and Jha M. 1979. *The Sacred Complex of Kashi*. Concept Pub. Co., Delhi.

Vishvakarma, Ishvar Sharan 1987. *Kashi ka Aitihasika Bhugola*. (Historical Geography of Kashi: From the earliest times to CE 12th century); in Hindi. Ramananda Vidya Bhavan, New Delhi.

Wadley, Susan S. 1983. The rains of estrangement: Understanding the Hindu yearly cycle. *Contributions to Indian Sociology* NS 17 (1) : 51-85.

Wilkins, W.J. 1882. *Hindu Mythology*. 2nd ed. 1910. 8th imprint. Rupa & Co., New Delhi.

Young, T.D. 1979. Mississippi: a Personal view of its past and a hope for its future. *The Southern Quarterly* 17 (3-4): 47-57.

Zimmerman, Francis 1980. *Ritu-Satmya:* the seasonal cycle and the principle of appropriateness, *Social Science and Medicine* 14B : 99-106.

* * * * * * *

* * *

APPENDIX 1
List of Figures

Appendix 2

Publications on Banaras (Varanasi) by Rana P. B. Singh

***A. Research Papers*:**

1. —1980 a. Socio-cultural space of Varanasi. *Art & Archaeology Research Papers* (AARP, London, UK), special publication "*Ritual Space in India*", vol. 17: pp. 41-46.
2. —1980 b. Rural water supply and problem of health in village India, case of Varanasi District. [with Ram Bilas]. *Changing Scene of Rural Habitat in Developing Countries*, eds. Shogo Yuihama and Rana P. B. Singh. 24th International Geogr. Congress, Tokyo/Okayama (Japan): pp. 95-109.
3. —1980 c. Urban landscape of Varanasi: a cultural synthesis. [with R. L. Singh]. *National Geographical Journal of India* (Varanasi), vol. 26 (3-4): pp. 113-123.
4. —1982. Image of Varanasi city: reflection on Geography of Tourism. *Frankfurter Wirtschafts- und Sozialgeographische Schriften* (Frankfurt/ Main, Germany), Heft 41: pp. 161-174.
5. —1985. The personality and lifeworld of Varanasi as revealed in Shivaprasad Singh's novel: a study in literary geography. *National Geographical Journal of India* (NGSI, Varanasi), vol. 31 (4): pp.291-318.
6. —1986. Shiva's universe in Varanasi. *Varanasi Through the Ages*, eds. T.P. Verma, et al. Bhartiya Itihas Samkalan Samiti, Varanasi, Pub. 4 : pp. 303-311.
7. — 1987 a. Toward myth, Cosmos, Space and Mandala in India, a search in the Geography of Belief Systems. *National Geographical Journal of India*, vol. 33 (3): pp. 305-326.
8. —1987 b. The pilgrimage mandala of Varanasi/Kashi: a study in sacred geography. *National Geographical Journal of India*, vol. 33 (4), December : pp. 493-524.
9. —1988 a. Interplay of sacred space and sacred time in Hindu belief system. *Spiritual Attitudes and Environment* (*Geistenshaltung und Umbelt*), ed. Werner Kreisel. Abhandlungen zur Geschichte der Geowissenschaften und Religion/ Umwelt-Forschung, Band 1. Alano Edition herodot, Aachen (Germany): pp. 439-454.
10. —1988 b. The Image of Varanasi: sacrality and perceptual world. *National Geographical Journal of India*, vol. 34 (1), March : pp. 1-32.
11. —1990. Literary images, cultural symbols and intimate sensing: The Ganga river in Varanasi. *National Geographical Journal of India*, vol. 36 (1-2): pp. 117-128.
12. —1991 b. Panchakroshi Yatra, Varanasi: Sacred Journey, Ecology of Place and Faithscape. *National Geographical Journal of India,* vol. 37 (1-2): pp. 49-98.

13. —1993 c. Varanasi: The Pilgrimage mandala, geomantic map and cosmic numbers. *Banaras (Varanasi)*, ed. Rana P.B. Singh, ref. **B 5**: pp. 37-64.

14. —1993 d. The Ganga Ghats, Varanasi: The Riverfront landscape. *Banaras (Varanasi)*, ed. Rana Singh, ref. **B 5**: pp. 65-102.

15. —1993 e. Shiva's Universe in Varanasi. *Banaras (Varanasi)*, ed. Rana Singh, ref. **B 5**: pp. 155-162.

16. —1993 f. Sarnath: Cultural history, museum and tourist sites. Banaras *(Varanasi)*, ed. Rana Singh, ref. **B 5**: pp. 235-256.

17. —1993 g. Varanasi: Demographic Profile – From ancient to late 1820s and the present state. *Banaras (Varanasi)*, ed. Rana Singh, ref. **B 5**: pp. 279-288.

18. —1993 h. Varanasi: A World heritage city: The frame, historical accounts. *Banaras (Varanasi)*, ed. Rana Singh, ref. **B 5** : pp. 297-316.

19. —1993 i. Cosmic layout of Hindus' sacred city, Varanasi. *Architecture & Behaviour* (Lausane, Switzerland), Vol. 9 (2) : pp. 239-249.

20. —1994 a. Water symbolism and sacred landscape in Hinduism: A study of Benares. *Erdkunde* (Bonn, Germany), Band 48 (3), September: 210-227.

21. —1994 b. Modern Varanasi: Place and Society in Shivprasad Singh's novel *Street Turns Yonder*. *Writing the City*, eds. P. Preston and P. Simpson-Housley. Routledge, London (UK): pp. 220-240.

22. —1994 c. Time and Hindu rituals in Varanasi. *Geographia Religionum* (Berlin, Germany), Bd. 8: pp. 123-138.

23. —1994 d. The sacred geometry of India's holy city, Varanasi: Kashi as Cosmogram. *National Geographical Journal of India*, vol. 40: pp. 189-216. Reprinted with revision in : *Ancient Cities, Ancient Skies*, eds. J.M. Malville and L. Gujral, 1999. Aryan Publ. For IGNCA, New Delhi : pp. 59-80.

24. —1994 e. Varanasi: Cosmic order and cityscape. **I**. Sun images and shrines. *Architecture + Design* (New Delhi), vol. 11 (6), November-December : pp. 75-79.

25. —1995 a. Varanasi: Cosmic order and cityscape. **II**. Ganesh images and shrines. *Architecture + Design* (New Delhi), vol. 12 (1), January-February : pp. 99-101.

26. —1995 c. Varanasi: Cosmic order and cityscape. **III**. Shiva's universe and pilgrimage journeys. *Architecture + Design* (New Delhi), vol. 12 (2), March-April : pp. 83-85.

27. —1995 d. Sun shrines, images and alignment at Varanasi. *The Ley Hunter* (Cornwall, UK), No. TLH 123, Summer : pp. 20-26.

28. —1995 e. Visual Astronomy in the mythology and ritual of India: the Sun temples of Varanasi. [with John McKim Malville]. *Vistas in Astronomy* (Pergamon, Oxford, UK), Vol. 39 (4): pp. 431-449.

29. —1995 f. Cosmic order and Cityscape of Varanasi (Kashi): The Sun images and cultural astronomy. [with John McKim Malville]. *National Geographical Journal of India,* Vol. 41 (1), March : pp. 69-88.

30. —1996 a. The Ganga River and the spirit of sustainability in Hinduism. *Dialogues with the Living Earth. New Ideas on the Spirit of Place*, eds. James and Roberta Swans. Quest Books, Wheaton, IL, USA : pp. 86-107.

31. —1996 b. Varanasi: Shiva's universe and pilgrimage journey. *The Ley Hunter* (Cheltenham, UK), No. TLH 125, Autumn : pp. 24-29.

32. —1997 a. Sacred space and pilgrimage in Hindu society: the case of Varanasi. *Sacred Places, Sacred Spaces. The Geography of Pilgrimages*, eds. R.H. Stoddard and Alan Morinis. *Geoscience & Man*, vol. 34. Louisiana State University Press, Baton Rouge, USA: 191-207.

33. —1997 b. Sacredscape and urban heritage in India: Contestation and perspective. *Contested Urban Heritage*, eds. Brian Shaw and Roy Jones. Ashgate, London (UK): pp. 101-131.

34. —1997 c. Urban heritage in India: Towards orientation to planning. (with Ravi S. Singh). In, A. K. Singh, et el., eds. *Strategies in Development Planning*. Deep & Deep Publs., New Delhi :pp. 289-304.

35. —1998 . Sacred journey, Sacredscape and Faithscape: an experience of Panchakroshi pilgrimage, Varanasi (India). *The Pennsylvania Geographer* (Johnstown, PA, USA), vol. 36 (1): pp. 55-91.

36. — 2000 a. Kashi as Cosmogram: Sacred Geometry of Varanasi. In, J. M. Malville & L. Gujral, eds. *Ancient Cities, Ancient Skies*. Aryan Publ., New Delhi for IGNCA : pp. 58-81.

37. — 2000 b. The Sun and its temples at Varanasi: meaning and pattern in the three worlds of Kashi. [with J.M. Malville]. In, J.M. Malville & L. Gujaral, eds. *Ancient Cities, Ancient Skies*. New Delhi *for* IGNCA : pp. 82-99.

38. — 2000 c. Sacredscape, Faithscape and Cosmic Geometry : A Study of Holy Places of north India. [with J.M. Malville]. In, Esteban C. & Belmonte J.A. (eds). *Astronomy and Cultural Diversity*. (Proceedings, Oxford VI & SEAC 99 Int'nal Conf., June 21-29, 1999, La Laguna, Spain). OAMC. Santa Cruz de Tenerife: pp. 99-106.

39. — 2000 d. Change and continuity in village India: crisis and prospects in Chamaon, Varanasi. [with Gerhard Gustafsson, K. Lejonhud & K.I. Valvik]. *FENNIA, International Jl. of Geography* (Geogr. Society of Finland, Helsinki), vol. 178 (No.2): 203-214.

40. — 2000 e. Sustainable heritage tourism: Framework, perspective and prospect. [with Pravin S. Rana]. *National Geographical Journal of India,* vol. 46 (1-4): 141-158.

41. — 2001 a. The Structure of Peri-Urban Agricultural Environment in Varanasi Development Region. [with Chandra Sen]. *National Geographical Journal of India,* vol. 47 (1-4): 61-72.

42. — 2001 b. The Holy city and the Cultural Tradition of Pilgrimage Mandala in India: Cosmic Geometries of Kashi (Varanasi) and Gaya. *Cultural Approach in Geography at the turn of New Millenium*, eds. M.R. Hashemi and M. Papoli-Yazdi. University of Mashhad Press, Mashhad, Iran.

43. — 2001 c. Rationales for including Varanasi as Heritage City in the UNESCO World Heritage List. [with Vrinda Dar and Pravin S. Rana]. *National Geographical Journal of India* (N.G.S.I., Varanasi), vol. 47, 2001: 177-200.

44. — 2001 d. The Future of Heritage Tourism in Varanasi: Scenario, Prospects and Perspectives. [with Pravin S. Rana]. *National Geographical Journal of India* (N.G.S.I., Varanasi), vol. 47, 2001: pp. 201-218.

45. — 2002. Sacred Geography of Goddesses in Kashi (Varanasi). (with Ravi S. Singh, Pravin S. Rana). *Journal of Geography*, vol 3 (Sp. on Social Geography, 2000-2001, eds. H.N. Sharma and A.K. Bhagabati; Department of Geography, University of Guwahati), October: 11-35.

46. — 2004 a. The Ganga Riverfront in Varanasi, a Heritage Zone in Contestation. *Context: Built, Living and Natural* (DRONAH, Gurgaon, HR, India), vol 1, no. 1, June: pp. 25-30.

47. — 2004 b. Behavioural Perspective of Pilgrims and Tourists in Banaras; [with Pravin S. Rana], in, *The Tourist - A Psychological Perspective*; ed. Aparna Raj; Kanishka Pub., New Delhi: 187-206.

48. — 2004 c. Kashi as Cosmogram: The Panchakroshi Route and Complex Structures of Varanasi; [with Fukunaga, Masaaki], in *Pilgrimage and Complexity*, eds. John M. Malville and B.N. Saraswati; DK Printworld, Delhi for IGNCA: 87-98.

49. — 2004 d. Goddesses in Kashi (Varanasi): Visualised Space and Constructing Patterns; [with Ravi S. Singh], in, *Visualised Space: Constructions of Locality and Cartographic Representations in Varanasi*, eds. Martin Gaenszle and Jörg Gengnagel; (South Asia Institute, Heidelberg, Germany).

50. — 2004 e. Representation of Kashi through the Cartographic Art in the 19th Century. In, *Contribution of Banaras to Indian Art and Culture* (Proceedings of a National seminar, 22-24 March 2004); eds. Ananda Krishna and Mukul Raj Mehta. Indian Institute of Advanced Studies, Simla.

51. — 2004 f. Pilgrims to Kashi; [with John M. Malville], in *Pilgrimage and Complexity*, eds. John M. Malville and B.N. Saraswati; DK Printworld, Delhi for IGNCA.

B. Books:

1. —1989. ***Where Cultural Symbols Meet. Literary Images of Varanasi***. Tara Book Agency, Varanasi. ISBN 81-85403-36-8. (For a fully expanded version, see No. 9).
2. —1991 a. ***Sarnath. Cultural Heritage, Museum, Tourism***. [with Prem Lata]. Tara Book Agency, Varanasi. ISBN 81-85403-79-1.
3. —1991 b. ***Panchakroshi Yatra, Varanasi: Sacred Journey, Ecology of Place and Faithscape***. Tara Book Agency, Varanasi. ISBN 81-85403-84-8. (For a fully expanded version, see No. 7).
4. —1993 a. ***Varanasi Region. An Insight Guide to Tourist Places***. Tara Book Agency, Varanasi.
5. —1993 b. Ed. ***BANARAS (Varanasi): Cosmic Order, Sacred City, Hindu Traditions***. Tara Book Agency, Varanasi. ISBN 81-85403-92-9.
6. — 2002a. ***Banaras Region: A Spiritual & Cultural Guide***. Indica Books, Varanasi. [with Pravin. S. Rana]. *Pilgrimage & Cosmology Series: 1*. ISBN 81-86569-24-3.
7. — 2002b. ***Towards the Pilgrimage Archetype: The Panchakroshi Yatra of Banaras***. Indica Books, Varanasi. *Pilgrimage & Cosmology Series: 3*. ISBN: 81-86569-30-8.
8. — 2003. ***Where the Buddha Walked. A Companion to the Buddhist Places of India***. Indica Books, Varanasi. *Pilgrimage & Cosmology Series: 5*. ISBN 81-86569-36-7.
9. — 2004. ***Cultural Landscapes and the Lifeworld: Literary Images of Banaras***. Indica Books, Varanasi. *Pilgrimage & Cosmology Series: 7*. ISBN: 81-86569-45-6.
10. — 2005! ***Kashi & Cosmos: Ritualscape and Sacred Geography of Banaras***. In preparation.
11. — 2005 Singh, Rana P.B. and Michell, George. Eds. ***Banaras, the City Revealed***, Marg Publications, Mumbai. Forthcoming.

C: Report:

1. Singh, Rana P.B. (chairman) and Dar, Vrinda (associate) 2002 (April 15). ***The Riverfront and Old City Heritage Zone of Varanasi. Nomination Proposal for inscription in the UNESCO World Heritage List***. Varanasi Development Authority, Varanasi (India). 174pp + 70 figures/ maps (locational, site plans, cross sections), 70 plates of photographs, including historical outline Selected Bibliography, O&M plans, and by-laws.

Author Index

Subject Index

The Author

Prof. Rana P. B. Singh (b. 15 December 1950), MA, PhD, Professor of Cultural Geography at Banaras Hindu University, Varanasi, UP 221005, India. He has been working in the areas of cultural geography, cultural astronomy, peregrinology, literary images and sacred geography. He has been Visiting Professor of Geography at Virginia Tech (USA), Japan Foundation Scientist at Okayama, Indo-Swedish Visiting Professor at Karlstad, Ron Lister lecturer at University of Otago, NZ, Linnaus-Palme Visiting Professor at Karlstad University, Sweden, and Indo-Japan Cultural Exchange Professor at Gifu Women's University, Japan. As visiting scholar he gave seminars at many universities in Australia, Austria, Belgium, Bhutan, Denmark, Germany, Finland, Italy, Japan, Nepal, Netherlands, New Zealand, Norway, Singapore, Spain, Sweden, Switzerland, the USA (including Hawaii), and the USSR. He is the *Founding President* of the (a) Society of Pilgrimage Studies, SPS (fd. 1989), (b) Society of Heritage Planning & Environmental Health, SHPEH (fd. 1989), (c) Indo-Nordic Cultural Association, INCA (fd 1992), (d) Indo-Japanese Friendship Association, IJFAB (fd. 1989), and (e) 'Friends of Banaras' (fd 2003). He is a member of the SASNET (Sweden), JASNET (Japan) and AASNET (Australia). He is a Life Member of the NAGI, NGSI, SPS, and EMS; and executive member of the International Research Forum, IRF, on SAARC, Tokyo (Japan). During 1985-95, he has served as Assoc./ Executive Editor of the *National Geographical Journal of India*. He has been involved in studying, performing and promoting heritage planning, Eco-tourism and rural studies in the Varanasi region for the last two decades, as consultant, project director, collaborator and organiser. He has also served as Chief Co-ordinator to international projects, like (a) UNO-CHBP, New York on "Rural development in Indian Environment; case of Varanasi", 1977, (b) University of Colorado, Boulder (USA) and SHPEH on "Cultural Astronomy & Pilgrimage Systems: The Bathers in Varanasi", 1998-2000, (c) Xerox Co. Project on "Crossings: Kashi and Cosmos", 2000-01, (d) SAI Heidelberg (Germany) project on "Visualising Sacred Space and Religious Cartography of Varanasi", 1999-2002; (e) Centre for Environmental Tech., Imperial College (UK), on "Land use and Farming

Systems in Peri-urban areas around Varanasi City", 1999-2002.

The American Biographical Institute (USA) has honoured Prof. Rana Singh with 'International Peace Prize' 2003, 'American Medal of Honour' 2003, '2000 Millennium Medal of Honor' 1999, and by nomination of 'Outstanding Man of the 20th Century' 1999, and 'Man of the Year' - 1999, 2000, 2003. He was also honoured with International Biographical Inst., Cambridge in the "*Outstanding People of the 20th Century*" – 1999, and Marquis Who's Who (USA) in the "*Who's Who in the World*", 1999 – 2002.

He is also serving as chief co-ordinator to the international programmes like New York State Independent College Consortium for Study in India, NYSICCSI (Varanasi), since 1995, Friends World Program, Long Island University, Southampton, NY, FWP-LIU (Varanasi segment, Jan/ Feb.), since 2001, and Denis Religious Study Teachers Association India Study Programme, since 2001.

His notable academic contributions include Spatio-temporal dimensional theory of diffusion, Space articulation theory in Indian villages, Literary images and spirit of place, Ritual Mandala and sacrality of space and time, Pilgrimage mandala, Sacred geography and cosmic order of holy places, Geomancy and cultural symbolism in Hinduism, Concepts of sacredscape and faithscape. Cultural astronomy and ordering of sacredscapes and holy cities, architectural symbolism and heritage planning.

Eight students have obtained PhD degrees under his supervision. His publications include twelve monographs, twenty-two books, and over one hundred fifty research papers, including articles in journals like GeoJournal, Architecture & Behaviour, Erdkunde, Geoscience & Man, Pennsylvania Geographer, The Ley Hunter, and Place. On different aspects of Banaras and environs he has published fifty research papers and nine books. His recent publications include *Environmental Ethics* (1993), *Banaras (Varanasi): Cosmic Order, Sacred City, Hindu Traditions* (1993), *The Spirit and Power of Place* (1994), *Banaras Region: A Spiritual & Cultural Guide* (2002, with P.S. Rana), *Towards the Pilgrimage Archetype: The Panchakroshi Yatra of Banaras* (2002), *Where the Buddha Walked* (2003), and *Cultural Landscapes and the Lifeworld: Literary Images of Banaras* (2004). Presently he is working on *Kashi & Cosmos: Sacred Geography and Ritualscape of Banaras*, and *Sacred Geography of the Goddesses in South Asia.*

E-mail: ranapbs@sify.com ; ranapbs@bigfoot.com

Opinions about the book:

This is a pioneering and innovative work, dealing as it does with the changing mood of human culture, its people and landscape as reflected through the literary productions pertaining to Varanasi, which is considered to be the City of Light as also the Cultural Capital of India. The vivid and contrasting features of the urban personality of Varanasi are delineated using appropriate metaphors, milieus and contexts, while citing profusely the Puranic literature to justify its glory and heritage.

— Prof. R.L. Singh, *founding editor of the N.G.J.I.*

The book opened new doors of methodology, which should tempt others into further literary-geographical studies of this nature. And, for those of us afflicted with '*Banarasia*', another welcomed piece of literary '*Banarasia*'.

— Dr. Mark Katz, *Karlstad University, Karlstad, Sweden.*

For the stranger, Varanasi is a bewildering city. This book helps put the city in perspective by revealing its personality as interpreted in literature. It is also an important addition to the geographical literature because of its integration of geographical analysis with literary themes.

— Prof. Mary L. Nolan, *Oregon State University, Corvallis, USA.*

The book deals with the changing mood of culture, people and landscape as expressed in the literary works on Varanasi. …This work is one of the creation of masterly writings combining 'Text' and 'Context' through making the bridge of literary expression, imagination, documentation from the historical sources and after all the field study. … My own experiences in the city of Varanasi have been further enriched and made clear from this book.

— Prof. Masaaki Fukunaga, *CSAS Gifu's Women University, Japan.*

What city can be more suitable for such experiential studies other than 'the oldest city' which is situated on the 'Trishul' of Lord Shiva. Rana Singh has successfully attempted to capture the spirit of 'Varanasi through time' as evoked by the writings of authors from different temporal, philosophical, cultural, linguistic and religious backgrounds.

— Prof. Ramesh Dhussa, *Drake University, Des Moines, USA.*

Drawing on literary sources and social comment, as well as the physical geography of Varanasi, this book provides an excellent example of the Human Science approach (*Geisteswissenschaften*) of suiting the method of enquiry to the subject matter studied. The author seeks understanding (*Verstehen*) of a city and its heritage. He obviously cares deeply about Varanasi, which makes his criticism all the more relevant.

— Prof. L. Eugene Thomas, *University of Connecticut, Storrs, USA.*

The book is quite in tune with the academic trends of the time. The purport of the book is to project the holistic personality of the ancient city of Varanasi, the cultural capital of India, from two probable points of view: topophilic and topophobic, through the analysis of works of literature … from the ancient times up to the present day.

— Prof. A.K. Tripathi, *Banaras Hindu University.*

This is an unusual book, which highlights the socio-cultural traditions of a city on the basis of literary sources of ancient, medieval and modern times. …. It focuses on the intrinsic reality of the city, which is mostly based on the common experience of the lived landscape.

— Dr. D.P. Dubey, *Society of Pilgrimage Studies, Allahabad.*